Patrick O'Meara

The Enigmatic Tsar and His Empire

TRANSFORMATIONS DIFFERENTIATIONS PERSPECTIVES

MAINZ STUDIES ON THE MODERN AGE

Edited by Michael Kißener, Jan Kusber, Andreas Rödder and Matthias Schnettger

VOLUME 5 — first in English & to be devoted to a Rn: theme

PETER LANG

Alexander Kaplunovsky, Jan Kusber,
Benjamin Conrad (eds.)

The Enigmatic Tsar and His Empire

Russia under Alexander I. 1801–1825

PETER LANG

Bibliographic Information published by the Deutsche Nationalbibliothek
The Deutsche Nationalbibliothek lists this publication in the Deutsche Nationalbibliografie; detailed bibliographic data is available online at http://dnb.d-nb.de.

Library of Congress Cataloging-in-Publication Data
A CIP catalog record for this book has been applied for at the Library of Congress.

Cover Illustration: Illumination in the Cathedral Square in Honor of Alexander I's Coronation, by Fedor Alekseev (1802).
Source: The State Hermitage Museum, St. Petersburg, Photograph
© The State Hermitage Museum, Photo by Vladimir Terebenin

Style Editing and Proofreading - Jessica Hinds-Bond

Printed by CPI books GmbH, Leck

ISSN 2566-6215
ISBN 978-3-631-73283-0 (Print)
E-ISBN 978-3-631-73284-7 (E-PDF)
E-ISBN 978-3-631-73285-4 (EPUB)
E-ISBN 978-3-631-73286-1 (MOBI)
DOI 10.3726/b15714

Peter Lang – Berlin · Bern · Bruxelles ·
New York · Oxford · Warszawa · Wien

This publication has been peer reviewed.

www.peterlang.com

Acknowledgments

Our volume on the epoch of Alexander I, the "enigmatic tsar," is a collaborative undertaking in many ways. The idea started with the international conference "The Russian Empire 1790–1830: In Search for Narratives for the Alexandrine Age" held on March 23–25, 2017, at the Johannes Gutenberg-University Mainz. We are very grateful to Deutsche Forschungsgemeinschaft for financing the conference. The lively discussions on the conceptualization of the Alexandrine epoch at the conference were intellectually fun for the organizers. We are thankful to all who contributed and worked with us in the editing process with patience. We would like to express our gratitude to Semen Kaul for his careful support in preparing this volume. We are especially grateful to Jessica Hinds-Bond, who did a marvelous job in copyediting and proofreading. We also owe special thanks to the State Hermitage Museum in St. Petersburg and to Château de Versailles and Réunion des Musées nationaux in France for kindly supplying pictorial material. Last but not least we thank the publishing house Peter Lang for professional cooperation.

Mainz, March 2019
Alexander Kaplunovsky
Jan Kusber
Benjamin Conrad

Contents

Alexander Kaplunovsky, Jan Kusber

Alexandrine Russia as Laboratory

Much international research has been done on different aspects of the reign of Alexander I. Yet, the general character of the Alexandrine Age remains undetermined, and its main political trends are not identified. While the epoch of Catherine the Great is customarily connected to "Europeanization," "Enlightenment," and "Enlightened Absolutism," the history of the nineteenth century, of course deeply simplified, usually evokes such tropes as the "Gendarme of Europe" or "Tsar-Liberator." In contrast, the period of Alexander I's rule is often seen as separate from this history. It was a bright and heroic time, and the monarch's personality was ambivalent, "mysterious," and "indecisive," but the epoch in general lacks a clear political character. So far, historiography has only agreed to distinguish between a "liberal" first and a "conservative-mythical" second part of Alexander I's reign, with the 1812 Napoleonic invasion serving as the point of rupture. The Patriotic War of 1812 presents its own field of study, but at the same time it is also the takeoff time of secret societies and the Decembrist movement, another grand narrative of Russian history. Sometimes one gets the impression that these major topics are somehow subjects of research apart from Alexander's rule in general.

Existing studies focus on collective or individual biographies of the historical actors[1] or on the development of institutions and specific (including reformist) policies—be they social, religious, or economic. While impressive and profound in their own right, these case studies remain ultimately uncontextualized vis-à-vis each other. At the same time, historiographers of the Alexandrine era tend to focus on two main themes: administrative indecision and the unsystematic or unsuccessful realization of ambitious reform plans.

---

1 Grunwald. Alexandre Ier; Almedingen. The Emperor Alexander I; McConnell. Tsar Alexander I; Palmer. Alexander I; Hartley. Alexander I; Raeff. Michael Speransky; Mironenko. Samoderzhavie i reformy; Jenkins. Arakcheev; Kenney. The Vorontsov Party in Russian Politics. Pp. 260–316; Whittaker. The Origins of Modern Russian Education; Zawadzki. A Man of Honour; Martin. Romantics, Reformers, Reactionaries; Tomsinov. Arakcheev. Idem. Speranskii.

Recent studies of religious politics and thought, political language and imaginaries, education, and the history of medicine[2] (including a special case of imperial politics in former territories of the Polish-Lithuanian Commonwealth or Bessarabia[3]), source editions (new collections of historical material),[4] and the ongoing research projects of this volume's editors on legal reforms or the financial system, present a more coherent picture. They demonstrate that Alexandrine Russia may be interpreted as a "laboratory" in which different potential scenarios for modernization were designed, discussed, and tested—but also rejected and forgotten.

To be quite candid as to the initial idea of this volume, our very first aim was to find a coherent and more valid heuristic frame for the Alexandrine era. An international conference, "The Russian Empire 1790–1830: In Search of Narratives for the Alexandrine Age," was held on March 23–25, 2017, in Mainz, organized by chair of eastern European history of Mainz University. Generous financial support from the Deutsche Forschungsgemeinschaft made it possible to invite a few well-known experts in various fields of Russian and Eastern European studies, whose current research projects are explicitly focused on the Alexandrine epoch. Colleagues from Russia, Germany, and Canada submitted their papers to be read in advance of the conference. This procedure ensured intensive, fruitful work and discussions during the whole time of the conference.

Thus, the aim of the planned conference was to establish general narratives for the Alexandrine age, not so much from the traditional vantage point of the emperor and his inner circle but from the point of view of experts and elites who perceived the empire as a laboratory. These "men on the spot," whether officially sanctioned by the state or independently of it, drafted "maps" of the empire and its collective subjects and constructed social, political, and economic imaginaries of the empire. These actors, who envisioned the functions of the state and imagined its future, did so also in comparison and in entanglement with other states in Europe. Therefore, individual experts like local doctors, legal scholars,

2 Sambuk. Wächter der Gesundheit; Kusber. Eliten- und Volksbildung im Zarenreich; Parsamov. Dekabristy i russkoe obshchestvo; Polskoi. Konstituciia i fundamentalnye zakony. Pp. 94–150; Biktasheva. Kazanskoe gubernatorstvo pervoi poloviny XIX veka; Vishlenkova. The State of Health. Pp. 39–75; Idem. Zabotias o dushakh poddannykh; Idem / Il'ina. The science of rulership. Pp. 65–107; Idem / Savelieva (Eds.). Soslovie russkikh professorov.

3 Ganzenmüller. Russische Staatsgewalt und polnischer Adel. Also see recent studies on Bessarabia and Russian-Ottoman relations in the first half of the nineteenth century by Victor Taki, e.g., Taki. Tsar and Sultan.

4 E.g. Parsamov (Ed.). M.M. Speranskii; Idem (Ed.). Sergei S. Uvarov.

practical jurists, and amateur scientists must be considered alongside collective actors such as the Decembrists and the members of the so-called conservative elite and other networks.

A congruent theme and aim of the conference was to enhance the focus on the imperial interior by looking also at influential factors such war and international alliances. We structured our discussions around three topics: Russia's movement toward "political nations," alliances, wars, and integration processes; patterns of modernization and the diversity of actors; and finally, redistribution of power and the imperial administration designs in domestic politics. Despite extensive discussions across the whole conference, we did not come to (or rather, we wittingly rejected) the development of a consistent grand narrative as a common framework for the Russian empire under the "enigmatic" tsar. More workable and flexible seemed to be the alternative heuristic paradigm of "empire as a laboratory."

Now, what was and is the matter of this Alexandrine "laboratory" in a historical and analytical perspective? What is the utility in discovering Russian history of the early nineteenth century and describing its specific nature at the turn from premodern to modern times? To answer these questions, the specific characteristics of this imperial *Sattelzeit*—to use a term from Reinhart Koselleck and Jan Kusber[5]—must be defined and our analytical capabilities explained. We deliver not a theory or an abstraction but a descriptive paradigm.

In many ways, it can be suggested that the Alexandrine era was a time of exploration and revision of empire and state-building[6] as well as of the search for suitable models of modernization and stabilization.

The discovery of imperial spaces, cultures, and peoples was undertaken in Russia in the eighteenth century and beyond not only by—mostly foreign—scientists, adventurers, and clerics but also by the monarchs themselves. From these times comes Catherine II's famous statement concerning the prospective tasks of empire-(re)building, in which she reflected on the process and its challenges and projected further changes. The empress addressed this statement on May 29, 1767, from Kazan, to her correspondent and kindred spirit at that time, the French philosopher Voltaire:

> The laws about which so much has been said are after all not yet completed. And who can say if they are good. It is posterity and not us in truth who will be able to judge their goodness. Consider, I beg you, that they must serve both Asia and Europe. *And what*

5 See below, Pp. 21–46

6 GANZENMÜLLER / TÖNSMEYER (Eds.). Vom Vorrücken des Staates in die Fläche. Pp. 7–32.

> *difference in climates, in people, in habits, and even in ideas. Here I am in Asia, I wanted to see this with my own eyes. There are in this city twenty different peoples who do not at all resemble each other. Yet a garment must be made that will fit them all. They may well find themselves general principles, but what of the details?* And such details! I would say that there is almost a world to create, to unite, to preserve. I wouldn't even finish and still there are too many details of all kinds.[7]

Thus far it was a program and a view from above, concisely formulated, but, as mentioned by the empress, only partially implemented.[8] A remarkable part of this ambitious undertaking was the creation and establishment of "lawful monarchy" in Russia. It could be seen, in common with Russian political discourse at the turn of the nineteenth century, as a rhetorical as well as a substantive bridge to the Alexandrine epoch and to the commonplace "Europe" in this time. Taking the throne, Alexander I promised to establish a lawful monarchy "according to the laws and wish" of his "beldame" Catherine the Great.[9] However, the state- and administration-building as well as the judicial and educational systems that had been introduced under Catherine II were compromised or functioned insufficiently. The era was once again marked by a fundamental reorganization of the whole empire on every stage and territory. Even this language of politics, which Sergei Polskoy brilliantly analyzes in this volume through a focus on the historical semantics and *Begriffsgeschichte* of the essential political terms "fundamental laws" and "constitution," does more than simply show a drastic transformation of the political vocabulary during the Alexandrine period.[10] It also highlights the emergence among Russian social elites of a new "moving power," which was related to the general transformation of the social order and its imaginaries at that time.

Another bridge to the previous "glorious century of nobility" as well as to the subsequent nineteenth century of ambivalent shaping and balancing of imperial diversity can be seen in the Alexandrine era's division of empire into viceroyalties. As Victor Taki explains in this volume, "the creation of ministries and of the State Council in 1802–11 can be considered a step toward greater centralization and bureaucratization, [but] the division of empire into viceroyalties can be seen as a

---

7 Hoogenboom, Hilde. Catherine the Great (1729–1796), Letter on Voltaire from Kazan, May 29, 1767. Pp. 81–93, cite P. 86, emphasis added.

8 Omelchenko. "Zakonnaia monarkhiia" Ekateriny Vtoroi.

9 Polnoe sobranie zakonov Rossiiskoi imperii (hereafter PSZ) I. Vol. 26. № 19779. 12.03.1801. O konchine imperatora Pavla I, i o vstuplenii na prestol imperatora Aleksandra I.

10 On the concepts of constitution and fundamental laws in Russian political discourse at the turn of the nineteenth century, see below, Pp. 135–166.

return to the 'empire of the nobles' (*dvorianskaia imperia*) [...] as it created the preconditions for the strengthening of the regional elites."[11] By the same token, Alsu Biktasheva shows how local nobles, liberated and invigorated in terms of their rights and privileges, became important players in the administration and control of the empire.[12]

A new phenomenon under Alexander I was the realization that theoretical and practical work could not be done by high-profile and enlightened statesmen, "top minds," or laymen and unprepared representatives of the estates of the empire (such as deputies in Catherine's Legislative Commission). The new actors were (pre)modern experts who had both professional training and experience—bankers and financiers, economists, physicians, lawyers, scholars, and professors (whether from newly founded or modernized universities), as well as ministers, governor-generals, and local officials.[13] The articles in this volume by Benjamin Conrad,[14] Elena Vishlenkova,[15] Alexander Kaplunovsky,[16] Alsu Biktasheva,[17] and Elizaveta Sysoeva[18]—each derived from an innovative and ongoing research project—show that these new actors did not function only as discoverers or contractors working on behalf and under the strict control of monarchic power. Rather, they created "maps" *of* and drafts *for* the empire quite often on their own initiative. As Vishlenkova aptly demonstrates in her research on physicians in the first half of the

11 See below, Pp. 317–337.
12 See below, Pp. 287–299.
13 For example, the enhancement of imperial control over the population of Kazakh steppes and its incorporation into the empire at the turn of the nineteenth century was attended by the "assessment" of *adats* (tribal customs) and Sharia law by local administrative officials (see Sartori / Shablei. Sudba imperskikh kodificacionnykh proektov. Pp. 63–105). The establishment and development of governors' power in the first third of the nineteenth century always involved balancing interactions in the triangle between emperor, ministers, and local societies (Biktasheva. Kazanskoe gubernatorstvo).
14 "'Un bon systême de finances doit être regardé comme l'ame qui vivifie l'État.' European Experts and Russia's State Finances under Paul I and Alexander I," see below Pp. 95–116.
15 "The Time of State-Building Discoveries: Governing Techniques in Health Care and Education," see below Pp. 219–243.
16 "The Alexandrine Commission for the Compilation of Laws: In Search of Codifying Models for the Russian Empire," see below Pp. 167–217.
17 "Russian Governors during the Reign of Alexander I: Mechanisms of Appointment and Dismissal in the Context of an Administrative Reform," see below Pp. 287–299.
18 "Alexander I's Governor-General Experiment in the Volga Region: A.N. Bakhmetev's Experience," see below Pp. 301–315.

nineteenth century, the Alexandrine period was a large-scale pivot point between the eighteenth and the twentieth centuries, in which medical professionals were (self)established as an expert community and a powerful player in state politics and society—that is, by forging state, empire, and nation-building processes.[19]

This shift led the elites away from the imported ideal of a "well-ordered police state" (Marc Raeff[20]) and the rational spirit of the Enlightenment, which was disavowed after 1789. Cameralism and its ideals were paramount in the cosmopolitan "enlightened absolutism"[21] of the eighteenth century but were steadily replaced by the study and cataloguing of the social, national, religious, economic, and cultural heterogeneity of the Russian empire.

The French Revolution and the related rise of both romantic and official nationalism also impacted these processes. Russia proceeded not only toward European "political nations" but toward a "national path" of modernization, as it tried to create its own solutions for the challenges of the new epoch in Europe. These solutions were based on different imaginings among Russians of "historical past" and "traditions"—imaginings that drew variously on Russian and European antecedents. Speaking metaphorically, it was a movement into a commonplace "Europe" and simultaneously a return to its own "roots," which had been postulated and constructed by intellectuals[22] and political elites. Thus, the case of British philosopher and jurisprudent Jeremy Bentham, as is shown by Aleksandr Orlov in his article,[23] could provide a better understanding of this contrarily proceeding dynamic. Bentham's fresh ideas on codification attracted much attention from Alexander I and the members of the Unofficial Committee in 1803. Just a year later, however, the admiration that both the monarch and the members of the Unofficial Committee had for the British legal scholar, and for his original theo-

19 Besides Vishlenkova, see, for example, Renner. Russische Autokratie und europäische Medizin; Sambuk. Wächter der Gesundheit; Mogilner. Homo Imperii.

20 Raeff. The Well-Ordered Police State. Take note, however, that some historians would characterize Nicholas I's Russia as a timedelayed emergence of the "well-ordered police state" due to thought patterns, political discourses or institutions, and practices.

21 For a fundamental revision of this historiographical concept and political discourse, see Mörke. Die Diskussion um den Absolutismus als Epochenbegriff. Pp. 9–33.

22 Well known in this context is Nikolai Karamzin's *Memoir on Ancient and Modern Russia* (1811), which not only delivered a new vision and narrative frame for historical writing in Russia but was also a conservative statement and, as far we understand it, a warning, if not a threat.

23 "The Influence of British Jurists, Political Economists, and Educators on the Ideas of Russia Modernization during the Reign of Alexander I (1801–1825)," see below Pp. 117–131.

ries and recommendations on setting up ideal criminal and civil codes, waned. These recommendations proved impossible to implement within the attempted codification project. By then, the goals, objectives, and means to bring it about had already been changed and fixed. The mass of "autochthonous" Russian legislation should had been collected, systematized, refurbished, and presented as unique (*samobytnyi*).

The radical political imaginings of Decembrists and members of the so-called secret societies concerning the republican types of political order in Russia could, as Vadim Parsamov[24] and Lorenz Erren[25] argue, be described and understood from the same vantage point—that is, as a mindset and radical politicking situated between the two poles. As Parsamov points out, republicanism as a theory had been seen by Decembrists as rather older than monarchism; put in historical perspective, a republic was not a new stage in history but rather the revival of an old tradition. The way to the future was thus a movement back to imagined "traditions." Parsamov declares: "Pestel's republic was not a republic in general sense, but a *Russian* republic rooted in national history, thus all its citizens could only be *Russians*."[26] Of course, there was on this road a barrier that should has been rejected—namely, autocratic power. Otherwise, both the debates about the disposal of the "usurper" and the December 1825 uprising itself were acts of a laboratorial nature.

All these revisions and projects did not necessarily lead to an immediate and consistent (re)organization of the political, social, and cultural structures of imperial space. The actors who provided competitive expertise and imaginings and nurtured their exclusive ambitions not only identified issues but also caused new problems. To give only a couple of prominent examples in this regard: Rosenkampff's model of compiling Russian law versus Speransky's attempt to design a completely new legal code;[27] Speransky's "Introduction to the Code of State Laws" versus Novosil'cev's "Constitutional Charter of the Russian Empire." Both of these debates dealt with finding a new political framework for the Russian empire and for state institutions, either on the basis of conventional cameralistic ideas of state-building excepting evident specifics of the imperial body or even recognizing, including, and improving them.[28]

24 "Republican Types in Russian Political culture, 1815–1825," see below Pp. 245–262

25 "Russia a Republic? Some Remarks on the National Consciousness of the Decembrists," see below Pp. 263–283.

26 Parsamov. Republican types. P. 249–249. Pestel's idea has elsewhere been described by Lemberg. Die nationale Gedankenwelt der Dekabristen.

27 Kaplunovsky. The Alexandrine Commission, see below Pp. 167–217.

28 Gerasimov / Mogilner / Glebov. Novaia imperskaia istoriia. Pp. 154–70.

In that time, the expansion of the Russian Empire in every cardinal direction, amid international conflict and a state of war, was coupled with internal challenges to domestic stability in the face of near bankruptcy.[29] An unstable period of large-scale wars lasted until 1815, when the European international order was been established. However, the same wars brought new subjects under the Russian imperial umbrella, and their economic, cultural, and legal differences had to be negotiated and administered. This ambiguity of imperial expansion is the main topic of two contributions in this volume. Victor Taki[30] and Constantin Troianowski[31] focus their chapters on territories and political upheavals in Bessarabia and Volhynia from the perspective of processes of incorporating, establishing, and redistributing political power.

Even if we know how the story goes—with its unsystematic and indecisive reforms and various borrowings—Alexandrine-era Russia may be seen as a network of interconnected experiments and labors. These experiments were not exempt of tensions and failures, as could be well shown in the case of some radical and highly complex but also unfinished or abandoned reforms. This proactive way of contribution and participation was made possible by both the liberal spirit of the epoch, especially in the first decade of Alexandrine reign, and the monarch himself. Nethertheless Alexander's liberal attitude was often drowned out by his indifference, undecidedness, shifting opinions, and lack of will to provide clear opportunities for political participation or even to prohibit any initiatives "from below." These faults made coherent implementation of ideas and reform projects so difficult and, considered in perspective, increasingly became a serious obstacle in a growing modern state that remained under strictly autocratic rule.

Last but not least, the person of monarch himself remains an important player and factor in this Russia as "laboratory" at the turn to the nineteenth century. Jan Kusber gives in his contribution[32] a short overview of the epoch. He discusses Alexander's self-fashioning as a ruler by giving a short biographical sketch, followed by an analysis of the achievements of Alexander's rule and his politics on various

29 Hartley / Keenan / Lieven (Eds.). Russia and the Napoleonic Wars; see also the article by Benjamin Conrad on finance politics in this volume, Pp. 95–116.

30 "Construction of Center and Periphery in the Reign of Alexander I: The Case of Bessarabia, 1812–1828," see below Pp. 317–337.

31 " 'The Volhynian Revolution': An Episode from the History of Relations between the Polish Nobility and the Imperial Government in the Age of Alexander I," see below Pp. 339–360.

32 "Alexander I, the Russian Empire, and the 'Sattelzeit' 1790–1830," see below Pp. 21–46.

fields. Following this chapter is a contribution from Franziska Schedewie that offers new approaches and insights for biographical explorations into Alexander I.[33] Summarizing her just-finished research project on unofficial diplomacy within the imperial family, Schedewie uses epistolary interactions between Alexander I and his younger sister Maria Pavlovna, an informal tsarist diplomat, to study the politicization of cultural concepts and terms such as kinship, friendship, and loyalty. Finally Maike Sach shows in her article how Alexander I not only depended on state experts but also on people with whom he was personally fascinated, such as Madame de Staël, whose anti-Napoleonic vision of Europe guided Alexander. Beyond this (inter)personal dimension, Sach shows that European international politics in that time were settled not only at congresses, in cabinets, or even with weapons, but also in intellectual salons such as that of Mme de Staël.

Summing up, we hope to uphold a promise made at the beginning of this introduction—namely, to reduce accumulated frustrations among historiographers by repositioning the puzzles of established works and current research projects dedicated to the Alexandrine epoch. It is now up to the readers of this volume to share and build on this view of early nineteenth-century Russian empire as laboratory—or to disagree.

List of references

ALMEDINGEN, EDITH. The Emperor Alexander I. London, 1964

BIKTASHEVA, ALSU. Kazanskoe gubernatorstvo pervoi poloviny XIX veka. Bremia vlasti. Moscow, 2014

GANZENMÜLLER, JÖRG. Russische Staatsgewalt und polnischer Adel: Elitenintegration und Staatsausbau im Westen des Zarenreiches (1772–1850). Köln, 2013

GANZENMÜLLER, JÖRG / TÖNSMEYER, TATJANA. Vom Vorrücken des Staates in die Fläche Ein europäisches Phänomen des langen 19. Jahrhunderts. In: GANZENMÜLLER, JÖRG / TÖNSMEYER, TATJANA (Eds.). Vom Vorrücken des Staates in die Fläche Ein europäisches Phänomen des langen 19. Jahrhunderts. 2016. Pp. 7–32

GERASIMOV, ILIA / MOGILNER, MARINA / GLEBOV, SERGEI. Novaia imperskaia istoriia Severnoi Evrazii. Vol. 2. Kazan, 2017.

GRUNWALD, CONSTANTIN DE. Alexandre Ier. Le tsar mystique. Paris, 1955; ALMEDINGEN, EDITH. The Emperor Alexander I. London, 1964

33 "Foreign Policy and Diplomacy of Alexander I, as from His Family Letters," see below Pp. 49–61.

Hartley, Janet M. Alexander I. London, 1994

Hartley, Janet M./ Keenan, Paul / Lieven, Dominic (Eds.). Russia and the Napoleonic Wars. New York, 2015

Hoogenboom, Hilde. Catherine the Great (1729–1796), Letter on Voltaire from Kazan, May 29, 1767. In: Stephen M. Norris / Willard Sunderland (Eds.). Russia's People of Empire. Life stories from Eurasia, 1500 to the Present. Indiana University Press, 2012. Pp. 81–93

Jenkins, Michael. Arakcheev. Grand Vizier of the Russian Empire. A Biography. London, 1967

Kenney, James. The Vorontsov Party in Russian Politics. An Examination of the Influence of an Aristocratic Family at the court of St. Petersburg in the Age of Revolution. Yale, 1975. Doctoral dissertation, unpublished manuscript

Kusber, Jan. Eliten- und Volksbildung im Zarenreich während des 18. und in der ersten Hälfte des 19. Jahrhunderts. Stuttgart, 2004

Lemberg, Hans. Die nationale Gedankenwelt der Dekabristen (= Kölner historische Abhandlungen. Bd. 7). Köln, 1963

Martin, Alexander M. Romantics, Reformers, Reactionaries: Russian Conservative Thought and Politics in the Reign of Alexander I. DeKalb, 1997

McConnell, Allen. Tsar Alexander I. Paternalistic Reformer. New York, 1970

Mironenko, Sergei. Samoderzhavie i reformy. Politicheskaia bor'ba v Rossii v nachale XIX v. Moscow, 1989

Mogilner, Marina. Homo Imperii. A History of Physical Anthropology in Russia. London, 2013

Mörke, Olaf. Die Diskussion um den Absolutismus als Epochenbegriff. Ein Beitrag über den Platz Katharinas II. in der europäischen Politikgeschichte. In: Eckhard Hübner / Jan Kusber / Peter Nitsche (Eds.). Russland zur Zeit Katharinas II. Absolutismus—Aufklärung—Pragmatismus. Köln, 1998. Pp. 9–33

Omelchenko, Oleg. "Zakonnaia monarkhiia" Ekateriny Vtoroi: prosveshchennyi absoliutizm v Rossii. Moscow, 1993

Palmer, Alan Warwick. Alexander I. Tsar of War and Peace. London, 1974

Parsamov, Vadim. Dekabristy i russkoe obshchestvo 1814–1825 gg. Moscow, 2016

Parsamov, Vadim (Ed.). M.M. Speranskii: Izbrannoe. Moscow, 2010

Parsamov, Vadim (Ed.). Sergei S. Uvarov: Izbrannye trudy. Moscow, 2010

Polskoi Sergei. Konstituciia i fundamentalnye zakony v russkom politicheskom diskurse XVIII veka. In: Aleksei Miller / Denis Zdizhkov / Ingrid Shirle (Eds.). "Poniatia o Rossii": K istoricheskoi semantike imperskogo perioda. Vol. 1. Moscow, 2012. Pp. 94–150

RAEFF, MARC. Michael Speransky. Statesman of Imperial Russia 1772–1839. The Hague, 1957

RAEFF, MARC. The Well-Ordered Police State: Social and Institutional Change through Law in the Germanies and Russia, 1600–1800. New Haven, 1983

RENNER, ANDREAS. Russische Autokratie und europäische Medizin. Organisierter Wissenstransfer im 18. Jahrhundert. Stuttgart, 2010

SAMBUK, DARIA. Wächter der Gesundheit. Staat und lokale Gesellschaften beim Aufbau des Medizinalwesens im Russländischen Reich 1762–1831. Köln, 2015

SARTORI, PAOLO / SHABLEI, PAVEL. Sudba imperskikh kodificacionnykh proektov: adat i shariat v Kazakhskoi stepi. In: Ab Imperio. # 2 2015. Pp. 63–105

TAKI, VICTOR. Tsar and Sultan: Russian Encounters with the Ottoman Empire. London, 2016

TOMSINOV, VLADIMIR. Arakcheev. Moscow, 2003

TOMSINOV, VLADIMIR. Speranskii. Moscow, 2006

VISHLENKOVA, ELENA. The State of Health: Balancing Power, Resources, and Expertise and the Birth of the Medical Profession in the Russian Empire. In: Ab Imperio. #3 2016. Pp. 39–75

VISHLENKOVA, ELENA. Zabotias o dushakh poddannykh. Religioznaia politika v Rossii pervoi chetverti XIX veka. Saratov, 2002

VISHLENKOVA, ELENA / IL'INA, KIRA. The science of rulership: Domination through knowledge and the administrative reform of Russian education in the first half of the nineteenth century. In: Ab Imperio. # 1 2017. Pp. 65–107

VISHLENKOVA, ELENA / SAVELIEVA, IRINA (Eds.). Soslovie russkikh professorov. Sozdateli statusov i smyslov. Moscow, 2013

WHITTAKER, CYNTHIA U. The Origins of Modern Russian Education: An Intellectual Biography of Count Sergei Uvarov, 1786–1855. DeKalb, 1984

ZAWADZKI, WACŁAW H. A Man of Honour. Adam Czartoryski as a Statesman of Russia and Poland. Oxford, 1993

Jan Kusber

Alexander I, the Russian Empire, and the "Sattelzeit" 1790–1830

1. A "Sattelzeit" within the Russian Empire?

One may say that any period in history is a transitional one. This is of course true not only in general but also for the Russian Empire. The turn of the eighteenth to nineteenth century, a time period called Sattelzeit by the late Reinhart Koselleck, is perhaps a special one. Koselleck had not Russia in mind but the Germanies when he described the period between 1750 and 1830 as a slow and uneven breakthrough of modernity on various fields of society and culture.[1] Politically, the "Heiliges Römisches Reich Deutscher Nation" was in decay and swept away during the Napoleonic Wars and was reerected as the loosely organized "German Confederation."[2] Within this period dramatic changes took place that led to the long path of a many-faced modernity. How about Russia?

Whereas the Catherinean age after the Pugachev uprising was a period of relative internal stability,[3] the Alexandrine age was not. The War of 1812 shook empire and society in the short and long run. The internal reforms of the great empress gave the empire in many ways a frame in which to develop; the rule of her grandson pushed the reforms further—in some fields in a more experimental way. The Europeanization of the elite by enlightened, sometimes protonational concepts, the challenge of the French Revolution during the last years of Catherine's rule, the ongoing process of institution-building, which reached also the provinces and the provincial elites—all these trends can be seen as the launching pad for the path of modernity in what we may call "Sattelzeit" in Russia.[4]

In an autocratic empire, the ruler plays a crucial role when it comes to reforms and the possibilities of various strata of society to participate in or even direct

1 Koselleck. Einleitung. P. XV.

2 Kusber. Russland, Europa und der Untergang des Alten Reiches, Pp. 55–70. For the European context, see: Erbe. Revolutionäre Erschütterung; Fehrenbach. Vom Ancien Régime zum Wiener Kongress.

3 The most thorough overviews are still: De Madariaga. Russia in the Age of Catherine the Great; Kamenskii. Pod seniiu Ekaeriny; Dixon. Catherine the Great.

4 Kusber. Faszination und Ablehnung. Pp. 116–28.

them. Of course, the autocratic model of rule should not be misinterpreted as purely top down. The ruler must cooperate at least with the ruling elites in the search for a consensus and in the field of public discourse.[5] Alexander's father, Paul I, offers a striking example. The beginning of his reign was marked by high hopes for a new surge of enlightened reform. As Catherine II's heir to the throne, he styled himself as a countermodel to his mother, who in the last years of her reign made no active efforts in the ongoing reform processes, horrified by the developments of the French Revolution. Radical enlightenment in her opinion led to an attack on the divine rule of kings, and the developments in the Polish-Lithuanian Commonwealth cemented her denial of state political participation to her subjects. There was a difference between the Catherine II of 1767, who was interested in broad public discourse, and the Catherine II of 1796, who feared public discourse and reintroduced censorship.[6] Her son, Paul, with his "small court" in Pavlovsk, his memoranda on enlightened rule, and his participation in freemasonry activities, seemed to promise an alternative, more open type of ruler.[7] This was, in fact, not the case. Paul's five years in power were perceived as erratic and disastrous, in foreign and—even more—in internal politics.[8] He was dethroned and murdered, and Alexander, heir to the throne and already prepared for his duties as a ruler by his grandmother Catherine, was involved in this conspiracy.[9] What type of ruler would he be?

Even for those who knew him well, that was no easy question to answer. Imprisoned by expectations of court and society, positioned between father and grandmother (Catherine had supervised his upbringing and education from his birth), he behaved somehow enigmaticly, was often dilatory, and made contradictory statements. And yet, there can be no doubt that Alexander wanted to be an active player in the development of reforms. He and his advisors—from Frédéric César de La Harpe[10] and Viktor Kochubei to Ekaterina Pavlovna or even Aleksei

---

5 For a neomarxist approach, see: LeDonne. Absolutism and Ruling Class; Idem, Ruling Families in the Russian Political Order, Pp. 233–322. For scholarship that uses the methods of cultural history, see: Zorin. Kormia dvuglavogo orla; Wortman. Scenarios of Power. Pp. 73–118. For a comparative and spatial view, see: Rieber. The Struggle for the Eurasian Borderlands. Pp. 79–292.

6 See my forthcoming interpretation of Catherine: Kusber. Katharina die Große.

7 Smith. Working the Rough Stone.

8 Ragsdale (Ed.), Paul I; Idem. Tsar Paul and the Question of Madness; McGrew. Paul I of Russia.

9 D'Encausse. The Russian Syndrome. Pp. 176–91.

10 Andreev / Tozato-Rigo (Eds.). Imperator Aleksandr I i Frederik-Sezar Lagarp.

Arakcheev—saw the empire as a construction site.[11] This perception was embodied in the construction of the Alexander Column in front of the Winter Palace by Alexander's brother Nicholas after the former's death. Interestingly enough, this structure was an abstract column crowned by an archangel and may thus be read variously as either a personification of the tsar, who was called around 1813–14 "our angel," or as Russia itself, shielded by God and divine providence so as to become the most influential power in continental Europe in Alexander's time.[12] This meant that all of Alexander's advisors were convinced that the only way to undertake change and modernization was to maintain a stable order. But the extent and the type of changes wanted within this Russian "Sattelzeit" was under dispute.

Thus, this chapter functions as an introduction to this volume. First, I discuss Alexander's self-fashioning as a ruler by giving a short biographical sketch. Though already well known, the basic facts about his life and his times are important for the volume as one of its relevant contexts. Then, second, I discuss the achievements of Alexander I's rule and his politics on various fields to set the stage for this book's case studies, which aim to analyze the different and sometimes contradictory developments of the empire in depth.

2. Personality and Autocracy in a European Frame

Alexander I was the first child and eldest son of Paul I and his second wife, Maria Fedorovna.[13] He was born in St. Petersburg on December 12, 1777. Immediately after his birth, he was removed from his parents by his grandmother Catherine the Great, who decided to bring the boy up herself—as Empress Elizabeth had done with Catherine's own son in 1754. Catherine later on gave ground to rumors that she intended to appoint Alexander as her heir, instead of his father, Paul. Catherine personally supervised the education of Alexander and his younger

---

11 On the problems of conceptualizing the Russian Empire, see: Gerasimov / Kusber / Glebov a.o. New Imperial History and the Challenges of Empire. Pp. 3–32.

12 The Alexander Column was designed by the French-born architect Auguste de Montferrand, built between 1830 and 1834 with Swiss-born architect Antonio Adamini, and unveiled on August 30, 1834. The monument is topped with a statue of an angel holding a cross, as a triumphal column. It is the heaviest recorded monolith to have been quarried, moved, and erected. The statue of the angel was designed by the Russian sculptor Boris Orlovskii. The face of the angel is said to bear great similarity to the face of Emperor Alexander I. See: Liubin. Aleksandrovskaia kolonna.

13 Maria Fedorovna's influence during Alexander's reign cannot be overstated. See the most comprehensive biography: Butenschön. Maria, Kaiserin von Russland.

brother Konstantin, laying out her ideas in a special document entitled "Instructions for the Education of my Grandsons."[14] The young grand dukes were tutored by Frédéric César de La Harpe, a Swiss liberal who became one of the directors of the Helvetic Republic after his tutorship of the royal family. Alexander later claimed that he owed La Harpe everything except his birth. The Grand Duke then claimed that he was a "republican."[15] This led to different interpretations, to varied expectations, and—later on—to disappointments.[16]

Even in his youth, Grand Duke Alexander felt trapped between the court of his grandmother and the "small court" of his parents. He tried to please both. Reticent, suspicious, and conceited, he was considered affected and insincere. But he was also known for his kindness and sentimentality. In fact, he never let anyone, liberals or conservatives, dominate him. He avoided open conflict, yet he always seemed to get his way, which made him a skillful diplomat and politician. Napoleon later confessed that he had been outwitted by the tsar.[17]

Outwardly, the emperor was handsome and charming. Frederick William III, King of Prussia, and his spouse, Luise, were deeply charmed by him when they first met. In 1807, after the negotiations near Tilsit, Napoleon wrote home to Josephine how fond he was of Alexander. All three would later change their impressions.[18]

On September 28, 1793, Grand Duke Alexander married Princess Louise Marie Auguste of Baden, who had converted to Orthodoxy as Elizaveta Alekseevna. Elizaveta was a niece of Paul I's first wife and had been invited to Russia along with her younger sister by Catherine II. The princess was said to have fallen in love with Alexander I immediately. But again, Catherine exercised her influence: she arranged the wedding when the betrothed were 14 and 15. Louise, then Elizaveta, gave birth to two daughters, who both died in infancy. Alexander soon lost interest in his wife and took a string of mistresses.[19] His longest affair was with Princess Maria Naryshkina, who gave birth to several of his children.[20]

---

14 Black. Citizens for the Fatherland. Pp. 74–76, 130.

15 Gielgud. Memoirs of Prince Adam Czartoryski. P. 111.

16 The best example is, perhaps, Alexander's relation to Adam Jerzy Czartoryski. See: Zawadski. A Man of Honour.

17 Martin. Romantics, Reformers, Reactionaries. Pp. 91–109.

18 Bailleu. Briefwechsel König Friedrich Wilhelms III.

19 Solov'eva. Elizaveta i Aleksandr.

20 Elizaveta Alekseevna herself may have had a closer relation with Alexander's friend Adam Jerzy Czartoryski, and there is some speculation about her relation to the famous

Alexander took no precautionary measures during the aforementioned plot against his father, a plot in which Alexander was involved. The new emperor was enthusiastically welcomed by the rest of the country. Young, intelligent, and well educated, he brought hopes of a more liberal and humane regime. Alexander I immediately demonstrated his liberal credentials by appointing an Unofficial Committee to seek ways to transform Russia through new reforms.[21] Was a constitutional monarchy the aim?[22] The committee was composed of such personal friends and associates of his youth as Prince Adam Jerzy Czartoryski, Count Pavel Stroganov, Prince Viktor Kochubei, and Count Nikolai Novosil'cev. The Unofficial Committee issued manifestos restoring the charters of Catherine II to the nobility and towns, granting pardons to those who had suffered under the previous tsar and allowing the purchase and sale of land by all free individuals.[23] New universities were opened in Kharkov, Kazan, Dorpat, and Vilna. Existing educational establishments were awarded new freedoms.[24] One of the most famous institutions founded by Alexander I was the Tsarskoye Selo Lyceum in 1811. Many famous Russians were educated there, including Alexander Pushkin[25]. When he was a lyceum student in the 1810s, the young poet paid tribute to Alexander I's role in the war against Napoleon and the liberal transformations at the start of his reign. Gymnasia were also founded in the governmental capitals of the empire.[26]

Alexander's reforms soon ran into resistance of members of the royal family, the court, and the nobility, foremost the so-called senatorial party led by the Zubov brothers . Even La Harpe advised Alexander not to rush into things. Finally, the emperor himself began to fear that any weakening of autocratic power would

---

Alexander Pushkin in her later years. On the difficult relations between Alexanderand his wife, see: KYLOV-TOLSTIKOVICH. Pocelui Psikhei.

21 ROACH. The Origins of Alexander I's Unofficial Committee. Pp. 315–26; MCCONNELL. Alexander I's Hundred Days. Pp. 373–93.

22 This question cannot be answered without the help of *Begriffsgeschichte*, or broader historical semantic analysis. What was meant by "constitutional" and "constitution"? Well ordered? See the articles of Alexander Kaplunovsky, Sergei Polskoy, and Vadim Parsamov in this volume.

23 For more on this, see: DEMKIN. Dnei Aleksandrovykh prkrasnoe nachalo.

24 FLYNN. The University Reform of Tsar Alexander I; WALKER. Popular Response to Public Education. Pp. 527–43; KUSBER. Eliten- und Volksbildung im Zarenreich. Pp. 277–342, 367–414; ANDREEV. Rossiiskie universitety. Pp. 372–406.

25 SINEL. The Socialization of the Russian Bureaucratic Elite. Pp. 1–31.

26 WALKER. Popular Response to Public Education. Pp. 527–43.

only help strengthen other groups, such as the bureaucracy; the Senate and the ministry reforms may serve as examples.[27] Also the laws concerning the Jews, who came into the Russian Empire with the partition of the Polish-Lithuanian Commonwealth, carried the sense of compromise with the elites. Personally convinced that Jews should have the same legal status as other subjects, Alexander left the legislative work to a commission under the presidency of Gavriil Derzhavin, minister of justice. The restrictions persisted.[28]

At this time Russia was being slowly drawn into the Napoleonic Wars. Although relations with France were initially cordial, the tsar's position began to change around 1802. He was dismayed at Napoleon's successes, yet he saw no strategic interest in helping Austria and its allies in their struggle against the Corsican upstart. Alexander felt personally offended by the murder of the Bourbon Duke d'Enghien in Baden and by the coronation of Napoleon as emperor in 1804.[29] Russia finally joined the anti-Napoleonic coalition in April 1805, but it was defeated by the French army at the Battles of Preussisch-Eylau and Friedland in the first half of 1807.[30] This led to a new orientation for Russian foreign policy.[31] The conference was held on the "neutral ground" of a raft with two grand white tents, hastily built by the French in the middle of the river. The main tent had a large green letter N on it facing the French side of the river and a large A facing the Russian (see fig. 1). The Prussians noted sourly that there was no initial for their king.

27 Narkiewicz. Alexander I and the Senate Reform. Pp. 115–36.

28 Hildermeier. Die jüdische Frage im Zarenreich, Pp. 332–36. The best study on this topic is still: Klier. Russia Gathers Her Jews. See also: Pękacz. To What Extent Did Prince Adam Czartoryski. Pp. 403–14.

29 Kusber. Russland, Europa und der Untergang des Alten Reiches. P. 61.

30 Wilms. Napoleon. Pp. 459–61. From a contemporary Russian viewpoint, see: Maikov. Zapiksi Grafa L.L. Beningsena.

31 Vneshniaia politika Rossii. Vol. 2. Dok. 194. Pp. 613–19; Vol. 3. Dok. 36. Pp. 110–16.

Figure 1. The Treaty of Tilsitz 1807 by Adolphe Roehn (1808). Copyright bpk | RMN – Grand Palais | Gérard Blot | Jean Schormans

The participants were ferried to the raft on June 25 for the first meeting. The French boat spurted so that Napoleon reached the raft first and went to greet the tsar as he arrived. This moment of greeting was a striking symbol for the communication between both ambitious rulers. The meetings continued for several days, punctuated by entertainment in the evenings, with both Napoleon and Alexander quartered in Tilsit, dining together every day and often talking alone together far into the night. They took to each other, hugged each other when they met, walked along holding hands, and exchanged cravats and handkerchiefs. Alexander had already told the Russian Orthodox Church to withdraw its 1806 anathematization of Napoleon as the Antichrist.

The treaty between France and Russia was signed on July 7, and the one between France and Prussia on July 9. Russia and Prussia were to join the Continental System, the blockade intended to destroy Britain's commerce, by closing their ports to British ships and neutral ships engaged in British trade. Prussia, treated with humiliating contempt, was made to give up territory for the creation of the new Grand Duchy of Warsaw, for Napoleon's ally the King of Saxony, and for the Kingdom of Westphalia for his youngest brother, Jerome Bonaparte. Prussia also had to reduce its army to forty thousand men and pay a huge indemnity to the French, meanwhile submitting to a French army of occupation until the money was handed over.[32] Many influential Russians and Prussians regarded the treaties as shameful capitulations, and they did not last.[33]

Alexander was shaken by the defeat of the Russian army and grew exasperated at his enforced friendship with Napoleon. He changed greatly over the years. As his former illusions and romanticism faded, the burden of governing a large empire began to weigh heavily on his shoulders. He faced growing resentments and resistance at court from very different personalities and groups, positioned around his mother. The successful, short war against Sweden in 1808–9 and the acquisition of the Grand Duchy of Finland, which was granted a high degree of autonomy[34] like the Baltic provinces in 1801, did not calm others' resentment of his agreement; the Continental Blockade became a serious problem over the years.[35]

Despite his doubts and hesitations, Alexander pressed on with his domestic reforms. Speransky—"the only clear head in Russia" (Napoleon)—rapidly increased his influence and activities in domestic politics between 1807 and 1812. In 1808 Speransky proposed to the emperor the memorandum "On Improvement of the Folk Education," which introduced and described the necessity of broad educational reform in the Russian empire, and which was partially implemented. One year later Speransky drew up a fundamental project, the "Introduction to the Code of State Laws." The title of this document is rather misleading because it pivotally reframed the political and social body of the Russian empire, for example with a legislative parliament (*duma*), a state council as the main executive institution, and also (or even more essentially) with the modernization and codification of civil rights.[36] Alexander estimated his work highly, but, as usual, was hesitant. In the end, Speransky could not convince the emperor to sign this radical document.

Without explanation, the tsar dismissed Speransky from office in March 1812, at the eve of the Napoleonic invasion.[37] Europe expected the war: On December 31, 1810, Russia withdrew from the Continental System and reopened trade

32 Stamm-Kuhlmann. König in Preußens großer Zeit. Pp. 252–58.

33 Kusber. Das Zarenreich und die Deutschen Staaten im Banne Napoleons. Pp. 192–99.

34 Butenschön. Maria, Kaiserin von Russland. Pp. 248–49.

35 Hildermeier. Geschichte Russlands. Pp. 725–29.

36 Gerasimov / Mogilner / Glebov. Novaia imperskaia istoriia. Pp. 154–70.

37 Christian. The Political Ideals of Michael Speransky. Pp. 192–213; Chibiriaev. Velikii russkii reformator; Morozov. Gosudarstvenno-pravovye vzgliady M.M. Speranskogo.

with Great Britain. Napoleon moved a great army of six hundred thousand men into the Grand Duchy of Warsaw, ready to force a decisive battle with the Russians. When the tsar did not respond, Napoleon invaded Russia on June 24, 1812.[38]

The French attack spurred Alexander into action. He declared that he would not lay down arms until the last enemy soldier had been expelled from Russian soil. The tsar vowed never to sign peace, not even if he had to retreat to the very end of the Russian Empire. Commanded by Prince Michael Andreas Barclay de Tolly, the Russian army drew the invaders deep into the interior, employing scorched-earth tactics. This caused widespread anger and frustration among the population. In a rare concession to public opinion, Alexander appointed his critic Prince Mikhail Kutuzov as commander-in-chief of the Russian forces.[39] On September 7, 1812, Kutuzov engaged Napoleon at the Battle of Borodino. Both sides suffered heavy losses, with a third of the French and half of the Russian army killed or wounded. After a conference at the village of Fili on September 13, Kutuzov fell back on the strategy of his predecessor and decided to retreat. This opened up the road to Moscow, which was captured by the French army on September 14. But it was a Pyrrhic victory, as the city was abandoned by its residents and caught fire. Alexander regarded the fire of Moscow as a divine punishment for his sins and his role in his father's death. He was heavily criticized for enabling the Grande Armée's attack on Moscow; one of the most prominent voices was his sister Ekaterina Pavlovna.[40] Despite losing Moscow, Alexander refused to surrender. A month later, the French invaders were forced to leave the ruined city and retreat toward Smolensk, harried all the time by mounted Cossacks and irregular troops. The effect of the invasion, the occupation, and the mobilization of society on the second half of Alexander's reign cannot be overstated.[41] On December 14, 1812, the Grande Armée was finally thrown out of Russia. Intoxicated by victory and against the advice of Kutuzov, Alexander decided to pursue Napoleon through Europe and invade France. The Russian emperor often rode into the field of bat-

---

38 There is abundant historiography on the wars of 1812. For a classic Soviet account, see: Tarlé. Napoleon in Russland; Mühlstein. Der Brand von Moskau; Zamoyski. Napoleons Feldzug in Russland. For the Russian perspective (and rich source material), see: Lieven. Russland gegen Napoleon.

39 On the Russian generals around 1812 see the collective biography: Bezotosnyi. Rossiiskii generaltitet epokhi 1812 goda.

40 Tarlé. Der Brand von Moskau. P. 63.

41 On this effect, see most recently: Belov. 1812 god v sud'be russkogo goroda. See also: Katzer. Russland 1812 und 1825, Pp. 117–39; Wortman. Myth and Memory. Pp. 145–79.

tle himself. At the Battle of Lützen on May 2, 1813, when advised to retreat to a safe distance after coming under heavy fire, he replied that his fate were not here.

The Russian army crossed the French border in spring 1814 and entered Paris on March 31.[42] Alexander rode on a white horse once presented to him by Napoleon. The French emperor was forced to abdicate on April 6 and exiled to the isle of Elba off the coast of Italy.

On April 10, 1814, Alexander ordered an Orthodox Easter mass to be celebrated in the place where King Louis XVI had been guillotined in 1793. Two weeks later, the State Council, Holy Synod, and Cabinet of Ministers awarded the emperor the title of "Alexander the Blessed."[43]

Although the French had plundered and pillaged Russia, Paris escaped the same fate. The tsar was gracious toward the former empress Josephine and her children. At the Château de Malmaison, he acquired the collection of paintings belonging to Napoleon's first wife for the Imperial Hermitage.

The victorious powers met to redraw the map of Europe at the Congress of Vienna.[44] In 1815, Alexander signed the Holy Alliance with the Habsburg monarchy and Prussia as a bastion against revolution. The introduction could be read as a manifesto of the views of Alexander at that time:

> THEIR Majesties the Emperor of Austria, the King of Prussia, and the Emperor of Russia, having, in consequence of the great events which have marked the course of the three last years in Europe, and especially of the blessings which it has pleased Divine Providence to shower down upon those States which place their confidence and their hope on it alone, acquired the intimate conviction of the necessity of settling the steps to be observed by the Powers, in their reciprocal relations, upon the sublime truths which the Holy Religion of our Saviour teaches.
>
> They solemnly declare that the present Act has no other object than to publish, in the face of the whole world, their fixed resolution, both in the administration of their respective States, and in their political relations with every other Government, to take for their sole guide the precepts of that Holy Religion, namely, the precepts of Justice, Christian Charity, and Peace, which, far from being applicable only to private concerns, must have an immediate influence on the councils of Princes, and guide all their steps, as being the only means of consolidating human institutions and remedying their imperfections.[45]

---

42 For a detailed analysis, see: Rey. 1814, un Tsar à Paris.

43 Kusber. Russland 1812 als europäisches Ereignis. Pp. 7–15; Idem. 1812 und die Folgen. Pp. 47–63.

44 For an excellent overview, see: Duchhardt. Der Wiener Kongress, Jarrett. The Congress of Vienna.

45 The Parliamentary Debates from the Year 1803 to the Present Time, Vol. 32. London 1916. Pp. 355–57. In French: Corpus Juris Confoederationis Germanicae oder

The tsar dreamt of heading a different world order rooted in God. He saw himself guided by a common Christian faith, a belief and worldview that were viewed critically by contemporaries in Europe and in Russia. The events of 1812 and lingering pangs of conscience over his father's murder led Alexander to immerse in mysticism. Pseudoreligious and mystical cults flourished throughout the country. After the war with revolutionary France, the emperor grew increasingly conservative. Russia entered another period of stagnation, although it would be a misinterpretation to conclude that Alexander refrained from thinking about reforms. Continued interest in reforms is evident in the Kingdom of Poland's constitution, which was created at the Vienna Congress; the projects of Nikolai Novosil'cev for a new political order for Russia, which included regionalization and participation and were often discussed in conjunction with a Russian constitution;[46] the Bessarabian constitution; and the abolition of serfdom in the Baltics.[47]

Alexander's leading statesman was now the loyal but reactionary Count Aleksei Arakcheev. Supported by the tsar, he created a network of military settlements, which combined the dual hardships of army service and agricultural labor. In Russia, Arakcheev's name became a byword for a military state and reactionary repression.[48]

In 1818, Alexander was alarmed by rumors and reports of a revolutionary conspiracy among the imperial guards. The authorities were particularly suspicious of masonic lodges, with their surreptitious rituals and mystical symbols. In 1822, the emperor signed a decree banning all secret societies, including masonic lodges.[49]

The tsar's growing conservatism forced Alexander Pushkin, who had once lauded what he called the "wonderful first days of Alexander," into the arms of the opposition. When notes of criticism crept into his writings, the poet was banished from St. Petersburg. After that, Pushkin was generally scathing toward the emperor, whom he called weak and sly.[50]

Staatsacten für Geschichte und öffentliches Recht des Deutschen Bunds. Pp. 290–91. See also: Schaeder. Autokratie und Heilige Allianz; Pyta. Idee und Wirklichkeit der "Heiligen Allianz." Pp. 315–45; Idem. Konzert der Mächte und kollektives Sicherheitssystem. Pp. 133–73; Ghervas. Réinventer la tradition; Menger. Die Heilige Allianz.

46 Kusber. Kann der Zar König sein. Pp. 253–70.

47 Hildermeier. Geschichte Russlands. Pp. 740–44.

48 There is still no better work on Arakcheev than: Jenkins. Arakcheev. On the military colonies, a still useful classic is: Pipes. The Russian Military Colonies. Pp. 205–19. See also (on the so called *Arakcheevshchina*): Tomsinov. Arakcheev. Pp. 193–234.

49 Donnert. Die Freimaurerei in Russland. Pp. 133–44; Faggionato. From a Society of the Enlightened to the Enlightenment of Society. Pp. 459–87.

50 Lauer. Aleksandr Pushkin. Pp. 86–88; 92 f.

The final years of Alexander's life were unhappy. Disillusioned with power and fame, he felt that he had lived his life in vain. This sense of disenchantment was particularly evident during the great flood of St. Petersburg on November 7, 1824. From the windows of the Winter Palace, the tsar watched as the wild elements raged out of control, killing hundreds of people. The autocratic ruler of a great empire, Alexander was yet unable to do anything to save his subjects, until the murderous winds died down at the will of God. The following day, the emperor toured the city, seeing for himself the traces of destruction.[51]

What had happened to the kind and compassionate man who had offered so much hope for liberal reforms at the start of his reign? In the intervening years, Alexander had lost many of his illusions regarding both himself and Russia. There was no more talk of the transformations that had previously been his whole raison d'être. Changes, it seemed, were not possible without reducing the power of the throne. The disappointed tsar realised that autocracy and freedom were incompatible.

There was another important reason why Alexander did not want to attempt any more reforms—or even to rule Russia. He was disappointed in the executive, the people, and the country as a whole. Alexander was convinced that there was no point doing anything worthwhile in Russia because the people were unworthy. He readily granted a constitution to the Kingdom of Poland and to the Grand Duchy of Finland, because these nations were in his opinion orderly, competent, and virtuous. But, for the tsar, Russia itself was a different matter.

Alexander I did not seem comfortable in his own country. A Russian sovereign had never spent so much time abroad since Peter the Great.[52] Accompanied by a small entourage, he traveled across Europe in an open carriage. Alexander Pushkin called him a nomadic despot. The emperor possibly sought solace in the ever-changing scenery or the solitude of a traveler on the road. He said that he was weary and wanted to abdicate. Once he had pursued glory and recognition; now he desired anonymity. Hence the persistent rumors that he faked his own death to become a hermit.

By this time, Alexander had left Princess Maria Naryshkina and returned to his wife, who was increasingly suffering from poor health. The couple decided to travel to the south of Russia, setting off from St. Petersburg in September 1825. While the tsar was visiting the Crimea in October 1825, he caught a fever and died

---

51 Butenschön. Maria, Kaiserin von Russland. P. 325.

52 Hartley. It Is the Festival of the Crown and Scepters. Pp. 246–68. On his diplomatic activities after 1815, see: Orlik. Rossiia v mezhdunarodnykh otnosheniiakh. Pp. 11–22; Dodolev. Rossiia i problemy Germanskoi Konfederacii. Pp. 124–47.

in the port of Taganrog on the Sea of Azov on November 19, 1825. The unexpected death of Alexander I and his nocturnal funeral attended only by close friends gave rise to many myths. The most popular legend is that he did not die at all and that someone else was buried in his place. The sovereign allegedly retreated to Siberia, later resurfacing as Feodor Kuzmich, a wandering pilgrim known for his righteous life who died in a forest near Tomsk in January 1864.[53]

3. Heritage, Perspectives and Interpretations

Alexander was dubbed by Marian Dziewanowski as "indecisive" and as "Russia's mysterious tsar" some twenty-five years ago;[54] he was named an "autocratic idealist" by Manfred Hildermeier much more recently.[55] The epoch in general, however, lacks a clear political character. So far, historiography has tended to distinguish between a "liberal" first and a "conservative-mythical" second part of Alexander I's reign, with the 1812 Napoleonic invasion serving as the point of rupture.[56] Due to its two hundredth anniversary, the Patriotic War of 1812 has been in focus among Russian (and foreign) historiographers.[57] Although this war presents a separate field of study, it, along with the secret societies and the Decembrist movement, is deeply interwoven in historiographies with both parts of Alexander's reign, the reforms, the way the empire was viewed by the elites, the involvement in European and international affairs, and the despondent emperor in his late years. Overall, the epoch of Alexander I is highly underresearched—in contrast to the reign of his grandmother Catherine II or his nephew Alexander II.

A congruous theme and aim of the studies presented here is to show how the European development of the age was transferred into the imperial interior and influenced by such factors as war and international alliances. This angle is all the more important considering that the expansion of the Russian Empire to

53 This legend is a popular topic in prerevolutionary historiography. See, for example: Romanov. Legenda o konchine imperatora Aleksandra. On all facets of this legend, see: Troubetzkoy. Imperial Legend.

54 Dziewanowski. Alexander I.

55 Hildermeier, Geschichte Russlands. P. 706.

56 See, for example: Palmer. Alexander I; Solov'ev. Imperator Aleksandr I; Sakharov. Aleksandr I; Arkhangel'skii. Aleksandr I. See the different interpretations in: Rey. Alexander I; Hartley. Alexander I.

57 See, for example, Elena Vishlenkova's study on the visual culture of 1812: Vishlenkova. Der Krieg von 1812 im Spiegel der visuellen Kultur. Pp. 126–39.

the west and south,[58] amid international conflict and a state of war, was coupled with internal challenges to domestic stability in the face of near bankruptcy.[59] An unstable period of large-scale wars lasted until 1815, when the European international order was established. However, the same wars brought new subjects under Russian imperial control, and their economic, cultural, and legal differences had to be negotiated and administered. One of the most important issues was of course the constitutional challenge by the Poles and the Finns. What did it mean that the Russian emperor as king of Poland and grand duke of Finland guaranteed constitutional freedom and autonomous rights, while the other imperial subjects acted within the framework of a more or less enlightened autocracy? Was regionalization of administration a real option for Alexander and not only for Nikolai Novosil'cev?

Some of Alexander's contemporaries were sympathetic to the reform changes. In the year 1824, a year before Alexander's death, Count Langeron, as Allan McConnell quotes, wrote that the contemporaries of Catherine the Great would not recognize their country if by chance they come back on earth, because: "between the Russia of 1790 and that of 1824 there is a distance of three hundred years."[60] This is a remarkable judgment, insofar as Peter the Great's contemporary Friedrich Christian Weber or Catherine's contemporary August Ludwig Schlözer were similarly enthusiastic in the beginning of their respective eras but not the end. The recent biography by Marie-Pierre Rey adopts this view of Langeron. Other contemporaries were not that optimistic: Nikolai Karamzin, in an 1811 memorandum to Alexander I, expressed disappointment and skepticism of the tsar's achievements. He became further convinced of the necessity of undivided autocratic power and urged Alexander to order the empire top down.[61]

On an international, even global—if one takes the expansion in the northern Pacific into account[62]—stage, Russia had become a major actor, not only due to the power of the army and the victories won over Napoleon, but more importantly due to the constant interest of Russian diplomacy and the tsar personally in European matters. International and multilateral plans for peace were on Alexander's table, whether drafted by Adam Jerzy Czartoryski or Vasilii Malinovskii before

58 For the expansion in the southern Caucasus, see: Nachtigal. Verkehrswege in Kaukasien. Pp. 54–116.

59 Hartley / Keenan / Lieven (Eds.). Russia and the Napoleonic Wars.

60 McConnell is quoted in: Rey. Alexander I. Pp. 377 f.

61 Pipes. Karamzin's Memoir on Ancient and Modern Russia. See also: Martin. Romantics, Reformers, Reactionaries. P. 97.

62 Winkler. Das Imperium und die Seeotter. Pp. 256–82.

1812[63]—or by himself.[64] More religious was Alexander's influence on the Holy Alliance, a term and concept mocked by Metternich as holy nonsense. Religion governed Alexander's thinking, even impacting internal policies, as we will see when it comes to the Bible Society.

Alexander I and the elites of the empire perceived Russia as on par with Great Britain and France and, of course, the Habsburg monarchy and Prussia. The tsar helped to greatly modify the image of Russia and Russians in Western Europe. Napoleonic propaganda had been partially successful in portraying Russians as barbarians. After 1812 the Russians were welcomed as liberators, but for example during the Siege of Mainz in winter 1813–14, the Russian troops were described as wild Cossacks or Mongols.[65] This winter is remembered in Germany as the Cossack winter. But in 1814–15 this hostile impression faded, ceding to a more nuanced, positive discourse.[66]

The trip that Alexander I made through Western Europe in these years was decisive for the country's evolution. The tsar's charm and seductiveness convinced western European elites of Russia's full-fledged membership in Europe.[67] Even after 1821–22, when the Holy Alliance was transformed into an instrument of repression, designed to stabilize and support authoritarian monarchies in their combat against revolution, Alexander continued to promote a European course, although in a more regressive way. He would do so until his death. As Elena Vishlenkova has pointed out, even a monument in remembrance of the Patriotic War of 1812 was planned in a classical European style: the first plans for the Cathedral of Christ the Saviour looked a bit like St. Peter's Basilica in Rome.[68]

But does this all mean that Alexander neglected the interests of the Russian Empire or the Russians? Such is the judgment of conservative contemporaries and, following them, of conservative Russian historians. Although the Patriotic

---

63 RAGSDALE. Russian Foreign Policy. Pp. 504–29. For more detail, see: SCHIPPAN. Die Französische Revolution von 1789. Pp. 353–61; GRIMSTEDT (Ed.). Czartoryski's System for Russian Foreign Policy. Pp. 19–91; SKOWRONEK. Antynapoleonskie końcepcje Czartoryskiego.

64 VNESHNIAIA POLITIKA ROSSII. Dokumenty Rossiiskogo Ministerstva Inostrannykh Del. Vol. 2. Pp. 138–46.

65 See the entries of second half of 1813 in: PUSHIN. Diaries of the 1812–1814 Campaigns.

66 For examples from the German press: FREYBURGER WOCHENBLATT. # 2, Mittwoch, den 5. Januar 1814. P. 13; MAINZER ZEITUNG. # 1, Donnerstag, den 5. Mai 1814. Front page.

67 On the tsar's self-fashioning at the congress of Aachen in 1818, see: DUCHHARDT. Der Aachener Kongress. Pp. 99–102.

68 VISHLENKOVA. Der Krieg von 1812 im Spiegel der visuellen Kultur. Pp. 133–37.

War of 1812 is nowadays spoken of as a heroic moment of Russian national greatness, since at least the time of the renowned historian Evgenii Tarle, Alexander I has been absented from the (metaphoric) galleries of heroes of that year. These conservative historians neglect to realize that the "European dreams" of Alexander—to quote his sister Ekaterina Pavolvna in her letters from Tver, in which she accused her brother of indecisiveness—were the main ingredient for a Russian Empire as the leading power in the world. For Alexander, these notions—Europeanism and Russianism—were closely connected.

Moreover, as in the age of Catherine the Great, in the course of Alexander's reign, the empire considerably expanded, both to the west and the south. In this perspective, the Treaty of Tilsit meant an opportunity, not a defeat. The annexation of Finland after a short, victorious war,[69] the gains in the Caucasus, the integration of Bessarabia after another war against the Ottoman Empire and, of course, the aforementioned creation of a Polish state under Russian control were the fruits of an expansionist dynamic that puts Alexander in one line with Peter I and Catherine II .

On the other hand, the expansion of empire and the engagement of the tsar on the international stage led to a decreasing awareness of internal developments. Alexander I was the first Russian ruler since Peter I to live and work abroad, in the theaters of war, and also in the numerous congresses before and after Vienna. His continuous engagement in service of Russia's power and geopolitical interests was, as Marie-Pierre Rey sums up, largely accomplished to the detriment of the domestic scene and its development. The long wars against France and its partners proved terribly costly on the demographic, financial, and economic level. After the heavy damages of the 1812 invasion, the cost of reconstructing territories was particularly high. But the consequences were also political: beginning in 1805, when diplomatic and strategic questions became more pressing with the lead-up to the Battles of Jena and Auerstedt; and culminating in 1812, when these questions assumed vital importance, domestic affairs found themselves either conditioned by diplomatic priorities or almost completely dropped. This neglect of domestic affairs may be one of the big differences from the beginning of the eighteenth century: whereas Peter gained acclaim for the reforms that he initiated as part of the Great Northern War, Alexander's reforms came under fire for their role in the fight against the usurper Napoleon and the idea of revolution.

But it is worth discussing whether it was only the first years of his reign that were crucial for domestic policies. These were the years when the spirit was re-

69 Scheibert. Die Anfänge der finnischen Staatswerdung. Pp. 351–430.

formist and a number of concrete initiatives were taken, including the founding of the ministries and the educational reforms with their new universities and gymnasia. Russian and Soviet history have fixed on these years, which were also marked by the rise and fall of Mikhail Speransky, due to the efforts to codify laws at this time. Yet, we will see in this volume that Russia as a country ruled by law was an idea that the tsar and the elites dealt with during the whole epoch.

Of course, the same is true when we follow the discourse on serfdom, which had not vanished from the agenda since the time of Catherine the Great.[70] During the reign of Alexander I, the educated public in Russia—facing Alexander's reforms and seeing the efforts of the peasantry in the Patriotic War—became more and more aware that serfdom was against humanity and an obstacle to modernization as well. In Russian discourse this had been clear since the debates of the Free Economic Society in the 1760s, though, as Susan McCaffray has pointed out, the discourse was alive but led not to emancipation but to minor measures to lighten the burdens of emancipation.[71] But by the end of his reign, a number of projects were on the table that would be valuable for the discussion in the time of Nicholas I and the liberation in the beginning of the reign of Alexander II.[72]

Last but not least it is important to keep in mind that the debates over liberalization and modernization of civil rights, and especially over property rights, at the beginning of the Alexandrine reign were still connected with the civil and property rights of nobility. A fundamental part of these rights was however the exclusive ownership of serfs, which had been provided to nobility not so long before. Thus, the liberation of the serfs in the Governorates of Livonia and Estonia in 1816 and 1818 bore the character of compromise and served as experiments in freeing the peasants without touching the property rights of the nobility.[73]

---

70 McCaffray. Confronting Serfdom in the Age of Revolution. Pp. 1–21.

71 See for example his decree to lighten the burden of poor peasants in the Government of Minsk: PSZ I. Vol. 35. № 27316. 23.3.1818. "Ob utverzhdenii vsekh sdelannykh po Mozyrskomu povetu, v oblegchenie krestian, rasporiazhenii i o rasprostranenii onykh na vsiu Minskuiu i na prochiia, ot Polshi priobretennye gebrnii." Pp. 170–72. O'Meara. The Opinion of One Ukrainian Landowner, Pp. 315–35.

72 Kiianskaia, Ocherki iz istorii obshchestvennogo dvizheniia Rossii, Pp. 205–50.

73 Kusber. Leibeigenschaft im Rußland der Frühen Neuzeit. Pp. 149–54. Donnert. Agrarfrage und Aufklärung in Lettland und Estland. Pp. 50–52. For an early attempt at describing the abolition of serfdom as a sole undertaking of the Baltic elite, see: Himmelstiern / Ludwig. Historischer Versuch über die Aufhebung der Leibeigenschaft in den Ostseeprovinzen.

Was the country, overall, more administered than governed, as historians have argued?[74] John LeDonne explains that

> The defining event in the administrative history of Alexander's reign was the creation of ministries in September 1802, followed by the gradual establishment of direct hierarchical relations between them and provincial agencies responsible for the management of individual sectors. Any forms of concentrated territorial management would involve the creation at the regional level of agencies combining various sectors under the authority of a delegate representing all the ministers, acting as their intermediary with the provincial agencies, and responsible to the emperor or a prime minister as the chief of a concentrated central government. The nature of government in the ruling elite—which saw the tsar emperor as the final arbiter of its political rivalries but considered the management of a vast empire its exclusive preserve, apportioned among a number of ministers, each defending his turf with tenacious determination—precluded the creation of such a delegate empowered to interfere in the operations of individual ministries, and hindered the establishment of a concentrated form of government in Petersburg. The deconcentration of government at the central level following the opening of ministries was incompatible with the acceptance of concentrated management at the regional level.[75]

In fact, at the economic and social level, little changed. The urban population was still about 4 percent of the national population, and despite the wars, demographic growth was unchanged. Russia lost its position as a global producer of iron. Technical innovation was slow both in its conception—at universities, institutes, and the academies—and in practice throughout the empire, although the technical breakthroughs that would take place in the reactionary reign of Nicholas I would be unthinkable without the educational reforms of Alexander I.

Historians have interpreted the apparently meager results during Alexander's reign as, dually, an increasing stubbornness against reforms and an increasing fear of a revolutionary coup d'état. And yet, Alexander was quite firm in resisting pressure from a court bristling with rumors and hostility to the Tilsit accord, his 1808 trip to Erfurt,[76] his conduct at the head of his Cossack regiments in the 1813 campaigns, and even his nonchalant behavior on hearing rumors of possible upheavals in the Semenovskii regiment in 1822–23. There is, at least, no doubt that Alexander was sincerely attached to reforms up until 1820–21, although he became more cautious and pessimistic.[77]

---

74 See the discussions in: Mironenko. Samoderzhavie i reformy.

75 LeDonne. Administrative Regionalization in the Russian Empire. Pp. 5–33. Cited P. 5.

76 Wilms. Napoleon. Pp. 486–489.

77 The number of laws and decrees signed by Alexander stands against a too pessimistic interpretation in: Tomsinov (Ed.). Zakonodatel'stvo imperatora Aleksandra I.

And in my opinion, we lack a proper explanation for Alexander's mysticism, which—from a contemporary view—was more than astonishing.[78] Universal Christian faith across a Europe that was deeply connected and at peace; the rise of the Bible Society;[79] and the Russian national consciousness and the modern concept of nationalism that rooted in the elites, led into somehow contradictory trajectories of history, embodied in Alexander himself. The Russian Empire lived its own specific path in the European "Sattelzeit."[80] The contribution of Alexander I, today one of the minor popular personalities among the Romanovs, is still to be fully discovered.

List of references

ANDREEV, ANDREI IU. Rossiiskie universitety XVIII–pervoi poloviny XIX veka v kontekste universitetskoi istorii Evropy. Moscow, 2016

ANDREEV, ANDREI IU. / TOZATO-RIGO, D. (Eds.). Imperator Aleksandr I i Frederik-Sezar Lagarp: Pis'ma. Dokumenty / Perevod s francuzskogo V.A. Mil'chinoi. Vol. 1. Moscow, 2014

ARKHANGEL'SKII, ALEKSANDR. Aleksandr I. Moscow, 2000

BAILLEU, PAUL. Briefwechsel König Friedrich Wilhelms III. und der Königin Louise mit Alexander I. Nebst ergänzenden fürstlichen Korrespondenzen. Leipzig, 1900 (Reprint Osnabrück, 1967)

BATALDEN, STEPHEN K. Printing the Bible in the Reign of Alexander I: Toward a Reinterpretation of the Imperial Russian Bible Society. In: GEOFFREY HOSKING (Ed.). Church, Nation and State in Russia and the Ukraine. London, 1991. Pp. 65–78

BELOV, A.V. 1812 god v sud'be russkogo goroda: Vliianie napoleonskogo nashestviia na sostaianie gorodskikh poselenii central'noi Rossii i zhizni obivatelei. Moscow, 2018

BEZOTOSNYI, V.M. Rossiiskii generaltitet epokhi 1812 goda: Opyt izucheniia kollektivnoi biografii. Moscow, 2018

BLACK, J.L. Citizens for the Fatherland: Education, Educators and Pedagogical Ideals in Eighteenth Century Russia. Boulder, Col., 1979

78 Although not overall convincing, see on this topic: ZORIN / SCHLAFLY. Star of the East. Pp. 313–42.

79 ZACEK. The Russian Bible Society and the Russian Orthodox Church. Pp. 411–37; BATALDEN. Printing the Bible in the Reign of Alexander I. Pp. 65–78.

80 HARTLEY. Is Russia Part of Europe? Pp. 369–385.

Butenschön, Marianna. Maria, Kaiserin von Russland: Die Württembergerin auf dem Zarenthron. Darmstadt, 2015

Chibiriaev, S.A. Velikii russkii reformator. Zhizn', deiatel'nost', politicheskie vzgliady M.M. Speranskogo. Moscow, 1993

Christian, David. The Political Ideals of Michael Speransky. In: Slavonic and East European Review. Vol. 44 (1966). Pp. 192–213

Corpus Juris Confoederationis Germanicae oder Staatsacten für Geschichte und öffentliches Recht des Deutschen Bunds, hrsg. v. Philipp Anton Guido Meyer, Teil 1. Staatsverträge. 3. Aufl. Frankfurt a. M., 1858. Pp. 290–91

De Madariaga, Isabel. Russia in the Age of Catherine the Great. New Haven, 1981

Demkin, Andrei V. "Dnei Aleksandrovykh prekrasnoe nachalo…": vnutrenniaia politika Aleksandra I v 1801–1805 gg. Moscow, 2012

D'Encausse, Hélène Carrère. The Russian Syndrome: One Thousand Years of Political Murder. New York, 1992

Dixon, Simon. Catherine the Great. London, 2009

Dodolev, M.A. Rossiia i problemy Germanskoi Konfederacii v pervye gody sushchestvovaniia Sviashchennogo soiuza (1815–1820). In: Rossiia i Germaniia. Vol. 1. Moscow, 1998. Pp. 124–47

Donnert, Erich. Agrarfrage und Aufklärung in Lettland und Estland: Livland, Estland und Kurland im 18. und beginnenden 19. Jahrhundert. Frankfurt a. M., 2008.

Donnert, Erich. Die Freimaurerei in Russland: Von den Anfängen bis zum Verbot 1822. Innsbruck, 2003

Duchhardt, Heinz. Der Aachener Kongress 1818. Ein europäisches Gipfeltreffen im Vormärz. München, 2018

Duchhardt, Heinz. Der Wiener Kongress: Die Neugestaltung Europas 1814/15. München, 2013

Dziewanowski, Marian K. Alexander I—Russia's Mysterious Tsar. New York, 1990.

Erbe, Michael. Revolutionäre Erschütterung und erneuertes Gleichgewicht: Internationale Beziehungen 1785–1830. Paderborn, 2004

Faggionato, Raffaella. From a Society of the Enlightened to the Enlightenment of Society: The Russian Bible Society and Rosicrucianism in the Age of Alexander I. In: Slavonic and East European Review. Vol. 79 (2001) # 3. Pp. 459–87

Fehrenbach, Elisabeth. Vom Ancien Régime zum Wiener Kongress. München, 2008.

Flynn, James T. The University Reform of Tsar Alexander I, 1802–1835. Washington, DC, 1988

Freyburger Wochenblatt. # 2, Mittwoch, den 5. Januar 1814. P. 13

Gerasimov, Ilya / Kusber, Jan / Glebov, Sergey / Mogilner, Marina / Semyonov, Alexander. New Imperial History and the Challenges of Empire. In: Ilya Gerasimov / Jan Kusber / Alexander Semyonov e.o. (Eds.). Empire Speaks out? Languages of Rationalization and Self-Description in the Russian Empire. Leiden, 2009. Pp. 3–32.

Gerasimov Ilia / Mogilner, Marina / Glebov, Sergei. Novaia imperskaia istoriia Severnoi Evrazii. Vol. 2. Kasan, 2017

Ghervas, Stella. Réinventer la tradition. Alexandre Stourdza et l'Europe de la Sainte-Alliance. Honoré Champion. Paris, 2008.

Gielgud, Adam (Ed.). Memoirs of Prince Adam Czartoryski and His Correspondence with Alexander I. Vol. 1. London, 1888.

Government of Minsk: PSZ I. Vol. 35. №. 27.316. 23.3.1818. "Ob utverzhdenii vsekh sdelannykh po Mozyrskomu povetu, v oblegchenie krestian, rasporiazhenii i o rasprostranenii onykh na vsiu Minskuiu i na prochiia, ot Polshi priobretennye gebrnii." Pp. 170–72

Grimstedt, Patricia K. (Ed.). Czartoryski's System for Russian Foreign Policy: A Memorandum. In: California Slavic Studies. Vol. 5 (1970). Pp. 19–91

Hartley, Janet M. Alexander I. 3d Impression. London, 1998

Hartley, Janet M. Is Russia Part of Europe? Russian Perceptions of Europe in the Reign of Alexander I. In: Cahiers du Monde Russe et Soviétique. Vol. 33 (1992) # 4. Pp. 369–85

Hartley, Janet M. "It Is the Festival of the Crown and Scepters": The Diplomatic, Commercial and Domestic Significance of the Visit of Alexander I to England in 1814. In: Slavonic and East European Review. Vol. 73 (1995) # 2. Pp. 246–68

Hartley, Janet M. / Keenan, Paul / Lieven, Dominic (Eds.). Russia and the Napoleonic Wars. New York, 2015

Hildermeier, Manfred. Die jüdische Frage im Zarenreich: Zum Problem der unterbliebenen Emanzipation. In: Jahrbücher für Geschichte Osteuropas. Vol. 32 (1984) # 3. Pp. 321–57

Hildermeier, Manfred. Geschichte Russlands: Vom Mittelalter bis zur Oktoberrevolution. München, 2013

Himmelstiern, Samson von / Ludwig, Reinhold Johann. Historischer Versuch über die Aufhebung der Leibeigenschaft in den Ostseeprovinzen, in besonderer Beziehung auf das Herzogthum Livland. Dorpat, 1838

Hartley Social + Military

Jarrett, Mark. The Congress of Vienna and Its Legacy: War and Great Power Diplomacy after Napoleon. London, 2013

Jenkins, Michael. Arakcheev: Grand Vizier of the Russian Empire. London, 1969

Kamenskii, Aleksandr B. "Pod seniiu Ekateriny ...": Vtoraia polovina XVIII veka. St. Petersburg, 1992

Katzer, Nikolaus. Russland 1812 und 1825: Patriotismus—Religion—Revolution, in: Lilia Antipow / Matthias Stadelmann (Eds.). Schlüsseljahre. Zentrale Konstellationen der mittel- und osteuropäischen Geschichte. Stuttgart, 2011. P. 117–39

Kiianskaia, O.I. Ocherki iz istorii obshchestvennogo dvizheniia Rossii v pravlenie Aleksandra I. St. Petersburg, 2008

Klier, John D. Russia Gathers Her Jews: The Origins of the "Jewish Question" in Russia, 1772–1825. DeKalb, Ill., 1986

Koselleck, Reinhart. Einleitung. In: Otto Brunner / Werner Conze / Reinhart Koselleck (Eds.). Geschichtliche Grundbegriffe. Vol. 1. Stuttgart, 1979. Pp. xiii–xxvii

Kusber, Jan. 1812 und die Folgen: Russlands Sieg über Napoleon als Erinnerungsfigur(en). In: Caroline Klausing / Verena von Wiczlinski (Eds.). Die Napoleonischen Kriege in der europäischen Erinnerung. Bielefeld, 2017. Pp. 47–63

Kusber, Jan. Das Zarenreich und die Deutschen Staaten im Banne Napoleons. In: Matthias Wemhoff a.o. (Eds.). Russen und Deutsche: 1000 Jahre Kunst, Geschichte und Kultur. Ausstellung im Neuen Museum, Berlin und Staatliches Historisches Museum Moskau. Essays. Petersberg, 2012. Pp. 192–99

Kusber, Jan. Eliten- und Volksbildung im Zarenreich während des 18. und in der ersten Hälfte des 19. Jahrhunderts: Studien zu Diskurs, Gesetzgebung und Umsetzung. Stuttgart, 2004

Kusber, Jan. Faszination und Ablehnung: Zur Diskussion um Rußlands Verhältnis zu Europa in der Zeit Alexanders I (1801–1825). In: Historische Mitteilungen der Ranke-Gesellschaft. Vol. 14 (2001). Pp. 116–28

Kusber, Jan. Kann der Zar König sein? Zur Diskussion um die Stellung "Kongresspolens" in den polnischen und russischen Eliten nach dem Wiener Kongress. In: Helga Schnabel-Schüle / Andreas Gestrich (Eds.). Fremde Herrscher—fremdes Volk. Inklusions- und Exklusionsfiguren bei Herrschaftswechseln in Europa. Frankfurt am Main, 2006. Pp. 253–70

Kusber, Jan. Katharina die Große: Legitimation durch Reform und Expansion. Stuttgart, 2019

Kusber, Jan. Leibeigenschaft im Rußland der Frühen Neuzeit. Aspekte der rechtlichen Lage und der sozialen Praxis. In: Jan Klussmann (Ed.). Leibeigenschaft. Bäuerliche Unfreiheit in der frühen Neuzeit.. Köln, 2003, Pp. 135–54

Kusber, Jan. Russland 1812 als europäisches Ereignis. In: Historische Mitteilungen der Ranke-Gesellschaft. Vol. 25 (2012). Pp. 7–15

Kusber, Jan. Russland, Europa und der Untergang des Alten Reiches. In: Michael North / Robert Riemer (Eds.). Das Ende des Alten Reiches im Ostseeraum. Wahrnehmungen und Transformationen. Köln, 2008. Pp. 55–70

Kylov-Tolstikovich, A.N. Pocelui Psikhei: Aleksandr I i imperatrica Elizaveta. Moscow, 2005

Lauer, Reinhard. Aleksandr Puškin: Eine Biographie. München, 2006

LeDonne, John. Absolutism and Ruling Class: The Formation of the Russian Political Order. New York, 1991

LeDonne, John. Administrative Regionalization in the Russian Empire 1802–1826. In: Cahiers du Monde russe. Vol. 43 (2002) # 1 (Jan.–Mar.). Pp. 5–33

LeDonne, John. Ruling Families in the Russian Political Order. In: CMRS. Vol. 28 (1987). Pp. 233–322

Lieven, Dominic. Russland gegen Napoleon: Die Schlacht um Europa. München, 2011

Liubin, D.V. Aleksandrovskaia kolonna. St. Petersburg, 2013

Maikov, P. M. Zapiksi Grafa L.L. Beningsena o voine s Napoleonom. St. Petersburg, 1900

Mainzer Zeitung. # 1, Donnerstag den 5ten Mai 1814. Front page

Martin, Alexander. Romantics, Reformers, Reactionaries: Russian Conservative Thought and Politics in the Reign of Alexander I. DeKalb, Ill., 1997

McCaffray, Susan P. Confronting Serfdom in the Age of Revolution: Projects for Serf Reform in the Time of Alexander I. In: Russian Review. Vol. 64 (2005). Pp. 1–21

McConnell, Allan. Alexander I's Hundred Days: The Politics of a Paternalistic Reformer. In: Slavic Review. Vol. 28 (1969). Pp. 373–93

McGrew, Roderick E. Paul I of Russia, 1754–1801. Oxford, 1992

Menger, Philipp. Die Heilige Allianz: Religion und Politik bei Alexander von Russland (1801–1825). Stuttgart, 2014

Mironenko, Sergei. Samoderzhavie i reformy. Politicheskaia bor'ba v Rossii v nachale XIX v. Moscow, 1989

? Mironenko (2016) see p.129

Morozov, B.I. Gosudarstvenno-pravovye vzgliady M.M. Speranskogo. St. Petersburg, 1999

Muhlstein, Anka. Der Brand von Moskau: Napoleon in Russland. Frankfurt a. M., 2008

Nachtigal, Reinhard. Verkehrswege in Kaukasien: Ein Integrationsproblem des Zarenreiches 1780–1870. Wiesbaden, 2016

Narkiewicz, Olga A. Alexander I and the Senate Reform. In: Slavonic and East European Review. Vol. 47 (1969) # 108. Pp. 115–36

O'Meara, Patrick. "The Opinion of One Ukrainian Landowner": V.N. Karazin, Alexander I, and Changing Russia. In: Maria Di Salvo et al. (Eds.). Word and Image in Russian History: Essays in Honor of Gary Marker. Brighton, MA, 2015. Pp. 315–35

Orlik, O.V. Rossija v mezhdunarodnych otnosheniiakh, 1815–1829: Ot venskogo kongressa do Adrianpol'skogo mira. Moscow, 1998

Palmer, Alan. Alexander I: Tsar of War and Peace. London, 1974

The Parliamentary Debates from the Year 1803 to the Present Time. Vol. 32. London, 1916

Pękacz, Jolanta. To What Extent Did Prince Adam Czartoryski Influence Alexander's "Jewish" Statute of 1804? In: Polish Review. Vol. 40 (1995) # 4. Pp. 403–14

Pipes, Richard. Karamzin's Memoir on Ancient and Modern Russia: A Translation and Analysis. Cambridge, Mass., 1959

Pipes, Richard. The Russian Military Colonies, 1810–1831. In: Journal of Modern History. Vol. 22 (1950) # 3. Pp. 205–19

Pushin, Pavel. Diaries of the 1812–1814 Campaigns. Translated by Alexander Mikaberidze (= Russian Voices of the Napoleonic Wars, Vol. 1). Tbilisi, 2011

Pyta, Wolfram. Idee und Wirklichkeit der "Heiligen Allianz." In: Frank-Lothar Kroll (Hg.). Neue Wege der Ideengeschichte. Festschrift für Kurt Kluxen zum 85. Geburtstag. Paderborn, 1996, Pp. 315–45

Pyta, Wolfram. Konzert der Mächte und kollektives Sicherheitssystem: Neue Wege zwischenstaatlicher Friedenswahrung in Europa nach dem Wiener Kongress 1815. In: Jahrbuch des Historischen Kollegs. Vol. 2 (1996). Pp. 133–73

Ragsdale, Hugh (Ed.). Paul I: A Reassessment of His Life and His Reign. Pittsburgh, 1979

Ragsdale, Hugh. Russian Foreign Policy, 1725–1815. In: Dominic Lieven (Ed.). The Cambridge History of Russia. Vol. II: Imperial Russia, 1689–1917. Cambridge, 2006. Pp. 504–29

RAGSDALE, HUGH. Tsar Paul and the Question of Madness: An Essay in History and Psychology. Westport, 1988

REY, MARIE-PIERRE. 1814, un Tsar à Paris. Paris, 2014

REY, MARIE-PIERRE. Alexander I: The Tsar Who Defeated Napoleon. DeKalb, Ill., 2012

RIEBER, ALFRED J. The Struggle for the Eurasian Borderlands: From the Rise of Early Modern Empires to the End of the First World War. Cambridge, 2014

ROACH, ELMO E. The Origins of Alexander I's Unofficial Committee. In: Russian Review. Vol. 28 (1969) # 3. Pp. 315–26

ROMANOV, NIKOLAI M. Legenda o konchine imperatora Aleksandra v Sibiri v obraze starza Fyodora Koz'micha. St. Petersburg, 1907

SAKHAROV, A.N. Aleksandr I. Moscow, 1998

SCHAEDER, HILDEGARD. Autokratie und Heilige Allianz. Darmstadt, 1963

SCHEIBERT, PETER. Die Anfänge der finnischen Staatswerdung und der Alexander I. In: Jahrbücher Für Geschichte Osteuropas. Vol. 4 (1939). Pp. 351–430

SCHIPPAN, MICHAEL. Die Französische Revolution von 1789 und Friedensvorstellungen in Russland bis 1825. In: Zeitschrift für Slawistik. Vol. 34 (1989). Pp. 353–61

SINEL, A.A. The Socialization of the Russian Bureaucratic Elite, 1811–1917: Life at the Tsarskoe Selo Lyceum and the School of Jurisprudence. In: Russian History. Vol. 3 (1976). Pp. 1–31

SKOWRONEK, JERZY. Antynapoleońskie Koncepcje Czartoryskiego. Warsaw, 1969

SMITH, DOUGLAS. Working the Rough Stone: Freemasonry in Eighteenth-Century Russia. DeKalb, Ill., 1999

SOLOV'EV, S.M. Imperator Aleksandr I. Moscow, 1995

SOLOV'EVA, D.V. (Ed.). Elizaveta i Aleksandr: khronika po pis'mam imperatricy Elizavety Alekseevny, 1791–1826. Moscow, 2013

STAMM-KUHLMANN, THOMAS. König in Preußens großer Zeit. Friedrich Wilhelm III. Der Melancholiker auf dem Thron. Berlin, 1992

STORCH, HEINRICH F. Rußland unter Alexander I: Eine historische Zeitschrift. Vols. 1–9. St. Petersburg, 1804–8

TARLÉ, EUGEN. Der Brand von Moskau. Leipzig, 1951

TARLÉ, EUGEN. Napoleon in Russland 1812. Zürich, 1944

TOMSINOV, VLADIMIR. Arakcheev. Moscow, 2002

TOMSINOV, VLADIMIR (Ed.). Zakonodatel'stvo imperatora Aleksandra I: 1812–1825 gody. Moscow, 2011

TROUBETZKOY, ALEXIS S. Imperial Legend: The Mysterious Disappearance of Tsar Alexander I. New York, 2002

VISHLENKOVA, ELENA. Der Krieg von 1812 im Spiegel der visuellen Kultur. In: Historische Mitteilungen der Ranke Gesellschaft. Vol. 25 (2012). Pp. 126–39

VNESHNIAIA POLITIKA ROSSII XIX I NACHALA XX VEKA. Dokumenty Rossiiskogo Ministerstva Inostrannykh Del. Seriia Pervaia. Pod. Red. A.L. Narochnickogo etc. Vols. I–IX. Moscow, 1962–70

WALKER, FRANKLIN E. Popular Response to Public Education in the Reign of Tsar Alexander I. In: HEQ (1984). Pp. 527–43

WILMS, JOHANNES. Napoleon: Eine Biographie. 3[d] ed. München, 2005

WINKLER, MARTINA. Das Imperium und die Seeotter: Die Expansion Russlands in den nordpazifischen Raum, 1700–1867. Göttingen, 2016

WORTMAN, RICHARD. Myth and Memory—Imperial Evocations of 1812: Alexander I and the Russian People. In: IDEM. Visual Texts, Ceremonial Texts, Texts of Exploration: Collected Articles on the Representation of Russian Monarchy. Brighton, Mass., 2013. Pp. 145–79

WORTMAN, RICHARD. Scenarios of Power: Myth and Ceremony in Russian Monarchy from Peter the Great to the Abdication of Nicholas II. New abridged edition. Princeton, 2013

ZACEK, JUDITH COHEN. The Russian Bible Society and the Russian Orthodox Church. In: Church History. Vol. 35 (1966). Pp. 411–37

ZAMOYSKI, ADAM. 1812: Napoleons Feldzug in Russland. München, 2012

ZAWADSKI, W.H. A Man of Honour: Adam Czartoryski as a Statesman of Russia and Poland, 1795–1831. Oxford, 1993

ZORIN, ANDREI L. Kormia dvuglavogo orla...: literatura i gosudarstvennaia ideologiia v Rossii v poslednei treti XVIII–pervoi treti XIX veka. Moscow, 2001

ZORIN, ANDREI L. / SCHLAFLY, DANIEL L. “Star of the East”: The Holy Alliance and European Mysticism. In: Kritika: Explorations in Russian and Eurasian History. Vol. 4 (2003) # 2. Pp. 313–42

Russia's movement toward the "Political Nations": alliances, finances, and circulation of knowledge

Franziska Schedewie

Foreign Policy and Diplomacy of Alexander I, as from His Family Letters

In the search for narratives of the Alexandrine age, we may add stories written in black ink or crayon on fine, water-marked, and often gold-rimmed paper: imperial family letters play an important role as sources for a new diplomatic history of the reign of Alexander I, as they provide evidence of the politicization of cultural concepts and terms such as kinship, friendship, and loyalty in the Russian monarchy around 1800. Unlike his immediate predecessors, Alexander I had a large family of brothers and sisters. Presumably, their letters' importance would have been even greater, had not two of his sisters, Aleksandra and Elena, died prematurely in 1801 and 1803, shortly after their marriages to Habsburg/Vienna and Mecklenburg, respectively. Also Ekaterina, who married abroad to Württemberg after the death of her first husband, died early. After Aleksandra's death, younger sister Maria Pavlovna—protagonist of the present chapter[1]—continued the correspondence with Archduke Joseph, her widowed brother-in-law, and when she left for Weimar, Empress Maria Fedorovna, Joseph's mother-in-law, took over.[2] Maria herself embarked on her new correspondence with her family members back in St Petersburg, including her brother Alexander.

To be sure, the source value of these documents does not reveal itself immediately. With few exceptions, Alexander's letters in particular hardly seem to convey straightforward explanations as to his mindset or decision-making, especially in matters of foreign policy.[3] Disappointingly, as one initially may be inclined to

---

1 Earlier versions of this paper were presented in Mainz and at the 2017 annual convention of the Association for Slavic, East European, and Eurasian Studies (ASEEES). At ASEEES, this paper was presented as part of a panel titled "Politicizing Friendship, Kinship, and Trust in the Russian Monarchy: 1762–1881."

2 See Landesarchiv Thüringen–Hauptstaatsarchiv Weimar (hereafter, LATh-HStA Weimar), HA A XXV. Korrespondenzen. O 15 (Joseph von Österreich von Maria Pavlovna, 1803–1804); Gosudarsvennyi Arkhiv Rossiiskoi Federacii (hereafter, GARF), F. 728. Op. 1. Kn. 2. D. 595. "Pis'ma imp. Marii Fedorovny k ertsgertsogu Avstriiskomu Iosifu, 1799–1807." – On the significance of Alexander's family, see also: Wortman. Scenarios of Power. Vol. 1. P. 247 f.; Idem. The Russian Imperial Family. Pp. 60–86.

3 The two major newer studies of Russian policies toward Germany under Alexander I tend to rely on classical diplomatic sources. See Iskiul'. Vneshniaia politika Rossii;

think, Alexander, vis-à-vis his family members, often displayed the complexion of a sphinx, which has become so well known for him. Further, previous analysis of the communication between the tsar and his relatives has shown that, as with others close to him, no matter how influential these individuals were (or thought they were), more often than not, the impact of their communication on the tsar's politics proved to be temporary, if not negligible. Alexander Martin's study of conservative thought under Alexander I amply demonstrates this lack of real influence for Ekaterina Pavlovna, the tsar's famous and ambitious sister, who waged plans for her brother's rule while she was residing at Tver with her first husband, George of Oldenburg.[4] Other historians assign rather passive roles to family members, particularly to the women married abroad, who wrote letters to keep in touch with the other reigning houses and at times to soothe the waves that their relatives had stirred.[5]

The present chapter seeks to make a different, complementary case by looking at the correspondence between Alexander I and his sister Maria Pavlovna.[6] In 1804, Maria Pavlovna had been sent off in dynastic marriage to the German duchy of Saxe-Weimar, and we can presume that she was there not only as the new hereditary princess and wife but also as an informal tsarist diplomat, fulfilling a core job of foreign representatives—that is, writing regular and extraordinary reports, and at the same time acting as an intermediary between her old and her new families, often charged with sensitive tasks. At court in the eighteenth and nineteenth centuries, personal relations, family correspondence, and networks served political ends.[7] Accordingly, and notwithstanding the aloof nature of Alexander's letters, this paper will show that even those instances in which communication seemed in vain and in which disenchantment and lack of revelation prevailed can be of great interest

---

Eich. Rußland und Europa. Iskiul' uses the abundant sources of the Russian state archives. Meanwhile, due to Romanov convention, family letters are kept in the court archives of the surviving correspondents. That is why Alexander and Maria Pavlovna's letters, for example, are kept in Weimar. Eich, who published her book in 1986, had no easy access to archives in the GDR or Soviet Union at the time. She concentrates on the three states of Southern Germany and sometimes refers to the correspondence of the Empress Elizaveta Alekseevna with her mother in Baden.

4 See Martin. Romantics, Reformers, Reactionaries. P. 108.

5 See Paulmann. Pomp und Politik. P. 93.

6 The letters are archived at LATh–HStA Weimar. HA A XXV. Korrespondenzen. Except for those letters to or from Maria Fedorovna (which are too numerous!), the letters that form the source material for my paper were recently published in Russian translation; see Dmitrieva / Schedewie (Eds). Perepiska iz trekh uglov.

7 See Fn. 1, ASEEES 2017 panel (description by Victoria Frede).

to historians. Tangible accomplishments and family members' successful impact (as ascertained by scholars) on the tsar's outlook and politics are not requirements for family letters to become interesting sources; nor even do we need outspoken explications or excuses on both sides. Examples show that mutual misunderstanding, even failure of communication, futile insistence, and embitterment produced a gap, or asymmetry, between correspondents, exposing differences in fundamental views, reflecting external influences, and highlighting the dynamics of opinions and politics in flux. Correspondents often wrote at cross-purposes. One can go so far as to maintain that such a gap reveals changes in Alexander's approaches to politics and diplomacy toward Germany. By the same token (since family relationships were reciprocal, though not always symmetrical), and perhaps even more importantly in terms of new diplomatic research interests, the "gap" reveals how these changes were received and handled by those affected. The gap is also intrinsically linked with notions and literal expressions of friendship, kinship, and loyalty.[8] The following analysis of Maria Pavlovna's and Alexander's correspondence uses these concepts as signal terms in their letters of 1808, at a delimited, but exemplary time span, which was the critical and mutually disappointing juncture of the lead-up to the Congress of Erfurt. But first, it is necessary to contextualize and explain why Maria Pavlovna should constitute a relevant research object—and Weimar a key prism for studying Russian foreign politics toward German states.[9]

1. Weimar and the Russian Court around 1800

During Alexander's period, the small duchy of Saxe-Weimar—so small as to be overlooked on any map of Germany, let alone Europe, and certainly tiny in comparison with the vast Russian Empire—gained major importance for the latter: and not only once, but twice, although in very different ways and under very different circumstances. The second time (which is beyond our focus here) was during the crucial period of 1816–19, when Weimar stood out as a center of liberal ideas and radical political opposition right before the reactionary Carlsbad Decrees.[10] The first time, however, was between 1798 and 1804, when the dynas-

8 As for friendship and patronage as a recent field of research, especially also with regard to asymmetry in relationships, see, for example: GRADUIRTENKOLLEG 1288. Freunde, Gönner, Getreue.

9 I draw the argument here from my published monograph: SCHEDEWIE. Die Bühne Europas.

10 Alexander and Roxandra Sturdza were at the conference in Carlsbad, as was August von Kotzebue; their involvement was a consequence, in one way or other, of the dynastic

tic marriage project was begun and accomplished. Given the continued overall structural importance of dynastic marriages at the end of the ancien régime, it is all the more important to know that the initiative for this project lay on Russia's side. The motives cannot have consisted solely in gaining the prestige of a marriage bond with the age-old House of Wettin or in gaining the cultural prestige of Weimar's *Dichter und Denker*—the poets and thinkers. The utmost secrecy and anxiety that surrounded the project[11] signify that what was at stake was much more volatile. Russia felt the need to curb Prussia's plans of expansion and to send out a similar signal to the Habsburg monarchy; but the supreme motivation may have been speculation on the dynastic inheritance (or rather, reestablishment) of the Saxon Electorate for the duke of Weimar—a replacement, in short, of the (younger) Albertine branch at Dresden by the (older) Weimar Ernestines. This vague, but extremely attractive inheritance prospect would have supplied a formidable stepping-stone for more influence on German affairs from within. Such motives underscore Weimar's importance for Russia and indicate the value, last but not least, of entrusting Maria Pavlovna as a steady reporter.

The princess took up her assignment immediately. Her daily letters, mostly to Maria Fedorovna, but also to Alexander and other addressees, make up more than five hundred folio, or a thousand pages, per year. Although circumstances at Weimar were already difficult in 1804–6, her first two years there, the letters of this period appear to be without below-surface conflict: political interests and outlooks between Russia and Weimar were still aligned. During the final stage of the Holy Roman Empire, Weimar was of structural importance on the political

marriage bond and the presence of Maria Pavlovna. The special link between Russia and Weimar (and the sources it produced) helps to explain both why Alexander I was so reluctant in following Metternich's politics—and why he did eventually do so.

11 "Voilá donc une bonne affaire d'arrangée, et que nous devons encore à vos soins," Empress Maria Fedorovna told her brother and confidant Alexander of Wurttemberg, after the accomplishment of their task of making the duke of Weimar believe that the idea of the valuable marriage project was his (a conviction that would last in the historiography until recently!). The empress and her brother were both at the same time counteracting a marriage project that their brother Frederick, future king of Wurttemberg, had devised for Maria Pavlovna and his own son. "Encore" in Maria Fedorovna's quotation refers to Alexander's previous efforts in arranging a marriage for the other imperial daughter, Ekaterina Pavlovna, to Bavaria, also an electorate of the Holy Roman Empire. This project (of Ekaterina's marriage) proved unsuccessful. See: Schedewie. Die Bühne Europas. P. 85. Quotation from: Rossiiskii Gosudarstvennyi Arkhiv Drevnikh Aktov (hereafter, RGADA). F. 2. D. 135. Projet de la Lettre pour mon frère Alexandre (22.04.1799). L. 124 ob.

map of Europe for Russia—as is reflected in the sovereign's personal correspondence. Even compared with those to his beloved sister Ekaterina,[12] Alexander's letters to Maria were truly sweet and often emotional. He consoled his sister when she received her first heavy blow, the death of her first son (and heir!) in March 1806. After the lost Battles of Jena and Auerstedt on Weimar territory in October of the same year, Alexander acquiesced to Maria Pavlovna's plea to treat her husband's[13] resignation from the Russian army (as required by Napoleon) as a fake, assuring her of his comprehension of the motives and his agreement to tell no one in Russia. All this time, Maria Pavlovna made sure to demonstrate to Alexander her continued loyalty in tangible and also symbolic ways: she addressed him as friend, *ami*; and in her correspondence with Maria Fedorovna, she amply employed all the attributes that Richard Wortman has identified as fundamental to Alexander's preferred scenario of an "angel on the throne."[14] "Dear Maman," she wrote to Maria Fedorovna in one letter, "you put me on the same level in your affection as Alexander; he is too perfect; he is the pearl of the family. I cannot accept this position, it belongs to him alone. His virtues, his adorable character make him deserve it."[15] Such phrases read like an exercise imposed by Maria Pavlovna on herself, as she coped with her initial tasks of defining her place in Weimar, in Russia, and in between.[16]

Yet the dissolution of the Holy Roman Empire in 1806 and, moreover, Weimar's integration into the Rhine Confederation changed the duchy's significance for Russia dramatically, effectively transforming Alexander and Maria Pavlovna's communication, too. Russia's previous marriage motives became obsolete. Henceforth, Alexander gave up his support for Weimar as a prospective base for further influence. Yet the Weimar government—always aspiring to its own ends of greater status and security—would not yield, but instead stubbornly kept on relying on a

12 As for publications and interpretations of Ekaterina and Alexander's correspondence, see: Martin. Romantics, Reformers, Reactionaries; Grand Duc Nicolas Mikhaïlowitch. Correspondance; Pingaud. L'Empereur Alexandre I. Pp. 379–95; Schiemann. Kaiser Alexander und die Großfürstin Ekaterina Pp. 540–66; Pushkin (Ed.). Pis'ma Velikoi Kniagini.

13 Charles Frederick (1783–1853), then hereditary prince of Saxe-Weimar-Eisenach.

14 See Wortman. Scenarios of Power. Vol. 1. Pp. 193–214. Maria Pavlovna used the term "angel" several times.

15 LATh-HStA Weimar, HA A XXV. Korrespondenzen. R 153 (Maria Pavlovna to Maria Fedorovna), Fol. 92 (28.09.1804).

16 Maria Pavlovna was engaged in a balancing act that was eventually to turn into a form of "double national loyalty." Schedewie / Utz. Russland, Deutschland und die Wartburg Pp. 139–58.

claim for consideration and patronage. Relations between Maria Pavlovna (who found herself caught in the middle) and Alexander became strained during the critical situation of 1808 and would eventually deteriorate, as is amply reflected in the letters. Their relations never really recovered, though they lasted until Alexander's death in 1825. As for the Erfurt Congress, the Russian grand duchess, tsar's sister and Weimar princess Maria Pavlovna saw the major summit of Alexander and Napoleon as a double challenge and defeat. Let us look next at the political implications and events leading up to the congress from her Weimar perspective.

2. Erfurt, 1808

Erfurt, a church-owned principality until it became Prussian in 1802 and then French in 1806, presented a piece of territory long coveted by the duke of Weimar (Maria's father-in-law, Carl August). As a Prussian (1802–6) and French (1806–14) exclave, Erfurt segregated parts of the duke's lands. Therefore, several advances had been made by the Weimar government to attain it. Since the dynastic marriage of 1804, the tsar had been the prime addressee and presumed advocate for Weimar's cause. Even in January 1808, right before the news of the upcoming congress reached her, Maria Pavlovna passed on the request for Alexander's intervention in her private letters to their mother, Maria Fedorovna. Here, she took up what may be the most typical diplomatic role of a private or semiofficial intermediary in an asymmetrical environment such as hers, and the unofficial character of the personal letter gave Maria Pavlovna greater freedom to express herself. She told her mother that Napoleon abused Erfurt, much unlike the duke, who would treat his subjects like a worthy sovereign. She also highlighted how Weimar was threatened by its neighbors' expansionist intentions.[17] Besides, as Maria Pavlovna wrote (anticipating rejection), her letter spared the tsar a moment of discomfiture.[18] Given the expressed personal hostility between Napoleon and the duke, Maria Pavlovna herself hardly believed it possible that the goal would be accomplished smoothly. Moreover, a letter (most probably unknown to her) from the duke's minister Voigt to his colleague reveals the actual misery of her situation. Voigt wrote:

---

17 This was a constant topic brought forward in such supplications, which can therefore be regarded to some degree as constitutive of the relationship between Weimar and the Russian court. The same applies for petitions for territorial gains or an increase in status. After all, Erfurt was not the only piece of terrain that the duke had in mind: the parallel, greater objective was Saxony.

18 LATh–HStA Weimar. HA A XXV. Korrespondenzen. R 155 (Maria Pavlovna to Maria Fedorovna). Fol. 302 f. (Weimar, 5/17.01.1808).

> I must admit [...] that, considering the hatred of the Russians [*National-Russen*] for the German princes, I have barely counted on the Russian ministry, and in such matters of politics it is obvious that a great monarch wants to be reminded and to be prepared. [...] I feel sorry for our dear hereditary princess, in case she should be blamed for anything. She is just subject to the directives of the St. Petersburg court, just like we are ourselves. [...] I considered it impossible that the sister of Alexander, eminent friend of an eminent victor, should not have aroused any interest. How lucky should we have been, had the great emperor met her in person.[19]

The talk is here about Napoleon. In other words, Maria Pavlovna was to secure the tsar's favor, on which the Weimar ministers were no longer inclined to rely; she was pitied as being fully dependent on the Russian court, while Weimar (except for the duke himself) was already placing its hopes on France. This whole matter was not only about Erfurt, as Voigt's letter shows how offhandedly Maria Pavlovna was regarded as a welcome political tool. For the princess herself, the minister's dream of her meeting Napoleon constituted a sheer nightmare, and by no means an advantage in the sense of an extension of the range of political options. Not only would she refuse to recognize Napoleon as a "great Emperor"; her and her Russian family's dread was that she might be abducted to France as a hostage. (Maria Fedorovna had even devised a coded language for her in case this should happen.) In their petty search of support for their duchy, the ministers had failed to notice that through the presence of the tsar's sister, Weimar had become a stage of European political scheming, quite regardless of their own political aims. Maria Pavlovna was now the only close (and letter-writing) relative of Alexander's to live in the Napoleonic sphere. The significance of this fact was clear to both Alexander and Napoleon. It was also exploited symbolically. For example, when Maria Pavlovna's daughter was born in 1808, both the Russian and French emperors became her godfathers. This move was in all likelihood insufferable for Maria Pavlovna, who did not talk extensively about it to her mother.

It was in this unhappy and intricate situation of Maria Pavlovna's that the two emperors also prepared their meeting—in Erfurt, of all places. In her first reaction to Alexander, Maria Pavlovna described herself as flabbergasted. Her letters of April 1808—written concurrently to Alexander and Maria Fedorovna—reveal the degree to which these plans for a congress shocked her. These letters contained not diplomatic glossing but rather the straightforward expression of political opinion and distress. In the letters to her mother, she first and foremost assigned blame to foreign minister Rumiantsev. Like all the other "misérables" around him, she

---

19 Andreas / Tümmler (Eds.). Politischer Briefwechsel des Herzogs. Vol. 2. Pp. 555 f. (Voigt to Müller, Weimar, 24.08.1807).

wrote, Rumiantsev, too, would allow the sovereign of this "grand nation [*Nation aussi imposante*]" Russia to expose himself unnecessarily to downright humiliation.[20] What Maria Pavlovna was referring to here was the traditional concept according to which another monarch—much less a hostile one—could not be encountered on one's territory without disgrace on the part of the visitor.[21] To Maria Pavlovna, this concept was well known, and besides, she had the memory of war and pillage two years earlier on Weimar territory. Thus, even at this early stage, the grand duchess solemnly declared her intention to leave Weimar for Russia should such an event take place: "My carriages are ready, and as soon as my brother departs, I will leave, too.—I believe death alone will stop me."[22]

At the same time, as early as her first letter, Maria Pavlovna made suggestions on how the fatal impression that this meeting would give to the world might be damped at the last minute. In the archival file, these passages are marked with crayon. The princess proposed that Alexander should live with his relatives at Weimar, not in the French fortress. Any idea that the Weimar court might want to derive any benefits for itself from this visit was strongly rejected. Now, as she wrote, the only task must be to save Alexander from a dramatic loss of authority in Russia. She wrote to Maria Fedorovna:

> The task is to protect my brother from further humiliation; he has to be reminded that Erfurt is a fortress, at least it bears the name of one. Perhaps our worthy Rumiantsev has forgotten about that! [...] So he [Alexander] shall come here. One can show him the monuments of their [the French] entry, especially at Jena, where Napoleon had granted his imperial word that there would be no pillaging, and on the same day, his soldiers were sent for plundering. But I don't want to talk about these old stories. Just think for one moment about what I have told you, dear mother, and perhaps you will agree that I´m frightened of the impression that will be produced in Russia, when one sees my brother travel to a country that belongs to Napoleon. Indeed, my brother will be staying at his place, and that cannot be his intention. This will be volume two of Tilsit! Maman, is it possible that one should wish to repeat those scenes?[23]

---

20 LATh-HStA Weimar. HA A XXV. Korrespondenzen. R 155 (Maria Pavlovna to Maria Fedorovna). Fol. 54 (Weimar, 23.03./4.04.1808).

21 See, for example, PAULMANN. Pomp und Politik. Pp. 37 f.

22 "[...] mes voitures sont en état, et [...] aussi-tôt après le départ de mon frère, je pars : je crois que la mort seule me retiendroit (...)" LATh-HStA Weimar. HA A XXV. Korrespondenzen. R 156 (Maria Pavlovna to Maria Fedorovna). Fol. 56 (Weimar, 24.03./5.04.1808). Her handwriting is barely legible here, a sign of her emotional agitation.

23 LATh–HStA Weimar. HA A XXV. Korrespondenzen. R 156 (Maria Pavlovna to Maria Fedorovna). Fol. 54 rev.–55.

Maria Pavlovna hated the idea, as she wrote, that her brother was about to throw himself into Napoleon's arms. She also feared that the meeting would seal a marriage plot for her sister.

3. Friendship, Kinship, and the "Gap" in These Letters

So much for the contents of Maria Pavlovna's letters before the congress. They provide a local perspective, but beyond that, Maria Pavlovna is also talking about Russian politics. She even writes of herself as a "Russian," physically underlining the word in order to strengthen its meaning. Alexander, she says, must not believe that the meeting is none of her business.[24] Her undiplomatic language is striking. Throughout this whole correspondence, she claims a thoroughly symmetrical relationship, writing of the tsar as "my brother" or "Alexandre" to her/their mother and addressing him as "bon ami" and "cher ami" (good friend) or "mon Alexandre" (my Alexander) in her letters to him. These were terms that she had employed in her very first letters of 1804–5. Expressions like "l'Emp[ereur]," which she frequently employed in letters to Maria Fedorovna starting in 1806 (when the war situation became more dangerous) and denoting hierarchy and asymmetry in the relationship, but also carefree reliance on defense and benefaction through a powerful brother as emperor,[25] are absent in this situation. In her letters to Alexander, the ideas of loyalty and friendship are strong. Hinting at, and thus recalling, the hardships of the past years, Maria Pavlovna claims that there is a "need for the sweetness of friendship,"[26] and she closes her letters as a "loyal, attached sister." As one can easily imagine in this tense situation, terms for Alexander like "tel ange d´Aléxandre"[27] are missing here. Instead, Maria Pavlovna tells the tsar that she must talk to him frankly as a friend and—as just mentioned—as a Russian. The underlining of the latter may indeed also be understood as a means to mobilize Alexander, to make him understand.

---

24 LATh–HStA Weimar. HA A XXV. Korrespondenzen. R 156 (Maria Pavlovna to Maria Fedorovna). Fol. 57–58.

25 See, for example, LATh–HStA Weimar. HA A XXV. Korrespondenzen. R 154 (Maria Pavlovna to Maria Fedorovna). Fol. 169 rev., (15./27.08.1806): "Ah! Quel bonheur de vivre sous la protection de l'Empereur, et comme on rend justiçe à ses intentions nobles."

26 "Mon bon ami, aprés des momens et des années comme les préçédentes, on a besoin de jouïr de la douçeur de l'amitié: la mienne Vous est connûe, jugez donc si je serai aise de Vous revoir!" LATh–HStA Weimar. HA A XXV. Korrespondenzen. R 156. Fol. 58. (This letter to Alexander I is enclosed as a copy in those to Maria Fedorovna.)

27 LATh–HStA Weimar. HA A XXV. Korrespondenzen. R 154. Fol. 82 (Maria Pavlovna to Maria Fedorovna, 6/18.03.1806).

Meanwhile, Alexander—through Maria Fedorovna—informed Maria Pavlovna of his "tendres amities." He then asked her to prepare her departure and wait for a messenger to arrive between May 10 and 15, who would tell her when exactly to start her travels.[28] Maria Pavlovna left on June 1, 1808.

What can be learned from these letters? On the one hand, Alexander's participation at the Congress of Erfurt (and his prior declaration to do so) substantiated a change of political action that consisted in the overcoming of traditional constraints. On the other hand, his sister Maria Pavlovna clung to the older approach and a view, shared with their mother, that the concession of such a visit and its accompanying ceremony was equal to subordination. The effect would be a dramatic loss of prestige at home and abroad. That is why Maria Pavlovna wrote to her mother that she was "less afraid of Napoleon himself than of seeing him eye to eye together with her brother."[29] For Alexander, in contrast, this convention had lost its categorical meaning; it was more important for him that the meeting took place. In pursuing his political ends, he accepted that his practical approach affronted his closest relatives, although he did feel obliged to explain his reasons for going to Erfurt in a lengthy letter to his mother.[30] Yet the "gap" that opened up between the different attitudes of the tsar and his sister in Weimar—and this is just one example out of a sequence—shows that such paradigmatic changes would not proceed without serious tension, or what in technical terms may be called

28 LATh–HStA Weimar. HA A XXV. Korrespondenzen. R 156. Fol. 61 (9.04.1808).

29 LATh-HStA Weimar. HA A XXV. Korrespondenzen. R 156. Fol. 76 (18/30.04.1808).

30 See SHIL'DER. Nakanune Erfurtskago svidaniia. Pp. 4–24. See also LIEVEN. Russia against Napoleon. Pp. 73 f. Interestingly, in her letter to Alexander of August 1808, as published in *Russkaia Starina*, Maria Fedorovna uses the very arguments brought forward by Maria Pavlovna in her letters of April. So by mere chronological order of these sources at least, Maria Pavlovna came up first with the argument. (In August, Maria Pavlovna was already in St. Petersburg.) There is no hint in Maria Fedorovna's letters to her daughter earlier that year that she discussed the implications of the congress with her, and a frank discussion of the kind is also hardly to be expected in her letters from St. Petersburg to Weimar. (See LATh–HStA Weimar. HA A XXV. Korrespondenzen. R 125 [Maria Fedorovna to Maria Pavlovna, 1807–1810].) Since her letters are enumerated, one letter (№. 33, written between March 31 and April 2) is apparently missing. She then tells her daughter to come to St. Petersburg: "viens viens dans mes bras" (LATh–HStA Weimar. HA A XXV. Korrespondenzen. R 125 25.03./6.04.1808, without Fol., underlining in original). As for Maria Pavlovna, she seems to have received all her information about the planned congress from Mr de Seebach, Oberstallmeister and general in Weimar, who traveled between Russia and Weimar. See also: JENA. Maria Pawlowna. P. 382.

"friction losses." If one were to appraise Alexander's conduct during the Erfurt episode, certainly one must agree that it was exactly by means of overcoming restrictive traditional forms that new forms of guaranteed peace were eventually facilitated, even made possible at all, in the early nineteenth century. Looking at Maria Pavlovna, we can see that the changes in the political ways of action could also lead to misunderstanding, frustration, and uncertainty. From her perspective, we must take into account Weimar's thwarted territorial interest in Erfurt, as well as the life-or-death uncertainty of what would become of them as a Rhine Confederation state if Alexander did not vigorously protect them. In those post- and prewar times, Maria Pavlovna was constantly worried about herself and her family in Weimar, but also about her brother's fortune and generally the fate of the imperial family in St. Petersburg. Finally, if Maria Pavlovna experienced a negative sensation, this was certainly much reinforced by the fact that Alexander would not answer the pleas and admonitions in her letters. The same stressful experience of silence or no reply can be found in other crucial situations in the course of developments between Russia and Weimar. In 1808, Alexander wrote to his sister with some sentimental impressions from Weimar—which he had visited during the congress—telling her how much he missed her presence there. We must rely on the archival files here, which are bound together and appear to have been undisturbed during the Alexandrine period.[31] According to the available documents, it was not until 1812 (i.e., almost four years later) that the tsar responded in greater detail and clarity to his sister's letters. By then, Maria Pavlovna was pressing him to alleviate the Rheinbund situation—and he countered with an articulate rejection. In his letter, Alexander reproached his sister for being too pessimistic and irrational in her arguments. He refused to give her or her father-in-law any advice and insinuated that she was not to expect anything of him. In fact, he expected something *of her*: he used Maria Pavlovna's presence in Weimar for an outright diplomatic commission for her. Once she was there, he proposed, she might as well convince Napoleon of the tsar's peaceful intentions.[32]

4. Conclusion

What, then, do we learn about the politicization of friendship and kinship in the Russian monarchy based on the interpretation of these family letters? To put it succinctly, the use of family letters as primary sources further accentuates

31 Maria Pavlovna ordered her son Carl Alexander to burn her documents.

32 LATh–HStA Weimar. HA A XXV. Korrespondenzen. R 101 (Alexander I to Maria Pavlovna). Fol. 55–60 (27.02.1812).

Alexander's period as an epoch of change. It shows how Alexander pursued his politics, here at the cost of uncertainty and embitterment on the part of those immediately involved and affected. Family letters are certainly not the only sources for analyzing these changes, but in specific ways, these letters open up insight into the mental disposition of the participants. As for Maria Pavlovna and her use of friendship, kinship, and loyalty as signal words in her letters, the example of the Erfurt episode shows that she was not and did not see herself in the role of a passive family member. Rather, she, too, "stirred the waves" and continuously strove to make her viewpoint known, even if it was to no avail. And as for Alexander I: perhaps Maria's departure for St. Petersburg did not leave him so impassive as he has so far given us the impression. Otherwise, it seems hard to explain why in his letters to his sister Ekaterina during the congress, he wrote of Maria Pavlovna as if she was there, equating her somewhat inscrutably with the biblical Mary of Clopas ["*Mme Cléophas*"]—a figure known as a first testimony of the resurrection of Jesus Christ, who is usually represented together with the Holy Kinship.[33]

List of references

ANDREAS, WILLY / TÜMMLER, HANS (Eds.). Politischer Briefwechsel des Herzogs und Großherzogs Carl August von Weimar. Vol. 2. Göttingen, 1954–73

DMITRIEVA, EKATERINA / SCHEDEWIE, FRANZISKA (Eds). Perepiska iz trekh uglov: Aleksandr I., Mariia Pavlovna, Elizaveta Alekseevna, 1804–1826. Moscow, 2017

EICH, ULRIKE. Rußland und Europa. Studien zur russischen Deutschlandpolitik in der Zeit des Wiener Kongresses. Köln, 1986

GRADUIRTENKOLLEG 1288. Freunde, Gönner, Getreue. Praxis und Semantik von Freundschaft und Patronage in historischer, anthropologischer und kulturvergleichender Perspektive. Albert-Ludwigs-Universität Freiburg, 2015. https://www.grk-freundschaft.uni-freiburg.de/

33 See: https://www.heiligenlexikon.de/BiographienH/Heilige_Sippe.html [2017-12-15]; GRAND DUC NICOLAS MIKHAÏLOWITCH. Correspondance. P. 20 (the editor deciphers "avec Marie, avec Mme Cléophas" as Maria Pavlovna in a footnote on this page). Another, profane and rather unlikely explanation might be that the editor mixed up letters: coincidentally, Alexander I was also in Weimar on the twenty-seventh, but his was the twenty-seventh of October three years earlier, when Maria Pavlovna's first son was born. While it is definite that he met her there, a possible error could be checked only with the help of the original files at RGADA, Moscow. As for Maria Pavlovna's itinerary and traveling activities, see LATh–HStA Weimar. HA A XXV. Korrespondenzen. R 156. Fol. 102 (20.05./1.06.1808)—Fol. 132 (7./19.05.1809); MÜLLER-HARANG. Maria Pawlowna. Pp. 244 f.

Grand Duc Nicolas Mikhaïlowitch. Correspondance de l'Empereur Alexandre Ier avec sa sœur la Grande-Duchesse Catherine, Princesse d'Oldenbourg, puis reine de Wurtemberg 1805–1818. St. Petersburg, 1910

Iskiul', Sergei. Vneshniaia politika Rossii i germanskie gosudarstva (1801–1812). Moscow, 2007

Jena, Detlef. Maria Pawlowna: Großherzogin an Weimars Musenhof. Graz, 1999

Lieven, Dominic. Russia against Napoleon: The Battle for Europe, 1807 to 1814. London, 2009

Martin, Alexander. Romantics, Reformers, Reactionaries: Russian Conservative Thought and Politics in the Reign of Alexander I. DeKalb, Ill., 1997

Müller-Harang, Ulrike. Maria Pawlowna—Reisetätigkeit. In: Jochen Klauss e.a. (Eds.). "Ihre Kaiserliche Hoheit": Maria Pavlovna. Zarentochter am Weimarer Hof. Katalog zur Ausstellung im Weimarer Schlossmuseum. München, 2004. Pp. 244–46

Paulmann, Johannes. Pomp und Politik: Monarchenbegegnungen in Europa zwischen Ancien Régime und Erstem Weltkrieg. Paderborn, 2000

Pingaud, Léonce. L'Empereur Alexandre I et la Grande-Duchesse Catherine Pavlovna. In: Revue d'histoire diplomatique. Vol. 25 (1911). Pp. 379–95

Pushkin, Evgenii (Ed.). Pis'ma Velikoi Kniagini Ekateriny Pavlovny. Tver, 1888

Schedewie, Franziska. Die Bühne Europas: Russische Diplomatie und Deutschlandpolitik in Weimar, 1798–1819. Heidelberg, 2015

Schedewie, Franziska / Utz, Raphael. Russland, Deutschland und die Wartburg: Politische Optionen und Repräsentationsstrategien in der Weimarer Festkultur, 1804–1836. In: Michael Maurer (Ed.): Festkulturen im Vergleich. Inszenierungen des Religiösen und des Politischen. Köln, 2010. Pp. 139–58

Schiemann, Theodor. Kaiser Alexander und die Großfürstin Ekaterina Pavlovna. In: Zeitschrift für Osteuropäische Geschichte. Vol. 1 (1911). Pp. 540–66

Shil'der, Nikolai. Nakanune Erfurtskogo svidaniia 1808 goda. In: Russkaia Starina. Vol. 98 (1899), Pp. 4–24

Wortman, Richard. The Russian Imperial Family as a Symbol. In: Jane Burbank / David L. Ransel (Eds.). Imperial Russia. New Histories for the Empire. Bloomington, 1998. Pp. 60–86

Wortman, Richard. Scenarios of Power: Myth and Ceremony in Russian Monarchy. Vol. 1. Princeton, 1995

? Eng. book on AI + family corr.
rather slight

Maike Sach

"… en Europe il fallait compter trois puissances: l'Angleterre, la Russie et Mme de Staël …": Salon Culture and the Formation of Networks during the Struggle against Napoleon

To be referred to as a great European power probably would have caused a witty comment by Germaine de Staël (1766–1817), French woman of letters on the verge of Romanticism, forerunner of comparative study of literature, early feminist, and last but not least famous *salonnière*.[1] She was already deceased when the above cited lines from the memoirs of Victorine de Chastenay—a French noblewoman who had made the acquaintance of both Mme de Staël and Napoleon—were published.[2] And yet, during Mme de Staël's lifetime, a broader European public would have agreed with this opinion because of her open opposition toward Napoleon, which was boldly manifested in eloquent conversation and both critical and fictional writings, and which found an attentive audience throughout Europe. For his part, Napoleon perceived Mme de Staël clearly as an opponent, as is proven by his reactions to her social and literary activities. Or to be more precise, he seemed to have been quite annoyed that Mme de Staël showed herself to be recalcitrant to his influence and acted as an opponent, one whom he could not defeat on his usual battlegrounds. The purpose of the present study is to explore the nature, the extent, and the limits of the influence that Mme de Staël was able to exert and that made her in some respects an inconvenient menace to Napoleon or at least a person difficult to counteract.

1 Mme de Staël has long been an object of research. See the following special lists of references and bibliographies: Dubé. Bibliographie de la critique sur Madame de Staël; Perchellet. Bibliographie staëliennes; Rous Besser. Germaine de Staël. Pp. 139–67. Among biographic approaches should be noted: Herold. Madame de Staël; Fairweather. Madame de Staël; Goodden. Madame de Staël; Winock. Madame de Staël; Appel. Madame de Staël.

2 The quotation's context: "Bonaparte l'avait persecutée de manière à ce qu'on dit qu'en Europe il fallait compter trois puissances: l'Angleterre, la Russie et Mme de Staël […]." Chastenay. Mémoires. Vol. 2. P. 445. For Chastenay's biography, see: Troussin. Une mémorialiste oubliée. Pp. 1–18.

1. Some Characteristics of the Source Material

Important reasons for Mme de Staël's influence on various levels can be found in her upbringing and her literary and political activities. Therefore the source material for this paper is mainly drawn from her own writings, especially her correspondence, oscillating always between private and public spheres;[3] her diaries;[4] and her unfinished memoir, depicting her peregrinations in the periods of 1797–1804 and 1810–12. She started composing her memoir during the winter of 1812–13 in Stockholm. It was posthumously edited by her son Auguste de Staël in 1821 and entitled *Dix années d'exil*.[5] When Mme de Staël died in 1817, a couple of redactions of the two main parts of the text existed, bearing resemblance to various literary genres like an autobiography, a pamphlet, a political or philosophical essay, a travel account, or a novel including dialogues—that is, conversations once held in a salon setting.[6] All the memoir fragments are part of a greater narrative, featuring her developing conflict with Napoleon. It is this form of representation—as Simone Balayé, expert and editor of some of her writings, rightly pointed out—that made Mme de Staël the best author and propagandist of her own myth as an adversary of Napoleon.[7]

2. Becoming Mme de Staël: Social Background

To characterize the circumstances defining Mme de Staël's life, habitus, and work, it is necessary to note that she was already born into—new—money and connections. Her parents, both of Swiss and Calvinist origins, were Jacques Necker and his wife, Suzanne Curchod. After their arrival in Paris, they had climbed the social ladder with breathtaking speed. As a bank director, Necker had earned a great fortune, but after some years he sold his share of the bank, transferred the management of all possessions to his wife, and turned to writing and publishing his ideas due to his deep commitment to enlightened ideas of

3 Staël. Correspondance générale. Vols. 1–9.

4 Balayé (Ed.). Les carnets de voyage.

5 The best annotated edition so far is: Staël. Dix années d'exil. For detail on the memoirs and a travel account, see: Cabak Rédei. An Inquiry into Cultural Semiotics; Sach. "Die Geographie de Napoleonischen Europa…".

6 On the history of the text, cf. the remarks of the editors Simone Balayé and Mariella Vianello Bonifacio in Staël. Dix années d'exil. Pp. 7–41. On switching between genres, see: Lot. De Dix années d'exil aux Considérations.

7 Balayé. Les rapports de l'écrivain et du pouvoir. P. 138.

the time.[8] The French king appointed him to the office of the minister of finance several times, although he withheld the official, prestigious title of Directeur du Trésor Royal because Necker was a bourgeois, a Protestant, and a foreigner.[9] Well aware of the critical state of public finances, Necker tried to encourage reforms and lent to the French state the enormous sum of two million livres from his own fortune.[10] Unfortunately, he was confronted by powerful opposition and its intrigues, forcing him to withdraw and to go into exile for some time.[11] His nonetheless brilliant career was actively supported in the sphere of society by his wife: long before his first appointment as minster in 1777, Suzanne Necker started to run one of the most influential prerevolutionary salons in Paris.[12] The various, complementary activities of Mme de Staël's parents gave her a notion of the importance of public opinion.[13]

3. Historical Context: Salons as Cultural and Political Institutions

What was so unique about running a salon, a complex social phenomenon without a clear and easy-to-apply cross-epochal definition? The development of salons correlated with social changes and new role models especially for educated women since the Renaissance. In France the influx of humanist ideals of education into the aristocratic culture at the royal court took place first and foremost in salons of the classical baroque type. These institutions offered women an adequate sphere as well as appropriate possibilities to present themselves as skilled, educated persons, as talented writers, as inspiring conversationalists, and as salon hostesses. A salon was the place to demonstrate refined taste, ready wit, and esprit—in other words, skills much appreciated in society and also meeting the needs of entertainment

8 Fairweather. Madame de Staël. Pp. 8–10, 29–31; Winock. Madame de Staël. Pp. 15–17, 19–26; Appel. Madame de Staël. P. 33.

9 Appel. Madame de Staël. Pp. 41 f.; Wehinger. Conversation, P. 72.

10 Mme de Staël, an efficient manager of her properties, retrieved the money after the fall of Napoleon. She officially called in the loan on July 1, 1814: Staël. Correspondance Générale. Vol. 9. Pp. 37 f.

11 Fairweather. Madame de Staël. Pp. 41 f., 72–75, 87 f., 108; Goodden. Madame de Staël. Pp. 33–35.

12 Heyden-Rynsch. Europäische Salons. Pp. 64, 119–121; Appel. Madame de Staël. Pp. 26–28; Fairweather. Madame de Staël. Pp. 23–28; Dubeau. Des livres et des hommes. Pp. 13–24; Gutwirth. Madame de Staël. Pp. 24–30.

13 Fairweather. Madame de Staël. Pp. 41, 110, 117 f.; Balayé. Madame de Staël et l'idée d'opinion publique. Pp. 173, 176.

and respecting courtly customs. The success of a salon was defined by the intellectual attractiveness of the salon hostess and her capability to create an inspiring atmosphere in her domicile.[14] Due to French cultural hegemony, the classical salon became the prototype for parallel developments at European courts and the formation of national variants.[15]

In the best of cases, salons were not limited to visitors of high social rank but were rather open to all cultivated and educated persons, who were regarded as equal because a person's position in a salon was defined by intellectual merits and accomplishments. But whether this promise could be kept depended on social conditions that differed across countries and periods.[16] Salons were free and easy but by no means informal. The salon hostess was always at the center; she was the one who set limits and rules, who decided to convene a regular meeting, the *jour fixe*. A salon was neither a formal association nor a club based on statutes and charging membership fees. No minutes were kept; what took place during a *jour fixe* in a respective salon, the course of the conversation, can only be reconstructed from memoirs and letters, which bear the emotional and subjective perspectives of their writers. The main purpose of all activities

---

14 Heyden-Rynsch. Europäische Salons. Pp. 37–56; Elias. Die höfische Gesellschaft. Pp. 120–22; Lepenies. Melancholie und Gesellschaft. Pp. 52–65; Wilhelmy-Dollinger. Die Berliner Salons. Pp. 23–44. For an overview of theroretical approaches in interdisciplinary perspective exemplified through German models, see: Seibert. Der literarische Salon. Pp. 159–220.

15 Albrecht. Kulturelle Hegemonie ohne Machtpolitik. Pp. 66–80; Heyden-Rynsch. Europäische Salons. Pp. 91–113, 132–175; Bernstein. Women on the Verge. Pp. 209–24. In the Russian tradition, men could also have formed the center of a salon; cf. Aronson / Reiser. Literaturnye kruzhki i salony. P. 36 f.; Andronikaschwili. Ekaterina II. P. 93; Sach. "… setzen Sie sich und erzählen Sie!" Pp. 87–89.

16 At the meetings in the house of the Marquise de Rambouillet, the founder of the French classical salon tradition, the bourgeois Vincent Voiture occupied a much higher position than Prince Louis II Condé because of the former's better command of the rules of poetry (Albrecht. Kulturelle Hegemonie. P. 77). But when servants of the Duc de Sully beat Voltaire, the philosopher waited in vain for an apology or some sort of satisfaction (Seibert. Der literarische Salon. P. 58). Nadezhda Durova (1783–1866), a Russian writer who, disguised as an officer, took part in the campaigns against Napoleon, reported how she at first was easily admitted to aristocratic salons in St. Petersburg. But after the first curiosity of the salon hostesses and their guests was satisfied, she was excluded because of her low social standing: Durova. God zhizni v Peterburge. Pp. 538 f. See also, on Durova: Kelly. A History. P. 48; Andrew. A Crocodile in Flannel. P. 59.

within a salon was conversation as a form of sociality.[17] Sociality means here—in the classical, early twentieth-century definition from the sociologist Georg Simmel—a social practice sui generis combining a certain sort of cultivated behavior, the observing of a certain ceremony including norms and rules of the *ars conversationis*, the art of conversation.[18] Frequent visitors, the *habitués*, formed the core of a salon.[19] It was also attended by occasional guests as a place of interest during a temporary stay on a journey or during the classical grand tour that completed a traditional aristocratic education. When Nikolai Karamzin visited Paris during his grand voyage in 1789–90, he was confronted with the aftermath of the French Revolution and a short break in salon activities and cultural sociality. Karamzin described the situation in April 1790, citing the views of a French abbot who deeply regretted the momentary absence of a place suitable for spending the evenings.[20]

But French salons were not only places to take part in educated amusement or to accomplish aristocratic education. During the age of Enlightenment they were quite prosperous and sometimes even changed into political arenas. In opening unique spheres and channels of communication to discuss new ideas in the arts, literature, or philosophy, salons not only met a need for entertainment but also launched a crucial process: as places of free speech in the context of sociality, salons served as locations where new, independent, and bourgeois elites could form themselves and where important structural transformations happened. It was, paradoxically, in the private space of the salon, as Jürgen Habermas has pointed out, where public opinion—which served at the time as a complement to the royal court—was constituted.[21] Or rather, as Ann T. Gardiner has argued in discussing Habermas's readings of Mme de Staël's practices, the salon was a site of "public-oriented privateness."[22]

---

17 For detail on the phenomenon and a general definition, see: Wilhelmy-Dollinger. Die Berliner Salons. Pp. 29–44.

18 Simmel. Soziologie der Geselligkeit. Pp. 177–193.

19 Wilhelmy-Dollinger. Die Berliner Salons. P. 38.

20 Karamzin. Pis'ma russkogo puteshestvennika. Pp. 370 f. Cf. also Berelowitch. La France dans le "Grand Tour." Pp. 193–209. On the diverse functions and effects of traveling and the role of travel accounts for the formation of cultural identities in the early modern period, cf. also: Witthoff. Grenzen der Kultur. Pp. 21–52, 277–302; and recently, on German examples: Voss. Reisen erzählen.

21 Habermas. Strukturwandel der Öffentlichkeit. Pp. 88 f., 94 f., 114 f.

22 Gardiner. Games in the Salon. P. 215; cf. also Staël. Du talent d'être amiable en conversation. Pp. 25–30; Wehinger. Conversation. Pp. 192–216.

4. The Future Mme de Staël's Training Place: Her Mother's Salon

Such was the general historical context in which Suzanne Necker established her own salon. Regular visitors, the *habitués*, could meet there famous encyclopedists like Diderot and d'Alembert and other proponents of the Enlightenment like Buffon, Gibbon, Marmontel, Galiani, Meister, Mably or Grimm, but also characters like the famous *salonnières* Mme Geoffrin or Geoffrin's opponent Mme du Deffand, to mention only some of the most important. The famous Mme Geoffrin, an early patron of Mme Necker,[23] was an influential *salonnière* with international connections including the British historian and politician Horace Walpole, Stanisław II Poniatowski (whom Mme Geoffrin hosted in her salon when he was on his grand tour and whom she visited in 1766 in Warsaw, after he has been elected to the throne of Poland and Lithuania), and both the princess of Anhalt-Zerbst,[24] and her daughter Catherine II, who hosted a salon of her own in St. Petersburg.[25] The prestigious connections that Mme Geoffrin kept up through a vast correspondence represented a sort of written conversation: Catherine II was well aware while composing her letters that they would be read aloud in the salon of Mme Geoffrin.[26] Such a practice—writing personal letters that were implicitly directed to a broader public—made it possible to take part in a debate or to raise a point for discussion without being physically present. It was precisely Mme Geoffrin, to whom Catherine reported her plans concerning her famous *Nakaz*,[27] a text officially forbidden in France after it had been published in various European

---

23 HAMON. Madame Geoffrin. Pp. 337–54.

24 HEYDEN-RYNSCH. Europäische Salons. Pp. 74–77; WOLFF. Inventing Eastern Europe. Pp. 242–57; HAMON. Madame Geoffrin. Pp. 313–17.

25 ANDRONIKASCHWILI. Ekaterina II. Pp. 89–105; BERELOWITCH. La vie mondaine sous Catherine II. Pp. 104–6; SACH. "… setzen Sie sich und erzählen Sie!" Pp. 93–95.

26 The letters of Catherine are edited in: GAMBURGER (Ed.). Pis'ma Imperatricy Ekateriny II k G-zhie Zhoffren. On the contact between Catherine II and Mme Geoffrin, see: HAMON. Madame Geoffrin. Pp. 489–98; HEYDEN-RYNSCH. Europäische Salons. Pp. 75 f. The letters of Mme Geoffrin to Catherine do not survive; cf. WOLFF. Inventing Eastern Europe. P. 247.

27 Catherine wrote to Mme Geoffrin in 1765 of her legislative projects; she also mentioned the topic in letters to other French correspondents visiting salons in Paris. These letters surely would have stimulated discussion of her actions as enlightened lawgiver; cf. GAMBURGER (Ed.). Pis'ma Imperatricy Ekateriny II k G-zhie Zhoffren. № 10. P. 276; № 12. P. 283.

languages.[28] But a salon was more than a place to build one's reputation. It was also an institution where a reputation could be instantly sullied, as Catherine II also knew quite well. In 1771 Mme Geoffrin took part in an intrigue to prevent Carloman de Rulhière from reading publicly from his manuscript *Anecdotes sur la révolution de Russie en l'année 1762*, which was critical of Catherine's image. Rulhière's text remained unpublished during his lifetime and that of the tsarina.[29]

Similar to the model of Mme Geoffrin, the salon of Mme Necker allowed for both philosophical and political discussions. But in clear contrast to other prominent salons, her salon had a clear purpose: to sanitize the public image of Jacques Necker, her husband.[30] Beyond that, the salon of Mme Necker was the formative intellectual training place, school, and academy for her young daughter.

Coming from a Calvinist family, the child was not sent to a convent school like the girls from noble or upper-class families in predominantly Catholic France.[31] Under these circumstances, young Germaine perhaps received an early notion of (religious) otherness and tolerance, helping her in later years to better perceive and understand cultural differences. She also became accustomed to attracting attention from a very young age: as her parents' pride and joy, she was presented as a prodigy and child genius to her mother's guests. Soon she became acquainted with the latest ideas of the Enlightenment, and very early in life she became a self-confident member of the country's intellectual and new social elite. But above all, she was introduced to a wide range of social practices of cultivated sociality, conviviality, and networking, which would define her habitus and concept of life.[32]

Due to political discussions in her mother's salon and to her beloved father's public functions, Germaine also took great interest in politics. But an appointment to public office was out of reach for women. Prospects of political activity consisted only in networkingand informal exercise of influence on decision- and opinion-

---

28 Plavinskaia. "Nakaz" Ekateriny II vo Francii. P. 18.

29 d'Armaillé (Ed.). La comtesse d'Egmont. Pp. 127–29; Dulac. Politique, littérature et mystification. Pp. 213–22; Hamon. Madame Geoffrin. Pp. 494–98. Rulhière died in 1791; soon after Catherine's death, the text appeared in print and also in the same year in English, German, and Dutch translation. Cf. Wolff. Inventing Eastern Europe. P. 273.

30 Heyden-Rynsch. Europäische Salons. P. 120; Bosse. Metamorphosen des literarischen "Contre-pouvoir." P. 39; Winock. Madame de Staël. P. 19 f.; Balayé. Madame de Staël et l'idée d'opinion publique. P. 173.

31 Appel. Madame de Staël. Pp. 24–30; Krapoth. Geist des Gesprächs. P. 253.

32 Heyden-Rynsch. Europäische Salons. Pp. 119 f.; Krapoth. Geist des Gesprächs. Pp. 256–61; Wehinger. Conversation. Pp. 192–202.

making.[33] After marrying Swedish diplomat Erik Magnus von Staël-Holstein, a marriage that provided her with the social and political status of an ambassador's consort,[34] she opened her own salon in 1786 in the Swedish embassy. Mme de Staël received numerous national and international guests in her salon, where she eagerly promoted liberal ideas. Her salon soon outshone and replaced her mother's salon as an important site of literary, philosophical, and political discussion.[35]

5. Mme de Staël as Parisian salonnière

In those years Mme de Staël also gained her first publicity and critical response as an author, especially as a female writer.[36] For the public, Mme de Staël was inspiring and provocative in all fields of her activity. During the era of the French Revolution, her salon became a meeting point for moderate revolutionaries and

---

33 GOODDEN. Madame de Staël. P. 35. The few positions in a royal court open to women implied possibilities as starting points for considerable influence, but they were at the same limited due to contemporary role models. Cf. BASTIAN. Kammerdame und diplomatische Akteurin. Pp. 261–76; DADE. Die königliche Mätresse als Diplomatin. Pp. 277–92.

34 The marriage was arranged. As the richest heiress in Europe, Germaine did not suffer from a lack of suitors; however, the Neckers wanted for her not only an aristocrat but also a Protestant. These crucial conditions excluded almost the entire French aristocracy, while Staël-Holstein, a Swedish baron and attaché, met the formal criteria, though he was heavily in debt. After some diplomatic activity between the French and Swedish courts, including an understanding pertaining to trade and the possession of Saint-Barthélemy, one isle of the Antilles, baron Erik Magnus of Staël-Holstein obtained a lifetime appointment as official ambassador of Sweden in Paris. The groom promised in a marriage contract, among other things, never to force his future wife to leave Paris, a point quite important to the bride and her parents (cf. APPEL. Madame de Staël. Pp. 45–48; SETH. Germaine de Staël and Marie-Antoinette. P. 48). As ambassador's consort, Mme de Staël wrote reports on social life at the royal court and in Paris: STAËL. Correspondance générale. Vol. 1. Pp. 87 f., 99–114, 136–49, 182–84, 217–33; PALME. Mme de Staël et la Suède. Pp. 96 f.

35 BOSSE. Metamorphosen des literarischen "Contre-pouvoir." P. 39; KRAPOTH. Geist des Gesprächs. P. 253; FAIRWEATHER. Madame de Staël. Pp. 66 f.; GUTWIRTH. Madame de Staël, P. 66; BALAYÉ. Madame de Staël et l'idée d'opinion publique. P. 173.

36 Besides some smaller pieces, she made her debut as a published philosopher and literary critic with: *Lettres sur les écrits et le caractère de J.-J. Rousseau* (1788), newly edited in STAËL. Œuvres complètes. Vol. 1. Pp. 17–110. For more on her writing and the response, see: GUTWIRTH. Madame de Staël. Pp. 50–75; WEHINGER. Conversation. Pp. 89–108. More generally on female authorship and the problem of celebrity, see: SCHLICK. Beyond the Boundaries. Pp. 50–63.

a sort of headquarters for opinion-making beyond mere conversation and correspondence.[37] Through collaborative work, political brochures were drafted and discussed, their print was organized, and texts were circulated in networks. To reach a greater audience, reviews and references in newspapers and journals in the growing media market were initiated as well. Mme de Staël eagerly took part in all these activities.[38] Beyond that, she was successful in a quite traditional manner of exerting influence—namely, winning allies through her eloquence, indirectly affecting processes of decision-making in securing important positions in the government for close friends such as Count Narbonne and Prince Talleyrand.[39] But she also generously supported friends who had to leave the country, exchanging crucial news with them and developing strategies to communicate secretly by organizing networks and using pseudonyms, cover addresses, invisible ink, and so forth.[40] Her connections and talents contributed to the freeing of General Lafayette, who had been arrested by antirevolutionary troops after fleeing France and was being held in a Prussian prison.[41] Paul S. Spalding rates the collaborative efforts of Mme de Staël and her fellows as:

> the first great template in modern times for international cooperation by private initiative to maintain communications with political prisoners and press state authorities by persisting lobbying and publicity to gain the captives' release. In effect, subsequent successful international campaigns to free such noteworthy prisoners of conscience as Alfred Dreyfus, Nelson Mandela and Aung San Suu Kyi would mimic the foundational achievement of Staël and her acquaintances.[42]

But she did not always succeed in her activities: she tried in vain to defend Marie Antoinette in an anonymously published brochure before the former queen's trial and execution in October 1793.[43] During the revolutionary period, Mme

---

37 See, generally: Fairweather. Madame de Staël. Pp. 79–225; Winock. Madame de Staël. Pp. 51–137; Appel. Madame de Staël. Pp. 57–112; Rous Besser. Germaine de Staël Revisited. Pp. 36–46.

38 See, in detail : Beausoleil. Germaine de Staël as Political Activist. Pp. 23–34.

39 Beausoleil. Germaine de Staël as Political Activist. Pp. 25 f.; Winock. Madame de Staël. Pp. 59, 145; Seth. Germaine de Staël and Marie-Antoinette. P. 53.

40 Beausoleil. Germaine de Staël as Political Activist. P. 26, cf. also ibid. Fn. 12. Mme de Staël was quite ingenious in organizing communication and the exchange of messages: Spalding. Germaine de Staël's Role in Rescuing Lafayette. P. 38.

41 In detail, see: Spalding. Germaine de Staël's Role in Rescuing Lafayette. Pp. 35–46.

42 Ibid. P. 46.

43 Staël. Réflexions sur le procès de la reine, par une femme. First published in August 1793; newly edited in Œuvres complètes. Vol. 3.1. Pp. 29–66.

de Staël was harshly attacked and denunciated by royalists and radical revolutionaries likewise. Even though they claimed different reasons for these attacks, the denunciations always came down to her capacity as an influential woman and a foreigner. Much like Marie Antoinette, she served as a scapegoat in an agitated public atmosphere and at a time when men wanted to push women's influence aside.[44]

In consequence, Mme de Staël left Paris, her birthplace and spiritual home, repeatedly, sometimes by her own choice to escape a dangerous situation and to make the best of it by traveling, sometimes by force. Her exile was quite privileged, due to her economic independence, but it was nevertheless painful. It would become a central topic of her life and of her writings.[45] She faced her first official banning from the city, for causeless charges, in 1795.[46] After her return she was kept under surveillance by the police, a painful situation that she had to experience again and again in the years to come, especially when Napoleon Bonaparte came into power.

6. Traveling through Europe

At first Germaine de Staël respected Napoleon for his military successes and hoped that his reforms would stabilize the young French republic and its vulnerable institutions and avert further damage.[47] They met for the first time in December 1797 and shared a mutual antipathy.[48] But she still perceived him as the lesser evil, a judgment that changed after his coup d'état in November 1799.[49] Napoleon, for his part, was annoyed by her criticism of his politics, criticism that spread out from her salon and became a contentious issue:

> Il lui revint que j'avais parlé dans ma société contre cette oppression toujours croissante dont je pressentais les progrès aussi clairement que si l'avenir m'eût été révélé. Joseph Bonaparte, dont j'aimais l'esprit et la conversation, vint me voir et me dit:« Mon frère se plaint de vous. Pourquoi, m'a-t-il répété hier, pourquoi Mme de Staël ne s'attache-t-elle

---

44 Seth. Germaine de Staël. Pp. 60 f.; Jasinski. Mme de Staël et la convention. Pp. 40–49.

45 Cf. Balayé. Absence, exil, voyage. Pp. 47–60.

46 Jasinski. Mme de Staël et la convention. P. 50.

47 Staël. Dix années d'exil. Pp. 46 f.; Fairweather. Madame de Staël. Pp. 237, 279 f.; Winock. Madame de Staël. Pp. 149–51; Cabak Rédei. An Inquiry into Cultural Semiotics. P. 29.

48 In the historical view of her memoirs the description of Napoleon is quite negative: Staël. Dix années d'exil. P. 49; Winock. Madame de Staël. Pp. 150–52.

49 Staël. Considérations. Vol. 2. Pp. 535–62. On her principal views, cf. Tenenbaum. Turning Honour on Its Head. Pp. 125–35.

> pas à mon gouvernement? Qu'est qu'elle veut? Le paiement du dépôt de son père [the private loan of 2 million French livres to the French government, mentioned above]? Je l'ordonnerai. Le séjour de Paris? Je lui permettrai. Enfin, qu'est-ce qu'elle veut?—Mon dieu, répliquai-je, il ne s'agit pas de ce que je veux, mais de ce que je pense. »[50]

Moreover, Mme de Staël shared her thoughts not only with her salon guests but also with readers of her writings, which increasingly provoked Napoleon. In her successful study *De la littérature considerée dans ses rapports avec les institutions sociales* (1800), she claimed literature's authority to morally judge rulers and therefore to protect society and its institutions.[51] Her vision also included the participation of women, for whom she claimed the right to equal education.[52] This was all quite aggravating for Napoleon, who had publicly declared himself to be unfond of women engaging in politics.[53] Napoleon, then First Consul, considered Mme de Staël's epistolary novel *Delphine* (1802) to be immoral, anti-Catholic, and anti-French, and he was utterly displeased when he heard of her relationship with Benjamin Constant, a well-known liberal politician and political philosopher. As a result Napoleon prevented Mme de Staël from returning to Paris after she left it for a journey.[54] In the years to come, Mme de Staël was not allowed to enter the city or to stay in the immediate vicinity; neither letters nor appeals to generosity were heard.[55] Her son Auguste de Staël, then seventeen years old, tried in vain to persuade Napoleon to let her return to Paris in 1807:

---

50 Staël. Dix années d'exil. P. 84.

51 Staël. De la littérature. Pp. 121–26, 285–308; Goodden. Madame de Staël. Pp. 83 f.; Winock. Madame de Staël. Pp. 180–84; Morrissey. Mme de Staël et Napoléon. Pp. 48–52.

52 Staël. De la littérature. Pp. 310–17; Morrissey. Mme de Staël et Napoléon. Pp. 53 f.

53 Cf. de Staël's description of a party at Talleyrand's: "Après dîner, il s'approcha d'une femme très connue en France par sa beauté, son esprit et la vivacité de ses opinions [i.e., the marquise de Condorcet]. Il s'arrêta devant elle droit comme un prince allemand. 'Madame, lui dit-il, je n'aime pas que les femmes / s'occupe de politique.—Vous avez raison, mon géneral, lui répondit-elle. Mais, dans un pays où l'on coupe la tête aux femmes, il est naturel qu'elles aient envie de savoir pourquoi.' Il ne répliqua point à cette repartie parce qu'elle était spirituelle." Staël. Dix années d'exil. Pp. 51 f. Cf. also Staël. Considérations. Vol. 1. Pp. 510 f.

54 Letter of Mme de Staël to Claude Hochet: Staël. Correspondance générale. Vol. 4. Pp. 592–95. Cf. also : Fairweather. Madame de Staël. Pp. 283–87; Winock. Madame de Staël. Pp. 201–4; Winegarten. Germaine de Staël & Benjamin Constant. Pp. 148–53.

55 In September and October 1803, Mme de Staël twice tried to convince Napoleon to end her banishment: Staël. Correspondance Générale. Vol. 5.1. Pp. 18 f., 54 f.

> Mais encore une fois, pourquoi votre mère veut-elle venir se mettre immédiatement à la portée de cette *tyrannie*, car vous voyez que je tranche le mot. Qu'elle aille à Rome, à Naples, à Vienne, à Berlin, à Milan, à Lyon; qu'elle aille à Londres si elle veut faire des libelles. Je la verrai partout avec plaisir; mais Paris, voyez-vous, c'est là que j'habite et je n'y veux que des gens qui m'aiment. Si je la laissais venir à Paris, elle ferait des sottises [...]. / Elle ne pourrait se tenir de parler politique [...] / Si je l'avait mise en prison, j'en reviendrais, mais de l'exil, non. Tout le monde comprend que la prison, c'est un malheur: il n'y a que votre mère qui soit malheureuse quand on lui laisse toute l'Europe.[56]

Banished from her beloved Paris, Mme de Staël turned toward Europe, which generously admitted her. She had already made her second visit to England—which she deeply admired for its political order[57]—by 1793, and she traveled through the German states in 1803–4. She stayed for some time in Weimar and Berlin. In 1804–5 she voyaged through Italy. Mme de Staël spent winter 1807–8 in Vienna, where she also made some Russian acquaintances.[58] She had easy access to the local elite everywhere she went, due to her connections as well as, more broadly, both the social and cultural institution of the salon. It was there where she made a lot of new acquaintances, formed new important ties, and met not only writers and politicians but also monarchs and their families.[59]

7. Place of Retreat and Strongpoint: Mme de Staël and Her Salon in Coppet

Between her journeys, Mme de Staël regularly spent time in Switzerland, at Coppet, an estate on Lake Geneva and a full-fledged barony that her father had had the foresight to purchase in 1784. The château de Coppet was located between France and the Italian and German states, formally under French authority, but far away from the official center of power.[60] This site, which became her place of asylum, was where she again unfolded her activities as salon hostess. The absence of a royal or imperial court removed the salon in Coppet in a certain sense from the structural antagonism of domestic salon versus court described above, in

---

56 Auguste de Staël's report is conveyed in: Lenormant. Coppet et Weimar. Pp. 122–25, quotation on p. 122 f.

57 Staël. Considérations. Vol. 2. Pp. 847–900; Pange. Le rêve anglais. Pp. 173–89.

58 For example, she met the future minister of education Sergei S. Uvarov and the historian Aleksandr I. Turgenev: Solovieff. Mme de Staël et ses correspondants russes. Pp. 9–18; Durylin. G-zha de Stal' i ee russkie otnosheniia. Pp. 225–42.

59 Staël. Dix années d'exil. Pp. 157–76; Balayé (Ed.). Les carnets de voyage. Pp. 21–259, 435–42; Cabak Rédei. An Inquiry into Cultural Semiotics. Pp. 85–151.

60 Hoock-Demarle. Coppet. Pp. 38 f.

which classical salons functioned as public-private complements to the court. In fact, Coppet became a center of its own, or to put it in Ann T. Gardiner's words: "Coppet was not a 'home' in any sense of the term, but a veritable 'house,' with all the differences in public and private that such a concept implies."[61] As expected, Mme de Staël's salon in Coppet became an object of interest as Prosper de Barante, statesman, historian, and member of the circle itself, has described it:

> Madame de Staël réunissait autour d'elle tous les hommes remarquables de Genève. Et tout ce qu'il y avait de distingué en France et en Europe, par l'intelligence, la renommée, la naissance et le pouvoir, ne traversait pas la Suisse sans être amené à Coppet, soit par d'anciennes relations, soit par une curiosité plus ou moins bienveillante.[62]

At Coppet, Germaine de Staël gathered a circle of writers and others into a community of collective and interdisciplinary thinking—or rather, into one of the first "think tanks" (Robert Morrissey),[63] later labeled as the *Groupe de Coppet.*[64] Besides her longtime companion Constant, already mentioned, the philologist and historian August Wilhelm Schlegel, whom Mme de Staël had once engaged as tutor for her children, the economist and historian Jean de Sismondi , and the Swiss writer Charles Victor de Bonstetten formed among others the core of this group of close friends promoting liberal ideas and political principles not in accordance with Napoleon's political ambitions.[65] This inner circle was complemented by a heterogeneous group of guests made up of old friends, new acquaintances, and opponents of Napoleon—as French bureaucrats and foreign diplomats were staying in Coppet sometimes for weeks and months—a clear difference from the Parisian habit to receive on a *jour fixe*. Professors and students from the Academy of Geneva dropped in, and travelers and aristocrats on grand tour from England, the German states, Scandinavia, the Russian Empire, or the United States stopped there on their way to Italy. Women came as well, including the German-Danish salon hostess Friederike Brun, Caroline von Humboldt, and Juliane von Krüdener,

---

61 Gardiner. From Group to Traveler's network. P. 172. Cf. also Craiutu. Moderation. P. 111.

62 Barante. Souvenirs. Vol. 1. P. 159.

63 Morrissey. Mme de Staël et Napoléon. P. 36; Gardiner. From Group to Traveler's Network. Pp. 153 f.

64 In detail, see: Rosset. Écrire à Coppet; Hoock-Demarle. Coppet. Pp. 37–46; Craiutu. Moderation. Pp. 109–24; Gardiner. From Group to Traveler's Network. Pp. 153–74; Balayé. Le Groupe de Coppet. Pp. 321–42; Beausoleil. Germaine de Staël as Political Activist. P. 26.

65 Craiatu. Moderation. P. 111. For a recent overview of the ideas of the major protagonists, see: Burnand / Poisson (Eds.). Comment sortir de l'empire?

often traveling for curative purposes or for their children's education, for which they would visit salons as places for learning for both girls and boys.[66] All would spend their time in Coppet in discussions, literary work, correspondence, and performances, making Coppet an important place of cultural interaction and transfer of ideas. In this way, exile—with its travels, tours to foreign salons, and activities in Coppet—led to the transformation of Mme de Staël's original Parisian salon into a European one, including an extensive dilation of its influence through transnational networks, of which it was itself a prominent part.[67]

8. Increasing Threat and Escape by Travel in 1812

The outcome of Mme de Staël's extensive voyages was not only a growing network but also a literary one that inspired her to write and to present to her audience different European cultures. In 1807 she published *Corinne ou l'Italie*, a novel that became a great international success but that again displeased Napoleon because there was not the slightest reference to his victories and achievements in Italy.[68] Finally, her magnum opus *De l'Allemagne* caused a major scandal in 1810: after having considered the remarks of the censor, Mme de Staël sent proofs to Napoleon as a sign of goodwill in order to end her disgrace and exile.[69] Napoleon criticized some passages and ordered their elimination, but Jean-Maric-René Savary, minister of the police, went much further. He commanded the destruction of both edition and printing plates and banished Mme de Staël promptly from France. Because she had exhibited enthusiasm about German literature and philosophy, she was accused to have written from an anti-French perspective.[70] Neither her protests nor her repeated,

66 Gardiner. From Group to Traveler's Network. Pp. 168–70. For an overview of the most important visitors, see: Jasinski. Liste des principaux visiteurs. Pp. 461–92. On the correspondence between members of the Groupe de Coppet, see: Solovieff. Aperçu. Pp. 493–512.

67 Cf. Balayé. Le Groupe de Coppet. P. 323. On the theoretical implications, see: Gardiner. From Group to Traveler's Network. Pp. 157 f.

68 Balayé. Les rapports de l'écrivain et du pouvoir. P. 153; Fairweather. Madame de Staël, Pp. 341 f.; Winock. Madame de Staël. Pp. 300–303; Goodden. Madame de Staël. Pp. 83 f.

69 Staël. Correspondance générale. Vol. 7. Pp. 258–60, 261 f.

70 Staël. Dix années d'exil. Pp. 193–200. The author included Savary's letter in her memoirs (Ibid. Pp. 200 f.), and she later included it in the beginning of *De l'Allemagne* (Staël. De l'Allemagne. Vol. 1. Pp. 5–7. Cf. also Fairweather. Madame de Staël. Pp. 367–74; Goodden. Madame de Staël. Pp. 193 f.

refused requests to be received in audience were fruitful; nor did attempts to mediate by Hortense, queen consort of Holland and Napoleon's stepdaughter, succeed: the verdict of exile was not repealed.[71]

Accordingly Mme de Staël took up residence in her Swiss château. But increasing surveillance by French secret police, the harassment of family members, and the prevented visits from friends depressed her more and more.[72] She feared imprisonment and planned to flee secretly from the threat of arrest. By autumn 1811, she dismissed the idea of immigrating to the United States because of the signs of the upcoming Anglo-American War, and she decided to flee to England.[73]

But when she left Coppet in May 1812, the direct route from Switzerland to England was closed due to the preparations of Napoleon's campaign to Russia, which would begin the following month. Finally she escaped to England, reaching it in 1813 via Austria, Russia, and Sweden with a small company including two of her children, Schlegel, Jean Rocca (her future second husband), and servants, among them one who furnished information on the voyage to the French secret police.[74]

Mme de Staël described her dangerous voyage impressively in her *Dix années d'exil.* It is striking how much the success of this particular journey during wartime is linked to the existence of old networks and cultural practices: due to her connections she was able to solve such practical and organizational problems as obtaining passports for all of her party while being constantly spied on within the Napoleonic sphere of influence.[75] Thanks to her reputation as a celebrated woman of letters and her connections as famous *salonnière*, she had easy access to the particular local francophone higher society on her way through the Habsburg lands, the Polish parts of the Russian Empire, and Russia herself. Her connections prooved crucial in gaining information concerning the currant military situation in order to avoid the French army already on the way to Moscow, where she was

---

71 Staël. Correspondance générale. Vol. 7. Pp. 262–67, 273–77.

72 Cf. her September 1811 letter to Napoleon: Staël. Correspondance Générale. Vol. 7. Pp. 461 f. Her fears were expressed in a letter to Mme Récamier in November 1811: Ibid. Pp. 501–3. A general description of this depressing time appears in: Staël. Dix années d'exil. Pp. 201–26. Cf. Jasinski. Liste des principaux visiteurs. Pp. 479–81.

73 Cf. the letter to Henri Meister, October 5, 1811: Staël. Correspondance Générale. Vol. 7. Pp. 487–89.

74 Napoleon received a detailed report on February 27, 1813: King. Un récit. P. 16, see also pp. 6–15.

75 Sach. Die Geographie des Napoleonischen Europa. Pp. 33–35.

also headed.[76] A German doctor, who served as Russian-language interpreter, accompanied the party on its way to Moscow.[77]

9. Imaging Russia in *Dix années d'exil*

In her memoirs, Mme de Staël presented a quite interesting narrative of the events, discussed from a political perspective but composed as an epic drama. The author herself appears as a fragile but brave woman persecuted by an abominable tyrant, Napoleon, who is determined to subdue Europe in order to extend his empire to the east; he has already conquered great parts of the continent. One of the last resorts seems to be Russia and her ruler, depicted as one of the tyrant's antagonists. The struggle against Napoleon is the dominating subject, also defining the liberal-minded author's judgments and perspectives, especially in dealing with Russia and her autocratic system and social situation, which she did not thoroughly analyze, as Anna Cabak Rédei has rightly pointed out.[78] Mme de Staël was well aware of the longstanding image of Russians as a barbarous people as well as current stereotypes in Western political or historical debates of Russia as a country of despotism and tyranny.[79] How well she subordinated her opinions to the need to fight against Napoleon becomes clear in her first remarks describing her entrance to the Russian Empire after Napoleon had already started his campaign:

> On n'était guère accoutumé à considérer la Russie comme l'État le plus libre de l'Europe, mais le joug que l'empereur de France fait peser sur tous les États du continent est tel qu'on se croit dans une république dès qu'on arrive dans le pays où la tyrannie de Napoléon ne peut se faire sentir. C'était le 14 juillet que j'entrai en Russie; cet anniversaire d'un jour qui a commencé la Révolution me frappa singulièrement: ainsi se refermait pour moi le cercle de l'histoire de France qui, le 14 juillet 1789 avait commencé et, quand la barrière

---

76 In detail on her route, look at the cartographic representations in: WINOCK. Madame de Staël. Unnumbered plate before P. 287. Cf. the scheme in: LIEVEN. Russland gegen Napoleon. Pp. 172 f., displaying the advance of the French army. Furthermore, see: BALAYÉ (Ed.). Les carnets de voyages. Pp. 279–86; KING. Un récit. Pp. 10 f.; SACH. "Die Geographie des Napoleonischen Europa..." Pp. 41 f., 52 f.

77 STAËL. Dix années d'exil. P. 256.

78 CABAK RÉDEI. An Inquiry into Cultural Semiotics. Pp. 230, 243.

79 SCHEIDEGGER. Perverses Abendland. Pp. 20–27; MERVAUD / ROBERTI. Une infinie brutalité. Pp. 101–51; LORTHOLARY. Le mirage russe en France. P. 273; MCNALLY. Das Russlandbild in der Publizistik Frankreichs. Pp. 83–88; MALIA. Russia under Western Eyes. Pp. 17–84; SCHAUB. Wahrnehmungen und Praktiken in den französisch-russischen Beziehungen. Pp. 319–40.

qui sépare l'Autriche de la Russie s'ouvrit pour me laisser passer, je jurai de ne jamais remettre les pieds dans un pays soumis d'une manière quelconque à l'empereur Napoléon.[80]

In Mme de Staël's view, Napoleonic rule could only have a negative impact on subject nations; the Habsburg Monarchy and Poland, both of which she crossed on her way to the Russian border, seemed to her to verify this idea.[81] Despite the outbreak of war, her description of her voyage through Russia sounds quite different. Mme de Staël sometimes seemed to feel more like a tourist than a refugee. In some cities—Kiev, Moscow, and St. Petersburg, for instance—she even did some sightseeing, and she regularly took the time for participant observations everywhere she went and left an enthusiastic description of Moscow before the great fire in 1812.[82] She was especially fascinated with the Russian people, to whom she attributed a form of lusty energy lacking in the West, an energy that she correlated with the trait of "barbarism."[83] But this common trope in debates on Russian identity was now revalued, infused with a clearly positive meaning, in light of the defense against Napoleon:

Heureusement pour eux, ils sont toujours ce que nous appelons barbares, c'est-à-dire conduits par un instinct souvent généreux, toujours involontaire et qui n'admet la réflexion que dans le choix des moyens et non dans l'examen du but; je dis heureusement pour eux, non que je prétende vanter la barbarie, mais je désigne par ce nom une certaine énergie primitive, qui peut seule remplacer dans les nations la force surprenante de la liberté.[84]

Generally, Mme de Staël described Russians of all social ranks as patriotic and willing to make sacrifices, and she illustrated this with anecdotes throughout the text. However, she herself had only heard of the loss of lives or material damages; she did not pass regions affected by destruction or plundering.[85] In 1813, as Mme de Staël was working on the first draft of her memoirs, Napoleon was not yet defeated, but the hopes that the author pinned on Russia, on the Russian people, and especially on the Russian ruler can be found everywhere in the text.

---

80 Staël. Dix années d'exil. P. 255.

81 Cf. Sach. "Die Geographie des Napoleonischen Europa…" Pp. 36–39; Cabak Rédei. An Inquiry into Cultural Semiotics. Pp. 152–80.

82 Cf. Staël. Dix années d'exil. Pp. 256–306; Sach. "Die Geographie des Napoleonischen Europa…" Pp. 40–45; Cabak Rédei. An Inquiry into Cultural Semiotics. Pp. 212–17.

83 Staël. Dix années d'exil. Pp. 268–69.

84 Ibid. P. 279.

85 Sach. "Die Geographie des Napoleonischen Europa…" Pp. 51–60.

10. The Tsar's Representation in *Dix années d'exil*

Besides the Russian people, the Russian emperor was of course an object of curiosity. In *Dix années d'exil*, Mme de Staël depicted Alexander I as an ideal ruler with intellectual capacities, wit, and education, who is not free from making mistakes—he once trusted Napoleon, after all—but who is able to correct false decisions.[86] The centerpiece of her portrayal of the tsar is the depiction of her reception at the imperial court in St. Petersburg on August 17, 1812, a meeting that was also attended by the imperial family.[87] Aware of Western stereotypes of Russian rulers as despotic, she described the tsar quite positively in comparison with an English statesman—to her an ideal figure:

> J'ai toujours considéré comme un signe de médiocrité cette crainte de parler du fond des choses qu'on a inspirée à la plupart des souverains de l'Europe; ils craignent de prononcer des mots qui auraient un sens sérieux et réel. L'empereur Alexandre, au contraire, s'entretint avec moi comme l'auraient fait les hommes d'État de l'Angleterre, qui mettent leurs forces en eux-mêmes et non dans les barrières dont on peut s'environner.[88]

In a sense, the meeting is presented as a classical conversation in a salon—in "public-oriented privatenesss"—between two educated persons in a free exchange of views on equal terms and in an atmosphere full of wit, as they listen to each other and flatter one another. At the same time, Alexander I is described in his manifest openness to discussion as the opposite of Napoleon, who had repeatedly refused to receive Mme de Staël. Furthermore Alexander is described in an important liberal keyword as "le meilleur citoyen de son empire."[89] The author presented him as a man of noble modesty, who even wished to improve the status of the peasants, and whose good character served, temporarily, as a substitute for a constitution, another important liberal keyword:

> Alexandre donne et retire sa confiance avec la plus grande réflexion. Sa jeunesse et ses avantages extérieurs ont pu seuls, dans le commencement de son règne, le faire soupçonner de légèreté, mais il est sérieux par l'âme autant que pourrait l'être un homme qui aurait connu le malheur. Alexandre m'exprima ses regrets de n'être pas un grand général; je répondis à cette noble modestie qu'un souverain était plus rare qu'un général et que soutenir l'esprit public de sa nation par son exemple, c'était gagner la plus grande des batailles et la première de ce genre qui eût été gagnée. L'empereur Alexandre me parla de sa nation avec enthousiasme et de ce dont elle était capable. Il m'indiqua le désir que tout le monde lui connaît

86 Staël. Dix années d'exil. Pp. 290 f.

87 King. Un récit. P. 11.

88 Staël. Dix années d'exil. P. 290.

89 Ibid. P. 285.

> d'améliorer l'état des paysans encore soumis au servage. "Sire, lui dis-je, votre caractère est une constitution pour votre empire et votre conscience en est la garantie.—Quand cela serait vrai, me répondit-il, un homme n'est jamais qu'un accident heureux." Superbes paroles, les premières, je crois, de ce genre qu'un monarque absolu ait prononcées! Que de vertus il faut pour juger le despotisme en étant despote et que de vertus pour n'en jamais abuser, quand la nation qu'on gouverne s'étonne presque d'une si rare modération![90]

Mme de Staël met Alexander at a time when he was inclined to introduce reforms,[91] but she also witnessed the opposite: conservative views and attitudes within the nobility.[92] As a matter of fact, Alexander was well aware of his guest's influence on the shaping of both his own public image and that of his empire in European minds. Consequently he also entered in a correspondence with her, started in 1814 with her request to be allowed to make his statements public through her writings.[93] However, in the course of 1812, her varied and versatile activities were especially needed in Sweden.

11. Lobbying for a European Alliance and Its Geopolitical Preconditions

At the time of Mme de Staël's audience at the Russian court, Alexander was about to go to Åbo (Turku) for an already arranged meeting with the former French general Jean-Baptiste Bernadotte, an old friend of de Staël's, who was heir to the

90 Ibid. P. 291. Similarly Mme de Staël stated elsewhere: "Je veux citer à cette occasion un mot de l'empereur Alexandre qui me paraît digne d'être consacré. J'avais l'honneur de le voir à Pétersbourg dans le moment le plus remarquable de sa vie, lorsque les Français s'avançaient sur Moscou, et qu'en refusant la paix que Napoléon lui offrit dès qu'il se crut vainqueur, Alexandre triomphait plus habilement de son ennemi que ses généraux mêmes. 'Madame de Staël, me dit l'empereur de Russie, vous n'ignorez pas que les paysans russes sont esclaves. Je fais ce que peux pour améliorer leur sort graduellement dans mes domaines; mais je rencontre ailleurs des obstacles que le repos de l'empire m'ordonne de ménager.—Sire, lui répondis-je, je sais que la Russie est maintenant heureuse quoiqu'elle n'ait d'autre constitution que le caractère personnel de Votre Majesté.—Quand le compliment que vous me faites aurait de la vérité, répondit l'empereur, *je ne serais jamais qu'un accident heureux*.'": Staël. Considérations. Vol. 2. P. 947, italics in the original.

91 Hartley. Alexander I. Pp. 82–94; Rey. Alexandre Ier. Pp. 275–91.

92 Staël. Dix années d'exil. P. 291.

93 Staël. Correspondance générale. Vol. 8. Pp. 502 f. For her letters, including the tsar's responses: [Lautier (Ed.)]. Lettres de l'empereur Alexandre Ier et de Madame de Staël. Pp. 5–22. Cf. also Durylin. G-zha de Stal' i ee russkie otnosheniia. Pp. 299–305; Cabak Rédei. An Inquiry into Cultural Semiotics. Pp. 186–95.

Swedish throne since he had been adopted as successor by the childless king in 1810.[94] Regarding the current political situation in Europe, an essential question was which position Sweden—a former, traditional ally of France—would adopt. Swedish-Russian relations were strained by the fact that the former Swedish province of Finland had become an autonomous Grand Duchy in the Russian Empire in 1809 after Sweden had lost a war. The revision of the Treaty of Fredrikshamn and therefore the restitution of Finland had become a political dream amongst the Swedish people and one reason for having chosen Bernadotte, a successful military leader and embodiment of the Franco-Swedish alliance, as crown prince.[95] Through an alliance with Napoleon against Russia, Sweden could probably regain Finland. But the Grande Armée had occupied Swedish Pomerania in early 1812 and thus aggravated Bernadotte.[96] As a result, Sweden and Russia began approaching an alliance in spring 1812, finally forming one together with England. At the same time, Sweden had not yet cut ties to France.[97] Against this background, there was a search for compensation for the Swedish loss of Finland—compensation that was found in the shape of Norway, still a part of the French ally Denmark. At this point, Bernadotte needed to publicly lobby for this solution, especially given the decidedly pro-French and anti-Russian public in Sweden.[98] This situation, in other words, offered a perfect task for Mme de Staël. It was no wonder that the French ambassador M. de Cabre was highly alarmed when Mme de Staël appeared in Stockholm in September 1812.[99] Her daily meetings with Bernadotte, as well as her weekly dinners at court, were a convincing sign for both the Swedish public

94 Palme. Mme de Staël et la Suède. P. 98; Palmer. Bernadotte. Pp. 52, 164–76; Fairweather. Madame de Staël. Pp. 276 f., 410.

95 Palme. Mme de Staël et la Suède. P. 98; Hartley. Alexander I. P. 95; Tuchtenhagen. Von "Tilsit" nach "Fredrikshamn." Pp. 23–43.

96 Palmer. Bernadotte, P. 185.

97 Rey. Alexandre Ier. P. 273 f.; Palmer. Bernadotte. Pp. 185–87.

98 The servant of Mme de Staël who also was an informant of the French secret police stated: "Je garantis, ajoute la personne de qui l'on tient ces renseignements, comme un fait certain et plus, que le fond du people suédois est absolument français, autant qu'on peut l'etre en france, et dans la bonne france. c'est a un tel point que j'en ai eté extremement frappé; ils sont anti-Russes au-delà de ce qu'il est possible d'imaginer. L'esprit à la Cour est absolument different d'après ce que j'ai pu entendre dire.": King. Un récit. P. 14.

99 Cf. an excerpt of one of the reports of the French ambassador: Balayé (Ed.). Les carnets de voyage. P. 335, Fn. 55; Winock. Madame de Staël. P. 427.

and for M. de Cabre that she was quite close to the crown prince.[100] The perspective that Mme de Staël adopted with regard to Norway was the following:

> Les Suédois se battirent en Finlande avec le plus grande courage, mais sans un chef guerrier sur le trône, une nation peu nombreuse ne saurait triompher de ses ennemis. L'empereur Alexandre s'empara de la Finlande par la conquête et les traités fondés sur la force, mais il faut lui rendre la justice de dire qu'il ménagea cette nouvelle province en souverain qui sait respecter la liberté dont elle jouissait. Il laissa aux Finnois / tous leur privilèges relativement à la levée des impôts et des hommes [...]. Enfin la grande idée du siècle, les limites naturelles, rendait la Finlande aussi nécessaire à la Russie que la Norvège à la Suède, et l'on peut dire avec vérité que partout où ces limites naturelles n'ont pas existé, elles ont été l'objet de guerres perpétuelles.[101]

Her line of argument was at once a thoughtful and honorable explanation of the Swedish defeat, a recognition of Alexander as a ruler respecting old liberties and privileges of his new subjects. At the same time, she introduced the originally French concept of natural boundaries, which could only provide a state with long-lasting, steady frontiers. This last element was exactly the same argument brought forward in a brochure written by August Wilhelm Schlegel and published anonymously using an acronym in February 1813 to propagate a European alliance.[102] The brochure complemented political discussions in Sweden and was circulated by Mme de Staël within her networks.[103] Besides circulating it, she also corrected rumors that she had penned it, or else she downplayed her role, as in the following letter to her acquaintance James Galiffe, dated May 7, 1813:

> Je vous écrit un petit mot par amour-propre d'auteur. Où avez-vous pris que je suis l'auteur du *Système continental*? C'est M. Schlegel qui l'a écrit, je ne me mêle point ainsi de politique. Si je publiais jamais rien là-dessus, ce serait pris d'un point de vue plus philosophique.[104]

Mme de Staël further rendered Bernadotte great service in forwarding and circulating relevant political information through her networks.[105] She would organize

100 KING. Un récit. P. 14; cf. PALME. Mme de Staël et la Suède. P. 99.

101 STAËL. Dix années d'exil. Pp. 311 f.

102 S[CHLEGEL]. Ueber das Continentalsystem und den Einfluß desselben auf Schweden.

103 Cf. her letter to the duchess of Saxe-Weimar, Louise von Hessen-Darmstadt, from April 1813: STAËL. Correspondance Générale. Vol 8. Pp. 238 f.

104 IBID. P. 247.

105 In November 1812, she asked Dorothea Benckendorff, Countess Lieven: "Je vous envoie un billet, Madame, pour Mme d'Engström [i.e., the wife of Lars von Engeström, then the Swedish minister of foreign affairs] dont je vous prie d'ouvrir la réponse, c'est le meilleur moyen. Je vous l'envoie ouvert, ayez la bonté, vous qui êtes toute

confidential communication or use cover addresses to share word from the Napoleonic sphere of influence.[106] She actively looked after Bernadotte's public image in Europe and tried to quash falsely planted and foreign-born rumors of internal troubles in Swedish politics.[107] She commented frankly on his political projects and warned of possible negative consequences in public opinion, a situation that she believed Napoleon would immediately try to utilize.[108] After she moved to London in 1813, she continued lobbying for Bernadotte's policy in general and, of course, for Norway as compensation for Sweden's loss of Finland.[109]

A Parisian salon was also the setting for a meeting between Mme de Staël and Thomas Jefferson, who had been ambassador in Paris in 1785–89 and president of the United States in 1801–9. She clearly referred to this old acquaintanceship as having originated in a salon—implying a sort of equality between her and him—when she tried in November 1812 to convince him to call for an end to the Anglo-American War, which was hindering England in the struggle against Napoleon:

> Tous vos anciens amis d'Europe, tous ceux qui pensait comme vous quand vous avez soutenu l'indépendance de l'Amérique, attendent de vous la cessation d'une guerre qui leur paraît une guerre civile car les peuples libres sont tous de la même famille. Oui, le plus grand malheur qui peut arriver aux Américains dans la guerre actuelle, ce serait de faire un véritable mal à leur ennemies, car alors les Anglais ne seraient plus en état de vous servir de rempart contre le despotisme de l'empereur de France, ou plutôt d'Europe. Quand il aurait renversé la liberté anglaise, c'est la vôtre qu'il s'attaquerait. L'Empereur, si

---

gracieuse en tout, de le cacheter après l'avoir lu et de le faire porter tout de suite. J'aurais une véritable humeur *s'il* ne venait pas. S'il vous avait vue, cela serait plus sûr qu'à présent.": Staël. Correspondance générale. Vol. 8. P. 121.

106 Cf. her letter to Thomas Jefferson on November 10, 1812: "Répondez-moi, *my dear sir*, sous l'adresse de votre consul en Suède, M. Speyer [...]": Staël. Correspondance générale. Vol. 8. P. 117 ; or her letter to the duchess of Saxe-Weimar on January 12, 1813: "PS: Si Votre Altesse veut me répondre, chez M. Tottie et Arfvedsen pour Mme Complainville.": Ibid. P. 169.

107 In a letter to Caroline von Humboldt of November 27, 1812, she wrote: "Peut-être avez-vous vu d'après la gazette de Prague qu'il y avait eu ici des conspirations, etc. Il n'en est rien, je ne connais pas de pays plus tranquille en Europe et où le prince soit plus universellement aimé et plus sûr d'être et de faire ce qu'il veut. Je voudrais bien que le pays où vous êtes imitât celui-ci. Il n'y a de bonheur que là où l'on n'est pas soumis à la grande horde [i.e. the French Grande Armée].": Staël. Correspondance générale. Vol. 8. P. 131.

108 Cf. her letter to Bernadotte on December 8, 1812: Staël. Correspondance générale. Vol. 8. Pp. 145–47.

109 Cf. her letters from London to Bernadotte: Staël. Correspondance générale. Vol. 8. Pp. 313–15, 349–51, 372 f., 386 f., 422 f., 467, 498 f.

> habile dans l'art de dissimuler, ne dissimule pas même la résolution d'écraser toute nation qui veut être indépendante.[110]

Her appeal to Jefferson did not succeed. The war, initially provoked by severe restrictions on neutral trade among other things, ended only after the defeat of Napoleon. However, in alienating Sweden from Napoleonic France in 1812, she was quite effective: at the end of the year, diplomatic ties were cut. In a dispatch dated November 24, 1812, the outgoing ambassador M. de Cabre named the people who had exerted decisive influence in the matter, emphasizing the contribution of Mme de Staël:

> Les efforts sont les mêmes pour porter le Prince Royal à me renvoyer et à rappeler Mr d'Obson [the Swedish ambassador in Paris]; il a resisté jusqu'ici car au milieu de son égarement il regrette ses nouvelles liaisons; mais il est complètement circonvenu par les Ministres de Russie, d'Angleterre et de Portugal, et surtout par Mme de Staël qui déploye un zèle d'âpotre pour la Russie et qui se plaît à représenter l'Empereur et tout son gouvernement comme occupés d'événements qui ébranlent le monde et empêchent la circulation de ses écrits.[111]

As far as her *Dix années d'exil* or other texts for publication were concerned, Mme de Staël remained quite vague on her concrete contribution to the alliance against Napoleon. But they all show "from a more philosophical perspective" the line of argument that she used in her various lobbying efforts for the formation of the European alliance against Napoleon and that was reflected more directly in her correspondence. Mme de Staël's capabilities of influencing and campaigning were extraordinary and correlated with the growing importance of public opinion. It was public opinion that was important for Napoleon, but it was impossible for him to control the place and the institution where public opinion was, to a large degree, formed through conversation: the traditional Parisian salon—always headed by a woman, a *salonnière*, and never by a general, consul, or emperor. As a gifted writer, an eager correspondent, a witty conversationalist, and last but not least a traveler, Mme de Staël, exiled from Paris was able to widen the area of influence of her salon and her networks far beyond the urban boundaries of Paris. However, her power and especially her influence on decision-making were always indirect, mediated. Her influence depended, on the one hand, on the openmindedness of counterparts with real (direct) power, and on the other, on need of these counterparts for her special talents. To put it differently, her influence depended on concrete and sometimes quickly changing historical circumstances.

---

110 Ibid. Pp. 114–17, quotation on p. 116.
111 Quoted from: King. Un récit. p. 19, Fn. 3.

12. The Changing Russian Reception of the Tsar's Portrayal in *Dix années d'exil*

Mme de Staël's contact with Alexander I can serve as an illustration for her sort of influence: in directing all her efforts to the forging of an alliance against Napoleon, she was well inclined to shape the public image of Alexander in her writings as an ideal, enlightened, and liberal ruler in order to make him acceptable to former opponents and liberal thinkers in Europe alike. When it came to the problem of serfdom, yet existing in Russia, she stressed the difference between the opinions of the liberal-minded tsar and the conservative Russian aristocracy, which was yet opposed to a solution that was surely to come in the future, after Napoleon's defeat. In the correspondence between Mme de Staël and Alexander after 1815, she tried to move him to counter illiberal developments in Europe, but he appeared to be unfond of the role that she wanted for him—especially with regard to the situation in France—that of advocate for liberal ideas.[112] She may have observed, before her death in 1817, the first signs of Alexander's transformation into a conservative ruler. After all she was spared from witnessing the fact that her two posthumously published historical and political books, *Dix années d'exil* and *Considérations sur les principaux événements de la Révolution française*, reflecting her life in exile, her thoughts on the history of the French Revolution, and the rise and fall of Napoleon could not appear in Russia due to censorship.[113] Nevertheless *Dix années d'exil* and other writings of hers eventually found a way to Russian readers and were received at that date quite positively, as a stimulation for a Russian literature on the verge of Romanticism.[114] The generation of young officers who, in 1825, would revolt, dissatisfied with the situation in autocratic Russia, sympathized with Mme de Staël as a courageous proponent of liberal ideals in her struggle with Napoleon.[115] Alexander Pushkin, who might have been interested in Mme de Staël's life and work in part because of the personal parallel of a strained relationship with a ruler, not only used reports of her visits in Russian salons for an unfinished historical novel[116]—he also defended her against criticism and

---

112 Cf. [Lautier (Ed.)] Lettres de l'empereur Alexandre Ier et de Madame de Staël. Pp. 6–22.

113 Durylin. G-zha de Stal' i ee russkie otnosheniia. P. 314; Jekutsch. Zur Rezeption. P. 92.

114 Leclerc. De Karamzine à Pouchkine. Pp. 376–88.

115 Jekutsch. Zur Rezeption. Pp. 94–108.

116 Pushkin. Roslavlev. Cf. Jekutsch. Zur Rezeption. P. 108; Fairweather. Madame de Staël. P. 401 f.; Debreczeny. The Other Pushkin. Pp. 140–43; Ebbinghaus. Puškin

recognized her positive description of the Russian people in *Dix années d'exil.*[117] Her portrayal of Alexander I, however, was by that time in Russia quite differently received than how it had been meant by the author: Tsar Alexander, once depicted as an ideal ruler and the antithesis to the tyrant Napoleon, had become the latter's Russian counterpart, a despot in the eyes of his subjects.

List of references

ALBRECHT, CLEMENS. Kulturelle Hegemonie ohne Machtpolitik: Über die Repräsentativität der französischen Salonkultur. In: ROBERTO SIMANOWSKI / HORST TURK / THOMAS SCHMIDT (Eds.). Europa—ein Salon? Beiträge zur Internationalität des literarischen Salons. Göttingen, 1999. Pp. 66–80

ANDREW, JOE. "A Crocodile in Flannel or a Dancing Monkey": The Image of the Russian Woman Writer, 1790–1850. In: LINDA EDMONDSON (Ed.). Gender in Russian History and Culture. Oxford, 1998. Pp. 52–72

ANDRONIKASCHWILI, SAAL. Ekaterina II—Kaiserin und Salondame zwischen Literatur und Politik. In: ROBERTO SIMANOWSKI / HORST TURK / THOMAS SCHMIDT (Eds.). Europa—ein Salon? Beiträge zur Internationalität des literarischen Salons. Göttingen, 1999. Pp. 89–105

APPEL, SABINE. Madame de Staël: Kaiserin des Geistes. München, 2011

ARONSON, MARK I. / REISER, SOLOMON A. Literaturnye kruzhki i salony. Leningrad, 1929

BALAYÉ, SIMONE. Absence, exil, voyage. In: SIMONE BALAYÉ (Ed.) Madame de Staël: Écrire, lutter, vivre. Geneva, 1994. Pp. 47–60

BALAYÉ, SIMONE. Le Groupe de Coppet: Conscience d'une mission commune. In: SIMONE BALAYÉ (Ed.). Madame de Staël: Écrire, lutter, vivre. Geneva, 1994. Pp. 321–42

BALAYÉ, SIMONE (Ed.). Les carnets de voyage de Madame de Staël: Contribution à la genèse de ses œuvres. Geneva, 1971

BALAYÉ, SIMONE. Les rapports de l'écrivain et du pouvoir: Madame de Staël et Napoléon. In: SIMONE BALAYÉ (Ed.). Madame de Staël: Écrire, lutter, vivre. Geneva, 1994. Pp. 137–54

und Rußland. Pp. 385–94; SACH. "Die Geographie des Napoleonischen Europa …" P. 54, cf. also Fn. 225.

117 PUSHKIN. O G-zhe Stal' i o A.M. M-ve. Pp. 22–26; JEKUTSCH. Zur Rezeption. P. 109; LECLERC. De Karamzine à Pouchkine. Pp. 385 f.; SACH. "Die Geographie des Napoleonischen Europa …" Pp. 71 f.

Balayé, Simone. Madame de Staël et l'idée d'opinion publique. In: Simone Balayé (Ed.). Madame de Staël: Écrire, lutter, vivre. Geneva, 1994. Pp. 173–83

[Barante, Prosper de]. Souvenirs de Baron de Barante de l'Académie française, 1762–1866. Claude de Barante (Ed.). Vols. 1–8. Paris, 1890–1901

Bastian, Corina. Kammerdame und diplomatische Akteurin: Die Princesse des Ursins am Hof Philipps V. von Spanien (1701–1714). In: Hillard von Thiessen / Christian Windler (Eds.). Akteure der Außenbeziehungen: Netzwerke und Interkulturalität im historischen Wandel. Köln, 2012. Pp. 261–76

Beausoleil, Marie-Ève. Germaine de Staël as Political Activist: Print, Privacy and Opinion in the French Revolution (1789–1799). In: Karyna Szmurlo (Ed.). Germaine de Staël: Forging a Politics of Mediation. Oxford, 2011. Pp. 23–34

Berelowitch, Wladimir. La France dans le "Grand Tour" des nobles russes au cours de la seconde moitié du XVIIIe siècle. In: Cahiers du monde russe et soviétique. Vol. 34 (1993) #1–2. Pp. 193–209

Berelowitch, Wladimir. La vie mondaine sous Catherine II. In: Anita Davidenkoff (Ed.). Catherine II & l'Europe. Paris, 1997. Pp. 99–106

Bernstein, Lina. Women on the Verge of a New Language: Russian Salon Hostesses in the First Half of the Nineteenth Century. In: Helena Goscilo / Beth Holmgreen (Eds.). Russia—Woman—Culture. Bloomington, Ill., 1996. Pp. 209–24

Bosse, Monika. Metamorphosen des literarischen "Contre-pourvoir" im nachrevolutionären Frankreich: Madame de Staël, Saint-Simon, Balzac, Flaubert. München, 1981

Burnand, Léonard / Poisson, Guillaume (Eds.). Comment sortir de l'empire? Le Groupe de Coppet face à la chute de Napoléon. Geneva, 2016

Cabak Rédei, Anna. An Inquiry into Cultural Semiotics: Germaine de Staël's Autobiographical Travel Accounts. Lund, 2007. URL: http://lup.lub.lu.se/search/ws/files/5680981/1299331.pdf [2017-11-03]

Chastenay, Victorine de. Mémoires de Madame de Chastenay, 1771–1815. Vols. 1–2. Alphonse Roserot (Ed.). Paris, 1896

Craiutu, Aurelian. Moderation and the Groupe de Coppet. In: Karyna Szmurlo (Ed.). Germaine de Staël: Forging a Politics of Mediation. Oxford, 2011. Pp. 109–24

Dade, Eva Kathrin. Die königliche Mätresse als Diplomatin: Madame Pompadour im Dienste der französischen Krone. In: Hillard von Thiessen / Christian Windler (Eds.). Akteure der Außenbeziehungen. Netzwerke und Interkulturalität im historischen Wandel. Köln, 2012. Pp. 277–92 d'Armaillé, Marie Célestine Amélie (Ed.). La comtesse d'Egmont, fille du maréchal de Richelieu, 1740–1773, d'après ses lettres inédites à Gustave III. Paris, 1890

Debreczeny, Paul. The Other Pushkin: A Study of Alexander Pushkin's Prose Fiction. Stanford, 1983

Dubé, Pierre H. Bibliographie de la critique sur Madame de Staël, 1789–1994. Geneva, 1998

Dubeau, Catherine. Des livres et des hommes: Suzanne Necker lectrice. In: Cahiers staëliennes. Vol. 58 (2007). Pp. 13–24

Dulac, Georges. Politique, littéraire et mystification: Échec à Rulhière. Un récit inédit de Diderot rapporté par D. Golitsyn. In: Dix-huitième Siècle. Vol. 23 (1991). Pp. 213–22

Durova, Nadezhda. God zhizni v Peterburge, ili nevygody tret'ego poseshcheniia. In: Nadezhda Durova (Ed.). Izbrannye sochineniia kaverlist-devicy N.A. Durovoi. Moscow, 1988. Pp. 485–540

Durylin, Sergei. G-zha de Stal' i ee russkie otnosheniia. In: Literaturnoe nasledstvo. Vols. 33–34. Moscow, 1939. Pp. 215–330

Ebbinghaus, Andreas. Puškin und Rußland: Zur künstlerischen Biographie des Dichters. Wiesbaden, 2004

Elias, Norbert. Die höfische Gesellschaft. Untersuchungen zur Soziologie des Königtums und der höfischen Aristokratie. Mit einer Einleitung: Soziologie und Geschichtswissenschaft. Frankfurt a. M., 1999

Fairweather, Maria. Madame de Staël. London, 2005

Gamburger, Andrei (Ed.). Pis'ma Imperatricy Ekateriny II k G-zhie Zhoffren. In: Sbornik imperatorskogo istoricheskogo obshchestva. Vol. 1. St. Petersburg, 1867. Pp. 253–93

Gardiner, Ann T. From Group to Traveler's Network: Thoughts on Reconfiguring Sociability in Germaine de Staël. In: Karyna Szmurlo (Ed.). Germaine de Staël: Forging a Politics of Mediation. Oxford, 2011. Pp. 153–74

Gardiner, Ann T. Games in the Salon: Jürgen Habermas on Madame de Staël. In: Roberto Simanowski / Horst Turk / Thomas Schmidt (Eds.). Europa—ein Salon? Beiträge zur Internationalität des literarischen Salons. Göttingen, 1999. Pp. 214–31

Goodden, Angelica. Madame de Staël: The Dangerous Exile. Oxford, 2008

Gutwirth, Madely. Madame de Staël, Novelist: The Emergence of the Artist as a Woman. Chicago, 1978

Habermas, Jürgen. Strukturwandel der Öffentlichkeit: Untersuchungen zu einer Kategorie der bürgerlichen Gesellschaft. Frankfurt a. M., 1990

HAMON, MAURICE. Madame Geoffrin: Femme d'influence, femme d'affaires au temps des Lumières. Paris, 2010

HARTLEY, JANET M. Alexander I. London, 1994

HEROLD, CHRISTOPHER. Madame de Staël: Herrin eines Jahrhunderts. München, 1960

HEYDEN-RYNSCH, VERENA VON DER. Europäische Salons: Höhepunkte einer versunkenen weiblichen Kultur. München, 1992

HOOCK-DEMARLE, MARIE-CLAIRE. Coppet, carrefour des influences. In: ANJA ERNST / PAUL GEYER (Eds.). Deutschlandbilder aus Coppet: Zweihundert Jahre *De l'Allemagne* von Madame de Staël. Hildesheim, 2015. Pp. 37–46

JASINSKI, BÉATRICE. Liste des principaux visiteurs qui ont séjourné à Coppet de 1799 à 1816. In: SIMONE BALAYÉ / JEAN-MICHEL CANDAUX (Eds.). Le Groupe de Coppet: Actes et documents du deuxième Colloque de Coppet, 10–13 juillet 1974. Geneva, 1977. Pp. 461–92

JASINSKI, BÉATRICE. Mme de Staël et la convention: Mai–octobre 1795. In: Madame de Staël et l'Europe: Colloque de Coppet (18–24 juillet 1966). Paris, 1970. Pp. 39–50

JEKUTSCH, ULRIKE. Zur Rezeption Mme de Staëls im russischen kulturellen Diskurs des frühen 19. Jahrhunderts um die Begründung einer romantischen Literatur. In: UDO SCHÖNING / FRANK SEEMAN (Eds.). Madame de Staël und die Internationalität der europäischen Romantik. Fallstudien zur interkulturellen Vernetzung. Göttingen, 2003. Pp. 75–110

KARAMZIN, NIKOLAI. Pis'ma russkogo puteshestvennika. In: NIKOLAI M. KARAMZIN (Ed.). Izbrannye sochineniia v dvukh tomakh. Vol. 1. Moscow, 1964. Pp. 79–601

KELLY, CATRIONA. A History of Russian Woman's Writing, 1820–1992. Oxford, 2005

KING, NORMAN. Un récit inédit du Grand Voyage de Madame de Staël (1812–1813). In: Cahiers staëliennes. Vol. 4 (1966). Pp. 4–23

KRAPOTH, HERMANN. Geist des Gesprächs und Gespräch der Geister: Mme de Staël—Pariser Salonkultur und europäische Begegnungen. In: ROBERTO SIMANOWSKI / HORST TURK / THOMAS SCHMIDT (Eds.). Europa—ein Salon? Beiträge zur Internationalität des literarischen Salons. Göttingen, 1999. Pp. 251–67

[LAUTIER, EUGÈNE (Ed.)]. Lettres de l'empereur Alexandre Ier et de Madame de Staël, 1814–1817. In: Revue de Paris, quatrième année. Vol. 1 (Janvier–Février 1897). Pp. 5–22

LECLERC, NATALIA. De Karamzine à Pouchkine: La réception de De l'Allemagne en Russie au début du XIXe siècle—un révélateur. In: ANJA ERNST / PAUL GEYER

(Eds.). Deutschlandbilder aus Coppet: Zweihundert Jahre *De l'Allemagne* von Madame de Staël. Hildesheim, 2015. Pp. 376–88

Lenormant, Amélie. Coppet et Weimar: Madame de Staël et la Grande-Duchesse Louise. Paris, 1862

Lepenies, Wolf. Melancholie und Gesellschaft. Mit einer neuen Einleitung: Das Ende der Utopie und die Wiederkehr der Melancholie. Frankfurt a. M., 1998

Lieven, Dominic. Russland gegen Napoleon: Die Schlacht um Europa. München, 2011

Lortholary, Albert. Le mirage russe en France au XVIIIe siècle. Paris, 1951

Lot, Marie-Christine. De Dix années d'exil aux Considérations: La traversée des genres. In: Cahiers staëliennes. Vol. 58 (2007). Pp. 69–81

Malia, Martin. Russia under Western Eyes: From the Bronze Horseman to the Lenin Mausoleum. London, 1999

McNally, Raymond. Th. Das Russlandbild in der Publizistik Frankreichs zwischen 1814 und 1843. In: Forschungen zur osteuropäischen Geschichte. Vol. 6 (1958). Pp. 82–169

Mervaud, Michel / Roberti, Jean-Claude. Une infinie brutalité: L'image de la Russie dans la France des XVIe et XVIIe siècle. Paris, 1991

Morrissey, Robert. Mme de Staël et Napoléon: Retour sur une question. In: Léonard Burnand / Guillaume Poisson (Eds.). Comment sortir de l'Empire? Le Groupe de Coppet face à la chute de Napoléon. Geneva, 2016. Pp. 35–55

Palme, Sven Ulric. Mme de Staël et la Suède. In: Madame de Staël et l'Europe. Colloque de Coppet (18–24 juillet 1966). Paris, 1970. Pp. 95–107

Palmer, Alan. Bernadotte: Napoleon's Marshal, Sweden's King. London, 1990

Pange, Victor de. Le rêve anglais de Mme de Staël. In: Madame de Staël et l'Europe: Colloque de Coppet (18–24 juillet 1966). Paris, 1970. Pp. 173–89

Perchellet, Jean-Pierre. Bibliographie staëliennes, 1994–2000. In: Cahiers staëliennes. Vol. 52 (2001). Pp. 147–86

Plavinskaia, Nadezhda. "Nakaz" Ekateriny II vo Francii v kontse 60–nachale 70-ch godov XVIII v.: perevody, cenzura, otkliki v presse. In: Sergei Karp (Ed.) Russko-francuzskie kul'turnye sviazi v epokhu prosveshcheniia. Materialy i issledovaniia. Moscow, 2001. Pp. 9–36

Pushkin, Alexander. Roslavlev. In: Pushkin, Alexander. Polnoe sobranie sochinenii. Vol. 6. Moscow, 1949. Pp. 198–213

Rey, Marie-Pierre. Alexandre Ier. Paris, 2009

Rosset, François. Écrire à Coppet: Nous, moi et le monde. Geneva, 2002

Rous Besser, Gretchen. Germaine de Staël Revisited. New York, 1994

SACH, MAIKE. "Die Geographie des Napoleonischen Europa lernt man nur durch Unglück ..." Germaine de Staëls Flucht vor Napoleon Bonaparte durch das Russische Reich im Jahre 1812 und ihr Bild von Russland. In: JAN KUSBER (Ed.). 1812 als europäisches Ereignis. Stuttgart, 2013. Pp. 16–72

SACH, MAIKE. "... setzen Sie sich und erzählen Sie!": Russische Salonkultur und russische Salonnièren seit der Zeit Katharinas II. bis in die erste Hälfte des 19. Jahrhunderts. In: BEA LUNDT (Ed.). Historische Geschlechterforschung. Stuttgart, 2007. Pp. 83–104

SCHAUB, MARIE-KARINE. Wahrnehmungen und Praktiken in den französisch-russischen Beziehungen (17. bis 19. Jahrhundert). In: HILLARD VON THIESSEN / CHRISTIAN WINDLER (Eds.). Akteure der Außenbeziehungen: Netzwerke und Interkulturalität im historischen Wandel. Köln, 2012. Pp. 319–40

SCHEIDEGGER, GABRIELE. Perverses Abendlandes—barbarisches Russland: Begegnungen des 16. und 17. Jahrhunderts im Schatten kultureller Missverständnisse. Zürich, 1993

S[CHLEGEL], A[UGUST] W[ILHELM]. Ueber das Continentalsystem und den Einfluß desselben auf Schweden. Hamburg, 1813 URL: http://opacplus.bsb-muenchen.de/title/BV001645967/ft/bsb10451527?page=5 [2017-11-28]

SCHLICK, YAËL. Beyond the Boundaries: Staël, Genlis, and the Impossible "femme célèbre." In: Symposium. A quarterly journal in modern literatures. Vol. 50 (1996) #1. Pp. 50–63

SEIBERT, PETER. Der literarische Salon—ein Forschungsüberblick. In: Internationales Archiv für Sozialgeschichte der deutschen Literatur. Forschungsreferate. Vols. 2–3 (1993). Pp. 159–220

SETH, CATRIONA. Germaine de Staël and Marie-Antoinette. In: KARYNA SZMURLO (Ed.). Germaine de Staël: Forging a Politics of Mediation. Oxford, 2011. Pp. 47–62

SIMMEL, GEORG. Soziologie der Geselligkeit. In: RÜDIGER KRAMME /OTTMAR RAMMSTEDT (Eds.). Georg Simmel: Aufsätze und Abhandlungen 1909–1918. Vol. 1. Frankfurt a. M., 2001. Pp. 177–93

SOLOVIEFF, GEORGES. Aperçu de la correspondance échangée entre membres du Groupe de Coppet. In: SIMONE BALAYÉ / JEAN-MICHEL CANDAUX (Eds.). Le Groupe de Coppet. Actes et documents du deuxième Colloque de Coppet, 10–13 juillet 1974. Geneva, 1977. Pp. 493–512

SOLOVIEFF, GEORGES. Madame de Staël et ses correspondants russes (Lettres inédites en français). In: Cahiers staëliennes. Vol. 1 (1962). Pp. 4–30

SPALDING, PAUL S. Germaine de Staël's Role in Rescuing Lafayette, 1792–1797. In: KARYNA SZMURLO (Ed.). Germaine de Staël: Forging a Politics of Mediation. Oxford, 2011. Pp. 35–46

STAËL, GERMAINE DE. Considérations sur les principaux événements de la Révolution françaises. In: LUCIA OMACINI (Ed.). De Staël, Madame. Œuvres complètes. Série III: Œuvres historiques. Vol. 2.1–2. Paris, 2017

STAËL, GERMAINE DE. Correspondance générale. Vols. 1–9. Vols. 1–7 ed. by BÉATRICE JASINSKI. Vols. 8–9 ed. by STÉPHANIE GENAND / JEAN-DANIEL CANDAUX. Paris, 1960–2017

STAËL, GERMAINE DE. De la littérature considérée dans ses rapports avec les institutions sociales (1800). In: STÉPHANIE GENAND / JEAN GOLDZINK (Eds.). De Staël, Madame. Œuvres complètes. Série I: Œuvres critiques. Vol. 2. Paris, 2013. Pp. 67–388

STAËL, GERMAINE DE. De l'Allemagne. Vols. 1–5. PAULINE DE PANGE / SIMONE BALAYÉ (Eds.). Paris, 1958–60

STAËL, GERMAINE DE. Dix années d'exil. SIMONE BALAYÉ / MARIELLA VIANELLO BONIFACIO (Eds.). Paris, 1996

STAËL, GERMAINE DE. Du talent d'être aimable en conversation. In: SIMONE BALAYÉ (Ed.). Cahiers staëliennes. Vol. 52 (2001). Pp. 25–31

STAËL, GERMAINE DE. Lettres sur les écrits et le caractère de J.-J. Rousseau. In: ANNE BROUSTEAU / FLORENCE LOTTERIE (Eds.). De Staël, Madame. Œuvres complètes. Série I: Œuvres critiques. Vol. 1. Paris, 2008. Pp. 17–110

STAËL, GERMAINE DE. Réflexions sur le procès de la reine, par une femme. In: LUCIA OMACINI (Ed.). De Staël, Madame. Œuvres complètes. Série III: Œuvres historiques. Vol. 3. Paris, 2009. Pp. 29–66

TENENBAUM, SUSAN. Turning Honour on Its Head: Germaine de Staël's Indictment of Napoleon. In: KARYNA SZMURLO (Ed.). Germaine de Staël: Forging a Politics of Mediation. Oxford, 2011. Pp. 125–35

TROUSSIN, RAYMOND. Une mémorialiste oubliée: Victorine de Chastenay. Communication à la séance mensuelle de 11 mai 2006. Académie royale de langue et de littérature françaises de Belgique. Brussels, 2007. Pp. 1–18 URL: http://www.arllfb.be/ebibliotheque/communications/trousson110506.pdf [2017-10-24]

TUCHTENHAGEN, RALPH. Von "Tilsit" nach "Frederikshamn": Der Ostseeraum in der Politik Russlands und Großbritanniens 1807–1809. In: JAN HECKER-STAMPEHL / BERND HENNINGSEN / ANNA-MAIJA MERTENS / STEPHAN MICHAEL SCHRÖDER (Eds.). 1809 und die Folgen: Finnland zwischen Schweden, Russland und Deutschland. Berlin, 2011. Pp. 23–43

VOSS, ANDREA. Reisen erzählen: Erzählrhetorik, Intertextualität und Gebrauchsfunktionen des adligen Bildungsreiseberichts in der Frühen Neuzeit. Heidelberg, 2016

WEHINGER, BRUNHILDE. Conversation um 1800: Salonkultur und literarische Autorschaft bei Germaine de Staël. Berlin, 2002

WILHELMY-DOLLINGER, PETRA. Die Berliner Salons: Mit historisch-literarischen Spaziergängen. Berlin, 2000

WINEGARTEN, RENEE. Germaine de Staël & Benjamin Constant: A Dual Biography. New Haven, 2008

WINOCK, MICHEL. Madame de Staël. Paris, 2010

WITTHOFF, EKKEHARD. Grenzen der Kultur: Differenzwahrnehmung in Randbereichen (Irland, Lappland, Rußland) und europäische Identität in der Frühen Neuzeit. Frankfurt a. M., 1997

WOLFF, LARRY. Inventing Eastern Europe: The Map of Civilization on the Mind of the Enlightenment. Stanford, 1994

Benjamin Conrad

"Un bon systême de finances doit être regardé comme l'ame qui vivifie l'État." European Experts and Russia's State Finances under Paul I and Alexander I

While searching for material on the government of Paul I and Alexander I that has not yet been considered by researchers in St. Petersburg's Rossiiskii Gosudarstvennyi Istoricheskii Arkhiv (Russian State Archive for History), it is always worth trying to order sources that contain the amendment "na francuzskom iazyke" (in French) in the description. Striking is the low number of Russian scholars consulting these sources for their research, as recorded in the archive's user list. This also appears to be the case for an 1809 memorandum that formed the basis of Mikhail Speransky's financial plan, which was in action from 1810 to 1812 and dominated Russian finance policy. Up until his banishment in 1812, Speransky was considered Emperor Alexander's most important advisor, as well as the person responsible for all of Russia's finances. And yet, instead of being written by himself, the memorandum lists Friedrich Würst, Ludwig Heinrich von Jakob, and Mikhail Andreevich Balug'ianskii, who formed a special committee of finances founded by Speransky, as its authors. The 1809 memorandum opened with the sentence, "Un bon systême [sic] de finances doit être regardé comme l'ame [sic] qui vivifie l'État."[1] This quote shows once again that a state without money cannot fulfil its tasks as it should. Therefore, a main research focus must be on this field of policy. In this chapter the role of dominant financial experts in Russian finance policy during the reign of Emperors Paul I (1796–1801) and Alexander I (1801–1825) will be examined.

---

1 "A good system of finances should be considered a soul that refreshes the state." Rossiskii Gosudarstvennyi Istoricheskii Arkhiv (hereafter, RGIA). F. 560. Op. 10. D. 338. "Idées préliminaires qui pourront servir de base au plan général à dresser sur le rétablissement des finances de Russie (Dec. 1809)." In modern French, "systême" would be written "système" and "l'ame" would be written "l'âme." It cannot be ascertained whether these differences in the quote came from incomplete knowledge of Würst, Jakob, and Balug'ianskii, or from language alteration. All deviations regardless of their origins are marked with "sic." For the significance of the memorandum, see: Heller. Die Geld- und Kreditpolitik. P. 79.

An examination of all Russian experts on finance of the time would go beyond the scope of discussion;[2] this article will focus on only two individuals, Ludwig Heinrich von Jakob (1759–1827) and Robert Voûte (1747–1823), who had an extraordinary influence on Russian finance policy. By analysing these two men, this article intends to contribute to the question of how an "expert" was defined and what paths he had to take to enter the Russian service. Furthermore, it is critical to investigate the kind of knowledge that the expert had and the facets of his knowledge that were transformed into real policy, or, alternatively, refused and not put into effect.

Lastly, the article contributes to cultural history by exploring problems of language and the process of acculturation that these two men from Western Europe underwent while living in Russia. Meanwhile, the provided framework shall help define the intensity of Europeanization of Russia under Paul I and Alexander I. Modern scholars refer to persons like Jakob and Voûte as experts, but this opinion is up for debate. In their self-descriptions and contemporary language, persons like Jakob and Voûte are called "conseiller" (French) and "sovetnik" (Russian), which translate into English as "councillor" or "advisor." These words of (self-)description—"expert" and "councillor"/"advisor"—convey different meanings. The term "expert" focuses on the knowledge that someone acquired before entering his current position, while the word "councillor" focuses on the more active role that a person plays in his occupation, including the transfer of knowledge into processes of all kinds. This chapter, then, closes with the very important discussion of terminology.

This article is in four subsections. The first subsection investigates the experts' origin and base of knowledge. Subsection two discusses Jakob's and Voûte's language—French—in terms of its use and the problems that it caused. The third subsection focuses on how their knowledge of financial topics was transformed into real policies or was rejected by the Russians. Finally, the last subsection discusses each man's reasons for leaving Russia, despite his high rank in Russian politics.

---

2 RGIA offers numerous memoranda in its collections; see RGIA. F. 560. Op. 10. Dd. 337–42.

1. The Experts and Their Background

Besides Speransky himself, Mikhail Speransky's (1772–1839) secret committee of finances consisted of three members, none of them of Russian origin. Friedrich Würst (1762–1831)[3] and Ludwig Heinrich von Jakob (1759–1827) were born in the states of the Holy Roman Empire. Mikhail Balug'ianskii (1769–1847)[4] was born in a Hungarian village that is today part of Slovakia, although he was most likely of Rusyn origin. Besides the Russian version of his name, used in this paper, various spellings exist, including Michel Balougyansky (French), Michael Baludjanski (German), Mihály Balugyánszky (Hungarian), Michal Baluďanský (Slovakian), and Michailo Baludians'kyi (Ukrainian).

Ludwig Heinrich von Jakob was born in the small town of Wettin in 1759 (see fig. 1). The town was the ancestral seat of the House of Wettin, which governed the Electorate of Saxony and the Polish-Lithuanian Commonwealth at that time. In 1789, Jakob became a professor of philosophy at Friedrichs University of Halle/Saale. Due to the Prussian defeat in the War of the Fourth Coalition seventeen years later and the subsequent French occupation, the university was forced to close. Before the war, Russia had already offered Jakob a chair at the University of Kharkov (now in Ukrainian as Kharkiv), where he taught as a professor of state science beginning in 1807. He quit the Russian service in 1816 and from that time held the position of professor of state science in Halle.[5]

Jakob drew Speransky's attention with an article entitled "Ueber Rußlands Papiergeld und die Mittel, demselben einen festen und unveränderlichen Werth zu verschaffen" (On Russia's paper money and ways to provide it with a stable and unvarying value). Jakob sent the article to Alexander I, who arranged for it to be sent to Speransky, who managed to get it translated into French and Russian. In October 1809, Speransky sent one thousand roubles to Jakob and ordered him to travel to St. Petersburg to take part in the committee of finances.[6] During their first meeting, Speransky asked Jakob to calculate the amount of all circulating Assignation roubles, while keeping the actual number secret.

---

3 Genealogisch-historisch-statistischer Almanach. P. 97.

4 Wurzbach (Ed.). Michael Baludjanski. Pp. 139–40.

5 Jakob. Denkwürdigkeiten. Pp. 128–272; Prantl. Jakob. Pp. 689 f.

6 Jakob. Denkwürdigkeiten. Pp. 207, 209, 211. The 1808 article was printed in 1817 in a modified version; see: Jakob. Ueber Russlands Papiergeld.

Figure 1. Ludwig Heinrich von Jakob by an unknown painter.

Source: Archive of the Martin-Luther-University of Halle-Wittenberg. Rep. 40I. J 2

Jakob's process was as follows. At first, he researched the last official amount of Assignation roubles, for the year 1788, as was stated in a 1786 *ukaz* of Catherine the Great (1729–96). It added up to 100 million Assignation roubles.[7] Since Jakob believed that authorities under Catherine had lied about the real amount of

7 PSZ I. Vol. 22. №. 16407, 28.06.1786 O.S. This article uses the Gregorian calendar. All sources dated in the Julian calendar are marked with the letters "O.S."

money, he assumed the real sum to have been between 140 and 150 million Assignation roubles. In 1808, the exchange rate of the Assignation rouble fell to one to three silver roubles. Considering these two facts, Jakob multiplied the 150 million Assignation roubles by three and calculated a total of 450 million Assignation roubles in circulation. As a last step, he added an amount of a few more million Assignation roubles, due to the fact that the last issuance of the Assignation roubles would take a year or two to have its consequences seen.[8]

Jakob's calculations were partly wrong. The right amount of circulating Assignation roubles in 1788 was in fact the 100 million stated in Catherine's 1786 *ukaz*. The authorities had not falsified the number. The calculated number by Jakob from 1808 was, however, correct. There were 477 million Assignation roubles circulating in 1808.[9] Although Jakob's calculations were not fully accurate, Speransky was most interested to hear the various assumptions connected to Russian paper money. In return, Speransky did not tell Jakob the truth. Instead, he told him:

> Je suis surpris de la sagacité de votre esprit; c'est comme si vous eussiez lû les procés verbaux de notre banque. Vous avez exactement diviné la somme circulante. Elle surpasse de beaucoup la somme de 400 millions.[10]

Speransky's statement that Jakob's calculations were absolutely correct is clearly untrue. Judging from Jakob's memory of the events, Speransky's statement must be seen as a courteous gesture. Jakob was in fear while giving Speransky his calculations, and he felt like it was a test.[11] Speransky could have denied Jakob the status of an expert and withdrawn the invitation to participate in the secret committee of finances, should he had calculated wrong.

Robert Voûte, the second expert under discussion here, was born in Amsterdam as a descendant of the Voûte family, a Protestant family originating in the South of France (see fig. 2). As Huguenots, the Voûtes resettled in Amsterdam in the sixteenth century, when the religious wars took place in France. After being the first representative of the bank and trade house of Hope & Co. at the Sejm of the Polish-Lithuanian Commonwealth in Grodno (now Hrodna in Belarus) in 1793, Voûte was made representative of the same house in Russia, when residing in Moscow and St. Petersburg in 1793 and 1794. His second stay in Russia lasted

8 Jakob. Denkwürdigkeiten. P. 214.

9 For this data, see: Brzheskii. Gosudarstennye dolgi, prilozhenie. P. 4.

10 "I am surprised by the sagacity of your mind. It is like you had read the minutes of our bank. You have exactly divined the sum circulating. It surpasses by far the sum of 400 million." Jakob. Denkwürdigkeiten. P. 214.

11 Ibid. Pp. 213 f.

even longer, from 1796 to 1798. During this voyage, Voûte was joined by his young nephew Pierre Voûte (1777–1845).[12]

Figure 2. Robert Voûte by an unknown painter.

Source: Voûte Vereniging, Amsterdam

12 Voûte Vereniging, Amsterdam (hereafter, VVA). "Dagboek en brieven van Pierre Voûte en diens oom Robert Voûte, geschreven gedurende hun avontuurlijke reis van Nederland via Engeland naar St. Petersburg in Rusland (05.1796–01.1797)." P. 85; Buist. At spes non fracta. Pp. 111–85. As with Balug'ianskii, different spellings of Voûte's name exist. However, he always wrote "Voûte," and therefore this version is used by the majority of scholars. Other spellings such as "Wout" are false. See: Amburger. Geschichte der Behördenorganisation. P. 206. wrong (falsch)!

At first, Voûte's task consisted of attending the deliberations of the Sejm of Poland-Lithuania in Grodno in 1793. In this session, the Sejm, under pressure from abroad, had to accept the second partition of the Polish-Lithuanian Commonwealth. Through this partition, Prussia gained many territories in the West, and Russia in the East. For Hope & Co., the transfers had a direct impact on loans: most loans given to Poland had not been given to the king or the state of Poland. Instead, they had been given to the owners of great estates among the Polish nobility, the magnates. After this second partition of Poland, many estates that had been declared to Hope as securities for the loans given to the magnates were now situated in Russia. This new development had an enormous impact on the capability of the magnates to pay the interest. Save for Adam Jery Czartoryski (1734–1823), nearly all the Polish magnates were forced to stop the payments to the Netherlands in 1793 or 1794, because they stood at the edge of bankruptcy.[13]

Full of negative impressions, Voûte left Grodno for Moscow. In his subsequent correspondence with the house of Hope in Amsterdam, he described Poland as a country of extreme disorder. In contrast, he described Russia as the rising power of Eastern Europe. Voûte later traveled from Moscow to St. Petersburg in order to convince Catherine the Great to cover the Polish magnates' loans that they owed to the Netherlands. The house of Hope was well known in Russia: during the Russo-Turkish War of 1787–91, Hope lent 53.5 million Dutch guilders to Russia. Although Voûte was received cordially in Tsarskoye Selo by Catherine, developments soon changed direction and devalued all previous talks.[14] The situation for Hope and the other Dutch bank houses deteriorated in 1795, when the third Polish-Lithuanian partition by the Habsburg Monarchy, Prussia, and Russia marked the end of the Polish-Lithuanian Commonwealth. With no existing Polish state, the interest or loans could definitely no longer be paid. Likewise unredeemable were the debts of Stanisław II August Poniatowski (1732–1798), the last king of Poland. Even the Czartoryski family was unable to pay interest or repay its loans. Due to some magnates' participation in the 1794 anti-Russian uprising, led by Tadeusz Kościuszko (1746–1817), some estates were seized by the Russians. An attempt by the Dutch bank house of de Haan to demand the given security by Count Michał Kleofas Ogiński (1765–1833), who held estates in the Voivodships of Vilna and Minsk (now Lithuania and Belarus), had proven ineffective.[15]

---

13 Buist. At spes non fracta. Pp. 111–21, 503 f.

14 Ibid. Pp. 120 f., 132, 151–54.

15 VVA. JJ8 G. "Emprunt pour le Compte du Comte Michel Oginski (1796)"; Buist. At spes non fracta. Pp. 156–58, 504.

Confronted with the unpaid debts, all Dutch bank houses joined forces in a treaty in May 1796 that authorized Hope to unilaterally deal with the matter.[16] Voûte was appointed as the representative and sent to Russia a second time. Although Voûte told his nephew Pierre that he had convinced Catherine II to accept responsibility for the Polish debts, no convention had been signed by November 17, 1796, the day Catherine died.[17] It is still doubtful whether Voûte had really convinced Catherine and her government to step in and pay for the debts. Archives have apparently no drafts of a treaty concerning the transcription of debts. Perhaps Voûte simply intended to create an explanation for a possible failure. However, Catherine's death was fortunate for Voûte. Catherine's son Paul I was approachable in the matter of Poland. Hence, Voûte achieved conventions between the houses of Amsterdam and Russia in 1797. According to these conventions, Russia acknowledged all interest and loan payments demanded by Voûte, not only the ones on Poland but also the debt that Russia had run into after the Netherlands supported it in the Russo-Ottoman War of 1787–91. Paul I's government accepted the unification of all Dutch loans given from the houses in Amsterdam and Antwerp into one new loan consisting of 88.3 million Dutch guilders.[18]

Tsar Paul I was so impressed by both Voûtes, Robert and Pierre, that he made them bankers of the court alongside José Pedro Celestino Velho (1755–1802) and Alexander Franz Rall (1756–1832). For the first time in Russian history, the court bankers established a company for their operations; this company was called "Voûte, Velho, Rall & Co."[19]. The company's formation happened only three days after the final *ukaz* of Paul I on the matter.[20] In order to hide Voûte's quick change of employer, it was his nephew Pierre who was listed first in the company's name. Robert Voûte was rather the fourth person in the company's name, hidden in the

16 VVA. JJ8 G. "Procuration des Interessés dans lés [sic] Emprunts de Pologne, autorisant Mr. Voûte a [sic] prendre les arrangemens [sic] convenables, soit a [sic] Pertersbourg [sic] Varsovie Berlin ou Vienne, pour la liquidation des dits emprunts etc. (13.05.1796 N.S.)."

17 VVA. "Dagboek" P. 78.

18 PSZ I. Vol. 25. № 18326a, 15.01.1798.

19 PSZ I. Vol. 25. № 18327, 18.01.1798; VVA. JJ8 A. "Circulaire (19.01.1798 O.S.)"; Amburger. Behördenorganisation. Pp. 206, 562, 576; Kozyreva. Pridvornyi banker A. Ral'. Pp. 205–11, 206.

20 PSZ I. Vol. 25. № 18326a, 15.01.1798.

phrase "& Co.,"[21] a detail not understood by all scholars.[22] All four members of the company were foreigners, comparable with Speransky's secret committee of finances eleven years later, where the only Russian member was Speransky himself.

The examples of Jakob and Voûte as experts on finances demonstrate that there was no formal procedure in place to acquire a highly ranked position in Russia. The Voûtes and Jakob obtained their positions in St. Petersburg only by being in the public eye and pleasing politicians who held high ranks, such as the tsar personally in the Voûtes' case or Speransky for Jakob. On the one hand, their expertise attributed to their success, but on the other hand, there was no formal way to apply for that kind of job.

2. French Language and Its Usage

Two hundred years after their family's flight from France, Robert and Pierre Voûte still spoke in French with each other.[23] Their mother tongue helped them significantly in Russia, as French had overtaken German as the main language of communication for interacting with foreigners in Russia under Catherine the Great. French was known and spoken, especially among the Russian nobility and politicians, as well as by the empress and emperor.[24] German was still widely used, but not by the nobility or in international relations. Germans represented the biggest group of Western non-Slavonic foreigners in Russia during the early modern period. They often held high-ranking positions in society, as can be seen in their professions in economy, education, or other spheres needing higher education and professional skills. During the Alexandrine age, half the academic staff at Kharkov University were of German origin.[25] Simultaneously, the German population of St. Petersburg can be summed up to around 20,000 individuals or 7 percent of all inhabitants of the city. Thus, Germans made up the second largest group of people after the Russians living in St. Petersburg, concentrating their population on Vasilyevsky Island.[26]

---

21 Buist. At spes non fracta. P. 172. Buist dates the founding of Voûte Velho Rall & Co. to February 19, 1798. It happened in fact exactly one month earlier; see VVA. JJ8 A. "Circulaire (19.01.1798)."

22 Heller described Robert Voûte himself as the first co-owner of "Voûte Velho Rall & Co." Heller. Die Geld- und Kreditpolitik. P. 53.

23 VVA. "Dagboek." Pp. 4 f., 29 f.

24 Offord. French and Russian in Catherine's Russia. Pp. 27–32.

25 Jakob. Denkwürdigkeiten. Pp. 182–92.

26 Busch. Deutsche in St. Petersburg 1865–1914. Pp. 18–21; Idem. Zwischen Anpassung und Selbstbehauptung. P. 125; Dal'man. Peterburgskie nemcy. Pp. 156–63.

In the sphere of nobility and international affairs, the use of French was expected and essential, just as it was in all countries of Europe. Although Jakob reports the nobility's frequent use of Russian at Kharkov,[27] members of St. Petersburg's high nobility habitually preferred French to Russian as they were sometimes more fluent conversing in French.[28] Therefore, correspondence and private conversations between Jakob and Speransky, including the statement cited from Speransky above, occurred in French.[29] Likewise, the already mentioned 1809 memorandum by Würst, Jakob, and Balug'ianskii was composed in French,[30] much like nearly all memoranda by foreign experts in that period.[31] While traveling for weeks from Berlin to St. Petersburg by carriage, the Voûtes most likely conversed in French with their travel companion Karl von Nesselrode (1780–1862).[32] Nesselrode would later serve for over forty years as a Russian foreign minister, even though he was only barely able to read or write the Russian language.[33]

Judging from the immense networks of Robert Voûte and Ludwig Heinrich Jakob, neither the use of French among the nobility and state officials nor the use of German in trade matters appeared to be a problem for foreigners in St. Petersburg. What can then be learned from this multilingual sphere in Russia? On the one hand, it manifests the process of integration that Russia had undergone in the eighteenth century. Without the French language of the nobility and elite, or the German language of economic matters, Russia would probably not have attracted so many foreigners to enter the country's state service and therefore would have lost out on knowledge that was ultimately conveyed to Russia. On the other hand, the widening social gap between the poor and the rich, like in any other European country, was only exacerbated by having an elite language.

In May 1794, Robert Voûte was invited by St. Petersburg's Court of Conscience as a witness in the trial between the house de Bary from Amsterdam and its former partner in St. Petersburg, Michel Trosien. The invitation sent to Voûte by Councillor Vasilii Stepanov was written in Russian:

---

27 Jakob. Denkwürdigkeiten. P. 173.

28 Figes. Nataschas Tanz. Pp. 79–83. For the French language in Russian imperial culture, see: Lotman. La littérature russe. Idem. Rußlands Adel; Rosenzweig. Un siècle; Offord e.a. (Eds.). French and Russian in Imperial Russia.

29 Jakob. Denkwürdigkeiten. Pp. 209, 214.

30 RGIA. F. 560. Op. 10. D. 338. "Idées préliminaires (Dec. 1809)."

31 See RGIA. F. 560. Op. 10. Dd. 337–42; F. 560. Op. 22. D. 38.

32 VVA. "Dagboek." P. 18.

33 Figes. Nataschas Tanz. P. 81.

> Sankt-Peterburgskaia guberniia iz sovestnogo suda inostrannomu kupcu Robertu Voutu sim poveshchaetsia, chtob iavilsia, on, v sei sud sego mesiaca 16 chisla po utru v odinadcat' chasov maia 15 dnia 1794 goda.

On the invitation's back, a French translation was given:

> Traduction. Le Tribunal de Conscience de la Ville de St. Petersbourg avertit le Negociant etranger [sic] Robert Voute pour qu'il serende [sic] au dit Tribunal Le 16 ce mois à 11 heures du matin. Le 15 de mai 1794. Signé Conseiller Titulaire Wasilei Stepanoff.[34]

Evidently there are two different versions of the inviting authority. The Russian version names the "Sankt Peterburgskaya guberniya," while the French version holds "la Ville de Saint Petersbourg" as its authority. This small mistake certainly had no influence on the following proceedings, but problems accumulated. Two months later, Frederik Amburger, another Dutch witness, characterized parts of the proceedings as "absurdityd" (absurdity) and lamented the poor standard of translation from Russian into standard German. Additionally, he was confronted with documents in Russian that he was not able to read.[35] These problems of translation between German and Russian seem to have been very common. After living in Kharkov and St. Petersburg for nine years, Jakob remarked in his memoirs,

> Die guten Übersetzer aus dem Deutschen ins Russische sind aber so selten, daß man fast immer Gefahr läuft, verstümmelte Gedanken, wo nicht gar Unsinn in das Russische übergetragen zu sehen, nicht zu gedenken, daß die Übersetzung die Arbeiten außerordentlich verzögert.—Die deutsche Sprache zu erlernen, fällt den Russen so wie allen Ausländern ungemein schwer. Sehr wenige verstehen sie so gründlich, daß sie vermögend sind eine gute Uebersetzung aus dem Deutschen ins Russische zu Stande zu bringen. Die besten Uebersetzer begehen oft die lächerlichsten Fehler. Ich habe davon viele Hundert Erfahrungen gemacht.[36]

---

34 Conversely, here is a translation of the Russian version: "The Court of Conscience of the Governorate of St. Petersburg summon the foreign merchant Robert Voûte to appear before the named court on the 16th of this month at eleven o'clock in the morning. May 15, 1794." VVA. JJ8 I. "Vasilii Stepanov, St. Petersburg, to Robert Voûte, St. Petersburg (15.05.1794 O.S.)."

35 VVA. JJ8 I. "Frederik Amburger, St. Petersburg, to Barensfeld, Amsterdam (11.07.1794 O.S.)."

36 "Good translators for translating German into Russian are so rare to come by that one is always running the risk of translating it into twisted Russian thoughts. Not to mention that the process of translating delays the process of work enormously.—It is very hard for both Russians and other foreigners to learn the German language. Only a few understand it on a level where they are capable of producing a good translation from

It appears that Jakob's observation was not only valid for translations from German into Russian but also vice versa. Considering the general high standard of French in Russia, it is surprising to notice problems and misunderstandings in translations between these two languages. A good example are the drafts of another of Voûte's conventions with Russia, from 1797. The drafts are not identical, even though this convention could have led to an extremely important treaty concerning the transfer of millions of Dutch guilders. The Russian version read,

> Stat'i s Robertom Vutom postannovlennyia o peresrochke oplaty shikh Zaimov, na kakom osnovanie takovuiu peresrochku uchinit'.[37]

However, the French version read differently:

> Articles, desquels est convenu le Sieur Robert Voûte, concernant la manière de reconstituer les Emprunts dans les pays etrangers [sic] et d'en ecrire conformement a Mess. Hope.[38]

It is obvious that there is a difference between the overdraft of debts and the compilation of debts. Certain matters in the French version have been variously improved or worsened. The Russian version does not mention the house of Hope & Co., contrary to the French version, which clearly does. These discrepancies would most likely have been erased before this draft would have been transformed into a real treaty. But later developments led in a different direction. Interesting to note is that the final "Acte de Cession" between Russia and the Dutch houses represented by Voûte contained both a compilation and an overdraft of the Russian debts.[39]

3. The Roles of Both Experts

Disregarding the problems of translation, the Dutch scholar Marten Gerbertus Buist (1925–98) characterized Voûte's view on the Russian bureaucracy of 1793 in his extensive 1974 study on the bank and trade house of Hope & Co.:

German into Russian. The best translators often make the most ridiculous mistakes. I made this experiences hundreds of times." JAKOB. Denkwürdigkeiten. P. 266.

37 "Sections with Robert Voûte determining the overdraft of the debts to be repaid and fixing the basis on which this overdraft shall be done." Stadsarchief Amsterdam (hereafter, SAA). 735,1980. "Articles (02.11.1797 O.S.)."

38 "Sections, agreed to by Sir Robert Voûte, concerning the matter of compilation of the loans in foreign countries and writing them in conformity to the gentlemen Hope." SAA. 735,1980. "Articles (02.11.1797 O.S.)."

39 PSZ I. Vol. 25. № 18326a, 15.01.1798 O.S.

> All these bodies were headed by military men with no understanding of the job [...]. They spent more time talking than working, and every day saw decisions taken that conflicted with earlier ones.[40]

Many experts shared a negative view of Russia, which they saw as a powerful but badly administrated country. Remarks on stupid, poor, unskilled, corrupt, or ugly Russians can often be found in Jakob's memoirs. Jakob described buying serfs and avoiding intoxication or acts of theft as very difficult tasks for the Russians.[41]

How does someone act toward a country when holding such negative, even arrogant views of it? In 1797 and 1798, Voûte tried to find the best way to handle the Dutch debts for his houses in Amsterdam and Russia. His aim was to make Russia pay back all the debts as well as the interest. However, he also knew of the tough financial situation that the government and Paul I had inherited from Catherine the Great. As a form of compromise, and to prevent Russia from going bankrupt, Voûte split the repayment of the loan into two periods. During the first period, which ended in 1809, Russia only had to pay the accumulated interest, with a special clause that also allowed the country to repay nothing of the loan itself. In contrast, in the second period, beginning in 1810, the loan or its unpaid remainder had to be repaid step by step by the year 1829 at the latest.[42] This policy proved successful for Voûte. As mentioned before, Robert Voûte and his nephew occasionally held the position of court bankers of Russia. But indeed, his great diplomatic success came with a price. This chapter's appendix gives an indication of how high the foreign debts were in contrast to Russia's income in 1801. Russia's debt stood around 138 percent of the state's total income. More than one year's state income was meant to be transferred to the Dutch houses. Therefore it did not come as a surprise that the securities given by Russia had to be raised. Under Catherine, the securities that one toll in the city of Riga brought were enough. In 1798, not less than the whole state revenue, especially the tolls of the capital St. Petersburg, Livonia, and the small Russian part of Finland, had to be given to Hope as securities.[43]

---

40 Buist. At spes non fracta. P. 131.

41 Jakob. Denkwürdigkeiten. Pp. 159, 162, 164 f., 170–72, 182 f., 212.

42 PSZ I, Vol. 25, № 18326a, 15.01.1798 O.S. This split in two periods has not been observed by all scholars. Heller. Die Geld- und Kreditpolitik. P. 53, writes that the whole debt had to be repaid within twelve years by 1810, which would have been an absolutely impossible task. Better is: Marnei. The Finances. P. 138. A small mistake in Marnei's article is that she identifies the twenty-year-long second period of repayment as 1811–30, whereas it was actually 1810–29. For a correct assessment, see: Buist. De Russische staatsschuld. P. 294.

43 PSZ I. Vol. 25. № 18326a, 15.01.1798; Heller. Die Geld- und Kreditpolitik. P. 53.

These external and some internal debts created a situation that pushed Russia to the edge of bankruptcy. The first, pre-1809, period of repayment involved frequent use of Voûte's diplomatic loophole that allowed Russia to pay down only the interest. Alexander I made the one and only repayment of two million Dutch guilders, referring to the Dutch interest, in 1803.[44] It was not that the governments of Paul I and Alexander I did not intend to pay back the debts, but wars and other expenses simply gave them no other options than to postpone. Thus the debt was left at 86.3 million Dutch guilders to be repaid. Due to the fact that Russia had printed a lot of Assignation roubles, the sum of interest and loan debts corresponded to 243 million Assignation roubles or 82 percent of Russia's total state revenue in 1809.[45]

A misinterpretation of these numbers can lead to the thought that Russia's situation improved in the years 1801 to 1809. The share of Dutch debts to state revenue shrank from 138 percent to 82 percent. Unfortunately, this change mainly depended on the political climate. In 1810, Russia repaid 200,000 Assignation roubles to Hope,[46] left the Continental Blockade, and reduced its trade with France-ruled Europe, while Holland was incorporated into the French Empire. During this time, 86.1 million Dutch guilders accounted for 507 million Assignation roubles or 197 percent of Russia's revenue in 1810. This extreme increase was caused by the political alienation between the French and Russian Empires.

In his papers, Jakob recommended the use of a single sort of rouble instead of the silver, copper, and Assignation roubles then in circulation. Jakob rightly relied on his expertise here, as he had claimed in 1808 that the high count of Assignation roubles had to be reduced. Nevertheless, the overall amount of Assignation roubles doubled by 1816. An error that experts like Jakob could not avoid was including in the calculations long periods of peace, which simply did not occur. Every year new wars broke out, coalitions were formed, old ones were replaced, and new peace treaties were negotiated that claimed "paix et amitié parfait" (peace and perfect amity). The 1807 Treaty of Tilsit between France and Russia,[47] for example, resulted in only a five-year period of peace. In this case as in many others, time in the calculations got in the way of the repayments.[48]

---

44 SAA. 735,9. "Hope & Co., Amsterdam, à R. Voûte, Paris (22.06.1813 O.S.)." P. 373.

45 All currency conversions are made on basis of: Brzheskii. Gosudarstvennye dolgi, prilozhenie. P. 8.

46 SAA. 735,9. "Hope & Co., Amsterdam, à R. Voûte, Paris (22.06.1813 N.S.)." P. 373.

47 Perry (Ed.). Consolidated Treaty Series. Vol. 59. P. 234.

48 Jakob. Denkwürdigkeiten. P. 212.

Discrepancies were not limited to translations but also included mathematics. When Paul I ascended the throne, Russian authorities calculated the country's international debt at around 82.6 million Dutch guilders.[49] Voûte, however, estimated the international Russian debt differently. His calculations set the debt at 76.3 million Dutch guilder and added a reserve of twelve million guilders, which resulted in a calculation of the total Russian debt at 88.3 million Dutch guilders.[50]

Beginning in 1810, and continuing until the retreat of the French forces in 1813–1814, Amsterdam had been a part of the French Empire. It was for this reason that Russia began delaying the interest payments and loan repayment in 1810, finally stopping them in 1812. Once again the overdue payments and repayments were the focus of discussions and recalculations. Dmitrii Gur'ev (1751–1825), Russia's minister of finances, marked the sum at the time that the repayments had stopped in 1812 at 82.232 million Dutch guilders.[51] However, the house of Hope calculated the outstanding sum at 83.6 million Dutch guilders. In the final convention between Russia and the house of Hope, the latter sum was recorded.[52]

The reason for comparing the two different processes of calculation from the years 1798 and 1812 is the similar outcome. In both cases the non-Russian person's calculation of the data was found to be correct. It is startling and confusing that the Russian minister of finance and his officials were not capable of calculating the right sum or tracing the payments already made, especially in the case of the 1812 halt in payments.

Not only his membership in high social circles but also his position in the special committee of finances gave Jakob access to the transfer of information and provided him with information that he probably would have been unable to access otherwise. After a few months of belonging to the secret committee of finances, the members were granted access to the official, but secret, number of Assignation roubles. Jakob improved his unpublished 1808 memorandum, editing it in Halle in 1817, by including the data and therefore naming 577 million Assignate

49 Migulin. Russkii gosudarstvennyi kredit. P. 30; Heller. Die Geld- und Kreditpolitik. P. 53.

50 Buist. At spes non fracta. P. 167; Buist. De Russische staatsschuld. P. 294.

51 RGIA. F. 560. Op. 10. D. 71. "Dmitrii Gur'ev, Kratkoe obozrenie finansov s 1801 goda po nastoiashchee vremia (26.08.1814 O.S.)." Ll. 42–42 ob.

52 SAA. 735,9. "Hope & Co., Amsterdam, à R. Voûte, Paris (22.06.1813 N.S.)." P. 373; SAA. 735, 2005. "Calculation de P.C. Labouchère (1815)."

roubles as the Russian debts of 1811.[53] Similar numbers, like 572 million Assignate roubles, are mentioned in other scholarly materials, by experts who had access to the same knowledge base.[54]

4. Leaving Russia

After having worked in the secret committee of finances and the commission for the compilation of laws for more than two years,[55] Ludwig Heinrich Jakob suffered a serious setback in his position in St. Petersburg on March 17, 1812, when Mikhail Speransky was relieved of all his duties and banished from the city. Jakob continued working in St. Petersburg for four more years, although the mode of operation under the new head of the commission of laws, Baron Gustav Adolph von Rosenkampff (1764–1832) did not proceed at the same rate as it had under Speransky. Additionally, Jakob lost his main sponsor and friend.[56]

Between 1812 and 1816, Jakob's desire to return to Germany strengthened enormously. After the wars had ended, he finally received an offer work at the renewed university in Halle in 1816. Jakob's return was accepted by both the Russian government and Alexander I, which therefore released him from duty and rewarded him for his service with a title of nobility. Jakob's memoirs listed three arguments in support of his decision: First, his knowledge of the Russian language was incomplete. Even though his ability to converse in Russian had improved, he saw it as yet insufficient. Furthermore, his incomplete knowledge of French and the fact that only a few Russians knew German caused difficult working conditions. Second, Jakob described the attitude that the Russians had toward Germans as negative, hostile, and xenophobic. Third, his observations of the process of integration of Germans into St. Petersburg's society was that it very often involved the loss of the German language, a loss that Jakob wished to avoid for his family and descendants. He wrote:

---

53 Jakob. Ueber Russlands Papiergeld. P. 21.

54 RGIA. F. 994. Op. 2. D. 222. "Analyse du Manifeste du 11. Fevrier [sic] 1812 (1812)." L. 8; RGIA. F. 560. Op. 22. D. 38. "Zamechaniia professora Bule o kurse russkikh assignacii, o prichine upadka i o sposobakh vozvesti onoi (May 1812)." Ll. 60–79; RGIA. F. 560. Op. 10. D. 342. "Ideen über das Russische Papiergeld, die Ursachen des schlechten Courses desselben und die Mittel, diesen zu verbessern (1812)." Ll. 3–10. All sources contain similar numbers of 570 or 572 million Assignation roubles. Noncontemporary sources claim it as 581 million Assignation roubles, but this small difference is insignificant. See: Brzheskii. Gosudarstvennye dolgi, prilozhenie. P. 4.

55 See for this topic the article of Alexander Kaplunovsky in this volume.

56 Jakob. Denkwürdigkeiten. Pp. 218–60.

> Das russische Volk ist ohne alle moralische Kultur. [...] Sehr wenige besitzen solide Kenntnisse,—Gelehrsamkeit—nicht einer. [...]. Der bloße einfache Russe hat doch wenigstens noch die natürliche Güte des Menschen; aber der französirte Russe ist im allgemeinen die ekelhafteste Mißgeburt, die man sehen kann.[57]

The downfall of Robert Voûte, especially after his success of January 1798, was by far quicker that the one that Jakob experienced. Pierre Voûte had already left Russia in March 1798, officially due to a "faiblesse de nerfs" (weakness of nerves).[58] He recovered from his illness and planned to go back to Russia. But, at the influence of his uncle, Pierre officially resigned from the court banker company of Voûte, Velho, Rall & Co.[59] on September 25, 1798. Days after Pierre's letter of resignation had arrived in St. Petersburg, Emperor Paul I gave the order to rename the company of court bankers as "Velho, Rall & Rogovicoff." Nikolai Rogovikov (d. 1798) replaced Pierre Voûte, and the appendix "& Co." was simply erased without a replacement.[60] Both incidents were preludes to Robert Voûte leaving Russia. In December 1798, when the conversion of all precursory Russian and Polish bonds into new Russian ones was accomplished, and Robert Voûte's task for Hope had been completed, Voûte was finally able to leave Russia.[61]

The assumption can be made that Pierre's disease was used as an excuse to weaken Voûte's position. Apparently he fell victim to an intrigue at the Russian court, which nevertheless does not diminish his historical significance. Voûte paid attention to every detail in his surroundings, always keeping a certain case, that of Baron Richard Sutherland, in the back of his mind. Sutherland (1739–91), a British predecessor of the Voûtes during the age of Catherine the Great, had died in October 1791 under unknown circumstances. Many historians assume that he committed suicide.[62] Sutherland's case was of the highest importance for

57 "The Russian nation is without any moral culture. [...] Very few possess solid knowledge, eruditeness no one. [...] The ordinary Russian at least offers man's natural kindness; but the Frenchified Russian is in general the most disgusting monstrosity existing." Jakob. Denkwürdigkeiten. Pp. 267 f.

58 VVA. JJ8 A. "Circulaire (26.10.1798 O.S.)"; VVA. "Dagboek" P. 78.

59 VVA. JJ8 A. "Pierre Voûte, Amsterdam, à Joseph Velho et Alexandre Rall, St. Petersbourg (25.09.1798 N.S.)".

60 VVA. JJ8 A. "Circulaire (26.10.1798 O.S.)"; Amburger. Geschichte der Behördenorganisation. P. 206, writes that Voûte was replaced on September 27, 1798, by Rogovikov. This is untrue; the replacement took place in October.

61 Buist. At spes non fracta. Pp. 178 f.

62 Cross. The Sutherland Affair. Pp. 258 f.; Buist. At spes non fracta. Pp. 131 f., 141.

Robert Voûte, as is evident from his collection of all available material about the last weeks of Sutherland's life.[63]

5. Conclusion

Several things become clear across these two historical cases. First, the expertise of Ludwig Heinrich von Jakob, Robert Voûte, or others did not prevent any empress or emperor from waging wars. Therefore, state finances were not the most important guideline in ruling a country. Unfortunately, due to this fact, their expertise was limited to the moment in which they submitted their memoranda or had achieved their political aim.

The situation frequently changed in the years following the experts' delivery of advice, leading to new developments that they could not have foreseen. Jakob's calculations did not forecast the Assignation roubles doubling in circulation by 1816. Voûte definitely did not expect the Russian army to be victorious to the point where a conquest of Amsterdam seemed possible and the need for new compromises had to be created.

Second, Russia was regarded as a part of Europe, not only by the French elites but also by the experts. It is important to recall the expectations of the Dutch bankers who thought that the Russian state, when led by a German empress, would behave like the other European states. Previous empresses and emperors failed in obtaining loans from abroad, but this changed under the reign of Catherine II, based on the assumption that Russia would pay back its loans as all the other European states did. Both facts are indicators that a process of integration of Russia into Europe happened under Catherine the Great. The Alexandrine age marked a climax in the process of integration into Europe, in the case of state finances as well as in the field of foreign policy.

In the course of this article, many problems that occurred at the time were described. Problems of language and translation are an underestimated issue in that period. Normally, scholars tend to assume that the knowledge of French among all persons of importance in Russia was adequate. Very surprising is the observation of miscalculations by Russian authorities concerning financial matters in more than one case. Furthermore, some experts such as Jakob displayed a

63 VVA. JJ8 A. "Rd. Sutherland and J. Brown, St. Petersbourg, à Monsieur Digaut (13.10.1791 O.S.)"; "Ordre au Comptoir du Baron Sutherland Banq. de la Cour par le Prince Wiasemskoy (17.10.1791 O.S.)"; "Representation de la part des Commis du comptoirs du Baron Sutherland (19.10.1791 O.S.)"; "Ordre au Comptoir du Banquier Baron Sutherland par le Prince Wiasemskoy (30.10.1791 O.S.)."

lack of imagination. Problems were viewed from an idealistic point of view rather than a pragmatic one.

In the end, both experts left Russia after a certain amount of time. Voûte did so very quickly, whereas Jakob stayed longer. Both men were encouraged to leave Russia after events had taken place that altered their situation. Mobility of experts does not appear to be an extraordinary occurrence; rather, it was common in that time.

Can the examples of Voûte and Jakob contribute to the discussion as to what term—the modern "expert" or the traditional "councillor" or "advisor"—should be used to describe their expertise? This article suggests that the traditional notion of councillor was very close to the function that Voûte and Jakob fulfilled while living in St. Petersburg. From their point of view, business consisted not only of delivering expertise, memoranda, and other work, but also in the intention to reorganize their fields of knowledge for the benefit of Russia. Therefore, the term "expert" must be expanded and used in a way that includes the process of active policy-making.

Concerning the matter of state finances, Russia finally found its own solution in 1815. After the victory over the French Empire and its allies, the governments of the United Netherlands and Britain declared that they would accept half of Russia's Dutch debt. Dutch and British taxpayers, then, technically financed half of Russia's 1787–91 war against the Ottoman Empire, where most of the money was spent. Luckily, the house of Hope did not care where the money for Russia's debts came from. In November 1815, after years of waiting, the house of Hope wrote a note excusing the bondholders, and it restored its amicable tone toward Emperor Alexander I and Russia: "La cause de toutes de nations, celle de l'humanité, devoit [sic] passer avant tout" (The fate of all nations, of humanity is more important than everything else).[64]

This article, too, bears little relation to the book's title, even broadly understood!

64 SAA. 735, 2009. "Avis (09.11.1815 N.S.)."

Appendix: Russia's Foreign Debts in 1801[65]

a.) Dutch debt (all administered by Hope & Co., Amsterdam)[66]

- Accepted debts of the Polish-Lithuanian Commonwealth: 4.9 million Dutch guilders[67] = 6 million Assignation roubles ≈ 7 percent of the 1801 state income
- Accepted debts of Stanisław II August Poniatowski, the last king of Poland: 3.5 million Dutch guilders[68] = 4.3 million Assignation roubles ≈ 5 percent of the 1801 state income
- Accepted debts of the Polish-Lithuanian magnate families: 7.5 million Dutch guilders[69] = 9.2 million Assignation roubles ≈ 11 percent of the 1801 state income
- Combined debts of Russia at Hope & Co., Amsterdam: 53.5 million Dutch guilders[70] = 65.5 million Assignation roubles ≈ 81 percent of the 1801 state income
- Debt of Russia at the trade and bank house de Wolf, Antwerp: 3 million Dutch Guilders[71] = 3.7 million Assignation roubles ≈ 5 percent of the 1801 state income
- Reserve and Hope's commission: 15.9 million Dutch guilders[72] = 19.5 million Assignation roubles ≈ 24 percent of the 1801 state income
- Debts paid back under Paul I: 0 roubles, 00 kopecks[73]

b.) Genoese debt

- Debt of Russia at Regny & Co., Genoa = 3 million piasters[74] = 3.7 million Assignation roubles[75] ≈ 5 percent of the 1801 state income
- Debts paid back under Paul I: 0 Roubles, 00 kopecks[76]

Overall: 88.3 million Dutch guilders + 3 million piasters = 111.9 million Assignation roubles ≈ 138 percent of the 1801 state income

65 Russia's state income was calculated in 1814 by Dmitrii Gur'ev, the minister of finances, to have been 81,081,672 Assignate roubles in 1801; see RGIA. F. 560. Op. 10. D. 71. L. 11ob.

66 VVA. JJ8 G. "Procuration des Interessés."

67 SAA. 735, 1980. "Acte de Cession (30.06.1797 O.S.)."

68 Ibid.

69 Ibid.

70 PSZ I. Vol. 25. № 18326a, 15.01.1798 O.S.

71 Ibid.

72 Ibid.

73 SAA. 735,9. "Hope & Co., Amsterdam, à R. Voûte, Paris (22.06.1813 N.S.)." P. 373.

74 Brzheskii. Gosudarstvennye dolgi. P. 140.

75 The accordance of the exchange rate of Assignation roubles and piasters appears to be a coincidence; see Heller. Die Geld- und Kreditpolitik. Pp. 50, 54.

76 Ibid. P. 54.

List of references

AMBURGER, ERIK. Geschichte der Behördenorganisation Russlands von Peter dem Großen bis 1917. Leiden, 1966

BRZHESKII, N[ikolai]. Gosudarstvennye dolgi Rossii. St. Petersburg, 1884

BUIST, MARTEN G. At spes non fracta: Hope & Co. 1770–1815. The Hague, 1974

BUIST, MARTEN G. De Russische staatsschuld aan het einde van de 18de en het begin van de 19de eeuw. In: La dette publique aux XVIIIe et XIXe siècles, son dévelopment sur le plan local, regional et national. Brussels, 1980. Pp. 293–95

BUSCH, MARGARETE. Deutsche in St. Petersburg 1865–1914: Identität und Integration. Essen, 1995

BUSCH, MARGARETE. Zwischen Anpassung und Selbstbehauptung: Deutsche in St. Petersburg am Vorabend des Ersten Weltkriegs. In: STEFAN CREUZBERGER (Ed.). St. Petersburg—Leningrad—St. Petersburg: Eine Stadt im Spiegel der Zeit. Stuttgart, 2000. Pp. 123–34

CROSS, ANTHONY. The Sutherland Affair and Its Aftermath. In: Slavonic and East European Review. Vol. 50 (1972). Pp. 257–72

DAL'MAN, DITMAR. Peterburgskie nemtsy v XVIII stoletii: Krest'yane, remesleniki, predprinimateli. In: SERGEI ISKYUL' (Ed.). Nemtsy v Rossii: Peterburgskie nemtsy. St. Petersburg, 1999. Pp. 156–63

FIGES, ORLANDO. Nataschas Tanz: Eine Kulturgeschichte Russlands. Berlin, 2011

GENEALOGISCH-HISTORISCH-STATISTISCHER ALMANACH für das Jahr 1833. Weimar, 1833

HELLER, KLAUS. Die Geld- und Kreditpolitik des Russischen Reiches in der Zeit der Assignaten (1768–1839/43). Wiesbaden, 1983

JAKOB, LUDWIG HEINRICH VON. Denkwürdigkeiten aus meinem Leben. Herausgegeben von HANS-JOACHIM KERSCHER / MICHAEL MAHLOW. Halle/Saale, 2011

JAKOB, LUDWIG HEINRICH VON. Ueber Russlands Papiergeld und die Mittel dasselbe bey einem unveränderlichen Werthe zu erhalten. Halle/Saale, 1817

KOZYREVA, MARINA. Pridvornyi bankir A. Ral'. In: SERGEI ISKYUL' (Ed.). Nemtsy v Rossii: Peterburgskie nemtsy. St. Petersburg, 1999. Pp. 205–11

LOTMAN, YOURI. La literature russe d'expression française. In: YOURI LOTMAN e.a. (Eds.). Russkaia literatura na francuzskom iazyke XVIII–XIX vekov. Wien, 1994. Pp. 1053

LOTMAN, JURIJ. M. Rußlands Adel. Eine Kulturgeschichte von Peter I bis Nikolaus I. Köln, 1997

Marnei, Liudmila P. The Finances of the Russian Empire in the Period of the Patriotic War of 1812 and of the Foreign Campaigns of the Russian Army. In: Janet M. Hartley (Ed.). Russia and the Napoleonic Wars. Basingstoke, 2015. Pp. 136–47

Migulin, Petr. Russkii gosudarstvennyi kredit 1769–1899. Vol. 1. Kharkov, 1899

Offord, Derek et al. French and Russian in Catherine's Russia. In: Derek Offord e.a. (Eds.). French and Russian in Imperial Russia. Vol. 1: Language Use among the Russian Elite. Edinburgh, 2015. Pp. 25–44

Offord, Derek e.a. (Eds). French and Russian in Imperial Russia. Vols. 1–2. Edinburgh, 2015

Perry, Clive (Ed.). Consolidated Treaty Series. Vol. 59: 1806–1808. Dobbs Ferry, 1969

Prantl, Carl von. Jakob, Ludwig Heinrich von. In: Allgemeine Deutsche Biographie. Vol. 13. Leipzig, 1881. Pp. 689 f.

Rosenzweig, Victor. Un siècle de bilinguisme littérature. in: In: Youri Lotman e.a. (Eds.). Russkaia literatura na francuzskom iazyke XVIII–XIX vekov. Wien, 1994. Pp. 5474

Wurzbach, Constant von (Ed.). Michael Baludjanski. In: Biographisches Lexikon des Kaiserthums Österreich. Vol. I. Wien, 1856

Aleksandr Orlov

The Influence of British Jurists, Political Economists, and Educators on the Ideas of Russia Modernization during the Reign of Alexander I (1801–1825)

1. Introduction: Why British Influence?

All significant domestic reforms conducted in Russia from the sixteenth to the early twentieth century, including the revolutions of the latter period, can be mostly attributed to foreign policy factors. Being surrounded by strong and dangerous rivals (or enemies), Russia had to accelerate its modernization. That, naturally, made its government focus its attention on the experience of mature economies. Alongside with the need to modernize was a tendency to widely adopt economic innovations but to exercize extreme caution in political innovations in order to maintain power and to not stir revolution in the country. Russian and British researchers have made reference to this phenomenon,[1] which was best reflected in the words of Nicholas I when the imperial couple visited the Moscow Trade and Industrial Exhibition in 1831. The visit report, published in the popular newspaper *Severnaia Pchela* (Northern Bee; No. 256) said:

> More than two hours Emperor Nicholas Pavlovich … spent at the exhibition. Having found out that the children of industrialist [Mikhail] Titov had been to England and France, the emperor said that, in his opinion, education was necessary for doing things perfectly, but one also ought to travel abroad and learn from foreigners for the benefit of the home country, "to learn good, not evil."[2]

Before we turn to Alexander I and his time, some important observations should be made. British influence on the ideas of modernization in Russia first manifested during the reign of Peter I. The tsar used the latest British inventions, but he insisted that "In Russia 'the English freedom'" was futile, out of place: "like peas

1 Mironenko. Samoderzhavie i reformy; Idem. Aleksandr I i dekabristy; Liven. Rossiiskaia imperiia i ee vragi; Kross. Angliiskii Petr.

2 Quoted in: Orlov. "Shkoly dlia vsekh." P. 56.

thrown at a wall."[3] In contrast, Catherine II paid close attention to the works of English lawyer William Blackstone. However, Catherine's attitude toward his works differed from her attitude toward Charles Louis Montesquieu's famous volume *The Spirit of Laws* (1748), which she admitted to having "ripped off" to draft the "Order" of the Law Drafting Commission of 1767. Catherine II wrote to Friedrich Melchior, Baron von Grimm: "Je ne fais rien de ce qu'il y a dans son livre; mais c'est mon fil que je dévide à ma façon" (I don't do anything of what is written in [Blackstone's] book. It's rather a yarn to unwind in my own way).[4] Blackstone's work convinced Catherine II that the highest legislative and executive power in Russia should stay with the monarch, who recognizes the supremacy of law.[5]

The empress was actively engaged in the economy, focusing primarily on increasing foreign trade and improving the state's defensive capabilities. For this purpose, Russia invited various technical specialists, including naval officers, from England.[6] However, domestic industry interests required gradual liberation from the British influence: the underdevelopment of economic institutions in the feudal state could result in leading positions being taken by wealthy English entrepreneurs.[7] Catherine II encouraged Russian merchants to open trade offices in London for exporting their products at the greatest advantage, receiving added value, and sharing this value (in the form of money or goods) with Russia.[8] Accumulated funds could be used to carry out new reforms.[9] On the other hand, she continued (on a larger scale) a project begun by Empress Elizabeth Petrovna, the sending of Russian students to British universities. Ivan Tret'iakov and Se-

3 Maikov. Rasskazy Nartova o Petre Velikom. P. 82. This Russian idiom is similar to the English-language notion of "talking to a wall."

4 Quoted in: Kologrivov. Novonaidennyi trud Ekateriny Velikoi. P. 169. The letter is dated August 4, 1776, one month after the United States declared its independence from England.

5 Ibid. Pp. 169–77.

6 Kross. Britancy v Peterburge. Pp. 176–280; Orlov. "Teper' vizhu anglichan vblizi…" Pp. 37–48.

7 Demkin. Mezhdu dvumia embargo. Pp. 314–29. For more information, see: Idem. Britanskoe kupechestvo v Rossii.

8 Demkin / Preobrazhenskii (Eds.). Russko-britanskie torgovye otnosheniia v XVIII veke. P. 67. "Zapiska" (Note) compiled in the Commerce Board (1774) on the British merchant N. Cavanagh on Russian-British trade (copy).

9 These attempts failed and did not contribute anything to the treasury. Throughout the entire eighteenth century, only twelve of the more than five hundred Russians who visited England were engaged in trade: Kross. U Temzskikh beregov. Pp. 348, 352–54, 356, 358–61.

men Desnickii went to the University of Glasgow and attended lectures given by Adam Smith in 1761–64.[10] After completing law degrees in 1767 and returning to their home country, they contributed to the popularization of Smithianism in many ways.[11] Smith's influence in Russia would continue into the first quarter of the nineteenth century and later, fostered by the writings of French economist Jean-Baptiste Say.

Though Adam Smith's ideas were inevitably subject to adaptation in Russia, his writings resonatedly deeply with Russians—in some aspects even deeper than (and earlier than) with audiences in England. For example, in a chapter entitled "Of the Expenses of the Sovereign or Commonwealth" in book 5 of his famous *An Inquiry into the Nature and Causes of the Wealth of Nations* (1776), Smith argued that reasonable protectionism is necessary if without it some important branches of the domestic commerce could die in a competitive fight against foreigners, thus dooming a large part of the population to starvation. Moreover, he said, "Some particular branches of commerce, which are carried on with barbarous and uncivilized nations, require extraordinary protection."[12]

In Russia, the perception of economic innovations was accompanied by the spread of domestic and cultural Anglomania. English nannies took care of all Catherine's grandchildren, the eldest among them being Grand Duke Alexander Pavlovich (later Alexander I), who spoke English and no French at all until Swiss tutor Frédéric-César La Harpe was appointed to him.

2. British Experience as a Defense against the French Revolution

After becoming emperor in 1801, Alexander I had to face the challenge of the French Revolution. New conditions required him to reform the entire government and the economic system of Russia. The emperor's goal was to create a constitutional monarchy, with some elements of parliamentarism and an abolished serfdom. In this case, it was only England that could be exemplary—the only great power of the eighteenth century that was able to make a stout resistance to France, defending its own economy and safeguarding its basic political freedoms. For its part, Great Britain was extremely interested in allying with Russia. The French Revolution's (1789–99) destruction of the feudal system and of serfdom could not, in principle, be as popular in Russia as it had been in France and in

10 Ibid. Pp. 142–48.

11 Soplenkov. Vostochnye obshchestva i Rossiia. Pp. 64, 75–80.

12 Smit. Issledovanie. P. 526.

small German states that were inevitably affected by Paris. From the Russian ruling circles' point of view, there was nothing to learn from the French/German case.[13] The liberation of peasants from feudalism, carried out in the Habsburg Monarchy by Emperor Joseph II in 1781–82 set a poor example. Performed aggressively and uncompromisingly, it resulted in increased general discontent and triggered resistance of the nobility and aristocracy.

Given this context, my article analyzes the diverse Russo-British relations in the early nineteenth century. What exactly was Alexander I adopting, and how did he do so? How did this process evolve in relation to different areas of state life? Which British innovations took roots on Russian land, which did not, and why? What was the outcome of the emperor's reforms?

On the eve of war with France, Alexander I sought to quickly modify the governance system of the empire and to strengthen the financial security of the state. To attain the latter goal, he pursued the protection policy of Catherine II. Attempts were made to boost Russian foreign trade by means of state support. As discussed above, the role of the state was blessed by Smith's authority. There was one more mediator who popularized and adapted Smith for the Russians: Heinrich Friedrich von Storch, who was a Baltic German and the author of the six-volume work *The Treatise on Political Economy…*[14]

Educated in the spirit of the Enlightenment, Alexander I sought to carry out reforms based on the principles of "reason" and "utility" (rationalism and utilitarianism). For legal reforms, he turned to English philosopher Jeremy Bentham, through State Secretary of the Ministry of Internal Affairs Mikhail Speransky. Etienne Dumont from Switzerland mediated between Bentham and his Russian "customers." Speransky asked Bentham through Dumont to use the achievements of Smith's political economy to devise a holistic doctrine (presumably, acceptable for reforms under Russian conditions). "I believe, if we follow Mr. Bentham's plan, political economy will occupy a much more natural place; it will be easier to learn and will be more scientific," Speransky wrote.[15]

However, Bentham did not fulfill Alexander I's "order." He offered ready-made projects and did not want to change anything in them.[16] In the end, Russian authorities had to end their cooperation with Bentham. Public interest in the

13 To learn more about the relationship between Russian and German states in 1789–1815, see: Straube. Zur Deutschlandpolitik des Zaristischen Russland. Pp. 103–23; Iskiul'. Deutsch-russische Beziehungen. Pp. 178–96; Idem. Vneshniaia politika Rossii.

14 Storch. Cours d'économie politique; Shtorkh. Kurs politicheskoi ekonomii.

15 Quoted in: Pypin. Russkie otnosheniia Bentama. P. 812.

16 Medushevskii. Bentam. P. 121 f.

ideas of the English philosopher gradually subsided. And yet, the educated part of the Russian nobility "outgrew" the government's paternalistic policy. In such an environment, which would give birth to the Decembrists, Bentham's ideas about the need for the broad development of public opinion through parliamentarism and free press found fervent support.[17] There was a chasm between the two approaches to modernization, and this chasm eventually deepened. It did not allow the reforms of Alexander I to become irreversible.

Though the partnership with Bentham failed, Alexander I did not give up his plans for reform. Slow but steady progress occurred. Decrees (ukazy) of 1801 and 1803 paved the way for freeing peasants from serfdom. Books from Western European authors, translated and published in Russian, maintained the interest in vital issues of law, political economy, interaction between the state and the society, and so forth. Notably, as scholar Mikhail Alekseev asserts, a significant number of works were translated from the English language. Alekseev also observes a steadily growing interest in learning English among the Russian nobility in the late eighteenth and early nineteenth centuries.[18] After being appointed as an observer and member of the Comission for the Compilation of Laws in 1808, Speransky worked to develop a mechanism for future legal and political reforms.[19] In the same year, Count Aleksei Arakcheev was appointed minister of war. He launched reforms to optimize the management and supply system of the army. Admiral Pavel Chichagov, minister of the navy and a famous Anglophile, strengthened the Russian fleet with the support of high-ranking officers of British origin. Most notable among them was Scotsman Alexey Greig. Greig's father, Admiral Samuel Greig, had commanded the navy under Catherine II.[20]

Military reforms were paramount during the war between Russia and Napoleon. However, in between military campaigns, important public reforms took place. Since England was Russia's key—and sometimes sole—ally, Russo-British relations were on the rise, except during the Anglo-Russian War in 1807–12. As early as 1804, Alexander I, in cooperation with Prince Adam Czartoryski, suggested that British Prime Minister William Pitt's creation of a coalition would

17 More detailed information about Bentham's influence on the Decembrists can be found in: Miliukov. N. I. Turgen'ev v Londone. P. 71; Parsamov. Dekabristy i Franciia. Pp. 116–50.

18 Alexeev. The English Language in Russia. Pp. 153–55; Idem. Angliiskii iazyk v Rossii. Pp. 92–110; Idem. Russko-angliiskie literaturnye sviazi.

19 On this commission, see the chapter by Alexander Kaplunovsky in this volume, Pp. 167–217.

20 Kriuchkov. Aleksei Samuilovich Greig; Orlov. Angliiskie moriaki. Pp. 191–95.

ensure peace and stable development in Europe, safeguarded by the "new Code of International Law." Russia and England, bound by a permanent alliance, had to become guarantors of an equitable world order in the future, both in Europe and in neighboring Asian countries, primarily in the Ottoman Empire.[21]

Pitt, a Tory, formed his second ministry in May 1804. The Russian emperor hoped to gain the assistance of the illustrious organizer of two former anti-French coalitions. In his opinion, informal contacts were the best way to hold secret talks. One of his closest associates in the Unofficial Committee (Neglasnyi Komitet), Nikolai Novosil'cev, went to London under the pretext of studying the British legal system.[22] Before leaving, Novosil'cev received an instruction from Alexander I that he had prepared with Czartoryski. This instruction of September 11, 1804 (O.S.), laid out the emperor's views on the goals and methods of struggle against Napoleon. Talks between Novosil'cev and Pitt were to be kept secret from everyone, even the Russian ambassador in London, Count Semyon Vorontsov. It was expected that after drafting an agreement, Pitt would propose it to the ambassador on behalf of the British government.[23]

In addition to discussing specific issues of military cooperation, Novosil'cev was also instructed to determine with Pitt the main principles of postwar settlement in Europe. Alexander I believed that after the defeat of France, Europe highly needed a "new Code of International Law" that could guarantee every large and small country reliable protection from any aggression. The countries that adopted the code were to agree not to resort to war until a disinterested third party offered mediation. St. Petersburg and London, linked together in a permanent alliance, would become the guarantors of the new international order. All this would have contributed to establishing a single community of states in Europe—a potential prototype of a future equitable world order. The Russian emperor believed that such a great goal could force London to introduce certain changes to its Maritime Code,[24] since this code was "the only vulnerable point in the British Cabinet

21 Orlov. Soiuz Peterburga i Londona. P. 18 f.; Soplenkov. Doroga v Arzrum. P. 163.

22 Chartorizhskii. Memuary. Pp. 262 f. Novosil'cev's mission was thoroughly studied by Avgusta Stanislavskaia: Stanislavskaia. Russko-angliiskie otnosheniia. Pp. 341–43, 352, 358–65.

23 Solov'ev. Imperator Aleksandr Pervyi. P. 63. Nevertheless, Alexander I gave Vorontsov a general outline of his views: VPR 1. Vol. II. № 49. Pp. 135–38. Letter from September 10/22, 1804.

24 The Maritime Code secured a leading position for Great Britain in world trade. One of its first rules was the "right of visit" according to which, during war, the captain of any British ship of war could forcefully detain a neutral merchant ship on the sea and

policy that favors the enemy to harm England and inflates the discontent of neutral powers whose interests are infringed."[25]

In 1804, however, Pitt was skeptical about Alexander I's plans and suggested first defeating Napoleon and then agreeing on the principles of postwar settlement in Europe. The prime minister adamantly rejected all Russian proposals affecting Britain's vital interests.[26] In fact, Pitt refused to conduct any large-scale military operation on the continent in the near future.[27] He said that for his country the most efficient method of war was to concentrate forces on the British Isles until the French cleared up some coastal areas, thus creating the opportunity for troops to land.

Having understood that Pitt would not support his ideas, the Russian emperor had to yield in order to create a bilateral political and military alliance. The parties agreed to first root out the main factor of international instability—in other words, to defeat France militarily. And yet, the intention was to then renew the states according to Enlightenment ideals rather than restore decayed political regimes that had suffered a crushing defeat in the fight against France.[28]

Alexander I used all opportunities to sway public opinion in both Russia and Great Britain. He was one of the few Russian politicians of the early nineteenth century who understood the power of public opinion and who could use it to exert pressure on the powers that be. Russia published various treatises advocating the emperor's ideas about the need to create an equitable world order. For example, and perhaps at the instruction of Count Semyon Vorontsov, diplomat Vasilii Fedorovich Malinovskii published in 1803 the pacifist treatise *Deliberation on Peace and War*, which he had conceived in London in 1790 while working as an interpreter at the Russian embassy.[29] In 1811, the emperor appointed Malinovskii director of the Tsarskoye Selo Lyceum, a privileged educational institution for

---

take it to the British port if contraband of war was found on it. The absence of any clear definition of "contraband of war" allowed the British to abuse their power. The code had one more rule: a "paper blockade." The British authorities could declare (sometimes on paper only) any port of the belligerent to be blockaded. In this case, British ships had a right to seize all vessels that tried to approach that port: Stanislavskaia. Russko-angliiskie otnosheniia. P. 156 f.

25 VPR 1. Vol. II. № 50. P. 150.

26 Rose (Ed.). Select Dispatches. Part I. "Russian Dispatches." № 57–59. Pp. 88–96. Three letters of January 21, 1805 (N.S.) written by British Foreign Secretary Henry Phipps, Lord Mulgrave to Ambassador in St. Petersburg Lord Granville Leveson Gower.

27 VPR 1. Vol. II. № 79. Pp. 242 f.

28 Soplenkov. Doroga v Arzrum. P. 164.

29 For more information, see: Orlov. Vospriiatie v Rossii nachala XIX veka. Pp. 439–54.

preparing young nobility (among its students was the future poet Alexander Pushkin) for positions in public administration.

During his negotiations with British politicians, Alexander I always (except for the 1812 campaign) insisted that London send troops to the continent. Presumably, he believed that only shared time on the battlefield in the fight against Napoleon could guarantee postwar cooperation of European countries. Furthermore, Britain's active engagement in the war on the continent could prepare British public opinion to recognize the urgent need to create a system of collective security. In its turn, public opinion would influence the British government. The emperor, for example, suggested that Novosil'cev use every opportunity to support the idea of establishing a government in Great Britain that "would include representatives of all parties and all outstanding and talented statesmen, and, relying on such forces and full confidence of the nation, would be able to deploy all means at its disposal, and to firmly pursue its target."[30]

3. Postwar Russian Anglomania: Hope for Social Peace and Political Stability

In 1815, the collective war efforts, largely financed by England, ended with Vienna Congress and its establishment of a new system of international relations, guaranteeing Europe a lasting peace and economic stability. After the victory, Alexander I turned again to the idea of sociopolitical reforms. The British experience still had a strong influence on his activities. The emperor, in a letter to the Duke of Wellington, emphasized: "Great Britain is the best example of a system of state administration, and this model may well be transferred to postwar France."[31] However, Russia still needed time to reach France's level of modernization (at least in setting up a stable and functioning tax system able to accumulate funds for postwar economic recovery). Domestic finances and the economy were in a deplorable state. Consequently, Russia first needed to focus on the economy. Again, the interest in political economy came alive in Russian society.

Like Catherine II, Alexander I helped attract British industry specialists, scientists, doctors, and more to Russia. English engineers and mechanics[32] worked at Russian gun factories in Tula, Sestroreck, Olonec, Izhevsk, and other Ural cities. British doctors James Wylie (Iakov Villie), James Leighton, and Alexander

30 VPR 1. Vol. II. № 50. P. 151.

31 VPR 2. Vol. I (IX). № 16. Pp. 62. Letter from January 25 / February 6, 1816.

32 Zybin. Istoriia Tul'skogo Imperatora Petra Velikogo oruzheinogo zavoda; Bondarenko / Mikitiuk / Shkerin. Britanskie mekhaniki i predprinimateli na Urale.

Creighton[33]) were in charge of the entire medical service in the military, naval, and civil departments.

The liberal customs tariffs of 1816 and 1819 provided the British with ample opportunities to export goods to Russia (negative consequences of such measures became apparent rather quickly; thus, a protection tariff was adopted in 1822).[34] Nevertheless, it was impossible to carry out economic reforms solely through the financial contributions of foreigners. Therefore, Russia drastically needed the *raznochincy* (educated people of various ranks) to take up the cause.[35]

In addition, as Alexander I saw it, the spread of education among the population would help pave the way for more significant changes in the future and, hopefully, avert revolution.[36] At that time, there were concerns that education would urge Russia's lower classes to initiate a struggle against the authorities in order to improve their social standing, but Alexander I hoped for a different outcome. Historian Sergei Rozhdestvenskii noted that, in the emperor's education policy, he strove "to shift the gravity center from top (universities) to bottom (folk schools)."[37] For this purpose, the emperor decided to introduce the Lancasterian System (named after its founder, Quaker Joseph Lancaster) of mutual instruction, about which he had learned during his stay in England in June 1814. Alexander I had met with Quakers Stephan Grellet, William Allen, and John Wilkinson at the Pulteney Hotel in London: "The Quakers told him about the war, which, in their opinion, was illegal; they also told him about slavery against which they were fighting, about activities of the British and Foreign School Society (which popularized the Lancaster school system), and about what this society could do

---

33 Kross. Britancy v Peterburge. Ch. 4. Pp. 135–75.

34 Strakhova. Rossiiskii tamozhennyi tarif 1822 goda. Pp. 15–22.

35 In early nineteenth-century Russia, *raznochincy* referred to a category of educated people. Due to their education, they no longer belong to the unprivileged, tax-paying social group. However, they were not in active service. The *raznochincy* included clergy, merchants, petty bourgeoisie, peasantry, and low-ranking civil servants. Retired soldiers and the children of soldiers composed a significant part of this category: Wirtschafter. Structures of Society.

36 Religion—Orthodoxy together with the broad development of the Christian ecumenist movement—was also thought to help prevent revolution. For this purpose, the Russian Bible Society was set up in 1813 on the model of the British and Foreign Bible Society (founded in 1804). In 1817, the Ministry of Public Education was renamed as the Ministry of Religious Affairs and Public Education: Pypin. Religioznye dvizheniia. Pp. 20–303.

37 Rozhdestvenskii. Vopros o narodnom obrazovanii. P. 39.

in his great country."[38] Later the Quakers published a brochure highlighting their meeting with the emperor.[39]

At the instruction of Alexander I, Russian officials, students, and enthusiasts went to England, France, and German states to learn the fundamentals of this new pedagogy. Thus, in 1816, the Ministry of Education sent four students to London. In summer 1819, they returned to St. Petersburg, and the Lancasterian System was disseminated across the ministry schools and beyond.[40]

The Lancasterian System was prevalent in Russia from 1816 until the end of Alexander I's reign, although the "Semenovskii case" (more information to be provided later) would significantly cool the emperor's enthusiasm for training soldiers under the British method. It helped the country produce a large number of educated people, some of whom continued their self-education; to a certain extent, this system was ideologic preparation for the reforms of Alexander II because Lancasterian educators often told their students that it was morally impossible to keep a person—especially a Christian—enslaved.[41] The introduction of the Lancasterian System—like all of the emperor's postwar reforms—was intended to save public funds and to lay the foundation for a "tiers état" (third social class). His economic and social reforms were accompanied by preparations for an important political transformation on the European model—the adoption of the first Russian constitution (the State Charter of the Russian Empire). These developments reflect an ongoing interest in British achievements, which contributed to further development of Anglomania in Russian life and culture.

Conversely, in the late 1820s, Alexander's attitude toward the British experience changed. In October 1820, St. Petersburg witnessed the so-called Semenovskii Case—an attempted riot in the Semenovskii Lifeguard Regiment.[42] Considering this incident together with the onset of revolutions in southwest and southeast Europe, the emperor saw danger in undermining the postwar structure of Europe. In 1821, Alexander I received information about clandestine activities of secret societies (the future Decembrists). The conservatives' discontent was growing in the country. The emperor—who understood that the reforms had stirred up the country but not led to his intended goals—had to gradually abandon his reforms. This abandonment heavily stifled the political Anglomania of the Russian nobility,

---

38 Quoted in: Pypin. Religioznye dvizheniia. P. 404.

39 A Correct statement.

40 Orlov. "Shkoly dlia vsekh." P. 20.

41 For more information, see: Ibid. Pp. 61, 64.

42 For more information, see: Lapin. Semenovskaia istoriia.

but cultural and practical Anglomania were still developing and would once again induce a surge of political Anglomania during Alexander II's reforms.

4. Conclusion. The Priority of Anglo-Saxon Civilization: The Legacy of the Nineteenth and Twentieth Centuries

Thus, the following conclusions can be made. British influence on the ideas of modernization of Russia had deep roots. As a rule, this influence was more intensely felt during periods of reform, generated by the circumstances of foreign policy. England's economic development and political stability appealed to the leading powers in Russia. And yet, it was difficult to adopt the British system due to differences between the two countries. A mediator, who usually took the form of a Swiss (Etienne Dumont), Frenchman (Jean-Baptiste Say), or German (Heinrich von Storch) scholar, was needed. Russia thus assimilated an already adapted (mediated) experience that was often dramatically changed in the process of its assimilation. This process offered the advantage of assimiliating what had been learned by the mediators but the disadvantage of marking some unassimilatable ideas as "unacceptable, incomprehensible, and dangerous" in the national consciousness. For example, in 1849, an anxious year for all of Europe, poet Vasilii Zhukovskii (tutor to Grand Duke Alexander Nikolaevich, the future Emperor Alexander II) wrote to the viceroy (Namestnik) of the Kingdom of Poland and chief military advisor to Nicholas I, Prince Ivan Paskevich. First highlighting the growing role of Great Britain in European civilization in the first half of the nineteenth century ("It only remains to wish England, who is at the forefront of educated people, the high honor of leading them to welfare and, so to speak, of commanding the world at large to be consistent and calm"), Zhukovskii then harshly condemned the self-interested policy of the British rulers, who provoked revolutions in other countries:

> But this ship turned into a hostile vessel of filibusters. England, with all its national grandeur, is no more than global corsair. At first, it is a clandestine accomplice of all petty criminals, who overtly and stealthily destroys the public order in other peoples, and now it is an overt rogue, who proclaims the right of the strongest, as the ultimate result of the Christian civilization, and shamelessly raises the red flag of Communism in the countries, imitating the dirty crowds of mobs, erecting barricades in cities, with the purpose to rob, in the name of freedom.[43]

---

43 [Efremov (Ed.)]. Russkaia i Angliiskaia politika. Pp. 429 f.

The process of Russo-British interaction had always been strongly influenced by political relations. In the case of disputes or contradictions, Russian authorities (who were the main driver of reforms) refused to reform on a British (or on any Western) model. They paid attention to Russia's domestic experience, which was still affected by a mediated Western experience that would inevitably be borrowed in the future. The experience of English-speaking countries, particularly the United States, took precedence at that time because they were the countries that, by using their power, wealth, and authority on the international arena, had the greatest potential to influence the development of humankind.

However, such experience by itself had never been the main catalyst for modernization in Russia. In the foreseeable future, the main catalyst would be the need for domestic development, which was well understood by the ruling elite under the influence of many factors, including public opinion. Public opinion was not as strong as in Western countries; nevertheless, it was continuously fostered due to university education that was launched (and reformed) according to the Western model.

List of references

A Correct Statement of What Passed at a Conference between the Emperor Alexander and a Deputation from the Society of Quakers. London, 1817

Alekseev, Mikhail. Angliiskii iazyk v Rossii i russkii iazyk v Anglii. In: Uchenye zapiski Leningradskogo gosudarstvennogo universiteta. Vol. 72 (1944). Pp. 77–137

Alekseev, Mikhail. The English Language in Russia. In: Magazine of the English Association. Vol. 23 (1943). Pp. 153–55

Alekseev, Mikhail. Russko-angliiskiie literaturnye sviazi (XVIII vek–pervaia polovina XIX veka). Leningrad, 1982

Bondarenko, Fedor / Mikitiuk, Vladimir / Shkerin, Vladimir. Britanskie mekhaniki i predprinimateli na Urale v XIX–nachale XX vekov. Ekaterinburg, 2009

Chartorizhskii Adam. Memuary. Moscow, 1998

Demkin, Andrei. Britanskoe kupechestvo v Rossii XVIII veka. Moscow, 1998

Demkin, Andrei. Mezhdu dvumia embargo: britanskoe kupechestvo v Rossii v 1801–1807 gg. In: Iurii Poliakov (Ed.). Problemy istoricheskoi geografii i demografii Rossii. Moscow, 2007. Pp. 31–33

Demkin, Andrei / Preobrazhenskii, Aleksandr (Eds.). Russko-britanskie torgovye otnosheniia v XVIII veke: Sbornik dokumentov. Moscow, 1994

[Efremov, Petr (Ed.)]. Russkaia i Angliiskaia politika: Pis'mo V. A. Zhukovskogo k kniaziu Varshavskomu, grafu I. F. Paskevichu-Erivanskomu. In: Russkii arkhiv. Vol. 8 (1878). P. 426–36

Iskiul', Sergei. Deutsch-russische Beziehungen und das franzosisch-russische Bündnis (1807–1808). In: Jahrbuch für Geschichte Osteuropas. Vol. 40 (1992) #2. Pp. 178–96

Iskiul', Sergei. Vneshniaia politika Rossii i germanskie gosudarstva (1801–1812). Moscow, 2007

Kologrivov, Sergei. Novonaidennyi trud Ekateriny Velikoi. In: Russkii arkhiv. Vol. 6 (1908). Pp. 169–77

Kross, Antony. Angliiskii Petr: Petr Velikii glazami britancev XVII–XX vekov. St. Petersburg, 2013

Kross, Antony. Britancy v Peterburge: XVIII vek. St. Petersburg, 2005

Kross, Antony. U Temzskikh beregov: Rossiiane v Britanii v XVIII veke. St. Petersburg, 1996

Kriuchkov, Iurii. Aleksei Samuilovich Greig. Moscow, 1984

Lapin, Vladimir. Semenovskaia istoriia: 16–18 oktiabria 1820 goda. Leningrad, 1991

Liven, Dominic. Rossiiskaia imperiia i ee vragi s XVI veka do nashikh dnei. Moscow, 2007

Maikov, Leonid. Rasskazy Nartova o Petre Velikom: Prilozhenie k LXVII-mu tomu Zapisok Imper[atorskoi] Akademii Nauk. St. Petersburg, 1891

Medushevskii, Andrei. Bentam i principy konstruirovaniia racional'noi pravovoi sistemy v Rossii. In: Elena Alekseeva (Ed.). Diffuziia evropeiskikh innovacii v Rossiiskoi imperii: Materialy Vserossiiskoi nauchnoi konferencii, 10–11 noiabria 2009 g. Ekaterinburg, 2009. Pp. 120–29

Miliukov, Pavel. N. I. Turgen'ev v Londone. In: Vremennik Obshchestva druzei russkoi knigi. Vol. 3. Paris, 1932. Pp. 61–78

Mironenko, Sergei. Aleksandr I i dekabristy: Rossiia v pervoy polovine XIX veka. Vybor puti. Moscow, 2016

Mironenko, Sergei. Samoderzhavie i reformy: Politicheskaia bor'ba v Rossii v nachale XIX veka. Moscow, 1989

Orlov, Aleksandr. Angliiskie moriaki na russkom flote v Otechestvennuiu voinu 1812 g. In: Novaia i noveishaia istoriia. Vol. 2 (1997). Pp. 191–95

Orlov, Aleksandr. "Shkoly dlia vsekh": Lankasterskaia sistema obucheniia v Rossii v pervoi chetverti XIX veka (1814–1826 gg.). Moscow, 2014

Orlov, Aleksandr. Soiuz Peterburga i Londona: Rossiisko-britanskie otnosheniia v epokhu napoleonovskikh voin. Moscow, 2005

Orlov, Aleksandr. "Teper' vizhu anglichan vblizi...": Britaniia i britancy v predstavleniiakh rossiian o mire i o sebe (vtoraia polovina XVIII–pervaia polovina XIX vv.). Moscow, 2008

Orlov, Aleksandr. Vospriiatiie v Rossii nachala XIX veka idei "vechnogo mira" (na primere "Rassuzhdeniia o mire i voine" V. F. Malinovskogo). In: Viktor Bezotosnyi / Aleksandr Smirnov (Eds.). Epokha 1812 goda: Issledovaniia. Istochniki. Istoriografiia. Moscow, 2015. Pp. 439–54

Parsamov, Vadim. Dekabristy i Franciia. Moscow, 2010

Pypin, Aleksandr. Religioznye dvizheniia pri Aleksandre I. St. Petersburg, 2000

Pypin, Aleksandr. Russkie otnosheniia Bentama. In: Vestnik Evropy. Vol. 2 (1869). Pp. 784–819

Rose, John H. (Ed.). Select Dispatches from the British Foreign Office Archives relating to the Formation of the Third Coalition against France 1804–1805. London, 1904

Rozhdestvenskii, Sergei. Vopros o narodnom obrazovanii i social'naia problema v epokhu Aleksandra I. In: Sergei Platonov / Aleksandr Presniakov / Iosif Gessen (Eds.). Russkoe proshloe: Istoricheskie sborniki. Vol. 5. Moscow, 1923. Pp. 35–49

Shtorkh, Andrei. Kurs politicheskoi ekonomii, ili Izlozhenie nachal, obuslovlivaiushchikh narodnoe blagodenstvie. Moscow, 2008

Smit, Adam. Issledovanie o prirode i prichinakh bogatstva narodov. Moscow, 1962

Solov'ev, Sergei. Imperator Aleksandr Pervyi: Politika—diplomatiia. St. Petersburg, 1877

Soplenkov, Sergei. Doroga v Arzrum: rossiiskaia obshchestvennaia mysl' o Vostoke (pervaia polovina XIX v.). Moscow, 2000

Soplenkov, Sergei. Vostochnye obshchestva i Rossiia v istoriko-filosofskoi koncepcii A. Smita. In: Vestnik Moskovskogo gosudarstvennogo gumanitarnogo universiteta imeni M. A. Sholokhova. Seriia: Istoriia i politologiia. Vol. 1 (2012). Pp. 62–82

Stanislavskaia, Avgusta. Russko-angliiskie otnoshenia i problemy Sredizemnomor'ia (1798–1807 gg.). Moscow, 1962

Storch, Henri. Cours d'économie politique, ou exposition des principes qui déterminent la prospérité de nations. Vols. 1–6. St. Petersburg, 1815

Strakhova, Natal'ia. Rossiiskii tamozhennyi tarif 1822 goda. In: Vestnik Volgogradskogo gosudarstvennogo universiteta 4: Istoriia. Regionovedeniie. Mezhdunarodnye otnosheniia. Vol. 11 (2006). Pp. 15–22

Straube, Fritz. Zur Deutschlandpolitik des Zaristischen Russland 1789 bis 1815. In: Jahrbuch für Geschichte der sozialistischen Länder Europas. Vol. 19 (1975) #1. Pp. 103–23

Wirtschafter, Elise K. Structures of Society: Imperial Russia's "People of Various Ranks." DeKalb, Ill., 1994

Zybin, Sergei. Istoriia Tul'skogo Imperatora Petra Velikogo oruzheinogo zavoda, 1712–1834 gg. Vol. 1. Moscow, 1912

Inventory and perceptions of Imperial Frames: the diversity of actors and political imaginations

Sergei Polskoy

The Concepts of Constitution and Fundamental Laws in Russian Political Discourse at the Turn of the Nineteenth Century

> Our young men lie and prate, they understand nothing and do not know what they want when they see both the *constitution* and liberal rules all awry—but are we mature enough to think of *constitutions*?
> V.P. Kochubei to M.M. Speransky, November 2, 1820[1]

Speaking of intellectual unrest among the nobility after the end of serfdom, Konstantin Dmitrievich Kavelin (1818–85) noted that it was the constitution that "noblemen dream both in secret and openly [of] and put their hopes on." However, the problem as he saw it was that people were discussing "constitution" at crosshairs, conflating two meanings of the word: some saw it as "representative governance," and others as "internal improvement." The historian believed that "confusing the ideas of 'constitution' in these distinct meanings breeds thousands of misunderstandings among governments and nations, and even more so among people who with equal force wish happiness to their motherlands."[2] Kavelin's observation seems to hold true for the early nineteenth century as well—a time when differing notions of constitution led to differing views of political reality. The political lexicon of the late eighteenth and early nineteenth century contained several meanings of this word, meanings that more often than not remained distinct. When reading texts of the Alexandrine period, it is important to recognize how specific authors understood "constitution" and "fundamental laws." What did the emperor and his circle mean in their exchange on constitution? A correct understanding of political vocabulary of this time is all the more difficult because the Alexandrine generation experienced drastic transformations in the language of politics.

Indeed, the turn of the nineteenth century marked the peak of change in the political vocabulary—a change arising from the general transformation of the social order at that time. Reinhart Koselleck views the mid-eighteenth century as

---

1 V pamiat' gr. Mikhaila Mikhailovicha Speranskogo. P. 504.

2 Kavelin. Dvorianstvo i osvobozhdenie krest'ian. Pp. 151–52.

a "turning point" when "the classical topoi radically changed their meanings" and "old words started to mean new things, so that as they get closer to our modern times, they become so easily understandable that no translation is needed."[3] The notion of constitution is no exception here. Between the 1780s and the 1810s, it underwent crucial transformation and acquired meanings close to our contemporary ones. Constitution, as Olivier Beaud has noted, is directly linked to the notion of fundamental law: "il est difficile de faire une histoire du concept de constitution sans le mettre en relation avec le concept voisin de *lois fondamentales.*"[4] The changes that occurred to the concepts of constitution and fundamental law were part of a general shift in the social and political vocabulary. These two concepts can only be understood when seen in comparison with their peers, especially the notions of state, society, citizen, and liberty.

In Europe and America, the history of the ideas of constitution and fundamental law (*lex fundamentalis, loi fondamentale, Fundamentalgesetz*) has been studied within the scope of *Begriffsgeschichte* and the agenda of the Cambridge School.[5] Russian historiography cannot boast of many studies in the genesis of these notions.[6] In my article, I will attempt to trace the semantic changes these two key concepts underwent at the turn of the nineteenth century and investigate how these European concepts were adapted and used in the political language of the Alexandrine period.

1. The Development of the Concepts in the Context of European Political Thought of the Seventeenth and Eighteenth Centuries

The contemporary political notion of constitution, with fundamental law as its legal synonym, is a fairly recent development.[7] Three hundred years ago, the term had a legal, financial, religious, medical, physical, or astronomical meaning—but not a

---

3 Koselleck. Vvedenie. P. 25.

4 Beaud. L'histoire du concept de constitution en France.

5 Stourzh. Constitution. Pp. 35–54; Mohnhaupt / Grimm. Verfassung. Konstitution, Status, Lex fundamentalis. Pp. 831–62; Schmale. La France. Pp. 459–81; Idem. Constitution, Constitutionnel. Pp. 31–63; Beaud. L'histoire du concept de constitution en France.

6 See Makarov. Uchenie ob osnovnykh zakonakh. Pp. 370–81; Omel'chenko. K probleme pravovykh form rossiiskogo absoliutizma. Pp. 111–41; Timofeev. Konstitutsiia v Rossii. Pp. 23–32; Polskoy. Konstitutsiia i fundamental'nye zakony. Pp. 94–150.

7 Most contemporary dictionaries define "constitution" as, for example, "the basic law of a state, defining the foundations of its social and state structure, the administrative system, and the rights and duties of a citizen." See Tolkovyi slovar' russkogo iazyka.

political one. Seventeenth- and eighteenth-century dictionaries give evidence that the term was primarily understood according to its medical or judicial meanings.[8] The Latin noun *constitutio*, stemming as it did from the verb *constituo* (place, put, or establish), was used in the meaning of "establishment" or "institution." Following the example of Cicero, Quintilian and the authors of the *Codex Justinianus*, medieval Europe spoke of constitution as an established rule, legal resolution, or imperial or papal decree. A Frenchman in the first half of the eighteenth century, for instance, would associate it primarily with Clement XI's *Unigenitus* Bull, which split French society into supporters and opponents of Jansenism and gave rise to "constitutionalists" (constitutionnaires) and "anticonstitutionalists" (anti-constitutionnaires), referring respectively to opponents and proponents of the bull.[9]

According to Gerald Stourzh, "the term 'constitution' was apparently rather a latecomer in early modern political discourse."[10] Its medical, rather than legal, connotations allowed it to enter the political lexicon. In the seventeenth century, authors of political treatises started using the term metaphorically: the "body politic" of the state could be likened to a certain constitution, just as the body natural could have a weak or strong one. Constitution appears here as a certain "set" of the state's "body," which established the general features and principles of its existence, the governance of this corpus. In this meaning, constitution was close to Aristotle's *politeia*. But such terminological linkage did not arrive before the end of the seventeenth century. Earlier translators of Aristotle found other equivalents of *politeia*: res publica, policy, or commonwealth in English translations; *police* or *république* in French ones.[11] However, in the first half of the eighteenth century,

---

8 The first edition of the *Dictionary of the French Academy* (1694) speaks of the constitution as a certain establishment (*establissement*), most likely financial, that is adopted by a certain piece of legislation (e.g., rent or pension). The dictionary provides the following as an example of usage: "Il a pour cent mille livres de constitutions." Then constitution is discussed as a law, ordinance, or rule (again in the plural): "Cette République était gouvernée par de bonnes Constitutions." Next, the medical meaning (complexion) is given: "Bonne, forte constitution. Il est de bonne constitution, de mauvaise constitution," and the list concludes with a reference to philosophers who metaphorically apply the term to the structure of the world (constitution du monde). See: Dictionnaire de l'Académie Françoise. Vol. 1. P. 238.

9 Beaud. L'histoire du concept de constitution en France. Pp. 8–9.

10 Stourzh. Constitution. P. 84.

11 For example, French translator Louis le Roy thus explains the meaning of Aristotle's *politeia*: "La *police* est l'ordre de la cité ès magistrats, mesmement au souverain de tous : consistant toute la république en son gouvernement." (*Les Politiques d'Aristote*. Pp. 164–65). The same commentary has been preserved in the English translation of le

Bolingbroke and Montesquieu commonly associated *politeia* with constitution. As Bolingbroke wrote in 1733,

> By constitution, we mean, whenever we speak with propriety and exactness, that assemblage of laws, institutions and customs, derived from certain fixed principles of reason, directed to certain fixed objects of public good, that compose the general system, according to which the community hath agreed to be governed.[12]

Bolingbroke's definition is quite remarkable in its focus on what the idea of "state" implied for an eighteenth-century man. First, it was indivisible from that of society, which in turn was understood as a political association of citizens who had property and were endowed with a number of rights. In that sense, civil society (societas, societas civilis, populus) was the equivalent of state as a political entity (civitas, res publica). Second, the governance of this association of citizens was seen not as something entrusted to a separate, external institution but rather as an internal organization of the society wherein the governed consented to obey the rulers out of the principle of commonweal. Thus, until the end of the eighteenth century, both *politeia* and constitutions were seen as a public legal structure of civil society in its old meaning. This old usage of the notions of civil society and state collapsed in the French Revolution, when the divide between state and society materialized. Society was now construed as a space where private property holders coexisted freely in liberty and equality, free from political domination. The *state*, in its turn, was beginning to be understood as a separate political institution.[13] In this sense, people of the eighteenth century did not know the contemporary (bourgeois) opposition between state and society, which would become the pivotal point of nineteenth-century political thought.

Under the ancien régime, the system of governance in Europe was inextricably linked to the system of estates within society. Manfred Riedel has noted that

> the *societas civilis* is actually the name for the feudal Estate-based society that we see here and there in the political theory of the sixteenth and seventeenth centuries. [...] This name could be applied to any association of people enjoying individual rights or privileges and endowed with laws: cities, lands, kingdoms, principalities, counties, land estates big or small. [...] The structure of the concept was defined by the close, inextricable unity of the society and the authorities. Authority was always based on the power of the

---

Roy's book: "*Policy* is the order & disposition of the city in regard of Magistrats & specially in regard of him that hath soveraine authority over all, in whose government the whole commonweale consisteth" (ARISTOTLE'S POLITIQUES). The first English translation of *Politics* made directly from Greek (1776) explained it as a "form of government."

12 ST. JOHN [BOLINGBROKE]. Dissertation upon Parties. P. 157.

13 See RIEDEL. Obshchestvo, grazhdanskoe. Pp. 93–219.

A learned discussion but its focus is not on AI!

> "house"—be it the grand "houses" (i.e., dynasties or families) or the households of the landowners who, in the political sense, formed the community of the land. […] Privilege (as a priority right) was the central category of this society and defined the political and legal status of an individual within it, as well as their belonging to one of the "Estates" or "possessions" of which this society was composed.[14]

However, European political theorists often treated the political order described above, implying as it did the contract as a foundation of both private and public relations within society, as opposed to despotic regimes that knew no civil society or contractual relations. Thus constitution was possible only where the subjects had property and enjoyed some authority and were not themselves property of a despot. Seventeenth- and eighteenth-century European travelers found what served for them as examples of such barbaric forms of rule in Muscovy or the Ottoman Empire.[15]

In the seventeenth century, the word "constitution" was only rarely found in political treatises. A much more commonly occurring term was the notion of *leges fundamentalis*, the most important concept of early modern political law. In France, *lois fondamentales* was first used in 1576 to replace the *anciennes lois du Royaume*. In England, fundamental law had been associated with the Magna Carta since the early seventeenth century. In German lands, the *Fundamentalgesetz* first appeared in Pommerania's's *Regierungsform* of 1634, but as early as 1591 Friedrich Pruckmann, the chancellor of the Electorate of Brandenburg, wrote in his book *Paragraphus solute potestas* that Salic law was "*lex fundamentalis* florentissimi Galliae regni." Finally, descriptions of the Holy Roman Empire commonly mentioned its *constitutions et leges fundamentalis*, which primarily referred to the Golden Bull of 1356, the Augsburg Settlement, and the Peace of Westphalia.[16] Wolfgang

---

14 Ibid. Pp. 125–27.

15 Adam Olearius thus mused on the form of government in "Muscovy": "The politick Government of *Muscovy* is *Monarchical* and *despotical*. The Great Duke is the hereditary Soveraign of it, and so absolute, that no *Knez* or Lord in all his Dominions, but thinks it an honour to assume the quality of his Majesties *Golop*, or slave. No Master hath more power over his slaves, than the Great Duke hath over his Subjects, what condition or quality soever they be of. So that Muscovy may be numbred among those States, where of Aristotle speaks, when he sayes there is a kind of Monarchy among the Barbarians which comes neer Tyranny. For since there is no other difference between a legitimate Government and Tyranny, than that, in the one, the welfare of the Subjects is of greatest consideration, in the other, the particular profit and advantage of the Prince, we must allow, that Muscovy inclines much to Tyranny." See Olearius. The Voyages & Travels. P. 95.

16 Oestreich. From Contractual Monarchy to Constitutionalism. P. 324.

Schmale has noted that throughout the seventeenth and eighteenth centuries in Germany, defining the constitution was less of a problem than in France because, prior to the French Revolution, constitutions were construed as unchangeable bodies of the empire's fundamental laws.[17]

Before the mid-eighteenth century, political and legal thought knew no direct link between the constitution and fundamental laws. Whereas the former referred to a form of rule, the latter was associated with the contract between the governed and the ruler or with the common law (*ancient Custom, Coutume établie*). However, these concepts shifted in meaning throughout the eighteenth century. In *De l'esprit des lois* (1748), Charles Louis de Montesquieu used the term constitution as a political concept, a synonym for Aristotle's *politeia*, but he applied to the state in general rather than the city-state.[18] At the same time, Montesquieu made an important step toward defining fundamental laws, especially for monarchic rule. In his theory, the main difference between monarchy and despotism lay in the presence of unalterable laws securing the rights of estates. This definition of a "true monarchy" started to play a leading role in eighteenth-century political texts. Montesquieu saw constitution as a system of government that defines both legislation and social life. Similarly, Jean Jacques Rousseau, despite all his theoretical disagreements with Montesquieu, relied on the same understanding of constitution in his *Du Contrat social* (1762). In the same vein, Jean-Louis de Lolme wrote in his *Constitution de l'Angleterre* (1770) of the English constitution as a historically developed system of governance (*systems des Gouvernemens*), keeping close to the sense that the British themselves attached to their constitution.[19]

---

17 Schmale. La France. P. 468 ("En Allemagne, la notion de constitution faisait moins de problème qu'en France. [...] La raison en est simple, parce que le signifié ne faisait pas de doute: un corpus de lois fondamentales comme la Bulle d'Or de 1356, la paix de la religion d'Augsbourg, la paix de Westphalie de 1648 [...] formaient, sans nul doute, la constitution de l'Empire").

18 As noted by Olivier Beaud, constitution in its political meaning was a new word (borrowed from English) for an eighteenth-century Frenchman. Beaud explains that it is due to Montesquieu that "a élevé le mot de *constitution* à la dignité du concept, et il l'a fait en lui faisant endosser un sens désormais proche de l'ancienne *politeai.* [...] Assimilée à la *politeia* d'Aristote ou de Polybe, celle-ci acquiert un sens politique: elle désigne le mode d'agencement ou d'organisation des pouvoirs à l'intérieur de l'Etat. Montesquieu partage cette conception dans la mesure où, transposant la Cité à l'Etat, il use du mot de constitution pour qualifier la forme d'organisation de l'Etat" (Beaud. L'histoire du concept de constitution en France).

19 [De Lolme]. Constitution de l'Angleterre. P. 246.

A hugely important contribution to the development of constitution as a term was made in the mid-eighteenth century by Emer de Vattel (1714–67) in his *Le Droit des gens, ou Principes de la loi naturelle* (1758). This work would also have a significant impact on how constitution was perceived by American and French revolutionaries at the end of the century. Vattel was one of the first to provide a clear political definition of the term:

> Le règlement fondamental qui détermine la manière dont l'Autorité Publique doit être exercée est ce qui forme la Constitution de l'Etat. En elle se voit la forme sous laquelle la Nation agit en qualité de Corps Politique ; comment & par qui le Peuple doit être gouverné, quels sont les droits & les devoirs de ceux qui gouvernent. Cette Constitution n'est dans le fonds autre chose, que l'établissement de l'ordre dans lequel une Nation se propose de travailler en commun a obtenir les avantages en vûë desquels la Société Politique s'est établie.[20]

For Vattel, the nation plays a crucial role in shaping its constitution. By merging the concepts of constitution and fundamental laws, Vattel de facto provided the first modern legal definition of constitution as the aggregate of fundamental laws:

> Le *Loix* sont des règles établies par l'Autorité Publique pour être observées dans la Société. Toutes doivent se rapporter au bien de l'Etat & des Citoyens. Les Loix qui sont faites directement en vue du bien publique sont des *Loix Politique* ; & dans cette classe, celles qui concernent du Gouvernement, la maniere dont l'Autorité Publique doit être exercée ; celles en un mot, dont le concours forme la Constitution de l'Etat, sont les *Loix Fondamentales.*[21]

What Vattel did may amount to a breakthrough in understanding the concept—a breakthrough that paved the way for the first written constitutions. Scholars see his *Droit des gens* as a significant influence on the views of the United States' Founding Fathers, especially Thomas Jefferson.

The revolutionary turmoil of the 1770s–90s had a crucial impact on the transformations of political terminology. The constitutions that individual states adopted during the War of Independence were constitutional instruments par excellence that outlined the states' forms of governance. Adopted in 1787, the federal constitution implied the type of government already in existence.[22] Fol-

---

20 Vattel. Droit des gens. P. 31 (chapt. 3, par. 27).

21 Ibid. Droit des gens. P. 32. (chapt. 3, par. 29).

22 Thus, the constitution of North Carolina (1776) was titled "Constitution, or Form of Government," and the full title of that of Massachusetts (1780) was "Constitution, or Form of Government for the Commonwealth of Massachusetts." In the latter constitution, the word "constitution" appears as a synonym for "form of government": "Constitution of Government" (See: http://www.modern-constitutions.de).

lowing Vattel in their vision of constitution, the Founding Fathers merged the notions of constitution and fundamental laws and gave even more priority to the nation in constitution-building: it was the constitution that created the government, not vice versa.[23]

Written constitutions of the United States and its members would also impact semantic shift in France, where two understandings of the concept clashed during a new round of debate in 1788–89. One of them was the old view of constitution as a form of governance, a view championed by proponents of royalism and estate privileges; the other was a new, revolutionary view of constitution as an act guaranteeing equal rights and liberties to all citizens and thus establishing a new form of rule. French revolutionaries insisted that the nation needed a constitution that would provide civil freedoms to all and give the "Nation" an opportunity to express its will. France had no such constitution, and thus, they said, it had to be set up—an idea that enraged proponents of the old constitutionalism and the ancien régime. These royalists penned their own pamphlets in response to the revolutionary ones that were circulating and tried to prove that the French constitution had been around for centuries. The court historiographer Jacob-Nicolas Moreau wrote a treatise titled *Exposition et défense de notre Constitution monarchique Françoise* (1789), in which he could not help exclaiming angrily, "Une foule de brochures [...] contiennent cette effrayant assertion, *la France n'a point encore de constitution*. On en conclut, & tout le monde répète qu'il faut saisir l'occasion de lui en donner une."[24] The opponents of the "monarchic constitution" responded in kind, vigorously attacking those championing the privileges of the estates:

> On ne cesse de nous parler de *Constitution* : c'est le mot de ralliement de tous les Ordres privilégiés ; c'est avec ce mot qu'ils prétendent nous fermer la bouche. Menacer leurs Privilèges, c'est renverser la *Constitution*; comme s'il étoit de l'essence de la *Constitution Monarchique*, qu'il y eût des Ordres privilégiés.[25]

One of the first to arrive at a contemporary understanding of constitution during this round of debates was Emmanuel Joseph Sieyès, who offered his own definition of the term in chapter 5 of his famous political pamphlet *Qu'est-ce que le Tiers-État*

---

23 Thomas Paine, arguing against Edmund Burke, provided the following definition of constitution: "A *constitution* is a thing antecedent to a government, and a government is only the creature of a constitution. The *constitution* of a country is not the act of its government, but of the people constituting a government" (Paine. Rights of Man. Pp. 56–57). We must note that Paine's definition is indebted to a much-discussed 1789 treatise by abbé Sieyès and borrows some of its ideas.

24 Moreau. Exposition et défense. P. 190.

25 De l'organisation d'un état monarchique. Pp. 5–6.

(January 1789).[26] Building on the ideas of Vattel and American constitutionalists, he updated and clarified the definition of fundamental law, which he saw in constitution. Merging these notions once again, Sieyès thus confirmed that by the start of the revolution, the modern view of constitution was as an act establishing the rights of the nation and simultaneously consolidating the system of government based on popular representation. Thus constitution is a fundamental, "unalterable" law for those who hearken to the will of the nation in drafting and executing specific legislation—but it is not fully binding on the nation itself, which is free to change its constitution.

The debates came to an end when the *Declaration of the Rights of the Man and of the Citizen* (Déclaration des droits de l'homme et du citoyen) was adopted by the National Constituent Assembly on August 26, 1789. It marked the start of the first written constitution in France. The 1789 declaration, among other things, stated that "Toute société dans laquelle la garantie des droits n'est pas assurée, ni la séparation des pouvoirs déterminée, n'a point de constitution."[27] In revolutionary France, then, the understanding of fundamental law as an integral part of monarchic rule lost importance, while the *loi fondamentale* arose as a synonym for constitution. Moreover, as the revolutionary movement radicalized and de-Christianization advanced, constitution became a substitute for religion. Pointing out that some functions of religion were transferred to constitution, Schmale cites speeches and newspaper articles of 1793–94, where the adoption of these new meanings is most conspicuous: "Une *constitution* doit être le catéchisme du genre humain…," "… presque partout la *Constitution* remplace le culte … la *Constitution* nous conserve tout ce que les religions avaient de bon : la morale."[28] The constitutions drafted during the French Revolution (Declaration of the Rights of the Man and of the Citizen, 1789; Constitutions of 1791, 1793, and 1795) were considered exemplary and accepted as models for constitutions drafted in the first decades of the nineteenth century. At the same time, a utopian trust in constitution as a magical instrument for transforming society, while subsiding in France, was kindled across all Europe and spread like fire.

Summing up, within the political and legal discourse of the seventeenth and eighteenth centuries, constitution and fundamental laws had differing connotations: while constitution was used mainly to describe the form of government, the concept of fundamental laws referred to historically developing legal tradi-

---

26 [Sieyès]. Qu'est-ce que le Tiers-État. P. 74.

27 Constitutions des principaux états de l'Europe. P. 350.

28 Schmale. La France. P. 467.

tions that had been adopted as norms of political law. The idea that constitution could be directly expressed in fundamental laws or that it in itself formed the fundamental law of a state was explicitly expressed by Vattel in the mid-eighteenth century, but it was not until the 1780s and 1790s that it took root, beginning in prerevolutionary works of American and French authors. The most radical vision of constitution in the eighteenth century went further than simply identifying it with fundamental law, demanding that the latter should enshrine the principles of civil rights and liberties of the nation, as well as the legal guarantees thereof. However, this radical view, arising at the end of the century, was far from universal, and the "pamphlet war" around various understandings of this concept was still to continue for many years.

2. "Gosudarstvennye ustanovleniia" (State Establishments) and "nepremennye zakony" (Unalterable Laws) in Eighteenth-Century Russia

Eighteenth-century Russian authors who used the terms constitution and fundamental laws did so mostly in the domain of elite political discourse. The concepts were most actively referenced in the second half of the century, the period in which they were most consciously and successfully adapted.

In the first half of the century, both terms were still a rare occurrence in Russian political literature. This neglect of the notion of fundamental laws was largely due to the official position of the autocratic monarchy and its ideologues, who could not withstand the idea of any limitation on the monarch's will. Feofan Prokopovich made this case more than clear in his 1722 "The Right of the Monarch's Will" (Pravda voli monarshei), stating that "every autocratic Prince" (samodershavnyi gosudar') possesses "majesty,"—that is, sovereignty—and thus "should not follow the people's law [chelovecheskii zakon], and moreover, should not be brought to trial for violating the people's law. He should follow God's commandments, but he is answerable only to God if he violates them, and in no way could he be tried by his people."[29] The monarch is not subject to any law and, consequently, is not bound to comply with "foundational" (osnovatelnye) laws, a term that implied preserved, traditional law. Peter the Great's reforms challenged the latter, and Peter might have been Feofan's coauthor and was surely the commissioner of his work. Feofan did know the concept of fundamental law, but he never used it explicitly. He wrote that fundamental laws, including those determining the order of

29 Pravda voli monarshei. P. 22.

succession, can only exist in "indirect"—that is, limited—monarchy. Feofan brings up this issue when arguing that people cannot cancel their "own will," which had been expressed in the original contract. The people cannot dissolve the contract whereby they delegated their power to their sovereign. Feofan believed that this fact in turn mandated that they withstand "their monarch's disorderliness, or evil manners"—but with a notable exception: "unless at the first monarch's election there existed *certain agreements*, whether by good will of the monarch only or under oath, which would stipulate that in case of failure [of his duties] it was agreed to abandon the monarch."[30] In this case, "certain agreements" is a euphemism. The fundamental laws that loom behind the phrase are almost a political obscenity for the author, as law for him cannot be fully fundamental—that is, it cannot bind the sovereign's will in any way. Hence the definition of such monarchy as "indirect": it does not involve real sovereignty, or, as Prokopovich termed it, "Majestat." Prokopovich is here describing what the *verkhovniki* attempted in 1730 when they forced Anna Ioannovna to sign the document known as the Conditions. Anna famously agreed that, should she fail to execute the terms of the Conditions, she could be "deprived of the crown of Russia."[31] By doing so, Anna de facto relinquished her sovereignty, and the "direct" monarchy was replaced by an "indirect" one. Correspondingly, the Conditions and the Form of Government as compiled by the Supreme Privy Council equaled the fundamental laws of the state. Naturally, Prokopovich would not have approved of such an act of removing sovereign power from the person of the monarch.

After this plot of the *verkhovniki*, the issue *of fundamental law was not* brought up again until the latter half of the eighteenth century, when the governments of Elizabeth Petrovna and Catherine the Great made use of the "rhetoric of the monarchy," which implied that the "true monarchy" (*monarchie tempérée*) should rely on fundamental laws. Ivan Shuvalov's project, launched in 1760–61, provided that Elizabeth Petrovna's Legislative Commission (Ulozhennaia Komissiia) should crown its work with fundamental laws that specified the succession order and the rights of the subjects, especially of the nobility. At the same time, educated noblemen were discussing the issue of the highest estate's position in the Russian monarchy. Undeniably, the idea of monarchy limited by the rights of the estates, an idea borrowed from Montesquieu, had a significant impact on the political views of the noble elites during the 1760s. A good example can be found in the projects of Roman Vorontsov, who, while in charge

30 Ibid. P. 32.

31 Kurukin / Plotnikov. 19 ianvaria–25 fevralia 1730 goda. P. 36.

of Elizabeth's Legislative Commission (beginning in October 1760), attempted to do more than guarantee the nobility's rights—his plan was to codify them as the empire's unalterable law. In his opinion, the rights of other social groups (*sostoianie*) could only be outlined vis-a-vis those of the nobility, so the crux of part 3 of the *Novoye Ulozhenie* is chapter 22, wherein the rights of the "noble" are shown to be the foundation of the state's welfare. During the reign of Peter III, the father of his mistress initiated the abolition of mandatory service for the nobility. Together with Aleksandr Glebov, Peter III authored the manifesto *On Granting Freedoms and Liberties to the Russian Nobility* (1762). The manifesto contained an explicit, solemn promise of the monarch in the following form: "We, in Our Imperial word, most solemnly declare and promise, forever in the most trustworthy and inviolate way, to observe this in full force and privilege, and Our lawful Successors inheriting the throne from us should preserve it without any diminution, as this Our decree will for them be an *unassailable foundation* of the sovereign [*samoderzhavnyi*] Throne of All Russia."[32] This solemn oath made the manifesto of February 18, 1762, a fundamental law, limiting the power of the monarch vis-a-vis the rights of his subjects.[33] But alongside the "freedom" of the nobility proper, this limitation of the monarch's political will did not suit Catherine's plans. On February 11, 1763, she told the Commission for the Liberties of the Nobility that the status of the nobility "is retained with the liberty received." She even agreed to endorse whatever the "esteemed assembly would devise to improve the freedom of the nobility in Russia," upon the condition that the "autocratic power in the Russian state, which the empire had been ruled by since days immemorial, is preserved in full force."[34]

In 1762, Catherine herself resorted to the rhetoric of denouncing autocracy and called for the full compliance with hard law by the monarch in her July 6 manifesto, which was to explain to her subjects the reasons for deposing her hus-

32 PSZ I. Vol. 15. № 11.444, 18.02.1762. "On Granting Freedoms and Liberties to the Russian Nobility". In the original draft of section 3, chapter 22, of the *Ulozhenie* there is a phrase appearing in a black box. It reads that the freedom of the nobility will be an inviolable law for the monarch and that "neither Our successors after Our reign will do anything to abolish this, since preserving it will be an unassailable foundation of the autocratic throne of All Russia" (RGADA. F. 342, Op. 1, D. 63. Ch. II. L. 381).

33 This was well understood by contemporary thinkers: thus, M.M. Shcherbatov, in his critique of the 1785 *Zhalovannaia Gramota*, referred to the 1762 manifesto as the "*substantial law* of the state, as clearly shown in Art. 9." See Shcherbatov. Primechaniia vernago syna otechestva. Pt. 5. P. 9.

34 Quoted from: Omel'chenko. "Zakonnaia monarkhiia." P. 201.

band.[35] The author of the manifesto accuses Peter Fedorovich (Peter III) of having transgressed the country's traditions, assaulted Orthodox religion, and "defied laws both natural and civic." In this way, he was no longer a sovereign monarch (*monarque*) but rather an arbitrary one (*despote*): "he dreamt of his monarchic power, as if it had not been from God, and not for the benefit of his subjects, but accidentally fallen into his hands only for self-gratification, and therefore he let his despotism merge with arbitrary desire to provide all such *establishments of the state*, whichever his pusillanimity could devise to offend the people."[36] On ascending the throne, the empress as a "true monarch" gave a pledge and promises to establish fundamental law and to rule in full accordance with it: "here We must solemnly pledge in Our Imperial word to *legislate such constitutions of the state* which would guide the government of Our beloved motherland to run its course in full force and within its adequate borders."[37]

The statement that Peter III "overthrew" autocratic power was meant to emphasize that Catherine was simply restoring monarchy to replace the despotism that had been established by her husband's arbitrary rule. Most likely, the 1762 manifesto was written by Grigorii Teplov with the aid of Nikita Panin, who throughout his political career had insisted on the introduction of fundamental laws in Russia.[38] In 1762, Panin, writing in defense of his project of the Imperial Council, mused on the "inviolable" laws in a memorandum that argued against the empress's commentary on the draft manifesto on Senate reform and the establishment of the council: "No great empire, and especially that of Russia, can have a more reliable rule than monarchy—that is, sovereignty (*samoderzhavstvo*)—but it does not follow from here that the heir to the throne can with full legal right transgress all boundaries and do whatever he desires, defying [...] the inviolably established laws (*ustavy*) of his autocratic predecessor, such as spiritual faith, the

---

35 Manifest 6 iiulia 1762 goda.

36 Ibid. P. 218.

37 Ibid. P. 222. The official French translation of the manifesto, distributed among the diplomatic corps and published in European newspapers, explicitly stated the Empress's intent to "raffermir *les Constitutions fondamentales* de cet Empire & de notre Souveraine Puissance ébranlées par les malheurs passés." Quoted in: Pièces imprimées à Petersbourg au Senat, concernant la Révolution en Russie. In: Nouvelles extraordinaires de divers endroits (Gazette de Leyde). Livraison # 69 du 27 août 1762. Supplément.

38 The Danish ambassador Haxthausen, who was close to N.I. Panin, wrote on July 19, 1762, in his correspondence to the court that the manifesto was written by G.N. Teplov but that "Monsieur de Panin l'a corrigé et y donné la dernière main" (Quoted in: Ransel. The Politics of Catherinian Russia. P. 71).

security of his subject's property and their various statuses and conditions, and the sufficiently established form of government."[39]

Like translators of his period, Panin uses the word sovereignty (*samoderzhavstvo*) to refer to monarchic rule that, like all other forms of good polities (i.e., civilized societies and governments), requires fundamental laws. The fragment cited above makes quite clear what he called fundamental laws: in addition to preserving monarchic rule and Orthodox faith, these laws guaranteed the rights of the estates and retained the "form of government" unchanged, understood as "securing the Imperial throne against maleficent revolutions." This is actually the same form of government that Panin argued for in his draft plan for the Imperial Council, believing that the presence of fundamental laws was what distinguished monarchy from despotism to the utter benefit of the former.

Near the end of his life, working on the project of "unalterable laws" for his pupil Grand Prince Paul Petrovich (the future emperor), N.I. Panin, together with Denis Ivanovich Fonvizin, wrote *The Introduction to Unalterable Laws* (Vvedenie k Nepremennym Zakonam), wherein he most fully set out his vision of what fundamental laws were.[40] Panin and his supporters offer a reform program to Tsesarevich Paul Petrovich: "an enlightened and virtuous monarch, having found his empire and his own rights in such bad order and disarray, must begin his great service by immediately safeguarding the general security by means of *unalterable law.*"[41] This idea was dear for the tsesarevich, too—but of all such laws he cared most about the one establishing firm succession rights.[42] Therefore, at his coronation on April 5, 1797, he only promulgated the acts regulating imperial succession.[43]

In projects by ideologues of eighteenth-century Russian nobility, fundamental laws appear as an instrument of preserving estate-based society and thus are not linked to contemporary understanding *of* constitution. At the same time, these unchangeable rules, absent in despotic Russia as they were, became the primary "movers," aimed at and motivating future changes. Thus, Mikhail Miklhailovich

39 Arkhiv Sanktpetersburgskogo Instituta Istorii RAN (hereafter, ASPb.II RAN). F. 36. D. 400. Ll. 178 ob. – 179. Published in: Polskoy. Neizvestnaia zapiska N.I. Panina.

40 Fonvizin. Rassuzhdenie o nepremennykh gosudarstvennykh zakonakh. Pp. 254–66.

41 Ibid. Pp. 265–66.

42 In 1788, Paul Petrovich drafted a family agreement on the order of succession. It was promulgated as an official act on April 5, 1797 (PSZ I. Vol. 24. № 17910).

43 PSZ I. Vol. 24. № 17906 and № 17910. The preamble of the *Establishment of the Imperial Family* (Uchrezhdenie ob imperatorskoi familii) directly states that this act must be listed "among the *fundamental laws* of Our Empire" (PSZ I. Vol. 24. P. 525).

Shcherbatov postulated that Russia "is of monarchic rule," "as Her Majesty herself stated it in her *Nakaz*"; hence the monarch is no "lord of a patrimony [*votchinnik*] but the ruler and patron of his state [and] therefore must obey certain *fundamental rights*."[44] These were nothing else but fundamental laws, which must include, as Shcherbatov puts it, first, "firm foundation and rule *of the succession order*," and second, "*the preservation of an imperious faith* and the Monarch's confession thereof." These leading rules are followed by a short list of other inviolable rights: "the right to legislate, impose taxes, mint coins," "[the right to] courts and the right to defend oneself," and, last but not least, the "right for the name of nobility, in their various degrees, *under monarchic rule should be established inviolably*." Shcherbatov goes still further, arguing that there must exist "*a depository of laws*" (dépôt de lois), which he sees in the Senate. In addition, the Senate should not only be provided with "sufficiently fundamental state laws in its power but also manned with merited men [to match] its fundamental rights, so that it can safeguard the pledge entrusted to it [the Senate]."[45] At the end of his pamphlet "On Corruption of Morals" (O Povrezhdenii Nravov), Shcherbatov proposed the way out of the corrupt present to be through the reign of a noble monarch who would grant "*fundamental laws to the state*."[46] Here, he parted ways with Western political theory, which tended to see fundamental laws as more of a past heritage, rather than as a goal of the future political development.

Following the fashion of her times, Catherine II tried to demonstrate the "monarchic nature" of a Russian state where "unalterable laws" reigned supreme. Starting with her manifesto of July 6, 1762, wherein she promised to introduce such rules and establishments, she had been working on a number of potential fundamental laws. To be fair, she partly held her promise: the two Gramotas of 1785 fully matched the eighteenth-century standard of fundamental laws because they safeguarded the rights of the Estates.[47] On the other hand, Catherine did not want or dare to grant any political rights or guarantees to the nobility, a fact that annoyed the ideologues of the noble elites. Whether the rights previously granted would be safeguarded was a difficult question, which the empress herself understood well. She was trying to find a solution for a most complicated political equation: how to ensure that a guarantee of her subjects' rights would not weaken the authority of the monarch.

---

44 Sochineniia kn. M.M. Shcherbatova. Vol. 1. Col. 391.

45 Ibid. Col. 391–92.

46 O povrezhdenii nravov v Rossii kniazia M. Shcherbatova i Puteshestvie A. Radishcheva. Prilozhenie. P. 130.

47 See Griffiths. Ekaterina II i ee mir. Pp. 222-228.

Thus, as early as the latter half of the eighteenth century, the issue of fundamental (*korennye*) laws triggered a debate on Russia's development. The many ways that different political actors understood and explained these laws is a key aid in outlining their general principles and aims. The situation became more complex at the turn of the century as the old political terminology underwent drastic transformations.

3. "Constitution" in Early Nineteenth-Century Russia

The French Revolution significantly transformed the understanding of fundamental laws and re-actualized the notion of constitution in Russian political life.[48] As the *ancien régime* collapsed, leaving an indelible impression on Russian observers,[49] the once key concepts of state and society, citizen and subject, right and property, changed as well.

At the very start of the 1800s, high-profile social spheres once again became a venue for debates on fundamental laws. In the clashes between old-time "Catherinian" dignitaries and Emperor Alexander's "young friends" (closest associates of

---

48 During the years of the revolution, the concept of constitution entered the pages of Russian literature. In his *Letters of a Russian Traveler* (*Pis'ma Russkogo Puteshestvennika*, 1791–92 in periodical form, 1801 as a single volume), Karamzin said nothing about the French debates on the constitution that he must have witnessed, but he wrote much about the constitution of England, which he, like de Lolme, took to mean "system of government." Karamzin wrote that on his visit to the British Museum in July 1790, "the most interesting exhibit was the original of the Magna Carta, that glorious agreement between the English and their King John, signed in the thirteenth century and [since then] serving as the foundation of their constitution. Ask an Englishman what its main benefits are and he will say, 'I live where I want; I am secure in what I have; I fear nothing save the law.' [...] They are proud people, and most of all, proud of their constitution. I have been reading de Lolme here with utmost attention. The laws are good, but to make people happy, good laws must be obeyed well. [...] So, not their constitution, but enlightenment of the English is their true Palladium. Every civic institution should correspond to the character of the nation—what is good in England can turn evil elsewhere" (Karamzin. Pis'ma russkogo puteshestvennika. Pp. 565–66, 592).

49 Among them was Prince Boris Golicyn, who was one of the first to note the opposition between state and society in his *De l'influence des événements sur la formation d'une Constitution* (1790). Probably under the influence of revolutionary speeches and pamphlets, he talked of the "guerre continuelle entre le peuple et le souverain" in France—a country that, unlike England, did not develop the right sort of constitution ("D'un semblable ordre de choses il étoit impossible de voir naitre une *constitution* quelconque"). See Golitsyn. O vliianii sobytii na Konstituciiu. P. 200.

the tsar), both familiar and new meanings of the old concepts were prevalent. This debate of 1801–2, which was hidden from the public eye, summed up the changes that these concepts had undergone in the political discourse of eighteenth-century Russia. Those educated in the reign of Elizabeth Petrovna or early in that of Catherine II, who knew well the political theory of Montesquieu and Vattel, now faced the generation of their children or grandchildren who had imbibed the political ideas of the revolutionary years. Like the new fashions of Paris, which shocked the aged dignitaries, the new political language imported from France was seen as a hallmark of "debauched" youth. In this vein, the thirty-eight-year-old Count Fedor Rostopchin, a former favorite of Emperor Paul I and a retired official, complained about "young men" in his letter to Count A.R. Vorontsov on February 17, 1802:

> La race des jeunes gens est mauvaise. Ceux qui prétendaient que les costumes indécents des jeunes gens de Paris avaient perverti les meurs n'avaient pas si grand tort dans un certain sens, et ici on trouve à chaque pas des gens d'une origine noble, dignes par leur accoutrement et leur langage d'être adoptés par Danton et Robespierre. Il faut espérer que Dieu veillera sur un pays où on l'a adoré depuis tant d'années et qu'il maintiendra et Son culte, et le pouvoir souverain.

It was amid this complicated situation, which had gripped St. Petersburg since the coup d'ètat of March 11, 1801, that young Emperor Alexander I, while maneuvering among the opposing factions at court, openly made the case for political reforms. The emperor's "young friends" originally suggested implementation of a reform plan that was stated in a memorandum allegedly written by Chancellor Aleksandr Andreevich Bezborodko in 1799.[50] This text was as far away as possible from "the language of Danton and Robespierre." The author of the *Note on Compiling Russian Legislation* (Zapiska dlia sostavlenia zakonov Rossiiskikh) insisted that the emperor should not rule by arbitrary will but should rather "hold in reverence and compliance the *laws of his ancestors,* and those established by himself; in a word, having promulgated an act, he, so to say, is the first to honor it and comply with it, so that others would not even dream of evading the law." The

50 The original of the *Zapiska dlia sostavlenia zakonov Rossiiskikh* has not been discovered yet; all existing copies are unattributed and date from the early nineteenth century. The document has a number of anachronisms that argue for a date of 1801 rather than 1799. Thus, the author speaks of the upcoming coronation and the need for the emperor to take an oath during the event, but in 1799, when Emperor Paul I was still very much alive, this phrase would have been out of place. The only proof of A.A. Bezborodko's authorship is references to the *Zapiska* made by the emperor's "young friends." It can be supposed that the surviving copies are either the young friends' version of the *Zapiska*'s synopsis or comments made by an unknown author on the original text.

memorandum suggested that, at the emperor's coronation, he, "after reciting the Credo, will give a pledge in such words as would reveal to the people his immaculate wish to reign for the glory of the empire and for the public weal. Such oath could appear in force as follows..."[51] Unfortunately, the next lines are missing, but the memorandum makes self-evident that the pledge would imply a certain degree of limitation by fundamental laws. A draft of these laws follows later in the note as an outline of the rights and liberties of estates, and of the powers of the highest institutions of the state. In this sense, the *Note* presented nothing new since Ivan Shuvalov's first project of 1760.

Count Aleksandr Romanovich Vorontsov, called back to the capital from his provincial estate, was told in early May 1801 at his first meeting with the emperor that the latter wanted to "diminuer le pouvoir souverain" and grant Russia "une *Constitution* qui borne de son Pouvoir et donne droits grands." Finally, Alexander I asked Vorontsov, renowned for his civil virtue, to draft such a *gramota* (Charter).[52] Vorontsov immediately wrote to his brother in London, informing him of the event and assuring him that he was no "amateur du despotism" but that he (Vorontsov) still feared the consequences of such a rash action on the part of the emperor. Semyon Vorontsov's response was full of terror at the emperor's design. Prophesying an apocalyptic change in Russia's constitution, the latter Vorontsov wrote,

> ...faire des changements si essentiels dans l'empire le plus vaste de l'univers, dans une population de plus de 30 millions, dans une nation non préparée, ignorante et corrompue, et cela dans un temps où la fermentation des esprits est universelle sur tout le continent: c'est, je ne dis pas risquer, mais amener immanquablement les troubles dans le pays, c'est amener la chute du trône et la dissolution de l'empire.[53]

Despite his brother's warning, Aleksandr Vorontsov did start his first draft of the *gramota*, which would be known as the *Charter to the Nation of Russia* (Zh-

---

51 ASPb.II RAN. F 36. Op. 1. D. 400. "O vnutrennem upravlenii Rossii." Vol. 3. Ll. 15 ob., 16 ob.

52 Rossiiskii Gosudarstvennyi Arkhiv Drevnikh Aktov (hereafter, RGADA). F. 1261. Op. 3. D. 47. L. 54. Vorontsov used the Russian word *gramota* in his letter as a synonym for constitution. In subsequent letters, he switched to a more neutral and a more fitting translation of *gramota*—"une Chartre." Describing the *gramota* to his brother as constitution in French, he referred to the dictionary meaning of "the constitution of a monarch" (see, e.g., *Trevoux* 1771), that is, a monarch's decree or code of laws. In this case, it was a code providing the fundamental laws.

53 Pis'mo S.R. Vorontsova–A.R. Vorontsovu. 14(26) iiunia 1801 g. In: Arkhiv kniazia Vorontscova. P. 99.

alovannaya Gramota Rossiiskomu Narodu). In the final draft, he was assisted by other "young friends" of Emperor Alexander: Count Viktor Pavlovich Kochubei and Nikolai Nikolaevich Novosil'cev. The final version of the *gramota* in French is in the hand of the latter, and its translation into Russian was edited for style by Mikhail Mikhailovich Speransky. The preamble of the document quite explicitly stated that the *gramota* granted Russia fundamental laws. Alexander I was to declare his "will and intention to use all [Our] forces and diligence for the prosperity of Russia, reigning over the people [...] by *fundamental [korennymi] laws*." After that, the emperor was to pledge an oath: "We promulgate and promise, upon Our Imperial word, on Our own behalf and that of Our successors, [to honor] the articles following as *fundamental law*."[54] Alexander I was supposed to declare the articles of the *Zhalovannaia gramota rossiiskomu narodu* the foundational law during his coronation in Moscow. This act would have resembled both the procedure that Western political treatises described as characteristic of limited monarchy and the corresponding clause from the *Zapiska.* Ultimately, however, the emperor chose not to publish the *gramota* or to pledge his "oath" during the coronation, which took place in September 1801.

The *gramota* was critiqued by, among others, the emperor's former tutor Frederic Cesar de La Harpe, who as early as April 1801 had warned his pupil against following the example of the Antonine dynasty, who "failed to found the happiness of their peoples on solid establishments which would have reined in such emperors as Commodus, Caracalla, or Heliogabalus and kept them within the boundaries of law." Therefore, La Harpe continued, Alexander must "do a great service for your Nation. Protect it from arbitrary rule of your successors by such establishments that would give to the government the might it requires and to the people, a solid safeguard against tyranny."[55] But upon arrival in Russia, La Harpe changed his tune, and on September 3, 1801, he gave Alexander I the following recommendation:

> Sir, in the name of your people, preserve with utmost diligence the powers you are endowed with, the ones you will only use for their ultimate benefit. Do not give way to resentment that absolute power breeds in you. You have received this power in full compliance with the laws of your country, therefore have the courage to preserve it in full and indivisibly until the day when under your supervision all the works required to put an end

54 Otdel Rukopisei Rossiiskoi Nacional'noi biblioteki (hereafter, OR RNB). F. 637. D. 922. "Proekt vsemilostiveishei gramoty rossiiskomu narodu zhaluemoi." Ll. 1 – ob.2.

55 F.-S. La Harpe–Aleksandru. 17 aprelia 1801 g. (Plessis-Piquet). In: Andreev / Tozato-Rigo (Eds.). Imperator Aleksandr I i Frederik-Sezar Lagarp. P. 384.

> to it will have been completed; then you will choose to keep only those responsibilities that are required for a vigorous reign.[56]

La Harpe believed that the emperor was "born to save his people from despotic power" and must, therefore, first reform the judicial power and set up a code of laws, and then "grant beneficial civil liberty to his subjects." Like Semyon Vorontsov, La Harpe talks about the gradual course of reform and a "change of constitution" that cannot be brought about by simply granting a *gramota*. In this sense, the Vorontsov brothers' and La Harpe's understanding of constitution was still closely linked to mid-eighteenth-century political science and, most of all, with Montesquieu's ideas.

These ideas were also dear to another pair of brothers, the Zubovs (Platon Aleksandrovich and Valerian Aleksandrovich), who had developed their own "constitutional" projects. The anonymously-authored 1802 memorandum *On the Fundamental Laws of the State* (O korennykh zakonakh gosudarstva) was long ascribed to M.M. Speransky, even though its contents directly contradicted the ideas that this statesman would later elaborate. The document put forth a pro-aristocratic bias that Speransky never shared, and its general tone was far from that usually taken by Speransky. Although a number of researchers noted the "oddities" of what came to be known as Speransky's "early memorandum," historian Mikhail Mikhailovich Safonov convincingly proved that the real author of the memorandum was Count Valerinan Zubov, a member of the Permanent Council (Nepremennyi Sovet).[57]

In *On the Fundamental Laws*, Zubov argues that Montesquieu's *monarchie tempérée* and its principles should be implemented in Russia. Social transformation of Russia is much more desirable for him than political transformation, since it is only when social change is achieved that "true monarchy" can be established and fundamental laws can function. Following Montesquieu's line of thought on "point de noblesse, point de monarchie," Zubov concludes, "… in place of all intricate subdivisions of the free Russian people into the most free categories of nobility, merchants, etc., I see only two statuses in Russia: slaves of the monarch and slaves of the landowners [*raby pomeshchich'i*]." He continues: "given this subdivision of the people vis-à-vis the throne, how can we think of any *form of government* or of any *fundamental laws…*"[58] In this line, we can find both interpretations of constitution—the old (form of government) and new (fundamental laws)—though they are in

56 F.-S. La Harpe–Aleksandru. 3 sentiabria 1801 (St. Petersburg), In: Andreev / Tozato-Rigo (Eds.). Imperator Aleksandr I i Frederik-Sezar Lagarp. P. 397.

57 Safonov M.M. O tak nazyvaemykh rannikh zapiskakh M.M. Speranskogo. Pp. 101–17.

58 Speranskii. Rukovodstvo k poznaniiu zakonov. P. 239.

opposition to each other. The author of the memorandum suggests that the nobility should be first split into two categories as "higher" (those in the first four classes of the Table of Ranks) and "lower" noblemen. Then, the higher nobility should see the 1714 decree on primogeniture restored, while the lower nobility should be turned into a bureaucratic class and deprived of its noble rights and privileges. Thus, the higher class would be able to guarantee the functioning of foundational laws.

In another memorandum, *On the Rights of the Senate* (O pravakh Senata, 1802), Zubov wrote, "According to *Russia's true constitution,* the source, the beginning, and the end of all forces of the state is the Monarch."[59] As with *On the Fundamental Laws,* here we see an obsolete (from our contemporary position) semantics of constitution. At the same time, the notion of fundamental laws appears in the document as one of its "movers"—their implementation is delayed until after a significant social reform, which will result in the Russian noblemen acquiring the features of "monarchic nobility" *à la Montesquieu.*

Count Pavel Aleksandrovich Stroganov was the first person in Russia to offer a definition of constitution that resonated with our contemporary one. Stroganov was in Paris in 1788–89 at the time that the true meaning of constitution was being sharply debated, and he was much more influenced by the ideas of the "friends of the constitution" than by those of their opponents who argued that France already had a constitution and needed no other. Among Stroganov's files related to the work of the Unofficial Committee (Neglasny komitet), bound together in a single volume titled *Principes de la réforme du Gouvernement*, there is a memorandum *On the State of Our Constitution* (De l'état de notre Constitution). Though at the first glance, the title seems to refer to the prerevolutionary usage of the term, Stroganov made a clear case in this document for constitution as a legal recognition of the nation's rights:

> A mon avis une *Constitution* est *la reconnaissance légale des droits d'une nation* ou *les formes dans lesquelles elle peut les exercer.* Pour assurer ensuite la validité de ces droits, il doit exister une garantie à ce qu'un pouvoir étranger ne puisse pas empêcher l'effet de ces droits. Si cette garantie n'existe pas, le but de l'usage de ces droits, qui est d'empêcher qu'aucune mesure du gouvernement puisse être prise à l'encontre du véritable intérêt national, ce but, dis-je, serait manqué, & alors on pourrait dire qu'il n'y a point de *Constitution.*[60]

---

59 RGIA. F. 1167. Op. 16. D. 8. "Zapiska gr. Valeriana Zubova o pravakh Senata pri vsepoddanneishem pis'me 29 aprelia 1802 goda." L. 7.

60 RGADA. F. 1278. Stroganovy. Op. 1. D. 14. "Principes de la réforme du Gouvernement." L. 92. The memorandum has been published in: Nikolai Mikhailovich, Velikii Kniaz. Graf Pavel Aleksandrovich Stroganov. P. 40.

The last phrase in this passage is a direct reference to Article 16 of the French *Declaration of the Rights of the Man and of the Citizen* (1789). Stroganov found the main values of the declaration acceptable, and he agreed that they should compose the constitution of Russia as well: "Le bonheur des hommes consiste dans la sûreté de leur propriété & la liberté d'en faire tout ce qui ne peut pas être nuisible à autrui." Finally, Stroganov declared the concepts of constitution and fundamental laws to be equivalent and suggested that removing administrative arbitrariness would contribute to the preservation of property rights and freedom: "Les gardiens de ces règlements de l'administration sont *les lois fondamentales de l'État* ou, autrement dit, *la Constitution*."[61] However, he continued by saying that Russia already had some elements of the constitution, namely the well-established and implemented rights that were held by some of the Estates (*sosloviia*)—but that Russia lacked guarantees of these rights, which should thus be the main practical aim of the constitution. He therefore believed that when such guarantees were implemented, constitutional rule would have fully arrived in Russia.

Thus, Stroganov brought together the old understanding of fundamental laws as acts registering the rights of the Estates with the new usage of constitution as an instrument guaranteeing the rights of the nation. The latter, however, did not imply political unity, as it was subdivided into a number of the Estates. In his draft memorandum, Count Stroganov never called for full civic equality; on the contrary, the political society he envisioned was an estate-based type of ancien régime.

Historians ambiguously interpreted of the political program offered by the Unofficial Committee. Some, following the scared old dignitaries, believe that it was Jacobin-like and almost revolutionary. This view is hardly true, however, as most members of this "revolutionary committee" not only argued against the abolition of the estate-based societal structure but strove to strengthen and expand the privileges of the nobility. Studying how the "young friends" interpreted the idea of constitution can help outline their vision for the reforms. Historian Marc Raeff argues that by the start of the nineteenth century, there were two traditions of understanding constitution. One stemmed from English constitutionalism, as well as from the experience of the American and French Revolutions. According to this tradition, a constitution was

> a written document clearly stating the sources and character of political sovereignty, guaranteeing the basic rights of all citizens, establishing the mechanism of a representative parliamentary government, and, most important, confining the executive to a position subordinate to that of the elected legislative power.

61 Nikolai Mikhailovich, Velikii Kniaz'. Graf Pavel Aleksandrovich Stroganov. P. 41.

The second vision of constitution was found in Russia and was typical for Alexander I , members of his Unofficial Committee, and, later, M.M. Speransky :

> What they called constitutions should perhaps be termed "*fundamental principles of administrative organisation*." The term constitution conveyed to them the idea of an orderly system of government and administration, free from the caprices and demoralising tyranny of arbitrariness. To give Russia a constitution, therefore implied bringing clarity and order to the administration and basing the relationship between the government and the individual subject on the rule of law.[62]

Raeff's subtle observation seems only partially correct. Indeed, the "young associates" never called for an English or French constitution to be established in Russia, but their vision of constitution could not be reduced to its administrative component alone. For proof, we can turn to Stroganov's idea that constitution consisted of three parts: "the establishment of rights, the use of rights, and the guarantee thereof" (l'établissement des droits, la manière d'en faire usage & la garantie). At the first session of the Unofficial Committee, in June 1801, N.N. Novosil'cev suggested the following order of functioning:

> d'abord on devait se rendre compte de l'état actuel des choses, ensuite précéder a la reforme de ces diverses parties de l'administration et enfin couronner ces différentes institutions par une garantie offerte dans une *constitution* réglée d'après le véritable esprit de la nation.[63]

Novosil'cev evidently links constitution to the *esprit de la nation* rather than to the administrative system. The latter should be adjusted before the establishment of constitution, and only at the very end of reform should a constitution be granted that would enshrine its outcomes. Therefore, for the emperor's "young associates," constitution became a more distant objective than fundamental laws were for the eighteenth-century thinkers. In the views of Unofficial Committee members, a constitution must come as the final crowning piece in a long chain of reforms, especially in legislation, and the drafting of a new code of laws.

Drafts and sketches for such a code can be found in Novosil'cev's archives, among the files from his work in the *Commission for the Compilation of Laws* in 1803–4.[64] The first part of this draft code (Section 1) is titled "Constitution de l'Empire de Russie" and covers not only the rights and duties of the emperor, the succession law, and the statutes of the highest state institutions (ministries and

62 Raeff. Michael Speransky. Pp. 41, 42.

63 Nikolai Mikhailovich, Velikii Kniaz'. Graf Pavel Aleksandrovich Stroganov. P. 61.

64 The probable author of the project was Gustav Adolf von Rosenkampff (1764–1832), the first secretary of the Commission for the Compilation of Laws.

Senate), but also the rights of all subjects and estates. While the former had been routinely included in draft versions of unalterable laws in the previous century, the latter was a legal novelty for Russia.[65] It is therefore impossible to univocally assume that early nineteenth-century reformers saw constitution only as a set of "fundamental principles of administrative organization." Further, the first of the two traditions advanced by M. Raeff was relatively new across the world; even in the United States and France, constitution was more often linked to administrative forms. A short glance at the definitions provided in late eighteenth- and early nineteenth-century American and French dictionaries, or at abbé Sieyès's definition of constitutional laws, proves as much. It is little surprise, then, that the Russian projects also largely focus on the administrative organization of the constitution.

In their political memoranda, Stroganov and Novosil'cev viewed the constitution, already, as an act that guaranteed rights, outlined the borders of the state's authority over individual rights and liberties, and regulated the system of state administration. At the same time, for A.R. Vorontsov and his contemporaries, the political interpretations of constitution and fundamental laws were not the same: the constitution was (in a wider sense) was a form of government and (in a narrow sense) a specific decree of the monarch, while fundamental laws were unalterable establishments safeguarding the rights of the estates. This difference in the interpretations of the same key terms by Catherinian dignitaries and Alexander's associates indicates a change in the political discourse—a transformation achieved by differences in education, culture, and historical context. Mutual misunderstanding between these generations found its expression in different meanings suggested for the seemingly identical terms.

M.M. Speransky's projects commissioned by Alexander I, just like the works of the Unofficial Committee, always entailed a behind-the-curtain discussion of both constitution and fundamental law. In this respect, the *Introduction to the Code of State Laws* (Vvedenie k ulozheniu gosudarstvennykh zakonov, 1809) should be seen not as an original work by Speransky but rather as a continuation of a whole range of projects compiled in 1801–2 and motivated by the emperor's desire to "establish the authority of the government on a permanent

65 The public was informed of the plan for a new digest of laws: DOKLAD MINISTERSTVA IUSTITSII o preobrazovanii kommissii sostavleniia zakonov. It includes the *Glavnoie raspolozheniie knigi zakonov*, which reads in part that "Section 1 contains the *Gosudarstvennoie Postanovlenie*, or the laws on internal structure" (IBID. P. 38), and in the French version: "La Première contient *la Constitution de l'Empire* et les lois organiques" (IBID. P. 39).

foundation."[66] The 1809 project summed up all the previous designs of the reformers and was the most elaborate reform plan of its time. It included, among other things, the concept of representative power. If we compare Speransky's project with Novosil'cev's subsequent *Ustavnaya gramota*, the former offers a wider and more radical perspective, probably reflecting the ideas of Emperor Alexander himself and mirroring his political priorities. Its interpretation of constitution differs from the one expressed in what came to be known as Speransky's "early memorandum" of 1802–3, which, as we have seen, had been mistakenly ascribed to him and which was, in fact, the work of Valerian Zubov. The later works of Speransky (1820s), where the authorship undeniably belongs to him alone, almost never feature the term constitution.

The author of the *Fragment on the Legislative Commission* (Otryvok o komissii Ulozheniia, 1802), who is traditionally believed to have been Speransky, postulates that "every state has its own *constitution*, and the Code of Laws (*Ulozhenie*) must be in accordance with this *constitution*," but further into the text, he muses that "every Code of Laws should be founded on the rights of the people. … In Russia these should be assumed [to exist], because they actually do not exist as yet, although much has been written on them in charters (*gramotakh*) and manifestos. In despotic government (*pravlenii samovlastnom*), no Code of Laws can exist."[67] A very different understanding of constitution appeared seven years later in the Introduction to the *Code of State Laws*. Here Speransky spoke of constitution as a written law adopted by peoples or monarchs. Russia thus had no constitution and needed to introduce one:

> In almost all states, constitutions were established in various times, in a piecemeal fashion and usually amid violent political turmoil. The Russian constitution will owe its existence not to excitement of passions or to extreme circumstances but to beneficial inspiration of its supreme authority, which, having organized the political being of its people, can and has every opportunity to provide it with the most correct forms.[68]

In this fragment, Speransky sees constitution as an establishment of political and civil rights during the transition from a feudal to a republican system: "All political metamorphoses that have taken place in Europe reveal to us an incessant, so to say, struggle between the system of republics and the feudal system." Russia, he believed, was quite ready for such a transition: "the current system of government no longer corresponds to the state of the public spirit, and it is time the system

66 Speranskii. Plan gosudarstvennogo preobrazovaniia. P. 177.

67 Speranskii. Rukovodstvo k poznaniiu zakonov. Pp. 216–17.

68 Ibid. P. 341.

should be changed and a new order of things established."[69] The constitution proper in the text of the Introduction is referred to as "the state code" (*gosudarstvennoie ulozheniie*) and seen as identical with "fundamental laws of the state" (*korennye gosudarstvennye zakony*). Interestingly, ten years later, Alexander I, while discussing The *Constitutional Charter of the Russian Empire* (Ustavnaia gramota Rossiiskoi Imperii), ordered that constitution should be translated as *gosudarstvennoe ulozhenie*, just as it was in Speransky's project.[70]

The rise of the public sphere and the sharp growth of printed texts, especially journalism,[71] helped the new political terminology to spread quickly among audiences. Active adaptation of the new political terms became especially conspicuous after the wars of Napoleon, in the latter half of the 1810s. The emperor's famous speech at the Polish Sejm on March 15, 1818, almost immediately became known throughout Russia and generated rumors among the public.[72] This speech was widely credited with helping the new meaning of constitution achieve prominence. For instance, Sergei Nikolaevich Glinka wrote that "prior to 1818, no one in Moscow could speak the word *constitution*. It was Emperor Alexander I who first gave rise to the use of this alluring word."[73] At the same time, the government tried to prevent the *gramota* from sharing any association with European constitutions, whether revolutionary ones or those granted by a monarch. Novosil'cev , writing a manifesto for the Constitutional Charter (*Ustavnaia Gramota*) of the Russian

---

69 Ibid. P. 348.

70 Petr Andreevich Viazemskii, recalling an audience with Alexander I in summer 1820 on translating the Ustavnaia Gramota, wrote, "The translation of *constitution* and *libéral* as *gosudarstvennoe ulozhenie* and *zakonnosvobodnyi* belonged to the emperor himself." Quoted in: Mironenko. Samoderzhavie i reformy. P. 182.

71 At the beginning of the nineteenth century, Russian periodicals published a number of constitutional acts. See, for example, Konstituciia Italianskoi respubliki. In: Vestnik Evropy. Vol. 2 (1802) # 5, March. Pp. 71–79; Konstituciia Francuzskogo korolevstva. In: Syn Otechestva. Vol. 13 (1814) # XXVII. Pp. 193–97; Vol. 14, # XXXX V. Pp. 259–70; Novaia konstituciia Francii, izdannaia pod nazvaniem dopolnitel'nogo akta k gosudarstvennym konstituciiam. In: Dukh Zhurnalov. Vol. 3 (1815). # 20. Pp. 1063–71; Konstituciia Severo-Amerikanskikh oblastei. In: Dukh Zhurnalov. Vol. 38 (1820) # 2. Pp. 73–88; # 3. Pp. 97–116; # 4. Pp. 157–64.

72 Conservatively minded Fedor Rostopchin wrote to Semyon Vorontsov: "On regarde comme une constitution la liberté des paysans, qui est contre le voeu de la noblesse; mais on ne voudra pas restreindre son pouvoir et se mettre sous l'empire de la justice et de la raison." F.V. Rostopchin–S.R. Vorontsovu, 26 ianvaria 1819 (Paris). In: Arkhiv kniazia Vorontsova. Vol. 8. P. 363.

73 Glinka. Istoricheskii vzgliad na obshchestva evropeiskie. P. 118.

Empire in 1820, explicitly stated that the Ustavnaia Gramota established no new provisions—it only described the empire's constitution in the prerevolutionary sense of the word:

> The *Ustavnaia Gramota* ... introduces no novelty, nor any change in the system of government [*gosudarstvennoe ustroistvo*]. It is founded on our *state institutions*; it unites them, develops the principles they rest on, sets them in motion, and thus opens an opportunity to bring order and harmony to various branches of the administration.[74]

One of those who worked on the *Ustavnaia Gramota*, Prince P.A. Viazemskii, held a different opinion of the era's changes. For him, the state was directly associated with the government, and the government had to be controlled, with an integral part of this control found in the system of representative power. In March 1819, Viazemskii thus mused on the goings-on in a letter to Aleksandr Ivanovich Turgenev:

> Our government is being naughty as a child and says, "No one will see it anyway!" It is high time we should get it a tutor—national representation. The tutor will probably be somewhat stupid, but [he] still will calm down the child. The trouble is that the tutor may remember that he comes from a slave family and will too often say, "As you wish, master." This is the only thing I am afraid of; the rest is fiddlesticks, and I do not fear it. We will play with the government for these trifles, like children, and compare our trump cards—whose one wins after all![75]

The new understanding of constitution spread fast among the educated public, and in the same year of 1819 Alexander Sergeevich Griboedov wrote, for instance, "In Europe, and even among the peoples who have not yet got their own constitution, the general opinion demands that the guilty party should at least be brought to trial."[76] The phrasing is most interesting: a constitution can be "got"; it is an act granting rights and safeguards. In contrast, in the eighteenth century the majority among the educated public believed that constitution could be changed, but they would prefer not to do so, since constitution was seen as a traditionally established form of government in any country, and changing it marked a sure path to the collapse of the state.[77]

---

74 Quoted in: Mironenko. Samoderzhavie i reformy. P. 197.

75 Ostaf'evskii arkhiv. P. 204.

76 Griboedov. Sochinenia. P. 404.

77 One of the supporters of this "old" understanding of constitution was N.M. Karamzin. See: Kiselev. Karamzin i konstitucia.

Contemporary European constitutionalist trends found their fullest expression in the constitutional projects of the Decembrists.[78] Unlike Novosil'cev's *Ustavnaia Gramota*, where the statuses of the estates were retained while the estates themselves had no safeguards of their rights,[79] the constitutional projects of Nikita Mikhailovich Murav'ev and Pavel Ivanovich Pestel' included clauses on abolition of the estates and the introduction of universal civic freedoms. These clauses corresponded well to the idea of civic equality and protection of the rights of the man and citizen as crucial objectives of the new "republican" constitutions. Although they "Slavicized" the notion of constitution, consciously avoiding the very word,[80] both authors spoke of a basic, written law that codified the system of public administration and universal civic rights. Murav'ev spoke of a "charter of positive establishment" (*ustav polozhitelnogo obrazovaniia*), while Pestel' described constitution as the "most cherished state charter of the great Russian nation" (*zapovednaia gosudarstvennaia gramota velikogo naroda rossiiskogo*), which should serve "as a testament of improving the system of the Russian state."

The way that the Decembrists adapted the notion of constitution led them in the same direction as the government, forcing them to look for a Russian equivalent of the word and suggesting similar choices—*gramota* or *ustav*. This lexical agreement, reached in the latter half of the 1810s and early 1820s, suggested common understanding of the signified. Both Alexander I and his critics equally understood constitution as a fundamental law of a state, defining its structure and listing the citizens' rights, rather than as any form of government or a concept aligned with Aristotle's *politeia*. The political meanings seen in constitution by various social powers differed substantially, but terminological unity remained. These semantic transformations indicated an arrival of a new period, with its own problems, values, and ideals.

78 See the chapters by Vadim Parsamov and Lorenz Erren in this volume. Pp. 245–283.

79 Chapter 3 (Art. 78–98) of the Ustavnaia Gramota provided for the introduction of a number of "civic" freedoms for "all Russian subjects," which did not directly correspond to all the estates. Thus, Art. 91 read, "From now on and forever, the Russian people will have representation," but representative rights were conferred on a narrower circle of nobility, those possessing "real estate" (*nedvizhimoe imenie*) and "citizens" (*gradskie obyvateli*), who were enrolled in a special register (Art. 159, 161, 166, 171).

80 Murav'ev and Pestel' almost never use the term constitution. During the investigation of his case in 1826, Murav'ev spoke only of a "draft constitution" and "constitutional charter" (*kosnstitutsionnyi ustav*). In early drafts of his projects, the word appears only in the context of the English constitution. Pestel' never used the term at all.

Moreover, constitution was becoming a "moving power": just as, in the latter half of the eighteenth century, elites of the nobility advanced the idea that fundamental laws were needed to guarantee their security and property rights in what they saw as their state, the nascent nineteenth-century society sought constitution protection from the state's encroachment on their rights.

List of references

ANDREEV, ANDREI IU. / TOZATO-RIGO, D. (Eds.). Imperator Aleksandr I i Frederik-Sezar Lagarp: Pis'ma. Dokumenty / Sostavlenie, vstupitel'nye stat'i i kommentarii. Perevod s francuzskogo V.A. Mil'chinoi. Vol. 1. Moscow, 2014

ARISTOTLE'S POLITIQUES, or discourse of government, translated out of the Greek into French… by Loys le Roy called Regius. Translated out of French into English. London, 1598

ARKHIV KNIAZIA VORONTSOVA. Vol. 10. St. Petersburg, 1876

BEAUD, OLIVIER. L'histoire du concept de constitution en France. De la constitution politique à la constitution comme statut juridique de l'Etat (2009). In: Jus Politicum. Autour de la notion de Constitution. (2009) #3 http://juspoliticum.com/numero/autour-de-la-notion-de-constitution-24.html [12.10.2018]

CONSTITUTIONS DES PRINCIPAUX ÉTATS de l'Europe et des États-Unis. Vol. 3. Paris, 1791

[DE LOLME, J.L.]. Constitution de l'Angleterre ou État du gouvernement anglais comparé avec la forme républicaine et avec les autres monarchies de l'Europe. Amsterdam, 1771

DE L'ORGANISATION D'UN ÉTAT MONARCHIQUE, ou Considérations sur les vices de la monarchie Fransoise & sur la nécessité de lui donner une Constitution. Paris, 1789

DICTIONNAIRE DE L'ACADÉMIE FRANÇOISE. Vol. 1. Paris, 1694

DOKLAD MINISTERSTVA IUSTITSII o preobrazovanii kommissii sostavleniia zakonov i Vypiska iz podnesennykh EIV prisutstviem komissii raportov ob uspekhakh trudov eia. Pt.1. SPb., 1804

FONVIZIN, DENIS. Rassuzhdenie o nepremennykh gosudarstvennykh zakonakh. In: FONVIZIN, DENIS. Sobranie sochinenii. V 2 tt. Vol. 2. Moscow, 1959. Pp 254–66

GLINKA, SERGEI. Istoricheskii vzgliad na obshchestva evropeiskie i sud'bu moego otechestva. In: CAMUTALI, A.N. a.o. (Eds.). Nikolai I: lichnost' i epokha. Novye materialy. St. Petersburg, 2007. Pp. 118–32

? Hartley (Poland + Finland)

Golitsyn, B.V. O vliianii sobytii na Konstituciiu (1790). In: Frantsuzskii ezhegodnik 2010: Istochniki po istorii Frantsuzskoi revoliucii XVIII v. i epokhi Napoleona. Moscow, 2010. Pp. 192–236

Griboedov Aleksandr. Sochinenia. / Vstup. stat'ia, komment., sostav. i podgotovka teksta S.A. Fomicheva. Moscow, 1988

Griffiths D. Ekaterina II i ee mir. Moscow, 2013

Karamzin, Nikolai. Pis'ma russkogo puteshestvennika. In: Karamzin, Nikolai. Izbrannye sochinenia. V 2 tt. Vol. 1 / Sost., podgot. teksta i primech. P. Berkova. Moscow-Leningrad, 1964. Pp. 77–604

Kavelin, K.D. Dvorianstvo i osvobozhdenie krest'ian. In: Kavelin, K.D. Nash umstvennyi stroi. Stat'i po filosofii russkoi istorii i kul'tury. Moscow, 1989. Pp. 151–52

Kiselev, M.A. Karamzin i konstitucia. In: Novyi Mir. (2016) # 7. http://magazines.russ.ru/novyi_mi/2016/7/karamzin-i-konstituciya.html [12.10.2018]

Koselleck, Reinhart. Vvedenie. In: Slovar' osnovnykh istoricheskikh poniatii. Izbrannye stat'i v 2-kh tt. Vol. 1 / Per. s nem. K. Levinson; sost. Iu. Zaretskii, K. Levinson, I. Shirle; nauchn. red. perevoda Iu. Arnautova. Moscow, 2014

Kurukin, I.V. / Plotnikov, A.B. 19 ianvaria–25 fevralia 1730 goda: Sobytiia, liudi, dokumenty. Moscow, 2010

Les Politiques d'Aristote. Paris, 1576

Makarov, A.N. Uchenie ob osnovnykh zakonakh v russkoi iuridicheskoi literature XVIII i pervoi polovine XIX vv. In: Sbornik statei po russkoi istorii, posviashchennyi S.F. Platonovu. Petrograd, 1922. Pp. 370–81

Manifest 6 iiulia 1762 goda. In: Osmnadcatyi vek. Istoricheskii sbornik, izdavaemyi P. Bartenevym. Vol. 4. Moscow, 1869

Mironenko, Sergei. Samoderzhavie i reformy. Politicheskaia bor'ba v Rossii v nachale XIX v. Moscow 1989

Mohnhaupt, Heinz / Grimm, Dieter. Verfassung. Konstitution, Status, Lex fundamentalis. In: Reinhart Koselleck (Ed.) Geschichtliche Grundbegriffe. Historisches Lexikon zur politisch-sozialen Sprache in Deutschland. Vol. 6. Stuttgart, 1990. Pp. 831–62

Moreau, Jacob-Nicolas. Exposition et défense de notre Constitution monarchique Françoise. Vol. 2. Paris, 1789

Nikolai Mikhailovich, Velikii Kniaz'. Graf Pavel Aleksandrovich Stroganov. Vol. 2. St. Petersburg, 1903

Oestreich, Gerhard. From Contractual Monarchy to Constitutionalism. In: J.B. Collins / K.L. Taylor (Eds.). Early Modern Europe: Issues and Interpretations. Oxford, 2006. Pp. 166–86

Olearius Adam. The Voyages & Travels of the Ambassadors from the Duke of Holstein, to the Great Duke of Muscovy, and the King of Persia. Rendred into English, by John Devies. London, 1662

Omel'chenko, O.A. K probleme pravovykh form rossiiskogo absoliutizma vtoroi poloviny XVIII v. In: Omel'chenko, O.A. Vlast' i Zakon v Rossii XVIII veka. Issledovaniia i ocherki. Moscow, 2004. Pp. 111–41

Omel'chenko, O.A. "Zakonnaia monarkhiia" Ekateriny Vtoroi: Prosveshchennyi absoliutizm v Rossii. Moscow, 1993

O povrezhdenii nravov v Rossii kniazia M. Shcherbatova i Puteshestvie A. Radishcheva. Prilozhenie. Moscow, 1984.

Ostaf'evskii arkhiv. Vol. 1. St. Petersburg., 1899

Paine, Thomas. Rights of Man: Being an Answer to Mr. Burke's Attack on the French Revolution. (2nd edition). London, 1791

Polskoy, S.V. Konstitutsiia i fundamental'nye zakony v russkom politicheskom diskurse XVIII veka. In: Aleksei Miller / Denis Sdvizhkov / Ingrid Shirle. "Poniatiia o Rossii": K istoricheskoi semantike imperskogo perioda. V 2-kh tomakh. Vol. 1. Moscow, 2012. Pp. 94–150

Polskoy, Sergei. Neizvestnaia zapiska N.I. Panina i "Primechaniia" na proekt Imperatorskogo soveta (1762–1763 gg.). In. Izvestiia Samarskogo nauchnogo tsentra RAN. Vol. 12 (2010) # 6

Pravda voli monarshei vo opredelenii naslednika derzhavy svoei. St. Petersburg, 1722

Raeff, Marc. Michael Speransky: Statesman of Imperial Russia. The Hague, 1957

Ransel David L. The Politics of Catherinian Russia. The Panin Party. New Haven, 1975

Riedel, Manfred. Obshchestvo, grazhdanskoe. In: Slovar' osnovnykh istoricheskikh poniatii. Izbrannye stat'i v 2kh. Tt. Vol. 2. Pp. 93–219

Safonov M.M. O tak nazyvaemykh rannikh zapiskakh M.M. Speranskogo. In: Vspomogatel'nze istoricheskie discipliny. Vol. 22. Leningrad, 1991. Pp. 101–17

Schmale Wolfgang. Constitution, Constitutionnel. In: R. Reichardt / H.J. Lüsebrink (Eds.). Handbuch politisch-sozialer Grundbegriffe in Frankreich 1680–1820. Vol. 12. München, 1992. Pp. 31–63

Schmale Wolfgang. La France, l'Allemagne et la Constitution (1789–1815). In: Annales historiques de la Révolution française. (1991) # 3. Pp. 459–81

Shcherbatov, M.M. Primechaniia vernago syna otechestva na Dvorianskie prava. In: ChOIDR. Vol. 4 (1871)

Sochineniia Kn. M.M. Shcherbatova. Vol. 1. St. Petersburg, 1896

[Sieyès, E.J.]. Qu'est-ce que le Tiers-État. Paris, 1789

Speranskii, Michail. Plan gosudarstvennogo preobrazovaniia. Moscow, 2004

Speranskii, Michail. Rukovodstvo k poznaniiu zakonov. St. Petersburg, 2002

St. John, Henry [Bolingbroke, Nicholas Amhurst]. Dissertation upon Parties. In: Works of Bolingbroke. London, 1809. Vol. 3

Stourzh, G. Constitution: Changing Meanings of the Term from the Early Seventeenth to the Late Eighteenth Century. In: T. Ball / J.G.A. Pocock (Eds.). Conceptual Change and the Constitution. Lawrence, 1988. Pp. 35–54

Timofeev, D.V. Konstitutsiia v Rossii perovoi chetverti XIX veka: Poisk orientirov politicheskogo razvitiia. In: Vestnik Cheliabinskogo gosudarstvennogo universiteta. (2011) # 1. Istoriia. Vol. 43. Pp. 23–32

Tolkovyi slovar' russkogo iazyka S.I. Ozhegova i N.Iu. Shvedovoi. Moscow, 1993

Vattel, Emer de. Droit des gens; ou, Principes de la loi naturelle appliqués à la conduite et aux affaires des nations et des souverains. Vol. 1. Londres, 1758

V pamiat' gr. Mikhaila Mikhailovicha Speranskogo. 1772–1872. St. Petersburg, 1872

Refs suggest C18 orientat? rather than A's reign

Alexander Kaplunovsky

The Alexandrine Commission for the Compilation of Laws: In Search for Codifying Models for the Russian Empire

> It was in this institution that the fanciful and idyllic style so typical of Alexander I's early reign revealed itself with utmost clarity. There were high hopes laid on this commission, broadest and most vague objectives set for it, and when they had been achieved, the "commonweal," "general happiness," and "universal bliss" would have set in. Just as did many other undertakings of the same age, it suffered a devastating blow. It could never have achieved the expected results because the plan it had set out for itself was infeasible, and the de facto means that it had at its disposal were insufficient. Rather than the speculations that the commission's program was stock full of, the way of things was the ultimate triumphant.[1]

Such was the tough sentence that Aleksandr Nol'de, a lawyer and historian of law, pronounced to the 1804–26 Commission for the Compilation of Laws in his *Sketches on the History of Codifying Local Civil Law under Count Speransky* (1914). Nol'de's negative assessment rests on a simple formal criterion: the commission failed to set out or fully implement a complete legal code.[2] This criterion is usually taken as the ultimate measure of the commission's inefficiency and its lack of historical importance. However, in this article I will strive to demonstrate that the case of the Alexandrine Commission for the Compilation of Laws is among the most important in the history of law as well as legal consciousness and culture in imperial Russia. This institution can be seen as an experimental laboratory where—either ad hoc or with a goal in mind—the guiding principles and patterns of the "imperial rights regime" (as Jane Burbank described it)[3] were being formed. This regime, with its norms and practices, both represented and was contained by the Digest of the Laws

---

1 Nol'de. Ocherki po istorii kodifikacii mestnykh grazhdanskikh zakonov. Cit. Pt. I, Pp. 35–36.

2 Nol'de's actual frustrations applied to the missing codification of local laws in the Western—that is, the Polish and Lithuanian—provinces of the empire.

3 Burbank. An Imperial Rights Regime.

of the Russian Empire. The members of the commission could be simultaneously described as the subjects and actors of the Alexandrine reign, rich as it was in reform plans—but also in numerous political contradictions and environments.

At the very least, I can outline four fields of study relevant to this issue. The first one can be defined as a collective biography of legal experts as subjects and creators of meanings—a *thought collective* (in the words of Ludwik Fleck)[4] or an *epistemic community* (to refer to Burkart Holzner and Peter Haas).[5] This biography should be placed within the context of political communication and practices of power. One of the central pillars in Fleck's analytical model is the "social dimension" of the *thought collective*, the members of which are imagined as partakers of a certain stage in historical development of a field of thought, a culture, and a body of knowledge—in short, a specific style of thought. It is this dimension of the *thought collective* that, in my view, is of utmost research interest. I mean a reconstruction of a social and intellectual biography of both foreign and Russian legal experts who coexisted, communicated, and constructed ideas on the same platform. In the royal court and among the elites, they suggested and promoted universal principles, general norms, models, and discourses of the legal (or both legal and philosophical) foundations of their project of legal codification.

The second field comprises the concepts and codification projects. These projects of codifying or systematizing law balanced between the models of the *ulozhenie* and *svod*, gradually shifting toward the latter—that is, toward a compilation rather than a unified document. In other words, we can talk here of setting up a foundation for what Burbank, speaking primarily on the level of legal practices of the late empire, described as the *imperial rights regime*.[6] This regime can be described as both ad hoc governance and the legislative norms set up to support it. Both the governance and the norms were subject to the principle of flexible control of the imperial differences (and to the objectives thereof) and were mutually dependent, thus producing "different rules for different groups."[7]

---

4 It was on the basis of Fleck's theory that Thomas Kuhn later developed his concept of a "paradigm." See Fleck. The Genesis and Development of a Scientific Fact; Kuhn. The Structure of Scientific Revolutions.

5 The sociological concept of *epistemic communities*, originally suggested by Burkart Holzner, was later expanded by Peter Haas to cover network communities of experts and their influence over political decision-making in contemporary international relations. See Holzner. Reality Construction in Society; Holzner / Marx. Knowledge Application; Haas (Ed.). Knowledge, Power and International Policy Coordination.

6 Burbank. An Imperial Rights Regime.

7 Ibid.

However, I am not sure about Burbanks's view of the *imperial rights regime* or *imperial legal pluralism*, which refers to a "habitual practice" rather than an abstraction or theory: "The normality of legal pluralism in many forms—different rules for different groups, devolved authority to interpret and enforce them, sustenance of multiple and sometimes conflicting jurisdictions—explains in part why rulers, legal theorists, politically minded explorers, theologians, and other writers at that time do not seem to have needed a concept for it, or considered it worthy of debate. Legal pluralism was not an abstraction; it was a habit. More theoretically, it was a habitus."[8] The legal pluralism, as far as I can suggest, and the objective of flexible control of imperial difference were indeed part of the political and sociocultural realities in the Russian Empire (as well as in other empires). At the same time, due to the Russian Empire, they cannot be undeniably classified as byproducts of the ad hoc governance or of the routine of power politics. In the case of the Commission for the Compilation of Laws, we are in fact dealing with purposeful reflection over the relevant models of the rights regime and of the imperial legislation—*ulozhenie* versus *svod*, a unified versus compilative model. Simultaneously it is about its specific architects.

The third field is closely linked to the second, but, it focuses on reconstructing and describing the fundamental revision, identification, and systematization of the positive Russian legislation (the legislation in effect), organized by *branch of law*. Although legislation start-ups were shaped on an ad hoc basis over the whole eighteenth century, except for part of Elizabeth's and Catherine's reigns, legal experts and members of the Alexandrine commission were the first to conduct this work of systematization. They often found referential objects in continental European legal theories, systems, and models of codification—French, Prussian, or Habsburg—which they later appropriated.

Finally, the fourth research field opens the prospects of developing and modernizing the legal language and norms, as well as their interaction in the space of political authority. Draft versions of an *ulozhenie* were regularly presented to the emperor and debated at the Council of State and respective ministries. Printed at the Senate, they were sent to the governorates (*gubernii*) of Russia, and thus they circulated throughout the country and were discussed and incorporated within political discourses and the legal consciousness of the empire's political and administrative elites.

Having outlined both the basic issues and my analytical framework, I will limit my timespan, focusing only on the work of the Commission for the Compilation

---

8 Burbank / Cooper. Rules of Law, Politics of Empire. P. 279.

of Laws in the first decade of its existence. But to address this, it is important to take a brief look at the historiography of the problem.

1. "Codification proceeded only when Speranskii took over direction of the work…"[9]

> On that first evening Bolkonsky spent with him, having mentioned the Commission for the Revision of the Code of Laws, Speransky told him sarcastically that the Commission had existed for a hundred and fifty years, had cost millions, and had done nothing except that Rosenkampf had stuck labels on the corresponding paragraphs of the different codes.
>
> "And that is all the State has for the millions it has spent," said he. "We want to give the Senate new juridical powers, but we have no laws. That is why it is a sin for men like you, Prince, not to serve in these times!"
>
> Prince Andrei said that in order to do so, an education in jurisprudence was needed which he did not possess.
>
> "But nobody possesses it, so what would you have? It is a *circulusvitiosus* from which we must break a way out."
>
> A week later Prince Andrei was a member of the Committee on Army Regulations, and—what he had not at all expected—was chairman of a section of the Committee for the revision of the laws. At Speransky's request he took the first part of the Civil Code that was being drawn up, and with the aid of the *Code Napoléon* and the *Institutes of Justinian* he worked at formulating the section on Personal Rights.[10]

Although I do not aim to examine how reality and imagination are interrelated in a work of fiction, a very brief analysis of the fragment from Tolstoy's *War and Peace* quoted above will give us a glimpse of the problems that I have covered in my introduction to this chapter.

All the people mentioned in the passage, Prince Andrei Bolkonsky excepted, are historical characters. The "Commission for the Revision of the Code of Laws" that Tolstoy mentions is as historical as the Code Napoleon and the Institutiones Iustiniani.

---

9 Wortman. The Development of a Russian Legal Consciousness. P. 35.

10 Tolstoy. War and Peace. P. 463.

However, it was Mikhail Mikhailovich Speransky (1772–1839), rather than Prince Bolkonsky, who headed the commission in 1810–12 and who took part in setting up the Civil Code (*Grazhdanskoe Ulozhenie*). It was Speransky who, with his admiration of the French practice of legal codification, borrowed profusely from the Code Napoleon and sometimes even directly compiled its fragments to form a related segment of the Russian Civil Code. The fictional Bolkonsky, having immersed himself in legislative work in the commission, lost both his interest and his faith in the ultimate success of this undertaking after only a few months. Frustrated and disappointed, he withdrew from the political stage into his private life. The real-life Speransky, for his part, was a vigorous and indefatigable reformer and a pragmatic visionary who was soon consumed by the administrative realities of the "autocratic governance of the monarch." In May 1812, almost overnight, he was deprived of all his senior offices as a "French spy" and exiled from St. Petersburg, first to Nizhny Novgorod, and then, via Penza, to Siberia. In 1821 Alexander I pardoned Speransky and allowed him to return to St. Petersburg, where he continued his legal studies and legislative work. However, this time he did not attempt to set out an "ideal code of laws" for Russia, limiting himself instead to compiling and systematizing the corpus of positive law in Russia, unifying it into the *Svod* (Digest of Laws).

Returning to *War and Peace,* we should pay attention to one thing that the fictional Bolkonsky and the historical Speransky (as well as his fictional version) had in common: neiter of them had ever studied law or could be classified as legal experts. This background was what set them apart from another man mentioned in the fragment, Gustav Adolph von Rosenkampff (1764–1832). He is portrayed in the novel as a Baltic German, a narrow-minded official, sitting in his control room, perplexed by the grandness of the reformers' objectives—in contrast to the magnificent Speransky. In real life, Rosenkampff was descended from a Swedish noble family, graduated from the school of law at Leipzig University, worked for some time at the Collegium of Foreign Affairs in St. Petersburg, and then for many years served as a *Landrichter* (associate judge) and then a judge at a district (*uezd*) court in the Governorate of Livonia. In 1802, Russia's first minister of justice, Gavriil Romanivich Derzhavin (1743–1816), and the ober-procurator of the Senate, Osip Petrovich Kozodavlev (1753–1815), co-opted him to work on codifying legislation and legal reform in the Russian Empire. Later, the emperor and one of his closest associates, Nikolai Nikolaevich Novosil'cev (1761–1838), involved him in their separate discussions on forthcoming legislative tasks.

However, in the above passage from Tolstoy, reality and fiction overlap rather than diverge. As scholars including Viktor Shklovsky have shown,[11] Tolstoy's novel exhibits a good understanding of Alexander I's reign in general, and of the history of his legal reforms in particular. Speransky's reform projects, almost in their pure form, are woven into the fabric of Tolstoy's literary narrative. I used the word "pure" because Tolstoy's plot reproduced, in an almost unadulterated manner, both the historical knowledge and the myths that had been constructed and represented in opinion journalism, memoirs, art, painting, and historiography since the 1840s.[12] These myths typically featured a defense of Speransky as both a prominent reformer and a single-handed creator and architect of the Digest of Laws of the Russian Empire (see fig. 1).

11 Shklovkij. Material i stil v romane Tolstogo "Voina i mir." See also Ungurianu. The Use of Historical Sources in "War and Peace"; Feuer. Tolstoy and the Genesis of "War and Peace." P. 248.

12 These myths were started by Speransky himself in an 1821 memorandum to Alexander I titled *Obozrenie del dlia komissii zakonov* (A Review of the State of Affairs for the Commission of Laws): Otdel rukopisei Rossiiskoi nacional'noi biblioteki (hereafter, OR RNB). F. 731. M.M. Speransky. D. 908. "Komissiia sostavleniia zakonov. Obzor raboty ..., predstavlennyi Aleksandru I za 1804–1821 gg. 30.09.1821." Ll. 1–11, and also in *Obozrenie istoricheskikh svedenii o Svode zakonov* (A Review of Historical Evidence on the Digest of Laws, 1833). Among the biographies of Speransky, several deserve a special mention: Turgeneff. La Russieet les russes; Dmitriev. O zaslugakh grafa Speranskogo; Korf. Zhizn' grafa Speranskogo; Novakovskii. Biograficheskie ocherki; Chistovich. V pamiat grafa Mikhaila Mikhailovicha Speranskogo; Seredonin. Graf M.M. Speransky. In art, painting, and literature, see, for example: the engraving by Koz'ma Repinskii, Speransky's associate and secretary (see fig. 1); *Nicholas I Placing the Sash of the Order of St. Andrew on Count Speransky* (1880), a painting by the renowned battle and historical scene painter Aleksei Kivshenko; and the portrayals of Speransky on the Millennium of Russia monument in Novgorod (1862), and in Leo Tolstoy's *War and Peace* (1868) and Dmitry Merezhkovsky's *Alexander I* (1911–12).

Figure 1. *An engraving by Koz'ma Repinskii. The explication says: "On January 19, 1833, at the general session at the Council of State, His Majesty Emperor Nicholas Pavlovich, after the final consideration and approval of the Empire's Digest of Laws, rising from His seat, beckoned the Digest's compiler, Mikhail Mikhailovich Speransky, embraced him, and having taken off the star of the Order of St. Andrew, deigned to place it on him as a sign of His deepest gratitude for this immense work"* (GOSUDARSTVENNYI SOVET).

Even from its own time, the Alexandrine Commission for the Compilation of Laws has been historicized as an opposition between victimized hero (Mikhail Speransky) and triumphant mediocrity (Gustav Rosenkampff). The commission itself served more of a background role than a primary one. Other actors—if mentioned at all—appeared only insofar as they had anything to do with the narrative of Speransky's fall, pigeonholed as either his "sympathizers" or "treacherous conspirators."

Since the publication of Speransky's first biography, by Modest Baron von Korff, historiographers have treated the 1808–12 intermezzo of the Russian Tribonian's tenure as head of the commission as the institution's climax, one that was followed by tragic collapse. Korff, who worked on the Digest of Laws under Speransky in the Second Section, HIM (His Imperial Majesty's) Own Chancellery, simultaneously and retroactively managed to annihilate the prehistory and competing narratives of this work. Ultimately, he imagined Speransky as the Digest's only architect and inspiring force. As for Rosenkampff , the commission's creator and long-time de facto president, Korff admits his "sharp wit" and "large theoretical knowledge." Still, the picture that Korff (who relied on eyewitnesses' accounts) drew of Rosenkampff is that of an ambitious and vengeful schemer-cum-courtier, a German alien in Russia who knew neither the country nor its language and, consequently, had no idea of the legislation then in effect—that is, one who was ignorant of what should have been the primary focus of his studies:

> Rosenkampf, who originally had been totally unacquainted with our law in effect, to say nothing of its sources, had to devote almost all of his time to studying it. Having fired most of the Russian officials from the commission, he replaced them with Germans and Frenchmen and a number of translators, whom he sorely needed, as he knew no Russian. He went from one policy to another: embraced the historical school, drew tables of contents and marginalia for the new Code [Ulozhenie] as one of the theories prescribed, or fully immersed himself in comparative studies of foreign legislations—[whatever he did], he in fact created nothing new, but time and again would redo everything. His commission went along in the same slow and fruitless fashion as his previous ones. The public could not help wondering how a man who knew neither the country's laws, nor its customs and mores, nor even its language, could of all others have been selected for the task of setting up the Code of Laws for the world's greatest empire. It was at this moment that Speransky suddenly entered [the stage].[13]

This view has made its way, though in a less emotional or over-dramatized form, into the mythologems, uncritical interpretations, and narrow views that popu-

13 Korf. Zhisn Grafa Speranskogo. Vol. 1. Pp. 147 f., 157; Vol. 2. Pp. 30 f.; Korf. Deiateli i uchastniki v padenii Speranskogo; Bychkov. Speraskii v 1808–1811 gg.

late key texts of contemporary historiography. Marginalizing the chief protagonists of the commission's narrative, as well as its history, researchers are prone to take a leap from Catherine the Great's Legislative Commission (*Ulozhennaya Komissiya*) to the Digest of Laws—as can be seen from several examples. Richard Wortman, for instance, claims that codification in the commission moved ahead only after Speransky had taken control of its work in 1808. When Rosenkampff replaced him in 1812, says Wortman, the commission focused on the technical work of collecting and revising laws. Wortman (mistakenly) holds that the commission was set up in 1808 and that Rosenkampff did not become its head until 1812.[14] William Whisenhunt's treatment of the commission's history is even more recognizably simplified: "The commission was reorganized in 1804 and fell under the direction of Baron Gustav Rosenkampf. However, he [...] was unprepared for such work. Rosenkampf was a Baltic German who knew little of 'Russian law, Russian conditions and even Russian language.'"[15] The quote in this passage by Whisenhunt refers us directly to a book by Marc Raeff.[16] In his turn, Raeff's narrative is based on the Korff biography and the memoirs of Speransky's closest associates, Ludwig Heinrich von Jakob (1759–1827) and Nikolai Stepanovich Il'inskii (1759–1846).[17]. This completes the circle. Only at first glance, it could seem paradoxical that both Raeff and Whisenhunt elsewhere describe the personality and role of Rosenkampff in a more complex way.[18] His oversimplified and clearly negative portrayal in histories of the commission, as developed by nineteenth-century biographers and historiographers, thus stands even more impressive. Neither of the contemporary historians (Raeff and Whisenhunt) has offered any comment on such a glaring contradiction within their respective narratives.

---

14 Wortman. The Development. P. 35. This mistake has persisted in the Russian edition of the monograph. See: [Wortman] Uortman. Vlastiteli i sud'i. P. 95.

15 Whisenhunt. In Search of Legality. P. 45.

16 Cf.: "Baron Rosenkampf, though he had received excellent training in jurisprudence in Germany, and was an able and learned man, was quite unsuited for the task, as he was not familiar with Russian Law, Russian conditions and even Russian language. He was an ardent proponent of the historical and practical approach of codification. [...] Quite understandably, as a Balt, he wanted to prevent the absorption of local traditions in an uniform imperial code. [...] The Commission's time was idled away in useless researches and abstract definitions, without any concrete results emerging from all this labor." Raeff. Michael Speransky. P. 67.

17 Jakob. Denkwürdgkeiten aus meinem Leben; Il'inskii. Iz Zapisok.

18 Raeff. Michael Speransky. Pp. 38 f., 65 f.; Whisenhunt. In Search of Legality. Pp. 47 f.

Some historians of law, however, tend to describe Rosenkampff and his work in a more neutral and pragmatic tone.[19] As a rule, they address the history of the Alexandrine Commission for the Compilation of Laws while discussing the attempts to set up a civil or criminal code or to systematize the body of constitutional law.

Among prerevolutionary legal historians, two (Petr Maikov and Alexander Makarov) stand out as having paid more attention to the institutional history of the commission and to the projects of the code of laws developed by its staffmembers—as well as to the actors themselves. Makarov, who analysed Rosenkampff's draft memo on the *Foundations of the Laws of the Russian Empire* (1804)[20] in a 1926 article,[21] concluded that it was the first attempt to provide a systematized and legally verified exposition of the legal foundations of Russia's statehood. This document was modeled after the General State Laws for the Prussian States (Allgemeines Landrecht für die Preußischen Staaten).[22] In the case of Maikov, two of his works deserve mention. Both works were byproducts of his history of the Second Section of HIM Own Chancellery:[23] a Russian translation of Rosenkampff's memoirs and a concise history of the Commission for the Compilation of Laws. Maikov and Makarov were the first to postulate that both Rosenkampff's codification plan and the preparatory work of the commission members who had collected and systematized the existing legislation contributed to the future Digest of Laws. Both were responsible not only for its

19 Pakhman. Istoriia kodofikacii grazhdanskogo prava; Romanovich-Slavatinskii. Sistema russkogo gosudarstvennogo prava.; Latkin. Lekcii po istorii russkogo prava; Tagancev. Russkoe ugolovnoe pravo; Filippov. Uchebnik istorii russkogo prava; Feldshtein. Glavnye techeniia v istorii ugolovnogo prava v Rossii.

20 Rossiiskii Gosudarstvennyi Istoricheskii Arkhiv (hereafter, RGIA). F. 1260. Komissia sostavleniia zakonov. Op. 1. D. 177. "Poekty i status quo o gosudarstvennom postanovlenii ili zakonakh vnutrennego ustroistva. 1804 g."; Ibid. D. 179. "Proekty uzakonenii vnutrennego gosudarstvennogo upravelniia. 1804 g."; Ibid. D. 180. "Erster Teil des Gesetzbuchs. Staatsverfassung des Russischen Reichs. Erster Abschnitt. 1804 g."

21 Makarov. Entwurf der Verfassungsgesetze des Russischen Reiches.

22 On the history of legal codification in Prussia and the introduction of the General State Laws, see: Schäfer. Juristische Germanistik; Krause. Geschichte der Justiz- und Verwaltungsbildung in Preußen und Deutschland; Schröder. Das Verhältnis von Rechtswissenschaft; Kuhli. Carl Gottlieb Svarez und das Verhältnis von Herrschaft und Recht; Idem. Power and Law in Enlightened Absolutism; Koselleck. Preußen zwischen Reform und Revolution.

23 Maikov. Vtoroe otdelenie Sobstvennoi Ego Imperatorskogo Velichestva kanceliarii.

concept and its founding principles but also for its relatively fast compilation and publication.[24]

In the last decade, Makarov's and Maikov's arguments and empirical findings were examined by a new generation of Russian scholars, especially legal historians. Among others. T.Iu. Borisova, S.V. Kodan, R.S. Taborin, and D.V. Gorozhankina worked on the archival collections of the Commission for the Compilation of Laws, as well as the personal files and archives of its staff members.[25] An honorable mention should go to D.V. Gorozhankina, who in her thesis provided a more detailed description and analysis of the commission's projects of codifying and reforming the empire's system of court procedures.[26] This last case, until recently unknown among historiographers, is of utmost importance both for reconstructing and analyzing the commission's work in light of the problems mentioned above.

For her part, Borisova, relying on the analytical power and tools of *Begriffsgeschichte* and historical semantics, suggested an original interpretation of how the legal models of the *svod* (digest) and *ulozhenie* (code) correlated within the Russian Empire's legal system. Borisova sees the general notion of the code (*ulozhenie*) and the particular codification efforts as stemming directly from the universalist ideas of the Enlightenment. As such, they became the pillar of the absolutist policies of European monarchies, aimed at setting up a regular *policey* state. In the early nineteenth century, the *svod* and the Digest model rose in Russia as a replacement for the pan-European codificational "fashion" of the previous century, in tune with the coming era of official nationalism and of Russia's political and cultural emancipation. The Digest, as a "national approach to codification," was supposed to help preserve the "traditions" and the Russian legal norms and corpus of laws, which had come together historically and were sanctified by time. Borisova dates this "turn to the Digest model" to 1812.[27] Unfortunately, though the

---

24 MAIKOV. Baron Gustav Andreevich Rozenkampf; IDEM. Komissia sostavleniia zakonov pri imperatorakh Pavle I i Aleksandre I.

25 BORISOVA. Russian National Legal Tradition; IDEM. The Digest of Laws of the Russian Empire; GOROZHANKINA. Istoriko-pravovoi analiz sistematizacii ugolovno-processual'nogo zakonodatelstva; KODAN / TABORIN. Nesostoiavshaiasia kodifikaciia grazhdanskogo zakonodatelstva Rossii. TABORIN. Sistematizaciia grazhdanskogo zakonodatelstva.

26 GOROZHANKINA. Istoriko-pravovoi analiz sistematizacii. Pp. 17–52.

27 BORISOVA. Russian National Legal Tradition; see also SEVASTIANOV. K istorii kodifikacii russkogo prava v pervoi treti XIX veka. Like Borisova, Sevastianov dates the debates on codification models to 1811–12.

analytical tools of historical semantics and discourse analysis have often proved historiographically productive, Borisova only selectively applies them on an intentionally narrowed-down (and thus inadequate) empirical basis. The historical decision to take up a syncreticist model, combining the elements of *svod* and *ulozhenie* and preserving within it a body of autochthonous legislation draped in the rhetoric of "traditions," belongs to an earlier period. The emperor and his "young associates" from the Unofficial Committee chose this way, rather than the writing out of new codes steeped in natural philosophy and rationalism, as early as 1803, and the work in this project began the following year.

2. The "Lawful Monarchy" of the Silent Sphinx

Throughout the eighteenth century, there had been increasing conceptualization and permament will among the political elites to modernize the system of government in Russia after that of the cameralist monarchies of continental Europe. This project was (though not necessarily) combined with the creation and implementation of codified laws.[28] However, these plans encountered a number of challenges and had to deal with the specific configurations of power in Russia. In the eighteenth century, codification projects were entrusted to a number of commissions. By the time of Alexander I's accession to the throne, all this work, rather than becoming irrelevant or repellant, had become, if not a systemic issue in politics, than definitely a practical one, and a serious challenge.

Taking the throne, Alexander I promised to establish a lawful monarchy "according to the laws and wishes" of his "beldame" Catherine the Great.[29] This promise was verbalized in an official motto of his reign, which was engraved on golden and silver commemorative coronation medals: "Law is the guarantee of happiness for everyone" (see fig. 2).

28 See Kuhli. Carl Gottlieb Svarez; Mertens. Gesetzgebungskunst im Zeitalter der Kodifikationen.

29 PSZ I. Vol. 26. № 19779, 12.03.1801. "O konchine imperatora Pavla I, i o vstuplenii na prestol imperatora Aleksandra I."

Figure 2. The coronation medal of Alexander I.

Source: Private archive of the author.

In the first months of the new reign, discussions were focused on (radical) reforms of the state system, governance, and civil rights. In addition, due to the circumstances of the emperor's accession, discussions centered on the stabilization of royal power, on alliances and plots, and on the struggle for influence on the young monarch between the old and new "parties" at the court. Enthusiasm for reform soon gave way to the concept of gradual reformation, pragmatism, and the routine of state governance. Thus, the monarch's intention to limit his autocracy and to provide legal foundations and civil rights to his subjects (as sketched in Aleksandr Vorontsov's "The Charter to the People of Russia")[30] was never translated into reality. The codification or systematization of the existing body of law was, however, considered a relevant and attainable goal. There was no strong correlation or interdependence between liberalization of political and social order and codification. The Unofficial Committee decied to begin the reformation process not by providing a constitution but by creating and establishing a new code of laws in its first session, June 1801.[31]

But at that time, Alexander I and his supporters had neither any plan of codification (or systematization) nor personal resources to implement it, nor even a clear understanding of how these models work. The June 6, 1801, Royal Decree on

30 For more detail, see Sergei Polskoy's article in this volume, Pp. 135–166, as well as Zakharov. Rossiiskii i zarubezhnyi konstitucionalizm. Vol. 1. Pp. 17–34; Vol. 2. Pp. 34–60.

31 Nikolai Mikhailovich. Velikii Kniaz'. Graf Pavel Aleksandrovich Stroganov. P. 61.

Reorganizing the Commission for the Compilation of Laws of the Russian Empire (a commission originally set up by Paul I in 1796)[32] remained purely declarative. It focused more on articulating the existing legislation and court procedures, acknowledged and criticized by all levels of Russian society, than on offering programs and suggesting a new code:

> I have always known that, from the publication of the Ulozhenie [the Code of 1649] to our days—that is, for about a century and a half—the laws that the legislative power had issued in a varied and frequently contradictory manner—and usually for the sake of specific causes rather than general concerns of the state—had no connection with each other, no unity of purpose, no permanence in their effect. From this came a general confusion of the rights and duties of every person; darkness descended on the judge and accused alike; the execution of laws turned impotent; and they were prone to change at the first impulse of caprice or arbitrariness.[33]

The same decree assigned the administrative position in the reorganized commission to Count Petr Vladimirovich Zavadovsky (1739–1812), a move that the monarch and his "young associates" saw at the time as strategic. The task of codification demanded, as the decree put it, "a man who, in addition to vast knowledge of this sphere, would have sufficient awareness of the previous actions of the commission."[34] A high-profile dignitary in Catherine II's reign, Zavadovsky was quite experienced as a reformer and legislator. From 1784 to 1797, he headed the Commission for the Establishment of Public Schools, and, besides being a senator, he also presided over the ad hoc Commission for Drafting a Project to Reduce Clerical Duties in the 1780s.[35] Behind this unassuming name lay a large body of problems related to increasing the efficiency of paperwork within the system of state governance. Further (and something that often escapes scholars' attention), this commission also dealt with the modernization of Russian judicial practice, which was interwoven with the administration due to the conjoining of powers in the empire.

The task that the monarch now entrusted to Zavadovsky was initially regarded as an automatic revision of the existing legislation and of the legislative projects stored in the archives. It did not, however, exclude borrowings from "exemplary

---

32 PSZ I. Vol. 24. № 17697, 30.12.1796. "Ob imenovanii Komisii dlia sochineniia proekta Novogo Ulozheniia: Komissieiu dlia sostavleniia Zakonov." Op. cit. P. 258.

33 PSZ I. Vol. 26. № 19904, 6.06.1801. "O upravlenii Komissiei sostavleniia zakonov grafu Zavadovskomu." Op. cit. P. 683.

34 Ibid. P. 684.

35 Listovskii. Graf P.V. Zavadovskii; Golubcov. K biografii grafa P.V. Zavadovskogo; Khoteenkov / Cherneta. Pervyi ministr narodnogo prosveshcheniia; Kusber. Eliten- und Volksbildung im Zarenreich. Pp. 183–212.

legislation of other [foreign] nations, neighboring our lands, or those more famous for their enlightenment or for their best legal provisions."[36] Although the emperor's decree did not set a deadline for completing the codification, the text makes clear that it was to be completed in a few months. The proceedings of the Commission for the Compilation of Laws under Emperors Paul I and Alexander I, albeit very uninformative, do testify to the fact that its work somewhat intensified during the several months of Zavadovsky's presidency.[37]

Zavadovsky was quite right in an early report to the emperor when he observed that Russia had never had either its own "legal scholars" (*uchonykh zakonovedcev*) nor professionally trained lawyers and judges. The legislative material, he reported, was scattered over thousands of decrees, which "cannot be comprehended even by people best endowed with memory."[38] He was convinced that codification must not be equated with paperwork: "Lawmaking demands incessant reflection rather than [pure] activity." Zavadovsky pointed to the absence of a legal foundation for the codification of documents consistent with the ideals of the Enlightenment and that would ensure the subjects' welfare:

> There are only two laws that exalt Russia: the first, of Empress Elizabeth concerning the abolition of the death penalty, and the second one, of Catherine the Great on the prohibition of torture. … The laws can be brought to action only when the power is unified, but it should be an action of prudence, justice, and order; good civil laws are the highest gift that princes can leave to their peoples; they are the source of good morals, the protection of property, the establishment of public and private tranquility; they envelop the life of every citizen and protect with their touch his every step, providing him with comfort.[39]

---

36 PSZ I. Vol. 26. № 19904… P. 685.

37 RGIA. F. 1259. Komissia dlia sostavleniia zakonov. Op. 1. D. 1. "Delo ob uchrezhdenii Komissii sostavleniia zakonov, opredelenie zadach, naznachenii chlenov i sluzhashchikh."

38 RGIA. F. 994. Fond grafov Mordvinovykh. Op. 2. D. 122. "Pismo gr. Petra Vasil'evicha Zavadovskogo Aleksandru I o prichinakh zamedleniia raboty Komissii po sostavleniiu zakonov. 1802 g." L. 1 ob.; On the prereform system of judicial procedure and law enforcement, see Baberowski. Autokratie und Justiz. Pp. 11–37; [Wortman] Uortman. Vlastiteli i sud'i. Pp. 53–92, 236–42. Novel research, providing a detailed reconstruction and description of the daily life of provincial officials and governorate-level administrators in the first half of the nineteenth century, can be found in: Schattenberg. Die korrupte Provinz? (with a detailed overview of the historiography of the topic); Biktasheva. Antropologiia vlasti; Idem. Kazanskie gubernatory.

39 RGIA. F. 994. Op. 2. D. 122. L. 2.

Zavadovsky concluded that the "dilapidated building" of the Russian laws then in existence, "created for [a people of] different morals and in a different time," could not form the basis for the new code. He recommended that the emperor set up and approve, point by point, a new code, modeled after its "best European counterparts." At the time, the commission had at its disposal the Prussian code of 1794 (The General State Laws for the Prussian States). It included the norms of civil, family, criminal, procedural, and public law,[40] which other available codes did not do.[41]

These remarks by Zavadovsky, along with comments made by Frédéric-César de La Harpe (1754–1838), were presumably the basis for the decisions of the Unofficial Committee that Pavel Aleksandrovich Stroganov (1774–1817) duly entered in the journal of its proceedings on March 10 and 17, 1802. Adam Jerzy Czartoryski (1770–1861) and N.N. Novosil'cev recommended seeking advice from leading European lawyers and legal experts in drafting the code, though no specific names were recorded.[42] This was the only time that the issue of legal codification was brought up at the sessions of the Unofficial Committee. In this regard, it is important to note that, even at this early stage, the reformers came up with the idea of preceding codification (*ulozhenie*) with a collection of laws (*svod*) systematized by branch of law.[43]

However, the implementation of this plan did not begin until two years later. With the new ministries established, ministers and their deputies appointed, and the spheres of influence and competence demarcated, the drafting of a detailed codification plan commenced. During 1803, the drafting (and the search for qualified staff to make it possible) slowly passed from the zone of "common concern" of all members of the Unofficial Committee under the control of Novosil'cev and

40 It is important to note, however, that the introduction of the General State Laws in Prussia did not lead to the abolition of the whole corpus, the specific norms of common law (*ius commune*), or Saxon law. Outside the Polish provinces of Prussia, the General State Laws enjoyed a subsidiary (secondary) status—that is, the norms could be used in cases that were undefined or untouched in traditional legal sources. See Kuhli: Carl Gottlieb Svarez; Idem. Power and Law in Enlightened Absolutism; Krause. Geschichte der Justiz- und Verwaltungsbildung; Schröder. Das Verhältnis von Rechtswissenschaft.

41 For example, see the *Codex Theresianus* (1766) and *Allgemeines bürgerliches Gesetzbuch* (Josephinisches Gesetzbuch 1787) in the Habsburg Empire; and the *Codex iuris Bavarici* (1751), the *Codex Iuris Bavarici Iudiciarii* (1753) and the *Codex Maximilianeus Bavaricus Civilis* (1756) in Bavaria.

42 See proceedings of the sessions of the Unofficial Committee in: Nikolai Mikhailovich. Velikii Kniaz'. Graf Pavel Aleksandrovich Stroganov. Pp. 184, 193–194.

43 Ibid. P. 193.

the Ministry of Justice.[44] The committee realized that the theoretical and practical work of codification needed the input of "appropriate people" such as legal experts and lawyers who had both professional training and experience in judicial practice, rather than that of statesmen, widely educated scholars and dignitaries, or representatives of the estates of the empire. Despite the deficiency of such experts in Russia, they soon managed to find a candidate who could become a de facto head of codification work. Found among "their own" lawyers was none other than G.A. Rosenkampff.[45]

Rosenkampff was a practicing lawyer, but he was not, in the strict sense of the word, skilled as a legal scholar. However, he was apparently familiar enough with the theory of law. Moreover, his years at Leipzig (1782–85) fell during the period of codification in Prussia, with the respective projects publicized and widely discussed by legal experts and practicing lawyers on the pages of Prussian periodicals. Though the School of Law at Leipzig University had by that time lost its former fame, one of the professors who taught Rosenkampff was Christian Gottlob Biener (1748–1828). At the university, Biener lectured in natural law and the *ius gentium*. Biener was, along with Gustav von Hugo (1764–1844), one of the predecessors of the historical school in legal studies and a vocal opponent of codifications based on philosophical maxims and theories of natural law and rationalism, a view that affected the codification models and legal interpretations of his disciple Rosenkampff. In his comments on the famous cabinet decree of April 14, 1780, whereby Frederick II initiated the Prussian codification, Biener expressed his doubts about eliminating the foreign law—that is, the *ius commune*—among the German states and establishing a general national code for German lands. He claimed that all the universities, their law schools, and their graduating lawyers owed their existence solely to foreign codes (i.e., Roman law).[46]

---

44 Liubeznikov. Nikolai Nikolaevich Novosil'cov. Pp. 34–62; OR RNB. F. 526. Novosil'cov N.N. Op. 1. D. 4. Bumagi otnosiashchiesia do Komissii sostavleniia zakonov 1803 g.; ASPb.II RAN. F. 176. N.N. Novosil'cev. Op. 1. D. 1. "Uchrezhdenie Komissii Sostavleniia Zakonov i trudy sei komissii."

45 Maikov. Baron Gustav Andreevich Rozenkampf. Vol. 120. Pp. 140–43; Makarov: Entwurf der Verfassungsgesetze. Pp. 209–33.

46 See: Biener. Bedenklichkeiten bey Verbannung. Issuing the decree in the wake of the "case of Arnold the miller," Frederick II hoped that after the introduction of new laws, written in an understandable (i.e., German) language, the "whole current corporation of lawyers will be sent packing," deprived of "their elaborate clutter." After that, the king planned to concentrate on supporting merchants and men of art, who were expected to be most helpful for the general welfare of the state. See: Abdruck der allerhöchsten Königlichen Cabinetts=Order die Verbesserung des Justiz-Wesens

Rosenkampff's attracted the attention of the emperor and the members of the Unofficial Committee through a summer 1802 memo on reforming the judicial system and codifying the criminal and civil legislation of the empire.[47] The memorandum was drawn at the request of G.R. Derzhavin and O.P. Kozodavlev. Kozodavlev, who introduced Rosekampff to Derzhavin, had graduated from the School of Law at Leipzig ten years earlier than Rozenkampf and had known him since the latter's service in the Collegium of Foreign Affairs. Derzhavin, for his part, became Rosenkampff's patron and introduced him to the emperor in October 1802, soon after being appointed minister of justice. During this first, short audience, Alexander I invited his interlocutor to discuss his legislative ideas in detail with Novosil'cev and, in addition, to draft a project for reorganizing the Senate.

In his memoirs, Rosenkampff wrote that at this stage, his conversations with Novosil'cev focused on the problems of rights and privileges of the estates, judicial reform, and codification and reorganization of the Senate: "First of all, I was to learn Novosil'cev's opinions on this matter, but I could not examine the whole issue in every detail shortly, nor comprehend the idea that guide the tsar's councillor, whether he wished to reorganize the government as it was or continue toward constitutional monarchy; whether he wanted the whole nation to have liberty, all estates to participate in law-making and enjoy civil rights—or were these to be open for only some of them?"[48] These issues were of serious concern for Rosenkampff not so much because of his own political beliefs (he was a supporter of constitutional monarchy and abolition of the serfdom), but rather because of their practical importance for drafting the civil code. From his discussions with Novosil'cev, Rosenkampff concluded that two limiting preconditions were to be followed in the future codification work: the establishment of a constitutional monarchy and the abolition of serfdom were no longer on the agenda. A complex system of civil rights and judicial procedures would have to be worked out—a system that would have to fit into the hierarchy and variety of estate statuses, as well as into the confessional and ethnocultural differences between the empire's subjects and their communities.

---

betreffend. Potsdam, den 14. April 1780. In: Novum Corpus Constitutionum Prussico-Brandenburgensium praecipue Marchicarum. Vol. 6. Berlin 1781. Col. 1935–1944, Cit. Col. 1942; see also. Luebke. Frederick the Great and the Celebrated Case of the Millers Arnold. Pp. 379–408; Diesselhorst. Die Prozesse des Müllers Arnold.

47 The memorandum was published by N.M. Karamzin in *Vestnik Evropy:* G[ustav] R[ozenkampff]: Nekotorye zamechaniia na ugolovnye i grazhdanskie zakony v otnoshenii k Rossii. In: Vestnik Evropy. (1803) # 2. Pp. 141–56.

48 Maikov. Baron Gustav Andreevich Rozenkampf. Vol. 120. Cit. P. 150.

In summer and autumn 1803, the private meetings came to include not only Rosenkampff and Novosil'cev but other members of the Unofficial Committee, including Kochubei, Czartoryski and Stroganov. Rosenkampff, among others, noted in his memoirs that the men continued their discussions of such fundamental issues as lawful monarchy, abolition of serfdom, and civil liberties. But more attention was paid to specific reforms of the state system, already partially underway, as well their models and corrections, such as the establishment of the ministries, the reorganization of the Senate, and the codification of the law in effect. Rosenkampff's status at the meetings gradually changed from that of an "invited" commentator to that of a full-fledged participant and colleague. Simultaneously, he refined his model for future codification. Rosenkampff had a decisive conversation with the emperor on July 22, 1803:

> Every country, Sir, has its local foundations. The new code cannot be compiled other than in the way that the foundations of the existing law allow it. This is the law already known [to all] and the one Your Majesty would deign to order corrections and changes in, as You see fit. A code is nothing but a book of laws. Since the specific acts and law [in general] were not declared at once, but developed gradually, in the course of time; and since nobody can foresee the future circumstances, it is necessary to begin compiling the code on its existent foundations. [...] Your Majesty knows the Code of France. It does not include any rules that would not have existed for a long time in the law of some French provinces. One should also bear in mind that in both France and Germany, jurisprudence has been a scholarly field for centuries. In such countries it is easy to comprehend the content and the meaning of the variety of provisions in the code. In a small number of articles, their code covers everything that can be found scattered over the multitudinous body of previous legislation. But I am afraid that such an abstract work will not be understood in Russia. If we want to make the code understandable, we should [first] expose the sources wherefrom its provisions have been taken, and let time do the rest.[49]

Apparently, this idea was akin to the recommendations given by Alexander I's liberal and republican-minded tutor, F.-S. de La Harpe, who stated in 1801 that it was not preferable to force the endowment of all the subjects of the empire with equal civil rights and political involvement, nor to constitutionally limit the power of the monarch.[50] Among other things, Rosenkampff's idea managed to harmonize the horizons of political imagination with the field of real-life politics. Eventually, Alexander I endorsed Rosenkampff's suggestion and charged him with drafting the codification program and its "action plan." Simultaneously, the

49 Ibid. Pp. 171–72.

50 F.-S. Lagarp–Aleksandru 3 sentiabria 1801 (Sankt-Petersburg). In: Andreev / Tozato-Rigo (Eds.). Imperator Aleksandr I i Frederik-Sezar Lagarp. Pp. 394–97.

institutional base for the implementation of the project was being prepared. At the end of October 1803, the Commission for the Compilation of Laws was removed from the command of the Senate and subsumed under the Ministry of Justice,[51] with Novosil'cev appointed deputy minister.[52] Four months later, on February 28, 1804, the next step followed—the previous commission was dissolved, and a new one was established in its stead.[53]

Thus, long before the so-called codification dispute between Anton Friedrich Thibaut (1772–1840) and Friedrich Carl von Savigny (1779–1861), which was followed in Prussia and other German states by a turn toward a historical understanding of the law as the treasury of "national spirit,"[54] in the Russian Empire the guiding principle of codification (or, to be more precise, systematization) was found in what P. Maikov deemed a "historical and practical" approach.

3. The Commission for the Compilation of Laws: Its Personnel and Structure

> ... Of its [the Commission's] staff members, almost everyone did nothing, and moreover, there was hardly anyone capable of doing anything.[55]

> We were sent out of the main house and housed in a courtyard building, while the main one was taken by the Commission for the Compilation of Laws—a phantasm that a well-known mountebank used to fool the government with [...] When the new institution got hold of the house, the sign was to be changed. It now had to fit in three words: *Komissia Sostavlenia Zakonov* [Commission for the Compilation of Laws].The latter two words did not fit, but since Rosenkampff had suggested that the work of the commission should be over in three years, to save funds

51 On October 10, 1803, Petr Vasil'evich Lopukhin replaced Derzhavin as minister of justice.

52 PSZ I. Vol. 27. № 20995, 21.10.1803. "O bytii Komissii sostavleniia zakonov pod upravleniem ministra iusticii." P. 937.

53 PSZ I. Vol. 27. № 21187, 28.02.1804. "O preobrazovanii Komissii sostavleniia zakonov." Pp. 160–73.

54 See Thibaut. Über die Notwendigkeit eines allgemeinen bürgerlichen Rechts; Savigny. Vom Beruf unserer Zeit für Gesetzgebung und Rechtswissenschaft; Kaufmann. Anton Friedrich Justus Thibaut; Wendehorst. Ist der Kodifikationsstreit entschieden? Pp. 7–35; Fortunato. Vom römisch-gemeinen Recht zum Bürgerlichen Gesetzbuch. Pp. 327–38.

55 Korf. Zhisn grafa Speranskogo. Vol. 2. P. 312.

> it was decided to attach a piece of wooden board at each end of the sign. So it was done, and at first nobody noticed, but in about ten years, the wood rotted away, together with a letter at each end. *Komissia ostavlenia zakonov* [Commission for Abandoning Laws]—the sign read for several years, to the amusement of passersby.[56]

If we believe the anecdote reported by Nikolai Ivanovich Grech (1787–1867) in his memoirs, included by Dmitry Merezhkovsky in his historical novel *Alexander I* (1911),[57] and also featured in a number of semiacademic collections of "Russian literary anecdotes,"[58] then we find ourselves under the impression that the Commission for the Compilation of Laws was a commonplace in its contemporaries' cultural and historical memory. This commonplace, it would seem, was only to be remembered as the "Commission for Abandoning Laws" and "a mountebank's phantasm."

Concerning the personnel policy in the Commission for the Compilation of Laws, staff member Ludwig Heinrich von Jakob (served 1809–16), wrote in his memoirs that recruitment was done in an "extremely careless manner" ("Ueberhaupt ging *man* bei Besetzung der Stellen der Gesetz-Commission äußerst leichtsinnig zu Werke" [italics added]), since the recruiters followed "the universal Russian principle that any man is suitable for any job." Thus, concluded Jakob, "most of the Commission staff members [...] didn't have the slightest idea of

56 GRECH. Zapiski o moei zhisni. P. 235.

57 Unlike Grech's memoirs, the novel by Merezhkovsky places this anecdote into a directly opposite semantical context: "Legal, you say? Where? Prince, have you seen a sign in Liteiny that read "The Commission for the Compilation of Laws"? The letter "C" has fallen off, and it now reads "The Commission for Abandoning Laws." Isn't it more correct this way? Isn't it time to abandon laws? Why do we need them, if the tables of legislation are smashed against the stone of autocracy?" MEREZHKOVSKY. Aleksandr I. Op. cit. Pp. 33–34; A different version can be found in the memoirs of playwright Nestor Kukolnik. Recalling his father's (Vasilii Grigor'evich) work as a staff member at the Commission for the Compilation of Laws and as a professor of Roman law at the Higher School for Legal Studies, he wrote: "There were two commissions in St. Petersburg at the moment, one for compiling laws, and the other for canceling debts. The commission names were displayed on three different plaques each, as the artifice of the time would have it. Overnight, some pranksters changed some of the plaques, so the signs read: "Commission for the Compilation of Debts" and "Commission for the Cancellation of Laws." KUKOLNIK. Iz vospominanii N.V. Kukolnika. P. 97.

58 See, for example: OKHOTIN / KURGANOV. Russkii literaturnyi anekdot. P. 113.

legislation, nor experience, nor talent," and they were "accidental employees at this institution."[59]

It remains unclear who Jakob could have been referring to under the impersonal pronoun *man*. Of people endowed with the highest powers, save for the emperor himself, he could have meant Minister of Justice Petr Vasil'evich Lopukhin (1753–1827), his deputy N.N. Novosil'cev , M.M. Speransky , or G.A. Rosenkampff. Jakob obviously exculpated himself, and he also did not self-identify as one of the heavily criticized, incompetent appointees by protection.[60] The "universal principle" that the sharp-eyed foreign professor in Russian service and a devotee of learned impartiality claims to have noticed was indeed often named among the realities and practices of the system of administration and governance in the Russian Empire. At this point, one cannot help recalling the important observations made by Susanne Schattenberg in her historical and anthropological study of the practices and systems of rank promotion in civil service in early nineteenth-century provincial Russia. According to Schattenberg, the patron-client network of personal loyalties both in everyday life and in practices of political power functioned on the basis of a mutually binding reciprocal system of "gifting" and "receiving gifts." Those participating in the network were, of course, familiar with such abstract norms and concepts as law, legislation, *esprit de corps*, educatedness, and professional competence, but none of these norms were constitutive notions for contemporaneous actors, and consequently, they remain unhelpful for historiographical description and analysis today. Thus, Schattenberg concludes, it would be completely misleading now to describe these patron-client networks and practices in terms of "incompetence," "violations," "corruption," "arbitrary rule," or "lawlessness."[61]

---

59 JAKOB. Denkwürdgkeiten. P. 228.

60 A classic case of the paternalist practice of "job seeking" and rank promotion can be found in the diary of author and playwright Stepan Petrovich Zhikharev (1787–1860). Zhikharev mentions a private request made by Ivan Petrovich Arkharov (1744–1815), a retired infantry general and the former military governor of Moscow, on behalf of his neighbor, a landowner, "My dear friend, Petr Stepanovich [likely Valuev (1743–1814)]! Nikolai, a son of my good neighbor, is being sent to civil service. He is a simpleton, and his studies were very bad, so he must ask for protection. Dear friend, would you please be so kind to this fool of mine, give him a job at your chancery office and, should a case arise, if you find it fit, promote him up a rank or two, and we will be most pleased. He does stand in need of a salary, since he does not deserve it, and his father is very rich and will get still richer, because he lives like a hog." ZHIKHAREV. Zapiski sovremennika. P. 214.

61 According to Schattenberg, abstract legal norms, although existing on paper and featured in the discourses of political authority and the monarch's legal directives, remained "alien" to social and administrative reality on all levels of society. Laws and

However, it is due to other reasons that Jakob's harsh sentence on his colleagues in the Commission for the Compilation of Laws is to be analyzed in a critical manner. First, Jakob himself, having recently (1808) been invited to accept the chair of political economy at Kharkov University, was not a lawyer or legal expert by training and had no previous experience in jurisprudence. A philosopher and statistician, he had already gained prominence in Europe with his works on the theory of natural law (1795, 1802 [2nd ed.]) and on cameralistic "policey" legislation (1809).[62] Second, Jakob owed his own appointment to the commission wholly and personally to the monarch and Speransky, who took interest in the professor because of his hyperrelevant memorandum on paper money reform in Russia.[63] In October 1809, having read Jakob's treatise, Alexander I ordered that he should be immediately released from the university on vacation and sent to St. Petersburg with a consultative mission at "a special committee on certain important issues in the sphere of public law." After Jakob's arrival in St. Petersburg, Speransky explained to him the true reasons behind his transfer to the capital. Jakob was, upon personal request of the emperor, to become an expert and consultant on a special committee set up to oversee and implement financial and monetary reform, which aimed at improving the market situation of rouble banknotes. Both the committee's work and Jakob's participation in it were "top secret." As a cover job, Speransky provided Jakob with a place at the Commission for the Compilation of Laws—he would be an editor with the Criminal Code compilation team.[64]

---

decrees were neither "appropriated" nor "interpreted"—but simply ignored. SCHATTENBERG. Die korrupte Provinz? P. 88.

62 JAKOB. Philosophische Rechtslehre oder Naturrecht; IDEM. Grundsätze der Policeygesetzgebung und der Policeyanstalten; on L.H. von Jakob see also ABASHNIK. Ludwig Heinrich von Jakob. Pp. 895–927.

63 JAKOB. Ueber Russlands Papiergeld. Jakob wrote the memorandum in 1808 and originally circulated it among his friends and colleagues at Kharkov University. Following their recommendations, Jakob sent the memorandum to the curator of the Kharkov academic district, Count Seweryn Potocki (1762–1829), who, in his turn, forwarded it to Friedrich Würst (Fedor Khristianovich Virst, 1762–1831), at the time a member of the secret financial committee and the editor of Commercial Code at the Commission for the Compilation of Laws. In February 1809, Jakob used official channels to communicate his memorandum directly to the emperor. In October 1809, while on a lengthy visitation of the schools of the Kharkov academic districts, Jakob was surprised by a letter signed by Secretary of State Speransky, requesting his immediate arrival in the capital. JAKOB. Denkwürdigkeiten. Pp. 207 f. For mor details on the secret committee regarding financial politics and paper money, see the article by Benjamin Conrad in this volume, Pp. 95–116.

64 JAKOB. Denkwürdgkeiten. Pp. 205–17.

By then, Speransky had succeeded Novosil'cev as deputy minister of justice and board member at the Commission for the Compilation of Laws, thus concentrating de facto full control over codification work in his own hands.

Given these circumstances, Jakob's sudden arrival as a commission staff member was accidental in the strictest sense of the word. Jakob devoted most of his time to his work at the financial committee, but he also, at the behest of Speransky, helped draw up a draft version of the Criminal Code (*Ugolovnoye Ulozhenie*).[65] Deprived of his fallen patron in 1812, Jakob saw his career stall. On top of that, his personal and work relations with Rosenkampff, who once again assumed presidency at the Commission for the Compilation of Laws, were rather tense.

Throughout the whole period of the commission's work (1804–26), the search for candidates to fill vacancies was done by the order and at the initiative of the emperor, as well as N.N. Novosil'cev, P.V. Lopukhin, G.A. Rosenkampff, or M.M. Speransky. The selection criteria that they employed and the intentions that they followed—at least in commission matters—were as far from incompetent and corrupt as they could be, as Jakob would note in his memoirs. The individuals in charge were surely not dripping with the anti-Russian xenophobia and Germanophilia that M.A. Korff, a Baltic German, ascribed to his compartriot Rosenkampff. On the contrary, it is almost for certain that at the very top of the commission, there existed a tension between the Speransky party and that of Novosil'cev, Rosenkampff, and Lopukhin. This tension was based on personal loyalties and antipathies, on career path, or on differences in expert opinions and professional knowledge. All these factors came into play when the codification techniques and patterns and outcomes of work were assessed or judged for sense and relevance.

The patronage and clientele practices in rank promotion and vacancy filling, which coexisted endemically with (and often prevailed over) the official order enshrined in the Table of Ranks, are also quite conspicuous in the case of the Commission for the Compilation of Laws. Over time, its personnel included noble sons and relatives marked as "unsalaried." Among them were Novosil'cev's and Rosenkampff's nephews, Zavadovsky's son, and even renowned scholars such as Ignaz Aurelius Feßler (1756–1839). As a rule, these clientele appointees had jobs at the bottom of the commission's hierarchy, devoid of key prerogatives or often even clearly identifiable functions.[66] Among these editors and

65 Ibid.

66 RGIA. F. 1260. Op. 1. Dd. 7–11, 26, 75, 81, 863, 902–4; OR RNB. F. 731. Dd. 902–5, 916, 920.

section heads appointed by patronage or "opportunity" were also experienced officials and courtiers whose career developed under the auspices of influential statesmen or the emperor himself. One of these men was Iakov Aleksandrovich Druzhinin (1771–1849), a referendary (section head) at the commission's expedition and an editor for the Criminal Code. Other examples include the abovementioned Jakob and the *raznochinets* and "old-timer" (*starozhil*) in civil service N.S. Il'inskii, who started off as a scrivener at the Collegium of Commerce and eventually became the head of archives and the head of Civil Law at the commission.

In 1803–9, Novosil'cev acted as liaison and patron for the commission's leading staff members. Until his resignation as deputy minister of justice and member of the board (*prisutstvie*), Novosil'cev directly controlled the recruitment policy of the commission, as well as its codification work. In his memoirs, Czartoryski recalled that in searching for candidates to fill the commission's vacancies, Novosil'cev gave priority to people with "modern views" (*novymi vozzreniiami*).[67]

The commission's personnel, working as referendaries, under-referendaries, editors, assistant editors, or translators, were part of horizontally networked communities, united by specific ideological and political views, epistemological frameworks, and research paradigms. They possessed a common amount of specific knowledge, experience, and career ambitions. Also important here were their "social horizons" (L. Fleck), friendships, and collective and personal loyalties. The list of personnel included Rosenkampff (Civil Code, *principia iuris*), Georg Friedrich von Sahlfeldt (1769–1817, editor of local legislation for Baltic Governorates), Paul Wilhelm von Pomian de Pesarovius (1776–1848, assistant editor of local legislation for Baltic Governorates), Friedrich von Adelung (1768–1843, head of the commission's library), Johann Georg Neumann (1780–1855, assistant editor of local legislation for Baltic Governorates), Johann Gustav von Bellingshausen (1759–1820, under-referendary on general Civil Code, deputy archivist), Vasili Grigor'evich Kukolnik (1765–1821, professor of Roman law at Higher School of Legal Studies under the commission, Vyssheye Uchilishche Pravovedenia), Michailo Baludians'kyi (Mikhail Andreevich Balug'ianskii, 1769–1847, editor of the Code of Laws of state finances and public law), and Friedrich Würst (1762–1831, editor of the Commercial Code). All or most of theses men were (Baltic) Germans, studied law in German universities (or at universities in the Habsburg Monarchy), and worked at institutions of estate self-government and the regional administration in Courland or Livonia. With minor exceptions, all

67 Chartorizhskii. Vospominaniia i pisma. P. 239.

Interesting detail on Baltic German members.

of them were of the same generation and had similar social and educational backgrounds.

In constrast, members of the Speransky "party" were not united by either German or Slavic roots, by social background, or by university ties. Of individuals already mentioned, statesman, political economist, and lawyer Friedrich Würst, philosopher and economist L.H. Jakob, and economist and lawyer M. Balug'ianskii came close to Speransky only through their joint work at the abovementioned secret financial committee. According to Friedrich Leopold von Hauenschild (1785–1830), Speransky had a special liking for scholars from the Habsburg Monarchy and planned to recruit more of them into the commission.[68] Indeed, in 1808–12, when Speransky headed the work of the commission, a certain "Habsburg alliance" arose among its staff members. It included I.A. Feßler, F.L. Hauenschild, V.G. Kukolnik, and Balug'ianskii. Unlike Kukolnik and Balug'ianskii, who had been recruited and assigned to their positions by Novosil'cev, I. Feßler—-professor of Oriental studies, lawyer, theologian, and Freemason—had nothing to do with codification work or legal studies when he joined the commission in 1809. He had been invited to St. Petersburg by Alexander I and Speransky with a different mission in mind—to assist in setting up a Grand Lodge, which had been started in the capital in June 1810. As it was with Jakob, the commission was a smokescreen job for Feßler. His real task was to set out procedures and draft a statute for the newly created lodge.[69]

The lodge first met in the house occupied by the commission,[70] an event that had far-reaching repercussions in the political and personal fate of Speransky.[71] It also led to a major realignment in the balance of "party" configurations and loyalties, as witnessed by the same Hauenschild, who took part in the events. According to Hauenschild's coded diplomatic memorandum on Speransky, written in April

---

68 [Gauenshild]. M.M. Speranskii. P. 256.

69 For more details, see Vishlenkova. Zabotias o dushakh poddannykh. Pp. 118–22, 128 f.

70 [Gauenshild]. M.M. Speransky. P. 254. The text of the Hauenschild memo (as published by Bilbasov) appeared as an appendix to the latter's secret report of April 16, 1826. The Hauenschild memorandum was also quoted by Theodor Schiemann in the first volume of his *History of Russia under Nicholas I*: Schiemann. Geschichte Russlands. Vol. 1. Pp. 75–81.

71 In Elena Vishlenkova's opinion, the Grand Lodge could have been a key motive (if not the main one) in Alexander's ultimate decision to deprive Speransky of all important affairs and offices of state in March 1812: Vishlenkova. Zabotias o dushakh poddannykh. Pp. 126 f.

new to me

1826, the lodge's masters were Speransky (Master of the Chair), Hauenschild himself (First Observer), Rosenkampff (Second Observer), and Pesarovius (Brother Introducer).[72] We can only guess why the latter two chose to join the lodge and work with Speransky, given their disagreements and history of personal enmity. No further details are known, except that the existence of the lodge was threatened by a blunder or garrulousness on the part of Pesarovius, and that Rosenkampff soon started actively intriguing against Speransky.

The commission received its full share of government funds even after the setting of a legal foundation for the "lawful monarchy" stopped being a priority for Alexander I, and after his associates, who had previously guided and curated codification work, one by one resigned and were exiled from the capital. The emperor provided the commission with an impressive array of resources. Although structurally subsumed under the Ministry of Justice, the commission occupied a separate building (46 Liteinyi Prospekt), which was previously used by the Cadet School (*Iunkerskoye Uchilishche*, disbanded in 1804).[73] Its separate annual expenditure of 130,000 roubles on personnel salaries and operating costs alone equalled that of the whole Ministry of Justice. It is not the absolute sum of investments that is of importance here but rather their symbolic comparative value.[74]

The commission's personnel list, approved by the emperor, comprised forty-eight positions, including three referendaries (heads of expeditions), six under-referendaries, fifteen editors, fourteen assistant editors, and ten translators. In point of fact, according to my largely incomplete assessment, in the first decade of its existence the commission had up to ninety-five salaried staff members, and it was only between 1812 and 1816 that their number went down to about

72 [Gauenshild]: M.M. Speransky. P. 254.

73 G.A. Rosenkampf, N.S. Il'inskii, A. Povstansky, O. Goreglyad, P.P. Ikosov, and others lodged for many years in the house occupied by the commission.

74 As a point of comparison, in 1812 the total annual expenditure on personnel salaries and operating costs of administrative offices, and justice and social care (*prizrenie*) institutions in Moscow Governorate stood at 162,498 roubles; in St. Petersburg Governorate they stood at 164, 775 roubles in banknotes (with all readjustments of the early nineteenth century). In 1803, the Ministry of Justice, with its thirty employees, and the Ministry of Internal Affairs, with forty-nine, cost the treasury 68,650 and 70,750 roubles, respectively; and the three hundred members and employees of the similarly high status Academy of Arts received 146,000 roubles in salaries and payments. Cf. PSZ I. Vol. 44. Kniga shtatov. Part. 2. Shtaty po dukhovnoi i grazhdanskoi chasti. Carstvovanie gosudaria imperatora Aleksandra I. 1801–1812. Pp. 7–9, 18–19, 230–31.

thirty.[75] Referendaries were personally appointed by the emperor, and, in their turn, recruited the rest of the commission's personnel, including deputies, editors, editorial assistants, translators, and the clerical staff to carry out the paperwork. Those applying for a job at a codifying expedition or section had to be tested for legal knowledge. Everyone among the original rank-and-file personnel of the commission, who dealt with the immediate work of codification and systematization, had passed this examination.[76]

As mentioned above, from the time that the commission was set up/reorganized in 1804, it was answerable to the Ministry of Justice. On January 1, 1810, it was moved under the Council of State. A special collegiate body, the board (*prisutstvie*), which comprised the minister of justice, his deputy, and the permanent secretary (referendary of the first expedition), coordinated codification and controlled the work of the commission. Its day-to-day work was originally split between three expeditions, which were charged with codifying and systematizing both the legislation of the empire as a whole and the local law of the regions that either already had a special legal regime in place or were supposed to establish one in the future. The first expedition was responsible for developing the "legal foundations" (*principia iuris*), the imperial Civil Code, and judicial procedure. The second expedition focused on the Criminal Code, regional codes for "special regime" territories, (such as the Baltic Governorates or Left-Bank Ukraine), and "particular" codes. The third expedition dealt with translating foreign legislation and editing the texts of all the codes for "unity, clarity, and purity" of language. In April 1804, at the behest of Novosil'cev and Rosenkampff,[77] the board introduced the practice of regular (up to twice weekly) interexpeditionary meetings aimed at better coordination and improved efficiency of managing codification work, as well as better productivity.

As is commonly known among historiographers, Speransky's reorganization of the commission and drastic reduction of its personnel in 1809 opened a new

75 PSZ I. Vol. 28. № 21187, 28.02.1804. "O preobrazovanii Komissii sostavleniia zakonov." Pp. 160–73; RGIA. F. 1260. Dd. 7–11, 26, 75, 81, 863, 902–4; OR RNB: F. 731. Dd. 902–5, 916, 920.

76 See examples of such examinations in ASPb.II RAN. F. 176. D. 289. "Predmet, sluzhashchii materiei dlia dokazaniia svedennia o iuris-prudencii, sostavlennyi kollezhskim assesorom Antonom fon Riter-Mazurkevichem dlia Komissii o sostavlenii zakonov"; OR RNB. F. 526. D. 4. L. 209; RGIA. F. 1260. D. 1. "Ob obrazovanii Komissii sostavleniia zakonov, utverzhdenie ee shtatov, vypiski iz zhurnalov zasedaniia Komissii, otnosiashchiesia k ee obrazovaniiu." Ll. 57–60.

77 RGIA. F. 1260. D. 2. "Zhurnaly Prisutstviia komissii 1804 g." Ll. 28–29.

chapter in the history of legal codification in Russia.[78] Although the changes were sanctioned by an imperial decree signed on March 7, 1809,[79] the commission's leaders had decided in favor of structural change and of prioritization of codification tasks as early as November 19, 1808. This meeting came only three weeks after Speransky had first appeared as an observer at the regular sessions of the board,[80] and the decision largely relied on a report by Rosenkampff titled *On Further Scheduling of the [Commission's] Work and Reducing the Number of [Its] Officials*.[81] Since the report was presented at the same session as the discussion of structural changes, we might be able to consider Rosenkampff as a coauthor of the commission's 1808–9 reforms. However, this report's full text has so far proved impossible to locate, and this issue can not be solved until further information becomes available from additional sources.[82]

The emperor's decree of March 1809 in many ways differed from the original plan of reforms.[83] The decree established a new institutional structure within the commission and introduced a system of record keeping similar to the one used in the ministries. The commission's board (*Prisutstvie*) was renamed *Pravlenie*, but it preserved its full composition and retained the function of controlling the systematized plan of codification, overseeing the content of the codes and their articles, and deciding on the problems reported by heads of sections. The decree, however, placed the "bookkeeping" under the sole control of Speransky. A new entity to be established was the council, which was, from May 1809, tasked with revising and correcting the codification projects

78 Aleksandr Ivanovich Turgenev, who in 1808 was assistant editor at the section of Criminal Law, wrote to his brother in this respect: "I hurriedly left Moscow, since [I heard that] Speransky had been appointed member of our commission, and I feared big changes in it." Pismo A.I. Turgeneva N.I. Turgenevu 26.02.1808 g. In: PISMA I DNEVNIKI A.I. Turgeneva. P. 367; see also FATEEV. Akademicheskaia i gosudarstvennaia deiatelnost M.A. Balug'ianskogo. P. 35.

79 PSZ I. Vol. 30. № 23525, 7.03.1809. "Imennoi Ministru iusticii. O novom obrazovanii Komissii sostavleniia zakonov." Pp. 852–63.

80 The official appointment of Speransky was proclaimed on December 20, 1808, by Royal assent: RGIA. F. 1260. D. 1. L. 11.

81 RGIA. F. 1260. D. 6. "Zhurnaly Prisustviia komissii 1808 g." Ll. 31–42.

82 "Vsepoddaneishii doklad Prisutstviia" from December 29, 1808, whose text is similar to the Resolution of the Prisutustvie from November 19, 1808, includes however Rosenkampff's signature: OR RNB. F. 731. D. 907. Komissia sostavleniia zakonov. "Vsepoddanneishii raport o sostoianii raboty Komissii po sostavleniiu zakonov i uchilishcha pravovedeniia pri Komissii. 29 dekabria 1808."

83 RGIA. F. 1260. D. 6. Ll. 31–42.

approved by the board. The council comprised all board members, two heads of sections, and senators as appointed by the monarch. Here, too, bookkeeping was to be the concern of Speransky alone. Interexpeditionary meetings were promoted to the status of conference, where one of the members of the board was to act as president. Both new institutions—the conference and the council—now had a staff of clerks and translators, separate from the rest of the commission. Following the recommendations of section heads, the board scheduled weekly sessions of the conference and put on its agenda editorial decisions on the structure of the codes, to be made by heads of sections and their deputies.[84] Finally, the three existing expeditions were replaced by six sections with a more narrow specialization by branch of law: Criminal Code; Commercial Code; public law and state finances (including the Statute of the Police); Code of Laws for the Baltic Governorates; and Code of Laws for the governorates of Little Russia and Poland.

The board's resolution of November 19 had a clause establishing the priority areas of codification – the Civil, Criminal, and Commercial Codes (*ulozhenia*), with each including its own judicial procedure and a system of courts.[85] The March decree also had this clause (a key one for Speransky's codification plan), but it was formulated less directly: "Since a collection of regional laws (*svod zakonov provintsialnykh*) presupposes the functioning of general laws, the board (*pravlenie*) will not let the officials of these two sections be engaged elsewhere until it is time to compare these collections with general laws."[86] At the same time, the decree, as compared with the 1804 program,[87] more clearly accentuated the priority of imperial legislation and the subsidiarity of regional law.

The changes also touched the job structure: gone were the expedition referendaries, deputies, editors, and editorial assistants. Referendaries were replaced by section heads, whose subordinates were deputies, translators, and clerks. In absolute terms, the personnel of the commission under Speransky grew in number. The 1809 decree mentioned by name twenty-five section heads, their deputies and secretaries at the board, council, and conference. All in all, including assistants,

84 PSZ I. Vol. 30. № 23525, 7.03.1809. "Imennoi, dannyi ministru iusticii. O novom obrazovanii Komissii sostavleniia zakonov. S prilozheniem polozheniia o sostave i upravlenii onoi." Pp. 857–63; Ibid. № 23524, 7.03.1809. "Imennoi Senatu ob uchrezhdenii osobogo Soveta pri Komissii sostavleniia zakonov." P. 852.

85 RGIA. F. 1260. D. 6. Ll. 31 ob.–32.

86 PSZ I. Vol. 30. № 23525. P. 859.

87 PSZ I. Vol. 28. № 21187. Pp. 160–73.

translators, and clerks, the commission as of 1811 employed ninety-five people, at least half of whom started working there in 1804–8.[88]

It was in this reformed shape that the Commission for the Compilation of Laws was moved from the control of the Ministry of Justice to that of the newly created Council of State.[89] Speransky, who was then at the top of his career and the zenith of political influence as secretary of state, was busy drafting large-scale reforms of the state administration under the auspices of the emperor. He needed the commission as an important resource and a useful instrument of his vast modernization plans. At his initiative, the administrative structure of the commission was once again reformed. By the start of 1810, both collegiate, decision-making entities—the board and the council—had been replaced by a directorate (*direkciia*) that consisted of one director only—Speransky himself. A gifted politician and experienced courtier, Speransky understood well that under a cautious and hesitant monarch, radical and forceful top-down political reforming faced a high degree of opposition and could not proceed without either the neutralization of all political competitors or, at the very least, control of institutional resources staffed with professionals.[90] Inside these institutions, one of which was the Commission for the Compilation of Laws, Speransky needed to pull the levers of efficient control over the codification work and those who performed it. This model, created to fit specific circumstances and achieve specific tasks, remained productive and viable until March 1812—until, that is, the collapse of the political career of its architect, Speransky.

---

88 PSZ I. Vol. 30. № 23525. Pp. 862–63; RGIA. F. 1260. D. 902. "Formuliarnye spiski i spiski chlenov Komissii". Ll. 107–15.

89 PSZ I. Vol. 31. № 24064, 1.01.1810. "Obrazovanie Gosudarstvennogo soveta." P. 11.

90 Jakob, an eyewitness of these events, wrote in his memoirs, "Speransky liked to rule over what he had [with real,] absolute power, and it did not suit him to be subordinate to the council. Therefore it [the council] was officially fully disbanded in 1810, after doing nothing for several years, the commission became part of the Council of State. Since Speransky was the rapporteur [*dokladchik*] at the Council of State, he ruled here by the power of his reputation and eloquence. As the secretary of state, he was an intermediary between the monarch and the Council of State, and thus due to the combination of all of these, he single-handedly ruled the affairs of the Commission for the Compilation of Laws as he saw fit." Jakob. Denkwürdigkeiten. Pp. 227 f., op. cit. P. 228.

4. Models of Codification: The "German Method" versus the "Ideal Code"

> We work a lot at the commission, even though there is a lot of argument, especially around the *German method*, whereby to add importance to work, two-thirds of what is written is superfluous.—P.V. Lopukhin, 1808[91]

> Our Russian laws are a product of barbarism [...] these have been all borrowed from abroad, and long known elsewhere in the world. [...] Therefore in your labor, you need not be too concerned with Russian laws [...] follow your genius and set up an *ideal Code* for Russia."—M.M. Speransky, 1810][92]

In a speech on January 19, 1833, at the grand session of the Council of State, Emperor Nicholas I, who inherited the regnal motto from his brother (see fig. 3), set out the official narrative of the codification project. In record-breaking time, the project was completed: a systematized corpus of legislation was drawn together and promulgated.

Figure 3. The coronation medal of Nicholas I.

Source: Private archive of the author.

The emperor presented the Digest of Laws of the Russian Empire as his unique achievement and a star project of his reign. In a formal sense, this was true.

91 OR RNB. F. 526. D. 42. "Pis'ma Petra Vasil'evicha Lopukhina. 1804–1808." Lopukhin-Novosil'cevu 3.12.1808. Ll. 44– ob.

92 Jakob. Denkwürdigkeiten. P. 234.

Ironically, before Nicholas took off his star of the Order of St. Andrew and placed it on Speransky, the "compiler" of the Digest had been forced to hear a devastating critique of his early ("foreign") codification projects. The emperor did not need to name names—many statesmen present in the room well remembered the days of Speransky's directorate in the Commission for the Compilation of Laws, as well as the debates on the Civil Code projects at the Council of State. However, they must have been surprised by another clause in the monarch's speech – the one where he ascribed fully to himself the principles and solutions that had brought about the successful compilation and implementation of the Digest:

> Unfortunately, the evidence presented revealed to me that its [the Commission's] work was almost completely fruitless. The reason was far from difficult to discover: its lack of achievements stemmed mostly from the permanent desire to create new laws, while it was necessary [rather] to place the ones in effect on a firm foundation. This is what urged me to start, first and foremost, with defining the goal that the government should strive to attain in legislation. Of the routes pointed out to me, I selected the one completely opposite to those taken before. Instead of writing new laws, I ordered that the existing ones should be fully collected and set in order. The importance of this cause implored me to take in under my immediate control and to disband the previous commission.[93]

The formal success of the 1826–33 codification project, however, had a preceding history of its own—and this history was drastically different from the one propounded by Nicholas I.

In June 1803, Pierre Dumont (1759–1829) wrote to his friend Samuel Romilly (1757–1818) from St. Petersburg:

> We have a Livonian man here, Rosenkampff, a long-time president of the court in Dorpat, and now appointed, without a [required] title, to collect all the decrees—that is, all the laws in the empire—to set them straight and to remove all the contradictions and discrepancies. [...] This Herr Rosenkampff is a great admirer of Bentham. [...] He is somewhat superficial, but [he] has knowledge [...] He could manage the editorial work he has been entrusted with, if he only had the courage to curb his self-conceit; the problem is that he is afraid of being called a plagiarist if he uses thoughts that have first come to someone else's mind.[94]

Dumont had edited and brought to St. Petersburg a French translation of Bentham, under the title *Traités de legislation civile et penale*.[95] This book captured the minds

93 From Nicholas I's speech at the session of the Council of State, January 19, 1833: Korf. Zhisn grafa Speranskogo. Vol. 2. P. 300.

94 Pypin. Russkie otnosheniia Bentama. Pp. 805 f.

95 Betham. Précédés de Principes Généraux de Législation; Russian translation: [Betham] Bentam. Rassuzhdeniia o grazhdanskikh i ugolovnykh zakonopolozheniiakh.

of educated readers and remained a best seller for several weeks in St. Petersburg. Dumont did as much as he could to propagate Bentham's ideas in the highest circles of power. He met with Alexander I, Stroganov, Novosil'cev, Rosenkampff, and other high-profile dignitaries. Rosenkampff saw that the educated public, the monarch, and the members of the Unofficial Committee were all involved in lively exchanges about the book, and he admitted that Bentham had "an extraordinary talent, a sharp wit, and a keen eye, which shines through in many chapters of his book; as for the theory, the book is very well-elaborated as a single whole."[96] Bentham's works were soon translated into Russian and published in 1805 "by Royal order." However, the admiration felt by both the monarch and the members of the Unofficial Committee for the English legal scholar and philosopher, and for his original theories and recommendations on setting up ideal criminal and civil codes, quickly waned. His theories were impossible to implement within the attempted codification project.[97] By then, the goals, objectives, and means to bring the codification about had already been fixed: the mass of autochthonous legislation required some systematizing and "refurbishing."

Neither the preserved archives of the commission nor the draft papers of Novosil'cev pertaining to the work of the commission feature any reference to Bentham, whose ideas on codification had attracted so much attention from Alexander I and his Unofficial Committee in 1803. But these archives have preserved an 1804 copy of the *Intelligenzblatt*, a supplement to the *Jenaer Allgemeine Literatur-Zeitung*, where A.F. Thibaut published an article titled "Alexandrine Legislation in Russia."[98] One of the leading legal theorists in Europe and an ardent supporter of the codification effort, Thibaut fully agreed with the Novosil'cev-Rosenkampff plan, which had been previously published in full in German translation by Heinrich Friedrich von Storch (1766–1835) in the *Russland unter Alexander dem Ersten* magazine.[99] Thibaut admired the plan's perfection, its "all-encompassing system-

96 Maikov. Baron Gustav Andreevich Rozenkampf. P. 180. On Russian attitudes to Bentham and his correspondence with Alexander I, see: Pypin. Russkie otnosheniia Bentama; and also the articles by Aleksandr Orlov and Sergei Polskoy in this volume, Pp. 135–166.

97 Maikov. Baron Gustav Andreevich Rozenkampf. Pp. 178–83.

98 T[hibau]t. Alexandrinische Gesetzgebung. Col. 954–60; there is a Russian translation of this article with an abundance of mistakes and intentional semantical mistranslations (e.g., "alternant" vs. "revolution," "state" vs. "nation"), which to a great extent transform or distort the meaning of phrases in the original. RGIA. F. 1260. D. 1. Ll. 47–50 ob.

99 Storch. Annalen der Alexandrinischen Gesetzgebung. Pp. 209–67.

atic spirit"—conspicuous even at first glance—and the "wisdom" of the Russian monarch who had approved it. Thibaut ecstatically prophesied that the outcomes of this plan would "both politically and scientifically belong to the most beneficial symbols of modernity":

> With this course of action and under such rule Russia may hope to attain happiness and to enjoy perfect legislation—as much as mankind can achieve perfection. Even the most cultured European states have not attained this happiness, or if they have, it was by a revolutionary assault or painstaking and long preparation. It is most pleasing to see that the [...] author of the report has studied and made use of these preparatory efforts taken by other nations, attempting to bring their advantages together in his plan and at the same time trying to erect a building of his own on them as on a foundation. It is especially conspicuous to the author [of these lines] when it concerns the Prussian legislation, which is the best for our times—for instance, in the idea he borrowed that besides the general legislation, special provincial codes are needed to harmonize the particular constitutions and rights of some provinces with the universal principles [of law]. Given this zeal and the passing of decisions required to immediately satisfy this demand, alongside the general laws, Russia can be expected to implement this important part in a faster and more harmonious manner than [did] Prussia itself, where, after the General Law had been published, they are still working toward collecting provincial codes and setting them straight.[100]

Thibaut, who was known as a convinced adept of pan-German codification, was untroubled by the combination of *incorporation* and *codification* of laws. The codification model and technique as seen by Rosenkampff mandated the creation of a syncreticist code/digest: "the responsibility of the commissions lies neither in writing up a Code of Laws alone, nor [in] introducing laws in our land, be them [totally] new or [previously] created for other countries and peoples."[101] This fact makes it hard to agree with both the rhetoric of Nicholas I and the position of contemporary historians who draw numerous borderlines between the *Svod* as a systematized, "nativist" legislative corpus and the *Ulozhenie* as a codifed law that belonged to the cosmopolitan era of the Enlightenment.[102] Further, absolutist codes, despite all the monarch's rhetoric, legal scholars' efforts, and exercises in rationalist philosophy of the Enlightenment, preserved large layers of traditional laws and customs of the *ius communae*—layers that the codes were supposed to have replaced.[103]

---

100 T[HIBAU]T: Alexandrinische Gesetzgebung. Col. 953, 958.

101 PSZ I. Vol. 27. № 21187. P. 167.

102 See, for example, the works of Tatiana Borisova.

103 However, also well known is the opposite, in the case of the first edition of the Russian Digest of Laws—that is, the creation of legal norms by Speransky and his team that did not have any roots in "autochtone" legislations.

Ambitious as he was, Rosenkampff never tried to reinvent the wheel; his focus was rather on bringing the two models together within a codification project of his own. Alexander I and Novosil'cev shared his plan and bolstered it with official support. The commission personnel had to collect a body of positive (i.e., recorded) law, to fully revise the accumulated legal material and outline its lacunae. This task was impeded by the need to have the corpus of legislation (collected at the preparatory stage) analyzed, separated from the unstructured body of law,[104] and systematized by branch and area of state governance. Then it was to be restated in "clear and simple" language and assigned to various codes. Simultaneously, Rosenkampff, probably with the assistance of Novosil'cev, incorporated the principles of rational philosophy into legislation, thus developing its "foundations" (*principia iuris*): "[These] are the first, simplest, purest truths based on the sound judgments of human mind, on longtime experiments and observations, rigorously studied. Founded on the significant and potential benefits for the State, they are clear and undeniable and obviously encourage the public and private good, thus acquiring power and steadfastness."[105]

The codification plan mandated the creation of six compilative legal codes:

1. "Organic, or native [*korennye*]" laws established the rights of the monarch, the state regime, and the system of government. These laws involved "the exposition of the sacred rights of His Imperial Majesty and the emperor's family, of the relations of subjects to their Monarch; also, the governmental orders and decisions that have received the royal assent."[106]
2. "The foundations of law" or the "inalterable law of the state." For this part of the Digest/Code, Rosenkampff intended to scout the Russian positive law in effect for universal legal norms and principles that he had come to define as "the theory of law" or the *principia iuris*. Among the official sources that he intended to use for this segment were the "Instruction to the Legislative Commission" (*Nakaz*) of Catherine the Great (1767), the "Institution for the

104 Cf., tables of the laws: RGIA. F. 1260. Dd. 473 f.

105 PSZ I. Vol. 27. № 21187. P. 168.

106 Cf., the structure of the Digest of Laws of the Russian Empire (volume 1, the 1833 edition): Section I. On the Sacred Rights and Privileges of the Supreme Autocratic (*Samoderzhavnoi*) Authority. Section 2. The Institution of the Imperial Family. Digest of Institutions of State. Book 1. Digest of Institutions of the Council of State. Book 2. Digest of Institutions of the Committee of Ministers. Book 3. Digest of Institutions of the Senate. Book 4. Digest of Institutions. Book 5. Institution of the Chapters of Orders in the Russian Empire. Book 6. Statutes of Orders. Book 7. Statutes of the Awards for Meritorious Service.

Administration of Governorates" (1775), Peter the Great's "Military Statute" (1716), and several other pieces of comprehensive legislation. This segment would also deal with the status of legislative acts as such, their subdivision by branch of law, norms and procedures for promulgating legislation, their repeal or novelization, and finally, the issues of legal identity and legal capacity.

3. "General" legislation—that is, the civil laws in effect throughout the empire.
4. Criminal and police law.
5. Judicial procedure and the system of courts.
6. "Particular laws." This segment was supposed to accumulate all nongeneral norms of civil, criminal, judicial, and administrative law on all the territories (and pertaining to all the communities) that were endowed with special privilege or allowed to preserve (in full or in part) the use of particular norms of legislation. Another type of legislation falling within the same segment were regulatory statutes of trade and financial law.

Prior to 1809, the commission's codification work did not go beyond the boundaries of this hybrid Digest/Code model. Unwieldy in its over-complex architecture and large in the volume of legal material to be revised, it indeed demanded a lot of effort and time. Marginalia and code plans, together with other projects and proceedings of the commission's meetings held between 1804 and 1808 are preserved in hundreds of voluminous files at the Russian State Historical Archive.[107] Draft versions of the Foundations of Law and parts of the Civil and Criminal Codes have been analyzed in detail by A. Makarov, D.V. Gorozhankina,[108] and R.S. Taborin. Besides drafting the codes proper, the commission collected, revised, and registered more than twenty thousand legislative pieces within the corpus of positive law. These materials composed the archives of the commission. Another largescale enterprise (conducted as part of the preparation of the Criminal Code and the statutes of the courts) was a revision of judicial practices and court structure. Special questionnaires on legal practices and norms of local law (Fig. 4) were compiled and sent to regional

---

107 RGIA. F. 1260. Dd. 1–469.

108 Concerning the conclusions made by D.V. Gorozhankina, an important reservation must be noted. I cannot agree with her opinion, given without any explanation, that the reasons for failure of codification in the fields of criminal law and judicial procedure lay in the poor skills of the personnel of the Commission for the Compilation of Laws, with their allegedly insufficient theoretical knowledge, lack of practical experience, and poor command of codification techniques. GOROZHANKINA. Istoriko-pravovoi analiz sistematizacii. P. 52.

administrations and courts in the European governorates, Siberia, Left-Bank Ukraine, and the Baltic territories.[109]

Figure 4. Responses of the Vitebsk Governorate Administration (Vitebskoe Gubernskoe Pravelnie) and the First Department of the Vitebsk Principal Court to the commission's questionnare regarding the order of court procedures.

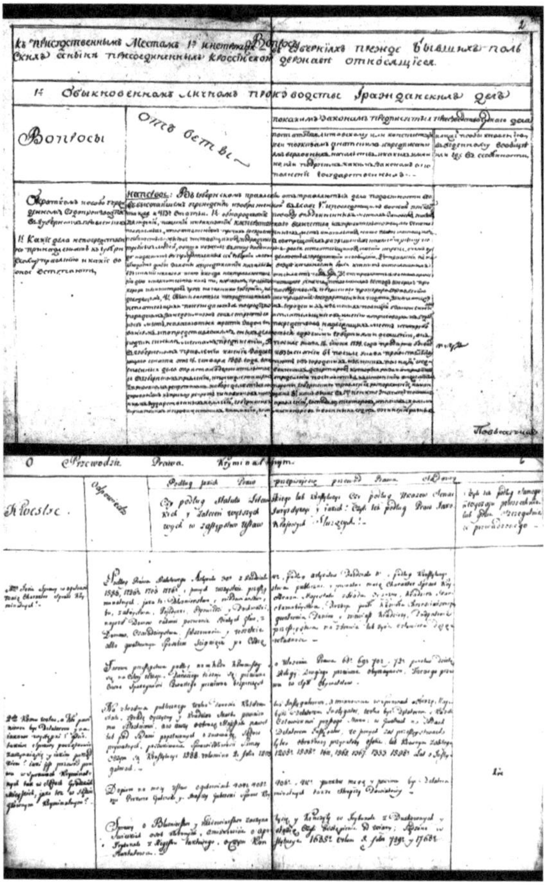

Source: RGIA. F. 1260. Op. 1. D. 51. "Otvety prisutstvennykh mest Vitebskoi gubernii na voprosy Komissii o poriadke sudoproizvodstva: ugolovnoi palaty, gubernskogo pravleniia, zemskogo suda, palaty grazhdanskogo suda, uezdnykh sudov, magistratov i nadvornykh sudov." Ll. 1 ob.–2, 5 ob.–6.

109 RGIA. F. 1260. Dd. 47–68.

With the rise of Speransky and his increased influence on Alexander I, as well as growth in the speed and scale of the reforms and Speranksy's political imagination, P.V. Lopukhin, N.N. Novosil'cev, and G.A. Rosenkampff more frequently had to deal with external doubts that the selected method was indeed the most relevant and the intended outcomes actually possible. The alternative often pointed out was the French Code. At the start of 1808, Rosenkampff (via the commission's board) was recommended to study a work by legal scholar Antoine Toussaint Desquiron, recently published under the title of *L'esprit des Institutes de l'empereur Justinien* (1807).[110] In his expert opinion, as presented in a March 1808 report to the board, Rosenkampff stated that Desquiron's book was indeed useful in studying French law, which was based on Roman law, but only as a guidebook for French lawyers and legal scholars. The commission, in his opinion, had already attempted a wider comparative study of the Russian law and an array of European legal systems, including the Roman, French, Prussian, Habsburgian, British, Swedish, and Danish.[111]

The outcomes of this study showed that Russia drew no special benefit from an article-by-article comparison of its codes with corresponding instruments of Roman law: "The Novorossiia Code can not be founded on the theory of Roman law. The laws of our country are known for their simplicity and clarity, drawing their provisions from practical considerations and respect of the local [norms], thus the whole theory of Russian law, derived from these, would convey the same sense."[112] Having made a number of conclusions and formal statements as a legal scholar reviewing a book by a colleague, Rosenkampff went on to a more urgent issue—that of the current codification plan and its deadlines for implementation:

> In France, editors had a complete collection of the [required] materials, as well as a theory of law, and legal studies as a systematized discipline, and on top of that, some attempts at more or less perfect exposition of laws; [...] moreover, editors in France were required to prepare an exposition only of the text of laws; but the commission had to start with the collection of pertaining materials, and had no theory of Russian law at its disposal, nor legal studies refined to a system. Thus, its duty was not only to relate the texts of laws, but to develop a legal theory;[113] in a word, its subject is every-

110 DESQUIRON DE SANT-AGNON. L'esprit des Institutes de l'empereur Justinien.

111 Cf., for example, RGIA. F. 1260. D. 237. "Sravnitel'nye tablicy proekta Grazhdanskogo ulozheniia, sostavlennogo Komissiei s francuzskim i prusskimi ulozheniiami." D. 506. "Vypiski iz prusskogo, shvedskogo i estliandskogo ugolovnogo zakonodatel'stva."

112 RGIA. F. 1260. D. 46. "Raporty chlenov Komissii o rassmotrenii imi sochinenii raznykh lic." Ll. 5 f.

113 As contemporaneous legal scholars (such as Jeremy Bentham or Paul Johann von Feuerbach) noted—and as historians of law concur—this section of the Code/Digest

> thing pertaining to positive legislation (*positio*), and also whatsoever composes the academic (*doctrinel*) part of legal studies. Its plans are larger, its duty more difficult, and its means more limited. However, if the course of the commission's work seems slow, it is nevertheless more reliable. In France they began [compiling] the code in 1791 and completed it in 1805. In Prussia, they have been working on the code for fourteen years.[114]

However, both the horizons of political imagination and the field of real-life politics had to yield to the pressure of drastic change, which in its speed and direction demanded shifting gears and coming up with new codification solutions. The appointment of Speransky as a commission boardman in October 1808, and as deputy minister of justice in December of the same year (replacing Novosil'cev) marked the first steps in a different direction.

But it was the codification project itself that underwent the largest transformation. Speransky steered the commission toward only two of the six intended segments—the Civil and Criminal Codes. The Code of Civil laws was Speransky's special priority, and he personally guided and controlled it.[115] The compilation of the Criminal Code he entrusted to his protégé Jakob. In one of their private exchanges, Speransky explained his new codification formula to Jakob in the following way:

> Our Russian laws are a product of barbarism. We can indeed find among them excellent decrees and superior formulations, but these have been all borrowed from abroad and long known elsewhere in the world. [...] Therefore, in your labor, you need not be too concerned with Russian laws. It is of course required that you do not offend the notions and prejudices common here too much. It would also be good if you can embellish your legal initiatives with references to the authorities of the Russian laws in effect. This will serve you as a recommendation [in the eyes] of our dignitaries, overburdened with prejudices and national pride. On the whole, you should but follow [the voice of] your genius and set up an *ideal code* for Russia.[116]

Describing this period in his memoirs, Rosenkampff lamented that the arrival of Speransky, with all his administrative novelties, effectively paralyzed the work

---

was the most problematic one because it aligned the legislation in effect with legal scholarship and theory of law. It would thus prove troublesome for both the commission's editors and Rosenkampff himself.

114 RGIA. F. 1260. D. 46. Ll. 6–7.

115 In this respect, I would like to refer to the "considerations" (*Predstavlenie*) that the Council of State submitted to the emperor on May 13, 1809. This document almost verbatim repeated the well-known *Introduction to the Code of State Laws* ("Vvedenie k ulozheniiu gosudarstvennykh gzakonov"). See RGIA. F. 1260. D. 77. "Plany i raznye predpolozheniia trudov Komissii sostavleiia zakonov." Ll. 39–50.

116 Emphasis added; see: Jakob. Denkwürdigkeiten. P. 234.

of the commission. The monthly reports were no longer commissioned by the emperor: the compilations that Rosenkampff had put together from the internal reports of the commission's personnel were deemed redundant. Consequently, the personnel's attitudes grew lax: "I have learned that Speransky talks of our work with very little respect. [...] I had always insisted on working regularly and in an orderly manner, but everyone was happy to get rid of what they saw as a constraint."[117] This is how Rosenkampff recalled the personally traumatic moment of winter 1808–9 (indeed, also a crucial time for the commission proper)—the moment when he lost his status of "codifier-in-chief" and was discredited in the eyes of the monarch who used to trust him. Deprived of his power and control over the commission, he was relegated to section head. Moreover, the Higher School of Legal Studies was suspended. This school was another brainchild of Rosenkampff's, which he had set up in 1804 to train lawyers and legal scholars.[118] Historiographers tend to see the school as a failed short-time experiment that had no impact on the subsequent development of jurisprudence or the training of professional cadres for courts and administrative agencies. My rather incomplete observations suggest, however, that the history of the school deserves at least a more focused study and cautious assessment. From 1805 to 1809, forty-three people graduated from the school, including Karl Ivanovich Cimmerman (Zimmerman), a staffmember of the Commission for the Compilation of Laws and subsequently senior official in the Second Section of HIM Own Chancellery; Nikolai Ivanovich Grech, a writer, journalist, and philologist; and Aleksei Ivanovich Smirnov, staff member of the commission and subsequently president of the First Department, Moscow Chamber of the Civil Court. Among the school's professors and instructors were G.A. Rosenkampff, A.I. Turgenev, V.G. Kukol'nik, M.A. Balug'ianskii, Petr Dmitrievich Lodii (1764–1829), and G.I. Terlach.

The consequences, then, involved more than just the matter of personal suffering, humiliated pride, and lost power on the part of a single official. The examples of codifications of law gone wrong under Catherine II and Alexander I clearly demonstrate that success here was impossible without the monarch's permanent involvement and unyielding control, as the successful finished codification project under Nicholas I substantiates. As early as 1805, Alexander I, who had promised to

117 Maikov. Baron Gustav Andreevich Rozenkampf. P. 400; see also G.A. Rosenkampff's report on the outcomes of the commission's work under Speransky in 1808–12: RGIA. F. 1260. D. 81. "O sostoianii del i o proizvodstve onykh v raznykh otdeleniiakh komissiei sostavliaiushchikhsia. 4.05.1812." Ll. 1–12 ob.

118 RGIA. F. 1260. D. 81. Ll. 10 ob.–11 ob.

turn Russia into a "lawful monarchy," regularly and for long periods of time turned his attention away from codification, focusing on other issues, primarily foreign policy. Having handed the commission and other important domestic policies fully over to Speransky in 1809, Alexander left the commission under Speransky's unrestricted rule and withdrew from participation or control. Such indifference of the "commissioner-in-chief" bode ill for both the intensity of codification and the quality of its outcomes.

Nevertheless, the compilation of the Civil Code (the new commission's main priority) sped up to its peak by 1810. Despite the widespread historiographical myth of Speransky's almost single-handed authorship, the real amount of work was carried out by the commission's personnel under the supervision of Rosenkampff, who continued as the curator of Civil Code. Meanwhile, Speransky, as much as time would allow, edited the texts that the commission sent to him, stringently correcting their heavy-handed legalese and the "German spirit."[119]

Speransky's efforts to draft an ideal legal code for Russia, just like his general attempts to arrive at the ideal political regime,[120] were doomed to fail. He faced opposition from Russian dignitaties, "overburdened with prejudices and national pride." More to the point, his plans were challenged by competing political projects. The 1809 model, developed by Speransky as an improved type of ideal regular state that incorporated some basic elements of the political and civil nation, paid little heed to the realities of the empire—or rather, it simply ignored them.[121] In March 1812, a large-scale political intrigue put an end to the career of Speransky the reformer. The plot was hatched by, among others, the emperor's sister Ekaterina Pavlovna, Minister of Police Aleksandr Dmitrievich Balashov (1770–1837), proponent of Finnish autonomy Gustaf Mauritz Armfelt (1757–1814), ideologue of Russian romanticist and official nationalism Nikolai Karamzin, French conservative Catholic philosopher Joseph Marie de Maistre (1753–1821),[122] and Baltic German legal expert Gustav Rosenkampff.[123]

---

119 This habit, as well as Speransky's permanent absence from the commission's offices, was witnessed by at least two commission staff members loyal to Speransky: H.L. Jakob and N.S. Il'inskii. See: Jakob. Denkwuerdigkeiten. Pp. 226–45; Il'inskii. Iz Zapisok. Pp. 433 f.

120 [Speranskii]. Plan gosudarstvennogo preobrazovaiia.

121 Excluded from the Speransky plan were Siberia, the Caucasus, Orenburg region, the Don region, and Novorossiia . See also: Gerasimov / Mogilner / Glebov. Novaia imperskaia istoriia. Pp. 154–70.

122 On Maistre, see: Parsamov. Zhozef de Mestr.

123 For more detail, see the works by Marc Raeff and Modest Korff cited in this chapter.

Within weeks of Speransky's exile from St. Petersburg, Rosenkampff returned as head of the Commission for the Compilation of Laws. Another comeback was the decision to revert to the original codification plan.[124] However, the Napoleonic Wars of 1812–15 (which led to devastating losses among the commission's personnel), the confiscation of Speransky's papers, and another change of ideological patterns in internal policy disallowed a return to the previous volume and pace of work. After 1814, separate segments of the Civil, Criminal and Commercial Codes were regularly submitted to the Council of State and usually returned to the commission to be revised.

At the same time, the commission, which in 1810 was moved out of the control of the Ministry of Justice and subsumed under the Council of State, was increasingly used as an expert body and publisher of legislation in effect. Between 1804 and 1822, it provided over two hundred expert opinions on various projects. Among the works of legislation audited by the Commission for the Compilation of Laws in this period were some voluminous works such as the Statute of Military Recruitment, a project of ending serfdom in Livonia, the Odessa city statute, the statutes of promissory notes and bankruptcy, a project to reform governorate administration, and one on improving the judicial system of the city and governorate of St. Petersburg.[125] On the one hand, this revealed the rising trust in the commission as a professional expert body and strengthened its role within the legislative system. On the other, being permanently distracted by urgent requests from the Council of State, the personnel of the commission had little time for their purported priority—legal codification.

5. Conclusion

To conclude, what are the grounds to interpret this model of codification as a forerunner to the official Digest of Laws of the Russian Empire, and in a wider context, as the laboratory and the first massive attempt to shape the foundations of the imperial rights regime?

First, as I see it, the codification technique itself—or, to be more precise, the technique of reductive systematization, hardwired to the Russian positive legislation *in effect* (to "its *own* legends, statutes, and laws")—excluded the whole mass of common unwritten law, just as the Digest of Laws of the Russian Empire would

124 RGIA. F. 1260. D. 81; D. 82. "Predstavlenie Soveta Komissii P.V. Lopukhinu o planakh raboty Komissii na budushchee vremia." D. 1. Ll. 32–33.

125 RGIA. F. 1260. D. 172. "Opis' del, ispol'zovannykh Komissiei dlia razrabotki raznykh proektov i polozhenii." Ll. 25–36 ob.

later do. Legal scholars and historians of law have defined this technique as incorporation of a "historical and practical" or "national" ("nativist") type. Minister of Justice P.V. Lopukhin, reporting to N.N. Novosil'cev in late December 1808 on the achievements of the commission, used the phrase "the German method" to describe this approach.[126] He was largely referring to the tedious long-windedness of the successive edits of legislative texts, as well as endless discussions at the regular meetings of referendaries and editors.

Second, the commission recognized a distinction between "general" (i.e., common throughout the empire) and particular (i.e., specific to a region) legislation. In the latter case, the commission's job was to systematize local legislative norms along the lines of the universal model. These local norms applied to those communities and territories within the empire that by the nature of their cultural and historical difference could not have been ruled by the law of the empire. Among the cases that the commission handled were the Baltic provinces and what used to be known as the "Polish" and "Little Russian" governorates. That regional laws were treated as subsidiary set the Russian case apart from the Prussian experience,e where the codified General State Laws had priority in Polish provinces only and elsewhere were subordinate to the Roman law or the French civil code, adapted and implemented in the Rhine provinces during the Napoleonic Wars. There were no plans whithin the comission to codify legislation for the empire's Muslim peoples and other "aliens" (*inorodtsy*). However, as Paolo Sartori and Pavel Shablei have shown, the strengthening of imperial control over the population of Kazakh steppes and its structural integration into the empire in this time was accompanied by the "recognition" of the *adats* and Sharia law by local administrative officials.[127] For its part, the recognition of historical, cultural, and legal difference of a certain community of imperial subjects would allow for the community's subsequent incorporation into the architecture of the Code/Digest on an ad hoc basis. Such flexibility did not preclude the idea of unification or the gradual replacement of the particular rights regimes by the general corpus of imperial legislation. From a long-term perspective, the "general" laws, being seen as more civilized, "rational," and "just," were supposed to become the universal norm. In other words, the Code/Digest model reflected the fragile balance between general and particular and the dilemma of variety versus *mission civilisatrice*—a balance and dilemma inherent in the imperial rights regime.

---

126 OR RNB. F. 526. D. 42. "Pis'ma Petra Vasil'evicha Lopukhina." A letter from P.V. Lopukhin to N.N. Novosil'cev, December 3, 1808, L. 7 ob.

127 Sartori / Shablei. Sud'ba imperskikh kodificacionnykh proektov.

Third and last, a distinction arose between the original texts of laws as exhaustive corpora of legislative sources and the Code/Digest as a product of systematization and compilation. In 1810, the Council of State informally requested that every article of the Civil Code should list legislative sources of the norms it proclaimed. In 1814, this request received official endorsement and was made compulsory for any work of legal systematization. In the seven years following 1815, Rosenkampff compiled and published the *Systematized Digest of the Laws of the Russian Empire* in twenty-two volumes—a comprehensive collection of the sources of Russian civil law. In this respect, an interesting comment can be found in a letter written on October 30, 1821, by Aleksei Nikolaevich Olenin (1763–1843), state secretary at the legal department of the Council of State. Sending the proceedings and the papers of the Council of State related to the Civil Code revision of 1814–15 to Speransky after his return from exile, Olenin explained the reasons for the fiasco of the past decade, as well as the new rules of the game:

> Some actions of the superior consultative estate, established in order to correct the laws and review important policies of state [...] may prove how far away [...] even the most clever of them can stray. [...] These otherwise very experienced men, fearing [...] the vicissitudes and temerity of the designs and thoughts of our times, dread discovering [...] some secret plot aiming [...] to topple the old regime. It is in this way, as [an attempt] to demolish our traditional laws and to replace them with completely new ones, that some members of the council saw the draft Civil Code. The small format of the book that contained the draft seemed dubious to them. Those used since the days of their very youth to the fact that even the incomplete collection of our civil laws occupies a large pile of paper, or a dozen volumes in folio and in quarto, were exceedingly surprised and even, if I am allowed to say so, scared when it had been announced that the whole mass of legislation could be contained in one book, conveniently published in octavo and quite large print—and it takes only 248 pages. Indeed, their longtime habit of seeing huge piles of existing legislation made it difficult to realize and to be persuaded that [...], with everything superfluous separated, the very essence of a law can usually be expressed in several lines only. [...] This is what I find hard, nay, almost impossible to prove in the absence of a general collection (*sobrania*) or digest (*svoda*) of the existing legislation, which should be arranged by the order of the articles in the draft Civil Code.[128]

If we accept Olenin's version of the events, then every conservative member of the Council of State who, as early as 1815, doubted that it was possible to fit the Civil Code within 248 pages of a printed book, deserved to be awarded the Order of St. Andrew for de facto compiling the multivolume texts *Complete Collection of the Laws of the Russian Empire* and *The Digest of Laws of the Russian Empire.*

useful, detailed & wide-ranging analysis

128 Maikov. Komissia. Pp. 263–65.

List of references

ABASHNIK, VOLODYMYR. Ludwig Heinrich von Jakob (1759–1827), ein hallescher Professor in Char'kov und Sankt Petersburg. In: ERICH DONNERT (Ed.). Europa in der Frühen Neuzeit. Festschrift für Günter Mühlpfordt. Vol. 7. Köln, 2008. Pp. 895–927

ANDREEV, ANDREI IU. / TOZATO-RIGO, D. (Eds.). Imperator Aleksandr I i Frederik-Sezar Lagarp: Pis'ma. Dokumenty / Sostavlenie, vstupitel'nye stat'i i kommentarii. Perevod s francuzskogo V.A. Mil'chinoi. Vol. 1. 1782–1802. Moscow, 2014

BABEROWSKI, JÖRG. Autokratie und Justiz. Zum Verhältnis von Rechtsstaatlichkeit und Rückständigkeit im ausgehenden Zarenreich 1864–1914. Frankfurt a. M., 1996

BETHAM, JEREMY. Précédés de Principes Généraux de Législation Et d'Une Vued' Un Corps Complet de Droit, Terminés Par Un Essai Surl'Influence des Tems Et des Lieux Relativementaux Lois. Paris, 1802

[BETHAM, JEREMY] BENTAM, IEREMIIA. Rassuzhdeniia o grazhdanskikh i ugolovnykh zakonopolozheniiakh s predvaritelnym izlozheniem nachal zakonopolozhenii i vseobshchego nachertaniia polnoi knigi zakonov i s prisovokupleniem opyta o vliianii vremeni i mesta otnositelno zakonov. Per. Mikhaila Mikhailova. St. Petersburg, 1805

BIENER, CHRISTIAN GOTTLOB. Bedenklichkeiten bey Verbannung der ursprünglich fremden Rechte aus Deutschland und Einführung eines allgemeinen National-Gesetzbuches. Halle, 1781

BIKTASHEVA, ALSU. Antropologija vlasti: kazanskie gubernatory pervoj poloviny XIX veka. Moscow, 2012

BIKTASHEVA, ALSU. Kazanskie gubernatory v dialoge vlastei. Pervaia polovina XIX veka. Kazan, 2008

BORISOVA, TATIANA. The Digest of Laws of the Russian Empire: The Phenomenon of Autocratic Legality. In: Law and History Review. Vol. 30 (2012) # 3. Pp. 901–25

BORISOVA, TATIANA. Russian National Legal Tradition: Svod versus Ulozhenie in Nineteenth-Century Russia. In: Review of Central and East European Law. Vol. 33 (2008) # 3. Pp. 295–341

BURBANK, JANE. An Imperial Rights Regime: Law and Citizenship in the Russian Empire. In: Kritika. Vol. 7 (2006) # 3. Pp. 397–431

BURBANK, JANE / COOPER, FREDERIC. Rules of Law, Politics of Empire. In: LAUREN BENTON / RICHARD J. ROSS (Eds.). Legal Pluralism and Empires, 1500–1850, New York, 2013. Pp. 279–94

Bychkov I.A. Speraskii v 1808–1811 gg. (Dopolnitelnye zametki k "Zhizni grafa Speranskogo"). In: Russkaia starina. Vol. 114 (1903) # 4. Pp. 29–40

Chartorizhskij, Adam. Vospominaniia i pisma. Moscow, 2010

Chistovich, Illarion. V pamiat grafa Mikhaila Mikhailovicha Speranskogo. St. Petersburg, 1871

Desquiron de Sant-Agnon, Antoine Toussaint. L'esprit des Institutes de l'empereur Justinien. Vol. 1. Paris, 1807

Diesselhorst, Malte. Die Prozesse des Müllers Arnold und das Eingreifen Friedrichs des Großen. Göttingen, 1984

Dmitriev, Fedor. O zaslugakh grafa Speranskogo russkomu zakonovedeniiu. St. Petersburg, 1852

Fateev, A.N. Akademicheskaia i gosudarstvennaia deiatel'nost M.A. Balug'ianskogo v Rossii. Uzhgorod, 1931

Feldshtein, Grigorii. Glavnye techeniia v istorii ugolovnogo prava v Rossii. Iaroslavl, 1909

Feuer, Kathryn Beliveau. Tolstoy and the Genesis of "War and Peace." Ithaca, N.Y., 1996

Filippov, Aleksandr. Uchebnik istorii russkogo prava (posobie k lekciiam). 5th ed. Iur'ev, 1905

Fleck, Ludwik. The Genesis and Development of a Scientific Fact. Chicago, 1979

Fortunato, Sérgio Fernandes. Vom römisch-gemeinen Recht zum Bürgerlichen Gesetzbuch. In: Zeitschrift für das juristische Studium. (2009) # 4. Pp. 327–38

[Gauenshild, Fedor]. M.M. Speranskii. In: Russkaia starina. Vol. 110 (1902) # 5. Pp. 151–62

Gerasimov Ilia / Mogilner, Marina / Glebov, Sergei. Novaia imperskaia istoriia Severnoj Evrazii. Vol. 2. Kasan, 2017

Golubcov, Vladimir. K biografii grafa P.V. Zavadovskogo. In: Russkii Arkhiv. Vol. 1 (1887) # 1. Pp. 118–28

Gorozhankina, Diana. Istoriko-pravovoi analiz sistematizacii ugolovno-processualnogo zakonodatelstva Rossijskoi imperii pervoj poloviny XIX veka. Ekaterinburg, 2006. Doctoral dissertation, unpublished manuscript

Gosudarstvennyi Sovet. St. Petersburg, 1901

Grech, Nikolai. Zapiski o moei zhisni. Moscow-Leningrad, 1930

Haas, Peter (Ed.). Knowledge, Power and International Policy Coordination. Cambridge, Mass., 1992

Holzner, Burkart. Reality Construction in Society. Cambridge, 1968

Holzner, Burkart / Marx, John. Knowledge Application: The Knowledge System in Society. Boston, 1979

Il'inskii, Nikolai. Iz Zapisok Nikolaia Stepanovicha Il'inskogo. In: Russkii Archiv. Vol. 17 (1879) # 12. Pp. 377–434

Jakob, Lugwig Heinrich von. Denkwürdgkeiten aus meinem Leben. Halle, 2011

Jakob, Ludwig Heinrich von. Grundsätze der Policeygesetzgebung und der Policeyanstalten. Kharkov, 1809

Jakob, Ludwig Heinrich von. Philosophische Rechtslehre oder Naturrecht. 2nd Ed. Halle, 1802

Jakob, Ludwig Heinrich von. Ueber Russlands Papiergeld und die Mittel dasselbe bey einem unveränderlichen Werthe zu erhalten. Halle, 1817

Kaufmann, Dörte. Anton Friedrich Justus Thibaut (1772–1840). Ein Heidelberger Professor zwischen Wissenschaft und Politik. Stuttgart, 2014

Khoteenkov, Vladimir / Cherneta, Valerii. Pervyi ministr narodnogo prosveshcheniia Rossiiskoi imperii P.V. Zavadovskii. Moscow, 1998

Kodan, Sergei / Taborin, Roman. Nesostoiavshaiasia kodifikaciia grazhdanskogo zakonodatelstva Rossii. 1800–1825 gg. Ekaterinburg, 2002

Korf, Modest. Deiateli i uchastniki v padenii Speranskogo. In: Russkaia starina. Vol. 109 (1902) # 3. Pp. 469–508

Korf, Modest. Zhizn' grafa Speranskogo. 2 Vols. St. Petersburg, 1861

Koselleck, Reinhart. Preußen zwischen Reform und Revolution. Allgemeines Landrecht, Verwaltung und soziale Bewegung von 1791–1848. Stuttgart, 1987

Krause, Peter. Geschichte der Justiz- und Verwaltungsbildung in Preußen und Deutschland. In: Christian Baldus / Thomas Finkenauer / Thomas Rüfner (Eds.). Juristenausbildung in Europa zwischen Tradition und Reform. Tübingen, 2008. Pp. 95–125

Kuhli, Milan. Carl Gottlieb Svarez und das Verhältnis von Herrschaft und Recht im aufgeklärten Absolutismus. Frankfurt a. M., 2012

Kuhli, Milan. Power and Law in Enlightened Absolutism—Carl Gottlieb Svarez' Theoretical and Practical Approach. In: Rechtsgeschichte—Legal History. Vol. 21 (2013). Pp. 16–30

Kuhn, Thomas. The Structure of Scientific Revolutions. Chicago, 1962

Kukolnik; Nestor. Iz vospominanii N.V. Kukolnika. In: Istoricheskii vestnik. Vol. 45 (1891) # 7. Pp. 79–99

Kusber, Jan. Eliten- und Volksbildung im Zarenreich während des 18. und in der ersten Hälfte des 19. Jahrhunderts. Studien zu Diskurs, Gesetzgebung und Umsetzung. Stuttgart, 2004

LATKIN, VLADIMIR. Lekcii po istorii russkogo prava. St. Petersburg, 1891–92

LISTOVSKII, IVAN. Graf P.V. Zavadovskii. In: Russkii Arkhiv. Vol. 2 (1883) # 3. Pp. 81–174

LIUBEZNIKOV, OLEG. Nikolai Nikolaevich Novosil'cov—gosudarstvennyi deiatel imperatorskoi Rossii pervoi treti XIX veka. St. Petersburg, 2013. Doctoral dissertation, unpublished manuscript

LUEBKE, DAVID M. Frederick the Great and the Celebrated Case of the Millers Arnold (1770–1779): A Reappraisal. In: Central European History. Vol. 32 (1999) # 4. Pp. 379–408

MAIKOV, PETR. Baron Gustav Andreevich Rozenkampf. In: Russkaia starina. Vol. 120 (1904). Pp. 140–85, 371–429

MAIKOV, PETR. Komissia sostavleniiazakonov pri imperatorakh Pavle I I Aleksandre I. In: Zhurnal ministerstva iusticii (Sept. 1905). Pp. 256–91; (Nov. 1905). Pp. 236–82; (Dec. 1905). Pp. 189–214

MAIKOV, PETR. Vtoroe otdelenie Sobstvennoi Ego Imperatorskogo Velichestva kanceliarii. 1826–1882. Istoricheskii ocherk. St. Petersburg, 1906

MAKAROV, ALEKSANDR. Entwurf der Verfassungsgesetze des Russischen Reiches von 1804: Ein Beitrag zur Geschichte der Kodifikation des russischen Rechts. In: Jahrbücher für Kultur und Geschichte der Slaven. Neue Folge. Vol. 2 (1926) # 2. Pp. 203–366

MEREZHKOVSKY. Dmitry. Aleksandr I. Moscow, 2014

MERTENS, BERND. Gesetzgebungskunst im Zeitalter der Kodifikationen. Tübingen, 2004

NIKOLAI MIKHAILOVICH, VELIKII KNIAZ'. Graf Pavel Aleksandrovich Stroganov. Vol. 2. St. Petersburg, 1903.

NOL'DE, ALEKSANDR. Ocherki po istorii kodifikacii mestnykh grazhdanskikh zakonov pri grafe Speranskom. Pts. I–II. St. Petersburg, 1914

NOVAKOVSKII, VLADIMIR. Biograficheskie ocherki IV. Mikhail Mikhailovich Speranskii. St. Petersburg, 1863

OKHOTIN, NIKITA / KURGANOV, EFIM. Russkii literaturnyi anekdot konca XVIII–nachala XIX veka. Moscow, 1990

PAKHMAN, SEMEN. Istoriia kodofikacii grazhdanskogo prava. 2 Vols. St. Petersburg, 1876

PARSAMOV, VADIM. Zhozef de Mestr i Aleksandr Strurdza. Iz isotrii religioznykh idei Aleksandrovskoi epokhi. Saratov, 2004

PISMA I DNEVNIKI A.I. Turgeneva. St. Petersburg, 1911

PYPIN, ALEKSANDR. Russkie otnosheniia Bentama. In: Vestnik Evropy. Vol. 1 (1869) # 2. Pp. 784–819

RAEFF, MARC. Michael Speransky, Statesman of Imperial Russia: 1772–1839. The Hague, 1957

ROMANOVICH-SLAVATINSKII, ALEKSANDR. Sistema russkogo gosudarstvennogo prava v ego istoriko-dogmaticheskom razvitii. Sravnitel'no s gosudarstvennym pravom Zapadnoi Evropy. Vol. 1. Osnovnye gosudarstvennye zakony. Kiev, 1886

SARTORI, PAOLO / SHABLEI, PAVEL. Sudba imperskikh kodificacionnykh proektov: Adat i shariat v Kasakhskoi stepi. In: Ab Imperio. (2015) # 2. Pp. 63–105

SAVIGNY, FRIEDRICH CARL VON. Vom Beruf unserer Zeit für Gesetzgebung und Rechtswissenschaft. Heidelberg, 1814

SCHÄFER, FRANK LUDWIG. Juristische Germanistik. Frankfurt a. M., 2008

SCHATTENBERG, SUSANNE. Die korrupte Provinz? Russische Beamte im 19. Jahrhundert. Frankfurt a. M. 2008

SCHIEMANN, THEODOR. Geschichte Russlands unter Kaiser Nikolaus I. Vol. 1. Kaiser Alexander I. und die Ergebnisse seiner Lebensarbeit. Berlin, 1904

SCHRÖDER, JAN. Das Verhältnis von Rechtswissenschaft, Juristenausbildung und Rechtspraxis in Deutschland seit dem 18. Jahrhundert. In: CLAES PETERSON / MICHAEL STOLLEIS (Eds.). Rechtswissenschaft als juristische Doktrin. Stockholm, 2011. Pp. 313–37

SEREDONIN, SERGEI. Graf M.M. Speransky: Ocherk gosudarstvennoi deiatel'nosti. St. Petersburg, 1909

SEVASTIANOV, FEDOR. K istorii kodifikacii russkogo prava v pervoi treti XIX veka. In: Vestnik RGGU. (2008) # 4. Pp. 203–21

SHKLOVKIJ, VIKTOR. Material i stil v romane Tolstogo "Voina i mir." The Hague, 1970

[SPERANSKII, MIKHAIL]. Plan gosudarstvennogo preobrazovaiia grafa M.M. Speranskogo (Vvedenie k ulozheniiu gosudarstvennykh zakonov 1809 g.). Moscow, 1905

STORCH, HEINRICH FRIEDRICH VON. Annalen der Alexandrinischen Gesetzgebung. Memorial des Justizministeriums. In: Russland unter Alexander dem Ersten. Vol. 3 (1804) # 8. Pp. 209–67

TABORIN, ROMAN. Sistematizaciia grazhdanskogo zakonodatelstva Rossiiskoi imperii, pervaia polovina XIX veka. Ekaterinburg, 2002. Doctoral dissertation, unpublished manuscript

TAGANCEV, NIKOLAI. Russkoe ugolovnoe pravo: Lekcii. Chast obshchaia. Vol. 1. St. Petersburg, 1902

T[HIBAU]T, ANTON FRIEDRICH. Alexandrinische Gesetzgebung in Russland. In: Allgemeine Jenaische Literatur-Zeitung. Intelligenzblatt. (1804) # 115. Col. 954–60

Thibaut, Anton Friedrich. Über die Notwendigkeit eines allgemeinen bürgerlichen Rechts in Deutschland. Heidelberg, 1814

Tolstoy, Leo. War and Peace / Translated with notes by Louise and Aylmer Maude. Oxford University Press, 2010

Turgeneff, Nikolai. La Russieet les russes. 2 Vols. Paris, 1847

Ungurianu, Dan. The Use of Historical Sources in "War and Peace." In: Rick McPeack / Donna Tussing Orwin (Eds.). Tolstoy on War. Narrative Art and Historical Truth in "War and Peace." Ithaca, N.Y., 2012. Pp. 26–41

Vishlenkova, Elena. Zabotias o dushakh poddannykh: Religioznaia politika v Rossii pervoi chetverti XIX veka. Saratov, 2002

Wendehorst, Christiane. Ist der Kodifikationsstreit entschieden? In: Attila Fenyves / Ferdinand Kerschner / Andreas Vonkilch (Eds.). 200 Jahre ABGB. Evolution einer Kodifikation Rückblick—Ausblick—Methode. Wien, 2012. Pp. 9–38

Whisenhunt, William. In Search of Legality: Mikhail M. Speranskii and the Codification of Russian Law. New York, 2001

Wortman, Richard. The Development of a Russian Legal Consciousness. Chicago, 1976

[Wortman] Uortman, Richard. Vlastiteli i sud'i. Razvitie pravovogo soznaniia v imperatorskoi Rossii. Moscow, 2004

Zakharov, Vitalii. Rossiiskii i zarubezhnyi konstitucionalizm konca XVIII–1-oi chetverti XIX vv. Opyt sravnitelno-istoricheskogo analiza. 2 Vols. Moscow, 2017

Zhikharev, Stepan. Zapiski sovremennika. Moscow-Leningrad, 1955

Elena Vishlenkova

The Time of State-Building Discoveries: Governing Techniques in Health Care and Education[1]

If we imagine that a society in its development moves toward a preselected point or a predictable visualization, then any part of the path that lies behind will be deemed incomplete and merely preparatory. What if this stretch is far from straight? Then the zigzagging path will seem deflected from the desired goal by concessions, reactionary advances, weak will, or bad planning. Both personal wishes and historical evidence may push a historian of Alexandrine Russia to accept such logic of historical narrative and take the path of judgmental reasoning. After all, the ideologues of Nicholas I's reign—that is to say, everyone who set up its tasks and interests in the social sphere—indicated a breakaway from the previous practice of public administration.

Summarizing in 1843 the outcomes of his ten-year administration at the Ministry of Education (Ministerstvo Narodnogo Prosveshcheniia), Sergei Uvarov commented on tables that illustrated the rise in the numbers of schools, teachers, pupils, and professors. He told a story of the decay that school education had experienced before his arrival on the job.[2] Such accounts were nothing new—members of the Holy Synod who once worked at the Bible Society looked back in sadness and talked of a decline in faith.[3] President of the Academy of Medicine and Surgery in St. Petersburg, Ia.V. (James) Wylie, lamented the decay of "medical matters" at the sessions of the 1828 committee that was set up for their reform.[4]

Despite these accounts of decay and restoration, this article will focus on continuity: a continuity outlined not on the institutional level (a field of frequent reforms) but rather in the techniques of administration in healthcare and education. These

1 The article was prepared within the frame of project № 16-06-00467 supported by Russian Foundation for Fundamental Research.

2 Uvarov. Desiatiletie Ministerstva narodnogo prosveshcheniia. P. 348.

3 Skinner. Russia's Scriptural "Reformation." Pp. 73–102.

4 Rossiskii Gosudarstvennyi Istoricheskii Arkhiv (hereafter, RGIA). F. 1294. Op. 5. D. 194. "Delo komiteta, uchrezhdennogo dlia razrabotki proekta preobrazovaniia medicinskogo upravleniia, nachavsheesia v 1828 g., v piati chastiakh. Chast' pervaia. 1828." Ll. 199–203.

two spheres had become priority interests of the Russian state in the late eighteenth century. Their techniques had been created as early as the reign of Alexander I, but they did not become widespread until his younger brother and successor, Nicholas I, took the throne, and they thus became associated with the latter's reign.

It is customary among researchers to assess a period in political history from the standpoint of what had been planned and how much of this planning came to fruition by a certain point in time. This sort of assessment is thus based on taking measurements at two, static points. However, the Alexandrine period fails this static measurement test: it had its periods of reforms and counte-reforms, of liberalism and reaction. Everything changed very fast, and at different moments the discrepancy between the original designs and the real state of affairs was too pronounced. Alexander I did not differ too much from his brother Nicholas in his desire to set up a well-furnished state, and both royal brothers might have been able to describe their vision of such an ideal. However, few of their contemporaries, including those endowed with power of political decision-making, could explain how this ideal could be brought to life on the banks of the Volga and Neva, rather than of the Thames or Rhine.

The experience of reform leading into the early nineteenth century had shown that importing forms of statehood characteristic of modernity was easier than making them work as they did in Berlin or Stockholm, let alone improving them. The second stage of ministerial reform, as outlined by M.M. Speransky in 1810, was in fact triggered by the need to devise a homemade mechanism to kickstart the state machinery. Speransky, the "luminary among Russian administrators," was by no means its only engineer and operator. People of quite radical political opinions agreed that transferring Western institutions into Russia did not guarantee their smooth functioning, which meant that they—each in his own segment—had to set up specific techniques of administration.

This article focuses on the discoveries made by three such men: M.L. Magnitsky, curator of the Kazan educational district; A.B. Kurakin, minister of internal affairs; and Ia.V. Wylie, chief inspector of military medicine.

1. Care of the Subjects' Bodies and Souls

It took almost a whole century to move the care of bodies and souls from the private sphere to the public and even the political.[5] Surely, the government's interests had for a long time been to reduce casualties in the army, protect the empire from

5 Amburger. Beiträge zur Geschichte; Alexander. Catherine the Great. Pp. 185–204; Idem. Bubonic Plague; Renner. Russische Autokratie; Idem. Progress through Power.

epidemics, and train high-quality clerks for the empire's numerous chanceries. But apart from that, the arrival of tutors, schools, boarding schools, and learned medical doctors was mostly the fruit of private initiative—that of Russian nobility or of foreigners residing in Russia.

Doctors in Russia were supervised and regulated by the Medical Collegium (a Russian counterpart of the Prussian Collegium Medicum and the Collegium Sanitatis, which merged in 1799 to form the Berlin Überkollegium). Its members were medical researchers, mostly foreigners or Russians with degrees obtained at European universities. These medical doctors worked under the control and supervision of a Russian government official. One of the most important functions of the collegium was licensing medical practice—that is, granting the right to work as a doctor in the Russian Empire. The collegium was also the central body to oversee provincial medical boards (*gubernskaia vrachebnaya uprava*). The government saw the boards as institutions set up to aid not the sick but rather provincial authorities, in solving judicial and administrative issues (forensic examinations, including cases of grievous bodily harm, army recruitment, and prevention of outbreaks of various epidemics).

By the start of the nineteenth century, Russia had a disproportionate network of private and state-run schools (*gosudarstvennoie narodnoie uchilishche*). These had very little connection with each other and with the country's only university, in Moscow.[6] Alongside with them, Russia had a network of theological seminaries (*dukhovnye seminarii*), which under Peter the Great were grouped into districts of spiritual education, with a theological academy (*dukhovnaia akademiia)* at the head of each district.[7] To train doctors, schools of surgery and medicine were merged into an Academy of Surgery and Medicine, and graduates of theological seminaries were forced to join it. There was never a single plan for establishing educational institutions, and nobody consulted the needs of the population or took its numbers into account. As a rule, schools were opened when and where there was somebody to establish them.

The government's desire to employ doctors and teachers was, further, limited by the scant budget. Throughout the eighteenth century and the first three decades of the nineteenth, the government consistently failed to assess how many doctors and teachers the nation required, or even to outline the limits of the necessary and the sufficient. Since the position of the medical officials and teachers at state-run

---

Pp. 29–54; Smirnova. Medicinskie chiny. Pp. 6–19; Becker. Medicine, Law and the State; Sambuk. Wächter der Gesundheit.

6 Kusber. Eliten- und Volksbildung.

7 Vishlenkova. Dukhovnaia shkola.

schools was quite low on the ladder of bureaucracy, their salaries (unless boosted by privileges established for foreign citizens) were rather low. These low salaries allowed for the presence of large numbers of teachers and doctors on the state's payroll. For instance, it was accepted that the number of medical officials should somehow correlate with that of structural units of the state: each administrative part of the Russian Empire, each army unit, and each vessel should have its own medical personnel (*lekari*). In 1802, the empire employed 1,519 medics, of which 422 were in the army, 218 in the navy, and 879 in regional medical boards, hospitals, and quarantine stations—and there were still 475 vacancies on the state payroll.[8]

Having received medical affairs under the control of his ministry, V.P. Kochubei, minister of internal affairs, discovered that there were significant numbers of vacancies and that the salary offered to prospective candidates was below subsistence level.[9] According to the 1799 staffing plan, a senior medic made 400 roubles a year, a junior medic, 180, and a candidate of medicine and surgery, only 150 roubles.[10] In contrast, the charter of 1804 provided a professor with a 2,000-rouble salary plus allowances for accommodation, travel, and firewood. Foreign doctors also netted a higher salary. Since the government did not need to bargain with Russian doctors, who were used to living very close to poverty, it had leverage to make them work for a very small fixed salary.[11]

The reconstruction of state that was characteristic of Alexander I's early reign revealed a change of priorities in the policies of the government. Education and healthcare, formerly peripheral matters, were now issues of special governmental priority.[12] This transformation likely came as the Alexandrine reformers were getting acquainted with the practices of administration in the leading countries of contemporary Europe, such as France, Prussia, the Habsburg Monarchy, and Sweden. Close connections, family ties, interaction at the international labor market where the Russian Empire hired university-educated professionals, and the practice of aristocratic grand tours all contributed to the rise of a cosmopolitan outlook. In the early years of Alexander's reign, the educational experience of the emperor's "young associates" was the foundation for the political construction of an empire of modernity.

---

8 Stoletie voennogo ministerstva. P. 75.
9 PSZ I. Vol. 28. №. 21866. P. 1156.
10 Stoletie voennogo ministerstva. P. 75.
11 PSZ I. Vol. 30. № 22974. P. 195.
12 Vishlenkova. The State of Health. Pp. 39–75.

While tracing cultural transfer back to its source, researchers almost always discover that the information that reformers had at their disposal was limited or distorted and that they had to rely on their imagination to fill in the gaps. This fact has nothing to do with "Russian naiveté" or the "derivative" nature of Russian modernization. Rather, it can be seen as a mechanism of primary adaptation at work. American visionaries followed the same path when they imagined the "German university" for the United States or adjusted the famous Prussian school system for the use in American public schools.

The area of public administration that dealt with healthcare was, in the early nineteenth century, known as the "state medical knowledge" (*gosudarstvennoie vrachebnovedenie*).[13] In Russia and many European societies, this field was then based on the works of the Austrian German cameralist J.P. Frank, who developed the concept of *medicinischen Polizey* (medical police).[14] To turn medicine into an affair of the state, Alexandrine reformers took the empire's "medical matters" through many transformations. Every few years, they changed the institution that controlled civil and military medical personnel, as well as hospitals and pharmacies: the Medical Collegium disbanded, and the medical expedition was set up at the Ministry of Internal Affairs (MVD, 1803); the medical department was created at the Ministry of Army (*voenno-sukhoputnykh del*, 1805); the military expedition was set up at the Ministry of Police (1810). Medical councils were set up at the Ministry of Education (1810) and the Ministry of Police (1811), and then the two councils were merged (1822). In this atmosphere of permanent reshuffling, reforms little touched provincial or capital medical boards.[15] Beginning in 1805, the control over medical matters was split between four ministries: navy, army, internal affairs, and education. All these reforms aimed to transform Russian medicine from a corporate affair into an applied sphere of public administration, and doctors thus also took up positions as officials at various government agencies.[16]

While the ministerial reform used the interests of the state to split doctors into several institutions, educators, on the contrary, were for the first time lumped together under one. The Ministry of Education (Ministerstvo Narodnogo Prosvescheniia) was created in the Russian Empire even earlier than its counterpart in Prussia. When the Prussian Oberschulcollegium was disbanded in 1808, it was replaced subsumed under the Ministry of Internal Affairs by the Department of Education (with its first president none other than famed scholar Wilhelm von

13 RGIA. F. 1294. Op. 10. Vn. op. 3. D. 47. "Zhurnal Medicinskogo Soveta. 1842." L. 381.

14 Stochik / Zatravkin / Stochik. Stanovlenie gosudarstvennoi mediciny. P. 48.

15 Poddubnyi / Egorysheva / Sherstneva. Istoriia zdravookhraneniia.

16 Vishlenkova. The State of Health. Pp. 39–75.

Humboldt). The two ministries were also different in their main objective: the one in Russia had to create a space for schools almost from scratch, while the one in Prussia dealt with centralizing the multitude of state-run schools of various types.

2. Expanding the Space for Schools

The institutional background of the Alexandrine educational reform has been described in detail by researchers. Six educational districts, each with a university at its head, were supposed to set up a network of semiautonomous corporations of scholars, who in their turn had to create and oversee schools. In 1804, the empire had fifty-three gymnasia and head schools (*glavnye narodnye uchilishcha*) and nine hundred petty schools (*malye narodnye uchilishcha*), with a total of 33,715 students.[17] In actuality, however, universities proved to be little more than ivory towers. In the first decade of their existence, the new universities were self-contained, isolated from the local community, which made some of them prone to intracorporate conflict, labor opportunism, and oligarchic democracy.

The vertical pattern of subordination almost collapsed. District curators met for their sessions in St. Petersburg (rather than in their districts) and thus did not observe the work of their universities and knew little about them. In a similar way, university professors could hardly imagine the methods of teaching and the level of knowledge at the schools (*uchilishcha*) that they were supposed to be overseeing. The officials at the ministry found it very difficult to make the professors submit reports, and the professors faced the same problem with teachers and principals of subordinate schools. Both the archives of the ministry and the materials of school committees at universities feature very scant collections of reports for the Alexandrine period. We face here precisely what I. Khristoforov (and later, A. Teslia) defined as "undermanagement"—that is, a situation wherein some objects under the authorities' control fell off the radar.[18] Socially and geographically distant objects and institutions remained invisible. This lack of information was partially compensated for by an administrative practice inherited from the previous century—that of unexpected inspections (visitations), followed by personnel reshuffling. This reshuffling was based on visitors' personal impressions, their written statements, and the documents archived at (or missing from) the chancery office.

17 Ziablovskii. Noveishee zemleopisanie. P. 323.
18 Khristoforov. Sud'ba reformy; Teslia. Mezhdu ideologiei i real'nost'iu.

Another problem was chronic resource poverty. Even though the staffing plans for education and healthcare officials were quite modest for such a big country, the government could not attract the number of candidates required for filling vacancies. International hires were very expensive (including organizational work, travel and accommodation allowances, increased salary, and privileges for foreigners in Russian service). The efficiency of foreigners was also low: some foreign doctors chose not to go to Russia after all; many officials did not know Russian and required the service of interpreters; and they would not tolerate direct orders from their superiors, could easily quit their service when the conditions changed, and were generally not as loyal as their Russian employees.

On top of that, the government had little funds to develop the infrastructure for healthcare and education. The problems of procuring the appropriate buildings, tools, textbooks, recent research literature, and medication were ubiquitous; students and patients were too expensive to maintain; travel expenses were too high. As a result, some disciplines were taught on paper only, some educators had to do multiple jobs, schools admitted fewer students than planned and lost more on their way to graduation, the medical boards went empty at times of conscription, state-employed medical workers engaged in private practice, and hospitals lacked beds and equipment.

On the one hand, there was more of everything than in previous eras, but on the other, the increasingly complex state needed more doctors and teachers but lacked funds for them. The existing institutions lacked officials, and officials were underpaid (inflation ate up almost 50 percent of the salaries and budget in state-run institutions during the wartime years of 1805–15).

As time advanced, the issue of lack of standards in education and medicine became more pronounced. Every boarding school or hospital, every teacher or medical professional, was guided by the most general—or personal—ideas of what was required. Although the Chief Office for Schools (*Glavnoie upravlenie uchilishch*) tried to work out educational standards, it was still impossible to do so quickly and in a conventionally acceptable way. This is also hardly surprising: in Prussian schools, a similar process of unification began under Minister K.A. von Zedlitz (1731–93) and lasted throughout the nineteenth century. The establishment of a single, state-controlled educational canon in Germany was advanced by ideologues of the German nation (in particular, the Grimm brothers), who rooted its solidarity in common cultural and educational values,[19] as well as by the General State Laws for the Prussian States of 1794. But the centrali-

19 WIELAND. Katalonien.

zation of the land administration could not terminate the large variety of local and confessional schools. Prior to the second wave of Prussian reforms (under Baron vom Stein and Fuerst von Hardenberg, 1810), the transformations adopted were often referred to as "paper reform."

3. The Practice of Licensing Control

Having reformed the system of control over doctors and medical work, Alexander's government soon found out that it was not working. With corporate control now removed, the government had devised nothing to succeed it. In 1807, the St. Petersburg medical board submitted information on one hundred medical professionals active in the capital to the MVD medical expedition. Likewise, upon request from the ministry, pharmacies reported the names of St. Petersburg doctors whose signatures appeared on medical prescriptions—a list that totaled 580.[20] A.B. Kurakin, newly inaugurated as minister of internal affairs was shocked by the huge discrepancy. He suspected that at least two hundred doctors in the capital practiced their art without the required license, and he opined that these were either foreigners or mountebanks and uneducated "empiricists."[21] Outside the capital cities, the situation might have been still worse. Mass violations of the emperor's decrees revealed that the ministry had no mechanisms of control at its disposal.

To be able to enter practice, all medical professionals had to pass an examination administered by special expert committees established by governmental orders[22]—a system of control analogous to the ones used at the time in Sweden, Prussia, Austria, and France. In Britain, the responsibility for control was exercised by medical corporations. After the Medical Collegium was disbanded, the right to issue doctor's licenses was conferred on the MVD medical council, the Academies of Medicine and Surgery in St. Petersburg and Moscow, imperial universities in Vilna , Dorpat , Moscow, Kazan, and Kharkov, and medical boards in provincial capitals. Thus the Alexandrine reformers terminated the corporate monopoly that professional elites had on the examination of practicing doctors' knowledge and competencies.[23]

20 PSZ I. Vol. 29. № 22539. P. 1199.

21 Ibid.

22 RGIA. F. 1294. Op. 11. D. 62. "Delo o provedenii ispytanii na poluchenie medicinskikh zvanii raznymi litsami. 1807." L. 3.

23 RGIA. F. 1294. Op. 1. Sviazka 50. D. 4. "Predstavlenie s izlozheniem pravil, koimi Medicinskii Sovet mog by rukovodstvovat'sia. 1808." L. 2 ob.

There was little opposition from the medical elites. The small body of professors of the Academy of Medicine and Surgery, who often doubled as members of the medical council, found managing the flow of license seekers to be extremely difficult. Newly established universities had too little time to fully deploy their medical departments. The universities in Kazan and Kharkov only managed to hire one or two professors of medicine.[24] To make licensing locally manageable, the medical council at the MVD suggested that provincial administrative offices (*pravleniia*) could be used as venues for examination (but not assessment) of potential licensees. Officials in the administration of the *gubernia* would receive exam questions in sealed envelopes from St. Petersburg, and the candidates' responses were sent to the capital for assessment, also under seal. In response, the ministry would either issue a license for medical practice and send it to the provincial capital or else refuse the license.[25] Officials at the provincial administration thus acted as agents who ensured that the examination answers were genuine and submitted by licensee candidates.[26]

However, medical councillors often reported to the minister that this system was vulnerable and prone to abuses. An 1807 inspection showed that practicing doctors throughout the country preferred to stay free from any state control. Kurakin admitted that the Medical Collegium alone was a more efficient controlling body than the ministries that had inherited the collegium's functions.[27] Officials at the Ministry of Army hired foreign doctors without consulting the Ministry of Internal Affairs. Universities awarded medical ranks without procuring the approval of the "chief medical agency."[28] Nobody had full information, and nobody saw to it that licensing orders be strictly followed.[29] How was medical governance possible, asked Kurakin, when the government had no data even on the number of medical officials themselves, and when no personnel files ("general register of medical ranks") were kept?[30] For the minister, the universal solution for administrative chaos lay in well-established bookkeeping and data collection.

24 RGIA. F. 733. Op. 49. D. 138. "Delo o prisvoenii prof. I.M. Shumlianskomu zvaniia zasluzhennogo professora i ob uvol'nenii ego. 1811–1817." L. 1 ob.

25 RGIA. F. 1294. Op. 1. Sviazka 50. D. 4. "Predstavlenie s izlozheniem pravil, koimi Medicinskii Sovet mog by rukovodstvovat'sia. 1808." L. 5.

26 RGIA. F. 1294. Op. 11. D. 62. "Delo o provedenii ispytanii na poluchenie medicinskikh zvanii raznymi litsami. 1807." L. 22.

27 PSZ I. Vol. 27. № 21105. P. 1109; PSZ I. Vol. 28. № 21866. Pp. 1153–61.

28 PSZ I. Vol. 29. № 22539. P. 1200.

29 RGVIA. F. 879. Op. 1. D. 31 "Perepiska s ministrom Kurakinim. 1808." L. 1.

30 PSZ I. Vol. 29. № 22539. P. 1199.

To put an end to private practice of herbalists, chiropractors, and medical quacks, as well as unlicensed foreigners, the minister ordered the MVD's medical expedition to make a list of "legitimate" medical professionals and send it to every pharmacy.[31] From then on, every prescription was required to list the doctor's first and last name and rank. The pharmacist, before selling medication, had to check the doctor's legitimacy in the register of licensed medical professionals (Russian Medical Register, *Rossiiskii medicinskii spisok*). The sale could proceed only if the name of the doctor was on the list.

Since the medical register had a controlling function, publishing it became an important affair of the state.[32] The register was to include doctors of all ranks and specializations who worked at all institutions. Officials at the Ministries of Army and Navy had to supply lists of military medics, the Office of the Court had to list physicians in service to the royal family, and the universities had to record all medical ranks awarded and medical licenses issued.[33] Provincial governors were responsible for the information on privately practicing doctors and retired medical officials, while the medical expedition at the MVD reported on medical professionals working under the medical boards. Finally, pharmacies recorded and submitted information on all prescriptions issued by unlicensed practitioners. This network finally established the practice of information exchange between various agencies. Officials of the medical expeditions were charged with bringing the collected data together into an alphabetically organized register, eliminating repetitions. By order of the government, owners of private pharmacies had to buy a copy of the register (reissued annually) and also pay for monthly installments with some addenda.[34] Selling medication in accordance with a prescription written out by an unlisted doctor now became punishable. Thus a medical professional not "white listed" was automatically marginalized, regardless of his type of degree and of the university that awarded it. In this way, Kurakin managed to set up a suprainstitutional system of control over doctors and their work. This system had its own problems (for instance, it often for years preserved the names of the doctors who died or were killed in action),[35] but it worked.

At about the same time, the Ministry of Education started to standardize the amount and content of knowledge that was require of medical professionals of

---

31 Ibid.

32 Rossiiskii medicinskii spisok.

33 PSZ I. Vol. 29. № 22539. P. 1200.

34 RGIA. F. 1294. Op. 1. Sviazka 62. D. 26. "O dostavlenii ministru dukhovnykh del i narodnogo prosveshcheniia svedenii. 1820." L. 7 ob.

35 Zatravkin / Shchepin / Oleinikova. Obespechennost' vrachami. Pp. 236–40.

various degrees and specializations. This process culminated in a collected piece of conventional requirements, *On the Rules for Examination of Medical Officials* (1810).[36] When the medical matters were taken out of the Ministry of Internal Affairs and subsumed under the Ministry of Police, officials at the latter spent significant time and effort standardizing the data collected in the course of medico-topographic studies of the Russian Empire. Aiming to turn accounts that were widely varied in content and genre into unified reports on human and natural resources of the Russian state, the officials set up a single questionnaire and added instructions on the language and structure of the report, as well as the study techniques.[37] By the 1830s and 1840s, this practice had turned medico-topographical studies from a private initiative of a small body of intellectuals (as it was in the Alexandrine period) into an act of state-sanctioned self-description, recorded by medical officials.[38]

A similar drive toward improved state control, unification, and standardization was on the agenda of the new generation of officials at the Ministry of Education, who succeeded the early nineteenth-century reformers.

4. From Setting Up Institutions to the Practices of Governance

The latter half of Alexander I's reign was marked by increased dissatisfaction among Russian dignitaries about the schools and especially universities set up at the start of the century. In the fifteen years of their struggling existence, they failed to produce quick results, develop a viable corporate culture, or take root in local communities. But it was not this that irked the government. As Rolf Haaser has shown, anarchist actions by Prussian students triggered revisionism in Russian governmental policies.[39] "Literature, science, justice, even the holiness of the altars—everything is in the hands of the universities," A.S. Sturdza, the Russian ambassador to Prussia, wrote to the emperor, "but there is nothing to prove that they administer [these] assets of state in a proper way."[40] Having hardly escaped student violence, Sturdza was made a member of the Chief Office for Schools—a strategizing body under the Ministry of Education. Once there, he initiated inspections of Kazan and St. Petersburg Universities. Like-minded members of the office used the radicalism of the youth, philosophic dissent, and professorial

---

36 O PRAVILAKH OB EKZAMENAKH medicinskikh chinovnikov. Col. 616–18.

37 GATINA. Vrachebnaia ekspertiza.

38 VISHLENKOVA / GATINA. Izlozhit' predmet scientificheski. Pp. 154–69.

39 HAASER. Ot bratstva po oruzhiiu. Pp. 31–63.

40 STURDZA. Zapiska o nyneshnem polozhenii Germanii. P. 153.

squabbles as bogeymen to scare the emperor into establishing a more stringent control by the ministry's officials over schools.[41] As was expected, inspections proved that the universities' "financial books" were ill kept, their budgets in disarray, the day-to-day life marred by conflicts between "parties." Inspections also saw a direct connection between student unrest and course content, and they shrouded foreign scholars invited to Russian service with a cloud of suspicion and accusations of ingratitude and disloyalty.

The newly appointed curators of the St. Petersburg and Kazan educational districts, D.P. Runich and M.L. Magnitsky, radically transformed the style and type of their relations with their respective university communities. Contrary to popular suspicion, they did not aim to close any schools but rather to turn their schools into regularly functioning bodies. Both treated professorial councils as the Other who did not understand the rules of the game and thus had to be civilized. Both curators had to modify the teachers' consciousness in order to improve training of officials in the service of the empire. In this respect, what Magnickii did in Kazan in 1819–26 amounts to a certain administrative experiment.

Having started his term as curator in St. Petersburg, Magnitsky first focused on improving written communication with Kazan University. The previous practice of observing university life solely through letters received from the rector was unsatisfactory to Magnitsky, who demanded that the secretary of the university council keep the books "in perfection" and send copies of entries to the curator.[42] This practice implied both information transfer in the proper sense and the use of a specific language for its implementation.[43] In the nineteenth century, many European countries saw legalese become the professional language of government administrators, which helped them strengthen their grip over other social groups. In case of Russian universities, communication in legalese meant that texts written by professors would be understandable to officials in the chancery rooms.

Magnitsky's determination led to some resistance from Kazan professors, many of whom were graduates of old German universities. Members of the professorial council tried to explain to the curator, as he recollected, that "language of administration (*delovoi slog*) is not part of linguistic art (*slovesnost'*) and should not be

41 The crisis of German universities was known in the Russian government circles. See: Andreev. Rossiiskie universitety. Pp. 473–76; Minakov. Russkii konservatizm. Pp. 235–37; Parsamov. Zhozef de Mestr.

42 Nacional'nyi Arkhiv Respubliki Tatarstan (hereafter, NART). F. 92. Popechitel' kayanskogo uchebnogo okruga. Op. 1. D. 599. "Zhurnal iskhodiashchikh bumag." L. 72 ob.

43 Levinson. Nekotorye nabliudeniia. Pp. 126–46.

studied by those who know the general rules of the latter."[44] In his turn, Magnitsky called the language of academic exchange "scholastic" and "hypocritical."[45] His clerks had to translate this language into one that was not only "universally comprehensible, but also pleasant and attractive."[46] This response shifted the blame for the ministry's incapacity onto the professors themselves.

Commissioned to rectify the faults discovered during the inspection, Magnitsky started with teaching the "right" language to the professors. He achieved this task by writing a body of texts (his "instructions") of an ideological nature.[47] These texts formulated the government's plans and the tasks that the university faced as a state-run institution. The latter included producing scientific knowledge, improving teaching techniques, publishing books, training officials and educators who would succeed the current generation, exerting governance over the educational district, and finally, setting all of the above "on the firm foundation of Christian religion."[48] In his weekly circular letters, the curator explained to the university council that stringent forms of bookkeeping had advantages over arbitrary texts. He also provided examples of negative consequences that would result from violations of unified style in the language of administration.[49]

Simultaneously, Magnitsky introduced formalized assessments of the students' knowledge and behavior: "excellent," "very good," "good," "average," "newly admitted or under examination," "improvable," and "under special control."[50] Now educators could not use narrative to characterize their student's personalities or command of the discipline. Every month, the curator would enter the grades reported by the university's departments into a single table,[51] and he expected

---

44 Magnitskii. Kratkoe rukovodstvo. P. 13.

45 Ibid. Pp. 85 f.

46 Ibid. Pp. 84 f.

47 Instruktsiia direktoru Kazanskogo universiteta. Col. 1199–220.

48 Ibid. Col. 1207.

49 NART. F. 92. Op. 1. D. 1247. "O razdelenii del universitetskogo pravleniia na dva razriada. 1820." Ll. 1–11 ob.

50 RGIA. F. 733. Op. 40. D. 205. "Prilozhenie k delu o revizii Kazanskogo universiteta i gimnazii general-maiorom P.F. Zheltukhinym: spiski professorov, studentov universiteta i raznye svedeniia o nikh, vedomost' ob uchenikakh Kazanskoi gimnazii, nastavleniia direktoru universiteta o vnutrennem i naruzhnom blagoustroistve dlia studentov universiteta, kratkaia vedomost' sostoianiia universiteta, tetradi studentov po frantsuzskomu iazyku, zhurnal iskhodiashchikh bumag po revizii gimnazii i universiteta i drugie dokumenty. 1826." L. 13.

51 RGIA. F. 733. Op. 39. D. 354. "Delo o predostavlenii otcheta o sostoianii Kazanskogo universiteta. 1821." L. 6 ob.

school principals to send him identical tables. Unlike Prussian reformers, whose objective in using registers was to monitor students' progress and to group them according to their academic success, Magnitsky's aim was to control the work of professors and schoolteachers and make decisions on their careers.

Mirroring the structure of the collegiums on the highest level of state administration, Magnitsky introduced a new office within the university's self-rule—that of an appointed director responsible for economic and financial matters. Using the director to limit the power of the rector and the professorial council, the curator split corporate governance into two segments and mandated that each of them report to him separately. In addition, members of the council and the board (*pravleniie*) had to send Magnitsky monthly memoranda (short abstracts of the proceedings) and, every fortnight, an "accident report."

In these reports, the curator was most interested in the cases of "disdain of colleagues," "guile" (*pronyrstvo*), complaints, slander, and insults. Magnitsky's determination to fight the abuse of corporate relations helped him legitimize his usurpation of the right of assessing a professor's academic qualities, a usurpation that betrayed his intention to have these qualities replaced by loyalty. Introducing a candidate for a position at the university, the curator usually listed his achievements in the following order: "exemplary behavior and Christian mindset" (*obraz myslei*), "laborious service, diligence, teaching in accordance with the spirit of the royally approved instruction to the rector of Kazan University," "excellent academic performance of his students," and finally, his merits as a researcher.[52] Citing his concern for the university's political reputation, the curator started editing and censoring professors' notes for their public speeches.

Magnitsky put an end to the practice of referring conflicts and arguments to the attention of university councils.[53] As a result, professors and adjuncts lost access to corporate self-regulation and to justice within their own estate. Dissenting opinions and complaints stopped being archived, and the right to adjudicate conflicts now solely belonged to the curator. Professors felt his unseen presence through his letters, which were read aloud at sessions of the council and the board, and his orders revealed that the curator knew the internal life of the university well. Many a professor in these years lived in permanent fear of being fired or forced to resign, which happened quite often and was based on the assessment provided by the director and rector. To prove their loyalty and

52 RGIA. F. 733. Op. 40. D. 113. "Delo ob uvol'nenii professora Pal'mina. 1824–1835." L. 42 ob.

53 ORRK NBL KFU. № 7831. "Pis'mo popechitelia M.L. Magnitskogo rektoru G.B. Nikol'skomu 14 fevralia 1822." Ll. 10–10 ob.

remain in service, professors strove to assist the curator in rectifying "universal harmful influence" (*obshchepriniatoe vrednoe vospitanie*).[54] In their public speeches and addresses, these newly made associates of Magnitsky's started to describe the westernization of Russia as a danger brought about by their foreign colleagues.[55] They began to criticize the theory of natural law and desecularize the university. The curator had thus set up an efficient mechanism for controlling the faculty.

Magnitsky tried his hand at both practice and theory of public administration. Before being placed at the head of the Kazan educational district, he had gained much experience in bookkeeping (including chancery management) at the Russian embassies in France and the Habsburg Monarchy, at the Ministry of Internal Affairs, at the legislative department of the Council of State, and at the Committee for Military Statutes and Regulations at the Ministry of Army.[56] In his letters, reports, and larger accounts of his Kazan experience, Magnitsky presented it as an "upheaval" in the Russian educational administration.[57] Magnickii saw his primary achievement as the creation of a cohesive system of education that suited the requirements of the Russian state and that deserved to be implemented in other educational districts of the empire.[58]

In 1826 Magnitsky was exiled to Revel, and he subsequently left the political stage. However, the administrative technique that he had developed found supporters even among his personal enemies, since the technique allowed for successful control of both the content of tuition and its quality. In the latter half of the 1820s, in addition to monthly memoranda and numerous reports, professors had to send to St. Petersburg their reviews of the disciplines that they taught, assessments of the state of affairs in these disciplines (in the form of annotated bibliographies), course syllabi, information on the textbooks that they recommended, and copies of their speeches from university events. To process this flow of highly specialized documentation, the government had to double the number of clerical staff at the ministry and employ officials with university education.

---

54 ORRK NBL KFU. № 4045. "Slovo o tseli istinnogo vospitaniia, proiznesennoe v torzhestvennom sobranii Imperatorskogo Kazanskogo Universiteta, byvshem iiulia 6-go dnia 1824 goda ordinarnym professorom i kavalerom Vladimirom Bulyginym." L. 119.

55 Ibid. L. 119 ob.

56 Minakov. Mikhail Leont'evich Magnitskii. Pp. 268–71.

57 RGIA. F. 733. Op. 39. D. 354. "Delo o predostavlenii otcheta o sostoianii Kazanskogo universiteta 1821." L. 7.

58 Sobstvennoruchnoe vsepoddanneishee pis'mo. P. 363.

5. A Drive toward Formalization

In the eighteenth century, the social, administrative, and financial position of doctors in the Russian Empire was established in an informal way—so to say, "manually." Everything depended on whether the doctor arrived in Russia on his own accord or through international hire (i.e., at the invitation of the Russian government); whether he had the status of a foreign-educated doctor or had graduated from a Russian school of medicine; whether he had an academic degree or only a certificate of a university graduate; whether he intended to join the service of the state or establish a private practice; and whether he wanted to live in a capital or a provincial town. On the basis of these and other choices, the doctor entered the network of informal ties, paternalism, and dependence on personal services and others' opinions of him.

A number of important initiatives aimed at weakening this personal dependence on patrons and enemies, and at making doctors in Russia more answerable to the state, were introduced in the Alexandrine period by the emperor's chief resident physician, president of St. Petersburg Academy of Medicine and Surgery, and chief medical inspector of the army Ia.V. Wylie.[59]

A pastor's son, Wylie had graduated from Edinburgh University and had worked in private practice as well as served as an army doctor in Russia. In the 1790s, the Medical Collegium made him first "doctor of medicine" and then "doctor of medicine and surgery." His patron Count Aleksandr Kutaisov helped him become chief resident physician to Paul I. In the coup d'etat that ended Paul's reign, it was Wylie who declared the emperor dead of apoplexy. Having earned the trust of Alexander I, Wylie followed the young monarch in his military campaigns and saved him from being taken prisoner in the Battle of Austerlitz.

The emperor's patronage gave Wylie power and financial opportunities, setting the ground for his rapid career rise. Having concentrated power in his hands, Wylie showed by his own example the efficiency of personal responsibility vis-à-vis the weakness of institutional change. With little to no participation by the ministry or its agencies, the chief inspector reorganized the field medicine system of the Russian army almost on his own.

Since being appointed member and then dean of the medical council at the Ministry of Education, Wylie spoke against the dispersal of control over medical administration across several ministries and the subdivision of state medical

59 Stoletie voennogo ministerstva. P. 27.

service into civil, army, and navy branches.[60] Almost all medical administrators agreed with Wylie that the split had led to a decrease in healthcare quality.[61] After the medical boards and the local-level (*uezd*) doctors were subordinated to officials on the governorate (*gubernia*) level, the state of affairs in civil healthcare worsened. This situation led to both a case of limited understanding and a clash of interests. In some instances, clerks blocked the initiatives by doctors who wanted to protect the interests of their patients in demanding more funds for sanitary measures. The doctors who suffered in such exchanges reported that officials could easily curb a physician's professional zeal by delaying papers recommending his rank promotion or an award at the *gubernia*'s chancery office, or by mentioning cases of misbehavior in his documents. This fear made medics quite unwilling to advance their own initiatives or to criticize *gubernia* officials, and it forced them to comply even with the crankiest of orders.[62]

An 1810 attempt by medical elites to reintroduce collegiate self-rule failed,[63] and in the following years, homeland war and foreign campaigns made any further such endeavors irrelevant. Wylie revisited this idea only in 1828, when he was made head of the Committee for Reforming the Administration of Civil Medicine.[64] Through his work for the committee, he proved the inefficiency of bureaucrats' control over healthcare. With their characteristic incompetence, they reduced administration to three issues only: bookkeeping, staffing lists, and budgeting. Each of the four ministries dealt with its own segment of medical officials: professors and students, civil, army, or navy medical professionals, respectively. But all of these entities, Wylie argued, were parts of the same whole, which chancery clerks failed to grasp. Meanwhile, the divided doctors were hindered by the cumbersome governance system in their attempts to use their knowledge to solve

60 RGIA F. 1294. Op. 1. Sviazka 52. D. 43. "O vybore uchenogo sekretaria medicinskogo soveta dlia otpravleniia del dekana za otsutstviem ego i o naznachenii komiteta dlia preobrazovaniia vrachebnoi nauki v Rossii. 1810."

61 RGIA. F. 1294. Op. 3. D. 7. "O rassmotrenii proekta instruktsii vrachebnym upravam. 1817." L. 2 ob.

62 RGIA. F. 1294. Op. 5. D. 194. "Delo komiteta, uchrezhdennogo dlia razrabotki proekta preobrazovaniia medicinskogo upravleniia, nachavsheesia v 1828 g., v piati chastiakh. Chast' pervaia. 1828." L. 204 ob.

63 RGIA. F. 1297. Op. 9 b. Kn. 71. D. 135. "Po predstavleniiu uchenogo sekretaria Medicinskogo soveta s mneniem o preobrazovanii medicinskogo dela. 1810." L. 396.

64 RGIA. F. 1294. Op. 5. D. 194. "Delo komiteta, uchrezhdennogo dlia razrabotki proekta preobrazovaniia medicinskogo upravleniia, nachavsheesia v 1828 g., v piati chastiakh. Chast' pervaia. 1828." L. 1.

complex issues of state—that is, to grapple with epidemics or to improve medical science and education.[65]

Committee members cited numerous written requests from inspectors of local medical boards, who asked for freedom from regional control. However, Nicholas I's government left in place the system of double control over medical officials—a system that was both "horizontal" (by regional authorities) and "vertical" (by professionals in the medical council). Both the *gubernia* offices and medical councils were answerable to the Minister of Internal Affairs, who had power to adjudicate their disagreements. Also preserved was the institutional division into civil, army, and navy doctors, since this division had been deemed rational from the standpoint of *raisons d'état*. Thus no return to the corporate state was possible.

Nevertheless, in the domain of administrative techniques, Nicholas I's government proved more pliable. It agreed to the medical elite's suggestion that relations within medical administration should be formalized—that is, a formal definition should be provided for statuses, contacts, and links between medical officials and other groups of civil servants. All this was possible by means of rank promotion. For the growing group of officials with medical education, the issue of being incorporated into the hierarchy of ranks, grades, and salaries was vitally important. Foreign doctors could well be satisfied with exclusive clauses in the hiring agreement or with lucrative private practice, but graduates of Russian medical schools needed a regulatory contract with the state.

As early as 1810, Wylie (as well as other leaders of the "service estates") developed a draft "general"—applicable to all physicians regardless of their institutional affiliation—correlation of ranks, grades, and job titles.[66] What he offered was a stringent scheme of medical service, adoptable only due to the scant financial resources of the Russian state and the low social background of most Russian doctors. In the first quarter of the nineteenth century, most graduates of the Academies of Medicine and Surgery in Moscow and St. Petersburg were impecunious graduates of theological seminaries. For them, leaving the clergy as an estate and being awarded a rank in the service of the state was an act of social elevation in itself. Judging by the information in the archives of the academies, the underside of this kind of democratization of the medical profession was the frequency of cases of drunkenness, scuffles, theft, and class disruption. Every year, culprits were expelled from academies and sent to the army as conscripts. This might explain the reason for a certain suspicious at-

65 Ibid. L. 98 ob.

66 RGIA. F. 733. Op. 99. D. 59. "Delo ob utverzhdenii proekta novogo polozheniia o proizvodstve v klassnye chiny medicinskikh chinovnikov. 1816–1817." Ll. 19–71.

titude toward subordinates on the part of Wylie, one that permeates his project. It seems that the chief medical inspector felt that medical students were quite capable of ingratitude, machinations, and deception, and that the Russian state should be systemically protected against these influences.

According to Wylie's project, graduates of medical departments would immediately be awarded a degree, but the corresponding rank (and the personal ennoblement that accompanied it) was available to them no sooner than after eight years in service.[67] All those who were deemed physically capable were sent to the army, and after eight years in the military they were allowed to transfer into civil service or to start a private practice.[68] Only two categories of medical professionals could avoid the army: those physically unfit or those majoring in pharmaceuticals. There was only one way to be exempted from civil service altogether: a maiming injury or permanent incapacity due to bad health. If the medical professional was sent to civil service and failed to serve two years, he had to repay his travel allowance, a sum that was quite substantial for distant provinces.[69] According to Wylie's plan, civil doctors had a 50 percent longer wait for promotion than did their colleagues in military service.[70] Fee-paying students, "those of unfree condition," and graduates of foreign universities were exempted from these requirements,[71] but by not entering the service of the state, they had to abandon hopes for ranks, grades, pensions, and awards.

Given the looming war, growing army, and permanent cadre deficiency, Wylie's priority was to guarantee a regular flow of medics into the army. He strove to make military service more attractive than its civil counterpart, especially private practice, which was intentionally made more difficult to enter. To be able to work in civil service, a graduate had to get higher grades at the final examinations and obtain a certificate of his ability to perform surgeries (thus making him eligible for the title of "medical surgeon"). Still, a doctor in civil service would have a lower salary than his colleague in the military, and he would not get free accommodation, uniform, or the service of an orderly.

In 1810, another Scotsman, general staff doctor in civil service Alexander Creighton, stood up against Wylie and his project, accusing him of acting to the detriment of the Ministry of Police. The head of civil medicine declared that

---

67 RGIA. F. 1294. Op. 3. D. 19. "O proekte kasatel'no proizvodstva i nagrad medicinskikh chinov. 1816." L. 7.

68 Ibid. L. 4.

69 Ibid. L. 6.

70 Ibid. L. 7.

71 Ibid. L. 5 ob.

it was wrong to make the final university examination definitive for the whole subsequent career of an *uezd* doctor, dooming him to poverty if he received a low grade.[72] Creighton reported to the members of the council how difficult it was to keep doctors in service in the Caucasus and Siberia, where they often had to survive adverse conditions of nature.

For a time, the war silenced the standoff between the two Scottish physicians of high renown. But after returning to Russian in 1815, Wylie revisited his rank promotion project. After a discussion in government circles (1816), the project received approval from the ministers of army, navy, and education, but it faced fierce opposition from the minister of police.[73] In the postwar years, the burden on the *uezd* doctors grew even heavier. Many of them were mobilized into the army, and those remaining had to fill the vacancies. Their salaries were still small, and continuing inflation made the situation worse. The minister of police thus claimed that it would be impractical to demand that candidates for unpopular vacancies should be a certified "medical surgeon." Almost no one wanted to apply for the job of an *uezd* doctor, and some *gubernii* stayed without any medical assistance.[74] The need to come to St. Petersburg to take examinations at the academy would make the lack of civil service doctors even more glaring, the minister continued, and the Russian Empire would lose altogether both its medical police and forensic medicine. On these grounds, Wylie's project was put on hold for four years. This time was thought sufficient for Russian universities and academies to train an ample number of doctors. But by 1822, the lack of doctors had not been rectified, and no unification of medical knowledge had been established. The project had to be put off again.[75]

In 1819 and 1822, salaries rose among doctors in the army and navy. In 1828, the committee asked Nicholas I's government to improve the financial position of civil medical officials by adding allowances for accommodation and travel.[76]

---

72 RGIA. F. 1294. Op. 5. D. 194. "Delo komiteta, uchrezhdennogo dlia razrabotki proekta preobrazovaniia medicinskogo upravleniia, nachavsheesia v 1828 g., v piati chastiakh. Chast' pervaia. 1828." L. 52 ob.

73 Ibid. Ll. 5–5 ob.

74 RGIA. F. 1294. Op. 3. D. 19. "O proekte kasatel'no proizvodstva i nagrad medicinskikh chinov. 1816." L. 57 ob.

75 RGVIA. F. 879. Medicinskii department voennogo vedomstva. Op. 2. D. 65. "Proekt Polozheniya glavnogo medicinskogo inspektora po armii o proizvodstve v klassnye chiny. 1822." L. 1 ob.

76 RGIA. F. 1294. Op. 5. D. 194. "Delo komiteta, uchrezhdennogo dlia razrabotki proekta preobrazovaniia medicinskogo upravleniia, nachavsheesia v 1828 g., v piati chastiakh. Chast' pervaia. 1828." Ll. 199–203.

Together with the expansion of staff in civil medical service, this salary bump made the profession more attractive. In 1834, after discrimination against civil doctors was finally eliminated in a series of amendments, the Council of State endorsed Wylie's project.[77]

This new project finally codified control over the medical profession, with its keys in two hands: the government and the professional elite. Civil and military officials preserved their right to set tasks for doctors in the interest of states. At the same time, rank promotion most crucially depended on formal criteria, such as a degree and term in service, rather than on the subjective opinion of superiors, though "Special merit" could speed up promotion if superiors commended a doctor for efficient work. This degree of formalization did not fully strip personal clout and patronage of importance, but it reduced their role, thus improving the status of medics as officials, as proved by Elisa Becker in her study.[78] The 1846 issue of the Russian Medical Register comprised over eight thousand individuals, with only a third of them in the military.[79]

To sum up, the new areas of concern for the state—education and healthcare—in the first quarter of the nineteenth century became the experimental ground first for transplanting forms of administration typical for modernity, and then for developing and testing corresponding administrative techniques. As always, innovations arose from the synthesis of eighteenth-century Russian experience and that of more successful Western neighbors. Researchers have said a lot about institutional reform, but the specifically Russian administration techniques still remain largely unstudied. It is in them, it seems, that the nature of the much discussed "Russian modernity" may lie.

An example of these techniques can be found in Magnitsky's administrative experiments in the Kazan educational district. To enable distant governance, the curator developed new channels of written communication that put the university corporation in the service of the ministry. His administrative innovations relied on objectivized (numerical) indicators of the state of affairs in various aspects of university life—education quality as assessed by numeric scale, infrastructural development as measured by room space, numbers of students and textbooks, and research output in terms of number of publications and university press editions. These statistics, together with practices of time management and a transformation

---

77 PSZ II. Vol. 9. № 7118. P. 397.

78 Becker. Medicine, Law and the State. P. 16.

79 Khanykov. Istoriia medicinskoi policii.

in the language of administrative work made university life transparent for the distant administrative gaze of the curator in St. Petersburg.

Introducing this technology helped make the faculty's work dependent on the amount of their responsibility and the formalized assessment of the efficiency of their work. In turn, these techniques helped select prospective faculty members, control budget expenditure, improve the discipline of both students and professors, make executing orders more efficient, and conform classes and all rituals of academic life to a set schedule. It also allowed for research, which was once classified as a kind of art or creative work, to be reimagined as "scientific production" commissioned by the state. The output of this production could be measured quantitatively by the number of publications and qualitatively by reviews and feedback from professionals in the field.

By means of this technique, Magnitsky managed to set Kazan University free from the tangling web of corporate conflict and the arbitrary rule of the director and his deputies. However, he failed (or never wanted) to fully reformat university life from hotbed of personal disagreement into smoothly functioning state institution with formalized internal relations. Rather, he transformed a horizontally organized network into a vertically structured community of officials ready to execute orders from their superiors and largely dependent on personal relations with the curator. In the 1830s, the administrative experience of the exiled Magnitsky was used and further perfected by his political opponent S.S. Uvarov in his attempt to set up a "system of education."

The invention of minister of internal affairs A.B. Kurakin was his efficient method of collecting data on licensed doctors. It pushed learned physicians, with their long-standing aversion to state control, to apply for a state-issued license. In the reign of Alexander I, the amount of information that state agencies had on their subordinate institutions became a crucial factor of administrative efficiency. When required information was missing, insufficient, or incorrect, control was weakened or lost. The Medical Collegium did not prioritize counting or listing the learned doctors in the Russian Empire. Although the state license was already a requirement, a large number of doctors had entered private practice without taking any exams. On taking control over medical matters, the minister forced professional elites to create a suprainstitutional system of control of medical licenses by means of the Russian Medical Register. The strict correlation between being entered on the register and having the right to prescribe medication at pharmacies served to reduce doctors' autonomy from the state. In other words, the state broke the chain of corporate interaction between doctors and their patients and introduced a new mediating link between them—itself.

The shrinking of autonomous self-rule and the privileges of the medical elites (who, in the Alexandrine period, were mostly foreign-born doctors) was accompanied by formalization of state service for medical officials. The Wylie project of rank promotion, originally proposed as early as 1810, made the conditions of physicians' work transparent and understandable, where earlier they had been situation-based and opaque. After the heavy slant in favor of the Ministries of Army and Navy had been removed, the project was adopted, and under Nicholas I it became a sort of regulatory agreement between the state and the members of the medical profession.

These research cases prove the idea that in the Alexandrine period the reform of public administration came in two stages: first, the old system of institutions was dismantled and replaced with the new one, imported from Europe; then new techniques were set up to work under the new system, relying on bureaucratic rationality and stimulating "vertical power." These techniques rose from critique of and dissatisfaction with the mechanical transfer of structural forms of the state into Russia. Although these techniques might have been tested or proposed in the final years of Alexander I's reign, their large-scale implementation took place during that of his successor, Nicholas I.

List of references

Alexander, John. Bubonic Plague in Early Modern Russia: Public Health and Urban Disaster. Baltimore, Md., 1980

Alexander, John. Catherine the Great and Public Health. In: Journal of the History of Medicine and Allied Sciences. (1981) # 2, Pp. 185–204

Amburger, Erik. Beitrage zur Geschichte der Deutsch-Russischen Kulturellen Beziehungen. Giessen, 1961

Andreev, Andrei. Rossiiskie universitety XVIII–pervoi poloviny XIX veka v kontekste universitetskoi istorii Evropy. Moscow, 2009

Becker, Elisa. Medicine, Law and the State in Imperial Russia. Budapest, 2011

Gatina, Zarina. Vrachebnaia ekspertiza s gosudarstvennom upravlenii Rossiiskoi imperii v pervoi polovine XIX veka. St. Petersburg, 2017. Doctoral dissertation, unpublished manuscript

Haaser, R. Ot bratstva po oruzhiiu k ideologicheskoi vrazhde: politizatsiia universitetskoi zhizni v Germanii i obraz Rossii v natsional'nom dvizhenii 1813–1819 godov. In: A.V. Gladyshev / T.A. Bulygina (Eds.). Istoriia i istoricheskaia pamiat': Mezhvuzovskii sbornik nauchnich trudov. Saratov, 2012. Pp. 31–63

C. Henze?

INSTRUKTSIIA DIREKTORU Kazanskogo universiteta, 17 ianvaria 1820. In: SBORNIK POSTANOVLENII po Ministerstvu narodnogo prosveshcheniia. Vol. 1. St. Petersburg, 1875, Col. 1199–220

KHANYKOV, IAKOV. Ocherk istorii medicinskoj policii v Rossii. St. Petersburg, 1851

KHRISTOFOROV, IGOR. Sud'ba reformy: Russkoe krest'ianstvo v pravitel'stvennoi politike do i posle otmeny krepostnogo prava (1830–1890 gg.). Moscow, 2011

KUSBER, JAN. Eliten- und Volksbildung im Zarenreich während des 18. und in der ersten Hälfte des 19. Jahrhunderts. Studien zu Diskurs, Gesetzgebung und Umsetzung. Stuttgart, 2004

LEVINSON, KIRILL. Nekotorye nabliudeniia otnositel'no iazyka gosudarstvennogo deloproizvodstva v gorodakh Sviashchennoi Rimskoi imperii v Rannee Novoe vremia. In: Arkheograficheskii ezhegodnik. 2006–2007. Moscow, 2012. Pp. 126–46

MAGNITSKII, MIHAIL. Kratkoe rukovodstvo k delovoi i gosudarstvennoi slovesnosti dlia chinovnikov, vstupaiushchikh v sluzhbu. Moscow, 1835

MINAKOV, ARKADII. Mikhail Leont'evich Magnitskii. In: PROTIV TECHENIIA: istoricheskie portrety russkikh konservatorov pervoi treti XIX veka. Voronezh, 2005. Pp. 268–71

MINAKOV, ARKADII. Russkii konservatizm v pervoi chetverti XIX veka. Voronezh, 2011

O PRAVILAKH OB EKZAMENAKH medicinskikh chinovnikov. In: Sbornik postanovlenii po Ministerstvu narodnogo prosveshcheniia. Vol. 1. St. Petersburg, 1875. Col. 612–26

PARSAMOV, VADIM. Zhozef de Mestr i Aleksandr Sturdza: Iz istorii religioznykh idei Aleksandrovskoi epokhi. Saratov, 2004

PODDUBNYI, MIHAIL / EGORYSHEVA, IRINA / SHERSTNEVA, ELENA. Istoriia zdravookhraneniia dorevoliutsionnoi Rossii (konets XVI–nachalo XX vv.). Moscow, 2014

RENNER, ANDREAS. Progress through Power? Medical Practitioners in Eighteenth-Century Russia as an Imperial Elite. In: Acta Slavica Iaponica. Vol. 27 (2009). Pp. 29–54

RENNER, ANDREAS. Russische Autokratie und Europäische Medizin: Organisierter Wissenstransfer im 18. Jahrhundert. Stuttgart, 2010

ROSSIISKII MEDICINSKII SPISOK, izdannyi po vysochaishemu ego imperatorskogo velichestva poveleniiu. Na 1809 god. St. Petersburg, 1809

SAMBUK, DARIA. Wächter der Gesundheit: Staat und lokale Gesellschaften beim Aufbau des Medizinalwesens im Russischen Reich; 1762–1831. Köln, 2015

J. Flynn ?

SKINNER, BARBARA. Russia's Scriptural "Reformation" in the Late Eighteenth and Early Nineteenth Centuries. In: Vivliofika: E-Journal of Eighteenth-Century Russian Studies. (2017) # 5. Pp. 73–102

SMIRNOVA, ELENA. "Medicinskie chiny" v rossiiskoi provintcii (XVIII–seredina XIX vv.). In: Novyi istoricheskii vestnik. (2011) # 2. Pp. 6–19

SOBSTVENNORUCHNOE VSEPODDANNEISHEE PIS'MO deistvitel'nogo tainogo sovetnika Magnitskogo, s podneseniem zapiski o narodnom vospitanii. In: Sbornik istoricheskikh materialov, izvlechennykh iz arkhiva I-go Otdeleniia S.E.I.V. Kantseliarii. Vol. 1. St. Petersburg, 1875. Pp. 363–74

STOCHIK, ANDREI / ZATRAVKIN, SERGEI / STOCHIK, ANNA. Stanovlenie gosudarstvennoi mediciny (vtoraia polovina XVIII–pervaia polovina XIX v.) Soobshchenie 1. Vozniknovenie kontseptsii medicinskoi politsii, organov upravleniia medicinsko-sanitarnym delom, vrachebno-sanitarnogo zakonodatel'stva. In: Problemy social'noi gigieny, zdravookhraneniia i istorii mediciny. (2013) # 1. Pp. 44–49

STOLETIE VOENNOGO MINISTERSTVA. 1802–1902. Glavnoe voenno-medicinskoe upravlenie. Istoricheskii ocherk / ed. by D.A. Skalon. St. Petersburg, 1902

STURDZA, ALEKSANDR. Zapiska o nyneshnem polozhenii Germanii. In: Rossiia—Russia. Kul'turnye praktiki v ideologicheskoi perspektive. Rossiia, XVIII–nachalo XX veka. Vol. 3. Moscow, 1999. P. 146–57

TESLIA, ANDREI. Mezhdu ideologiei i real'nost'iu. Vdol' knizhnoi polki. In: Russkii zhurnal. (2015) # 6. Available at: http://www.russ.ru/Mirovaya-povestka/Mezhdu-ideologiej-i-real-nost-yu [14.10.2018]

UVAROV, SERGEI. Desiatiletie Ministerstva narodnogo prosveshcheniia. 1833–1843. In: UVAROV, SERGEI. Izbrannye trudy. Moscow, 2009. Pp. 346–55

VISHLENKOVA, ELENA. Dukhovnaia shkola v Rossii pervoi chetverti XIX veka. Kazan, 1998

VISHLENKOVA, ELENA. The State of Health: Balancing Power, Resources, and Expertise and the Birth of the Medical Profession in the Russian Empire. In: Ab Imperio (2016) # 3. Pp. 39–75

VISHLENKOVA, ELENA / GATINA, ZARINA. "Izlozhit' predmet scientificheski": Russkie vrachi i ikh polevye issledovaniia (pervaia polovina XIX veka). In: Rossiiskaia istoriia. (2015) # 3. Pp. 154–69.

WIELAND, LEO. Katalonien: Kulturnation ohne Staat. In: Frankfurter Allgemeine Zeitung. 10.10.2007

ZATRAVKIN, SERGEI / SHCHEPIN, VLADIMIR / OLEINIKOVA, VALERIIA. Obespechennost' vrachami naseleniia Rossiiskoi imperii. In: Problemy social'noi gigieny, zdravookhraneniia i istorii mediciny. (2017) # 4. Pp. 236–39

ZIABLOVSKII, EVDOKIM. Noveishee zemleopisanie Rossijskoi imperii. St. Petersburg, 1818

Vadim Parsamov

Republican Types in Russian Political Culture, 1815–1825

Republican types are understood here as a project of state order that implied seizing political power from a monarch and giving it to the people by means of a coup—either a peaceful or a military one. It is this circumstance that puts republican models aside from projects of state-initiated reforms intended to liberalize but not replace the monarchical regime. A monarch who granted a constitution to his subjects enhanced their rights and liberties, but he did not change their status, since a granted constitution did not imply discussions and approbation by the people. For example, if a benevolent lord replaced socage with rent payments, he enhanced liberties of his serfs, but they did not become *free people* because of it. On the other hand, republics could have strict laws that limited rights and liberties of individual citizens, but it was thought that the laws resulted from the will of the people, thus the people as a whole remained free. In the first case, liberty was understood as an act, and in the second—as a status.

Unlike constitutional monarchies, which set spatial limits to hereditary power (the private life of the people was supposedly not regulated), republics had temporal limits for elected power, while citizens' private lives could also be subjected to its control. Titus Livy spoke of a change from a monarchy to a republican regime and explained that "you may reckon the beginning of liberty as proceeding from the limitation of consuls' authority to a year, rather than from any diminution of their power compared with that which kings had exercised."[1]

During the period under discussion, republican projects were mostly produced by secret societies that emerged in Russia soon after the end of the Napoleonic Wars. There was a Soviet tradition to rank politicians according to a scale of progressiveness: absolute monarchy—constitutional monarchy—bourgeois republic—socialist republic. Progress here meant the increase of liberty. Its minimal level was connected to absolute monarchy, and maximum—to a socialist republic. Viewed from this angle, moderates who were constitutional monarchists were set in opposition to republicans within the Decembrist movement. According to this Soviet tradition, Nikita Murav'ev's constitution, in which a monarch held executive powers, was contrasted with Pavel Pestel''s "Russian

1 Livii. Istoriia Rima. P. 64.

Truth" (*Russkaia Pravda*), which suggested a republic. However, scholars have long known that Pestel' also produced a project of constitutional monarchy at the same time: this was explained by a suggestion that he did not want to discourage moderate members of the secret society and tried to take their political interests into consideration. The republican Pestel' was thus considered to be more of revolutionary and more progressive that the constitutional monarchist Nikita Murav'ev.

This concept was retrospective in its character and was based on a assumption about the further evolution of the liberation movement toward socialist ideas. If one were to view political projects by the Decembrists in the context of traditions that influenced them, the resulting picture would be very different. The Decembrists saw republicanism as a theory older than monarchism. Thus, they saw republic not as a new stage in history but as a revival of an old tradition.

These ideas were presented in their most clear form by Pestel'. In his opinion, at the beginning of history there had been states based on social contact and natural equality of people. In Europe, these were the Greek cities-states and the republic of Rome, and in Russia—the republics of Novgorod and Pskov. Later, "since the time of the invasion of barbarians," privileged estates emerged. It was the beginning "of the rise of nobility. This was a good old time when it was possible to kill and rob with impunity. [...] Nobility based its claims on the right of the conqueror, its sword, its military prowess, [and] clergy [based its claims] on its spiritual authority, on chasubles, on education. Monarchs were powerless before them. Peoples suffered and dared not complain."[2]

These crimes had another consequence. Unwittingly, they caused desire for goodness and justice: "the course of centuries that cannot be stopped and that sooner or later destroys all monuments to errors and passions touched this state of affairs. From the abyss of evil, good emerged." As a result, a time of revolutions had been prepared, which Pestel' saw and called the "spirit of time."

Thus, European history was divided into three periods. The first was the time when original republics existed, when the people ruled themselves. The emergence of nobility fractured the people and the rulers, with aristocracy as a dividing wall. The people were turned into slaves, and rulers lost real power. Finally, the destruction of aristocracy renewed the direct connection between the people and the government. However, because the number of citizens had grown compared to antiquity, modern republics did not imply the direct rule of the people but rather became representative. A linear progress from monarchy to republic, which

---

2 Vosstanie dekabristov. Vol. 7. Pp. 295–96.

paralleled the progress of liberty, was replaced by a cyclical model which brought back republican rule, although in a slightly different form. But this was not all.

Pestel''s historical scheme offers an its unusual view of the correlation between power and liberty. Paradoxically, Pestel' stated that an absolute monarch, dependent on his aristocracy, was the weakest ruler. The people were turned into serfs, and the monarch was so weak that he could not "protect himself from claims and insults of this arrogant nobility."[3] Thus, the weaker the ruler, the less liberty there was. And the only strong rule that guaranteed liberty was the rule of the people, which united the ruler and the ruled. This had been the case for classical republics. In modern representative republics, the government and the people were not united in one person, but because there was no intermediary between them, the government had enough of power, and the people—enough of liberty.

Thus, Pestel' saw the difference between classical republics (with direct democracy) and representative rule not as a matter of quality but of quantity. Meanwhile, Benjamin Constant saw differences in quality here, and he connected these with historically changing views of liberty. In 1814, he wrote his famous pamphlet *De l'esprit de conquête et d'usurpation*, where he contrasted the liberty of the ancients with that of the moderns. The ancient republics understood liberty as direct involvement of the people in the governing of their state. At the same time, the heavier the weight of an individual person in national sovereignty, the heavier the sacrifice that was required of him. "This self-sacrifice was necessary so that the people could enjoy political rights in the highest degree, in other words, so that each citizen had his share in sovereignty. For this, institutions were necessary that would guarantee equality, impede the growth of individual wealth, destroy differences, [and] resist the influence of wealth, talent, and even virtues."[4] According to Constant, the ancients did not understand the joys of private life and thus fully dedicated themselves to public service. Slowly, however, "the progress of civilization, the development of trade, [and] communication between people increased and diversified innumerably the chances for individual happiness. To be happy, people only need to get full freedom in their activities, business, work, and fancies."[5]

Conclusions by Constant resulted from the view that civil rights do not guarantee individual freedom and happiness. These rights are necessary but not enough for all numerous interests and needs of modern man. To be a free citizen of the modern world did not mean to be a happy person.

---

3 Ibid. P. 296.

4 Constant. Cours de politique constitutionnelle. P. 205.

5 Ibid. P. 206.

The situation was different in Russia, where problems that were solved in France by the revolution were still relevant. The poet Viazemskii offered a rhetorical question: "I see Tsar's subjects, / But where are the citizens of the nation?" This question implied not only the liberation of the serfs but also civil rights for all subjects ("You will bring a book of eternal rights down to us"). A glance toward classical tradition allowed one to speak of the recovery of civil liberties that were lost. The roles were distributed as follows: the people that suffered from slavery, a tyrant who usurped the people's power, and a tyrannicide who returned power to the people.

The Union of Salvation discussed tyrannicide. Pestel' witnessed one such episode: "In 1816, or in 1817, I do not remember exactly where, during our discussion of the society, Lounin, in the presence of Nikita Murav'ev and myself, talked about killing the tsar on the Tsarskoselskaya Road by a masked group, when the time comes to act."[6] Why did they discuss the killing of Alexander I in 1816? At the time, the authority of the tsar was at its highest. The victor over Napoleon, "the king of kings," "friend of peoples, and savior of their freedom," Agamemnon—only good things were expected of him. All hopes for liberal reforms were centered on him. At the same time, the status of the monarch made Alexander I incompatible with a republican state. His physical removal was to symbolize transition from monarchy to republic, and the killing of a "tyrant" acquired theatrical characteristics. A mask is a symbol of tragedy, and it likely implied the use of a dagger, its other attribute, as a murder weapon.

Similar projects emerged among the Decembrists later. It was suggested that people who had lost their liberty were always ready to get it back, thus, as soon as the tyrant was removed, the republic would restore itself.

The naivete of these plans was as evident as their esthetic attractiveness to the members of the secret society. Thus an attempt by Pestel' to move from historical aesthetics to the field of real politics provoked Lounin's ironic comment of "tyrannicide" and an observation that Pestel' offered "first to write an encyclopedia, and then to start a revolution."[7] Although he thought that the republic had historical roots in Russia, Pestel' did not believe in its automatic resurgence after tyrannicide and "found it necessary to prepare a plan of constitution in advance and even to write the major part of laws and orders so that with the beginning of the revolution the new order could be introduced immediately, but I did not then have a thought of a provisional government."[8] Although Pestel' did not think then about

6 Vosstanie dekabristov. Vol. 4. P. 179.

7 Ibid.

8 Ibid.

the dictatorship of the provisional government, he, according to Sergei Petrovich Trubetskoy, was sympathetic to the Jacobin dictatorship. "At the fist general meeting for the reading and approbation of the articles, Pestel' in the speech read by him said that France enjoyed the rule of the Committee for Public Safety. All protested against this statement, and this left an impression unfavorable for him, which could not be broken and resulted in a lack of trust in him."[9]

Pestel' said that the goal of his republic was "the possible good for all and everyone,"[10] at the same time emphasized that "what is good for a part or for one unit should always give way to what is good for the whole: by the whole we see the entire people, or the mass of the people."[11] Thus, in Rousseau's terminology, the will of the whole should prevail over the will of all. The question was how this could be done in practice. Pestel' realized that democratic institutes—the separation of powers, public control over these, and so forth—was not enough to guarantee equality and liberty for all in the huge, multiethnic, and multireligious Russia. Equal civil rights for all were not enough, in his view, for the existence of a stable republican government. It was necessary to provide for equal opportunities to exercise these rights. A republican has more than a *right* to be a free citizen; he has a *duty* to do so. An introduction of civil equality in Russia did not imply the equality of ethnic groups, languages, religions, and so forth.

"One should remember," the Russian Truth reads, "what heterogenous parts this huge state is composed of. Not only are its regions ruled by different institutions, or following different civil law, but also, they speak different languages, have different religions; their populations are of different origins and belonged to different states in the past."[12] Since the priority was freedom of the people as a whole, freedom of an individual citizen was determined by his integration into the "totality, or the mass of the people." Pestel's republic was not a republic in a general sense but rather a *Russian* republic rooted in national history, thus all its citizens could only be *Russians*.

Pestel' placed his political ideal into its historical past and modeled a precedent of state order. Civil liberty was accepted as having always existed, thus movement toward it was thought to be a restoration of national traditions. A state that was new in fact was to acquire old—as Pestel' thought—or, to be precise, specific national characteristics, "so that the people who live in the whole space of the Russian state *all* were *Russians*." He offered the following measures to reach this

9 Trubetskoi. Materialy o zhizni. Vol. 1. Pp. 218–19.

10 Vosstanie dekabristov. Vol. 7. P. 115.

11 Ibid. P. 116.

12 Ibid. P. 127.

goal: "first, only Russian language should dominate the space of the Russian state. [...] Second, since the existing difference in the names of peoples and tribes that populate Russia would always make separate masses of people out of them and would never let them become homogenous, which is necessary for the commonwealth of Russia, all these different names should be abolished and united everywhere into the *general name* of Russians. Third, the same *laws* and the *same rule* should exist in all parts of Russia, so that politically and civilly all Russia in all its territories would be homogenous, uniform, and of the same thinking."[13] The state institutions would receive Russian names: the legislative body would be called the Council of the People (*Narodnoe veche*), the executive—the Council of the State (*Derzhavnaia duma*). St. Petersburg was to be renamed Petrograd, and the capital was to be transferred into a "more Russian" place—Nizhny Novgorod or Moscow.

According to Pestel', language was to be the main symbol of national sovereignty. He planned a wide-ranging language reform, which would have resulted in all loan words being replaced by words with Slavonic roots—what was seen as a recovery of Russian terms. In creating his new terminology, Pestel' fought against neologisms of the Petrine language reform. In contrast with Peter I, who replaced Russian words with foreign equivalents or introduced new terms as loan words, Pestel' returned to old words or created new terms based on Slavonic words. Out of the terms that emerged during the reign of Peter I, Pestel' replaced the following: *battalion*, *heraldry*, *governorate*, *emperor*, *chancellery*, *minister*, *secretary*, *system*, and *fleet*. His replacement terms included *srazyn*, *zapys* [note], *district*, *tsar*, *povytie*, *gosudarstvennuy glava* [state head], *dyak*, *obyem*, *stroenie* [framework], *obzor* [review], *pravila* [rules], *plaven'*.

Two different cultural traditions collided in Pestel's national project: a romantic idea of national uniqueness, and the Enlightenment "myth" of the uniformity of human nature. Philosophers of the Enlightenment thought that human nature was always the same. All differences between peoples, including ethnic ones, they interpreted as prejudice. Pestel' based his new state on Russian national and cultural tradition (i.e., rejection of loan words, introduction of national costume, translation of the capital to Nizhny Novgorod or Vladimir), but he did not follow the idea of cultural revival but rather aimed at unification, a goal alien to it. In this sense, he, like the philosophers of the Enlightenment, based himself not on historical past but on the idea of reason. Unlike the romanticists, who saw some mystical meaning in national traditions, Pestel' built his project on rationalist foundations. His reference to traditions was a just a formality.

13 Ibid. P. 149.

In his reform projects, Pestel' acted not so much as a Russifier but as a rationalizer. His ethnic policy that suggested merging of all peoples of Russia into one nation meant a creation of a new people—material for a rationally organized state. A unified culture, suggested by him, slightly recalled Russian traditions but in fact had nothing to do with these.

The constitutional monarchy project penned by Nikita Murav'ev should also be seen alongside other republican models because it did not imply a monarch granting a constitution to the people but rather the people taking power and granting some authority to the monarch: "the source of sovereignty is the people, who have the exclusive right to make *constitutional laws* for themselves."[14] Murav'ev's project differed from Pestel's not only in form—federation instead of a unified state, preservation of monarchy, nobility's land property, and so forth—but also in the understanding of liberty.[15]

Pestel' based liberty on laws ("the spirit of time aiming at liberty, which is based on laws")[16] and combined it with homogeneity, uniformity, and one way of thinking. Murav'ev interpreted liberty in a liberal rather than a republican sense. He disagreed with Montesquieu's statement that "Liberty is the right to do what is allowed by laws." Murav'ev countered: "How am I free, if laws oppress me, if everything I do needs permission of the authorities, if others enjoy privileges I do not have, if my person is ruled over without my consent? According to this definition, a Russian peasant is free: he has a right to marry, etc." Murav'ev understood liberty as a guarantee of the natural rights of one who lived in a society. Laws were to correspond to the "totality of his [the subject's] physical and moral qualities. All other law is abuse based on force, but force never establishes or justifies any law." Murav'ev then gave his definition of a social contract: "by coming together into political communities, people never could or would grant or change any of their natural rights, or renounce their right to exercise these [...] they are united and linked by social contract to work freely and usefully through mutual help and to protect personal safety and property by mutual cooperation." Here he argued not against the breach of social contract but against its radical interpretation. Murav'ev thought that the "mass of people could become a tyrant just as one person could."[17]

---

14 Druzhinin. Revoliucionnoe dvizhenie. P. 254.

15 On "constutution" and "fundamental laws" in political discourses in this time, see the chapter by Sergei Polskoy in this volume, Pp. 135–166.

16 Vosstanie dekabristov. Vol. 7. P. 174.

17 Druzhinin. Revoliucionnoe dvizhenie. Pp. 85 f.

Unlike Pestel', who embraced Rousseau's idea of unlimited sovereignty of the people, Murav'ev preferred the version by Helvétius, according to which the social contract guaranteed one's personal rights against the common will of the society. Helvetius did not define society as a collective person (*personne morale*), as Rousseau thought, but as a free union of individual persons who retained their right to personal happiness. "I state," wrote Helvetius, "that people pursue happiness, and it is not possible to distract them from this pursuit, that it would have been futile to attempt this, and dangerous to achieve, and that, consequently, it is only possible to make them virtuous by uniting personal interest with the interest of society."[18]

Personal freedom of a member of society was mirrored on the state level by the autonomy of territories within the state—that is, by federalism. Murav'ev's constitution suggested that Russia be divided into fourteen "states" and two "regions." Nizhny Novgorod, called *Slavyansk*, was to become its capital. "States" were to be divided into counties, and counties into districts. Each "state" was to be ruled by a government with separate legislative, executive, and judicial branches. The highest legislative body in the country was to be the People's Council (*veche*)—a two-chamber parliament that consisted of the High Duma, which included three representatives from each "state," and the chamber of people's representatives, one per every fifty thousand voters. Executive power would remain in the hands of the emperor. Other reforms included the abolition of estates and guilds and of serfdom, the preservation of communal land ownership, and the introduction of civil liberties: freedom of speech, press, worship, work, and movement.

Divergence between Pestel' and Murav'ev marked the beginning of a new stage of the Decembrist movement: replacement of the Roman-style tyrannicide with the idea of a military coup. The thought of killing the tsar did not disappear completely; it had only lost its bookish attractiveness. From now on the members of the secret society did not volunteer to kill the monarch but rather engage those who could undertake this actio. Search was conducted among the periphery of the Decembrist organizations, or outside these. This was the birth of Pestel's idea of a "doomed party," characterized by the absence of any external signs. A group of twelve, not members of the secret society, was to kill *all* the royal family, including women and children, and after that society would execute the murderers and "proclaim that it was revenging the royal family." Although the selection of the group and its leadership was to belong to a member of the society, the group was to include people with the characteristics of assassins. It is notable that although there was no lack of Brutuses, no one wanted to join the "doomed party." Alek-

18 Gel'vecii. Sochineniia. P. 262.

sandr Petrovich Bariatinskii, who was entrusted with the task of finding the killers, asked to tell Pestel' "that all royal guard officers are zealous in their service to the goals of the society: but this does not mean that it is possible to make a gang of murderers out of them."[19] Mikhail Pavlovich Bestuzhev-Riumin suggested that "to strike the monarch, [...] demoted soldiers be used."[20] However, to kill the tsar alone was seen to be a half-measure; Pestel' planned to kill the entire royal family, in his own words, in order to "avoir maison nette" (clean house).[21] Tyrannicide moved from the forefront to the political backstage. This is what repelled would-be Brutuses. Pestel' made a skeptical remark about Sergei Ivanovich Murav'ev-Apostol: "il est trop pur" (he is too pure).[22]

N. Murav'ev rejected the idea of tyrannicide when he began his work on the constitution. The idea of law does not sit easily with the idea of murder, especially that of a monarch, and it was impossible for Murav'ev to have double standards. Crimes were to be punished by the court, and all citizens were before it: according to Murav'ev's constitution, the emperor was only the "highest official of the Russian government." He was bound by the law just like any other citizen, and tyrannicide was a crime against a person, just like any other murder.

It is not a coincidence that the former republican Murav'ev wrote a monarchical constitution. At first glance, there was not much difference between a republic and a constitutional monarchy. In both cases, the people are recognized as the only source of power; they are ruled by their representatives. Mably even coined an expression—"republican monarchy." However, the difference was great in the context of tyrannicide. From antiquity to the French Revolution, tyrannicide was associated with republicanism, while constitutional monarchy guaranteed the life of the monarch. The thought of a provisional dictatorship immediately after the coup was rejected by Murav'ev as unconstitutional. Pestel' accepted the period of lawlessness and even bloodshed at the establishment of a republic, but Murav'ev rejected this way. A constitution was to be introduced immediately after the fall of absolute rule.

Whether the new order would be based on the consent of the tsar or on a military coup did not, in the end, matter all that much. The building of the new—not the demolition of the old—was emphasized. Just like Pestel', who in 1817 wanted "first to write an encyclopedia, and then to start a revolution," Murav'ev thought that the introduction of the constitution was to be preceded not by a dic-

---

19 Vosstanie dekabristov. Vol. 10. P. 280.

20 Ibid. Vol. 4. P. 138.

21 Ibid. Vol. 11. P. 72.

22 Ibid. Vol. 4. P. 138.

tatorship but by public discussion. This provoked an ironic remark by Aleksandr Viktorovich Podzhio (Poggio), one of Pestel's supporters: "Murav'ev looks for interpreters of Bentham, but we are to act, and not with quills." The new order was not to be born out of the death of the old one, but out of an inside-out transformation of the old: "Nous commencerons absolument par la propaganda" (We will absolutely start with the propaganda).[23]

Republican projects by the Decembrists were not limited to Pestel''s Russian Truth or Murav'ev's constitution. The Order of Russian Knights had plans of its own; not much is known about the order, but what little we do know makes it possible to see it as a society that brought up would-be tyrannicides. Its founders, Matvei Aleksandrovich Dmitriev-Mamonov and Mikhail Fedorovich Orlov, the descendants of Catherine II's favorites, were more closely linked to eighteenth-century traditions than any other Decembrists, and they united aristocracy and republicanism.

The Order of Russian Knights consisted of two large sections. One was an "inner order," made up of founding members, those who knew its secret goal. The external order had educational duties and was built on symbols and rituals. The external order had three hierarchal degrees, or languages. Ascendancy was paralleled by the education of the seeker in republican virtues. The first language—of Israel—consisted of Biblical symbols and themes that encouraged valor and love of freedom.

The second language—of Greece—included symbols of ancient Greek republics and was to imbue the seeker with the thought of necessary transformation of the society based on republican virtues. The secret goal of the order was revealed at this stage.

The third language—of Romans—had political meaning and the idea of tyrannicide. It pointed to the way to republicanism.

Dmitriev-Mamonov's republican project was aristocratic by nature. A senate was to play the central role in government; it was to include one thousand members, out of which two hundred would be hereditary peers, four hundred would be gentlemen, and four hundred would be commoners. Thus, gentry and nobility, which together constituted less than 1 percent of the population, received 60 percent of the parliament. Nation was understood in qualitative, not quantitative, terms. It was thought that a gentleman who knew his ancestors and their merit to the motherland would represent the nation better than would a commoner. The Order of Russian Knights was to receive manors, lands, and forts like the

23 Ibid. Vol. 11. P. 72.

Knights Templar or Teutonic Knights, and two hundred hereditary peers were to be granted townships and lands. Out of all civil liberties only freedom of the press was mentioned. Freedom of conscience was omitted. Moreover, Dmitriev-Mamonov threatened to exterminate the Skoptsy sect of Old Believers.

The order planned expansionist foreign policies. Turks were to be expelled from Europe; Greece was to be restored under Russian protectorate; and Russia was to be joined by all Slavic peoples, as well as by Hungary and Norway. In the East, Russia was to conquer Persia and move to India.

One should add that two relics were kept in Dubrovitsy, Dmitriev-Mamonov's mansion near Moscow: a bloodied shirt of Tsarevich Dmitri and the standard of Minin and Pozharsky. The first symbolized the end of the Rurik Dynasty, to which DmitrievMamonov ascribed himself as he was a direct descendant of Grand Prince Vladimir Monomakh, and the second was a symbol of popular rebellion against invaders and the beginning of national revival.

N.I. Turgenev was possibly also a member of the Order of Russian Knights. An entry from his diary—"everything in Russia should be done by the government, and nothing—by the people itself"[24]—is often cited as proof of his moderate political views but can be interpreted in a more radical sense. Turgenev did not express a blind belief in the benevolent actions of the government but rather doubted the republican virtues of the Russian people. Russians were not educated and did not understand why republic was preferable to monarchy. Strictly speaking, Turgenev was not an advocate of classical republicanism. His political ideal was Britain, and as far as Russia was concerned, this ideal belonged to the future, not to the past. While Pestel' saw liberty in laws, and Murav'ev saw it in their absence (freedom to do what was not considered illegal), Turgenev connected liberty with education and enlightenment. In his opinion, the laws of the state did not change anything by themselves but rather only recorded certain norms. If Russia was to abolish serfdom and introduce a constitution, serfdom would be restored immediately by the parliament, Turgenev thought.

It seemed necessary to educate the people so that they would realize the benefits of a republic. This education should be a state program and, if necessary, implemented by force. For Turgenev, the ideal ruler was Peter I, a "liberal tsar," who was opposed, if not to the institution of serfdom, then at least to its worst characteristic—trade in people. The prohibition of Peter I on "[selling] people as beasts, which is not done anywhere in the world, and which causes a great cry" was

24 Arhiv brat'ev Turgenevykh. P. 333.

cited by Turgenev as antiserfdom propaganda.[25] Thus, Turgenev concluded that "Peter was more liberal than all other emperors and empresses in this respect."[26]

Turgenev thought that Peter I was not merely a liberal but also a tyrannicide. The Decembrist associated him with Brutus. "Modern peoples distorted their views of law; thus, they do not know what patriotism is and which acts belong to it. The ancients gave them respect to and awe of Brutus, and they marvel at him, but [they] do not want to recognize actions similar to the actions of Brutus that took place in recent times. They marvel at Brutus blindly, unreasonably, otherwise Peter I would have been seen alongside Brutus. We glorify Brutus's patriotism but are silent about the patriotism of Peter the Great who sacrificed his son for the good of his motherland. Voilà de conséquence!"[27]

This inversion—in ancient Rome a son killed his father for the sake of freedom, and in Russia a father killed his son for the sake of enlightenment—was highly symbolic to Turgenev. In Russia, everything was different. In Britain, rulers were enlightened together with the people and understood the necessity of civil liberties, while in Russia, the government was more enlightened than the people, and thus the ideas of freedom came from above and were met with silent resentment by society. This was a clear reference to the reign of Alexander I. This parallel had a darker meaning: Alexander I was responsible for the murder of his father, Paul I—thus he was also an "unrecognized" Brutus.

In other words, Russia needed a liberal dictator like Peter I. In 1820, at Fedor Nikolaevich Glinka's residence, Pestel' gave a talk about the forms of government. During the discussion that followed, Nikolai Turgenev remarked, "Le président sans phrases" (The president is without words). It can be suggested that here a president means a head of a republic with the rights of a monarch—that is, a dictator. Did he mean someone in particular? I think it is possible to offer a tentative suggestion.

Turgenev's close friend and ally M.F. Orlov, a founder of the Order of Russian Knights, intended in 1820 to obtain a position as division commander, successfully obtaining one in Kiev in June. In a letter to P.A. Viazemskii , Orlov expressed his regret at his location: "my fate is not to be envied although many would find it so. It would have been a huge difference if I got a division in Nizhny Novgorod or in Yaroslavl; I would have taken to it like a fish to water."[28] It is not difficult to see why Orlov would have been happier with a division in a city closer to Moscow:

25 Ibid. P. 222.
26 Ibid. P. 311.
27 Ibid.
28 Orlov. Kapituliaciia Parizha. P. 224.

Dubrovitsy, Dmitriev-Mamonov's Moscow-area mansion, was turned into a fortress with cannons left from the War of 1812 and peasants trained as soldiers, in military uniform. As Yuri Lotman has observed, "together with Orlov's division, this [division] was a real threat."[29] This fact was likely understood by others, not only by Orlov and Dmitriev-Mamonov. Thus, Orlov, the ambitious general, was given command farther from the center, at Kishinev. But even the far-away Kishinev turned into a promising place for a military coup when the Greek uprising began. This event encouraged Orlov. Likely "to admire himself in the mirror of history," he wrote to Aleksandr Nikolaevich Raevskii: "I have sixteen thousand in arms, thirty-six cannons, and six Cossack regiments. One can make mischief with this."[30]

One document found by Semen Landa in a work by the Greek historian Philemon reveals what Orlov meant by "mischief." According to this information, Orlov had an agreement with Alexander Ypsilanti, the leader of the Greek rebels, that he would bring his division across the Prut and would enter "the principalities as an independent ruler."[31] This act would have meant more than support for the Greeks. Had he broken his oath of allegiance, Orlov would have become a rebellious general at the head of an army. He clearly had the notion of moving to St. Petersburg. This is confirmed by a speech that Orlov gave at the Moscow meeting of the Union of Prosperity in early 1821.[32] Mikhail Kirillovich Gribovskii reported to the government: "Orlov vouched for his division and insisted on the establishment of "Invisible Brothers," who would constitute the center and would rule everything; the rest should be divided into languages (according to peoples: Greeks, Jews, etc.), which would come to the center as rays of light and pay fees without knowing to whom they make payments: about printing presses to be established in forests, even about making of counterfeit bank notes to gather sums necessary for the society."[33] Clearly, this speech referred to a large-scale war against the Russian government where not only arms but propaganda and counterfeit money were to be used. The document found by Semen Landa reveals that Orlov intended to fight both in Russia, and in Europe, and this duality was also in accordance with the program of the Order of Russian Knights.

29 Lotman. Izbrannye stat'i. Vol. 2. P. 318.

30 Orlov. Kapituliaciia Parizha. P. 225.

31 Landa. Dukh revoliucionnykh preobrazovanii. P. 170.

32 Chernov. U istokov osvoboditel'nogo dvizheniia. Pp. 4695; Nechkina. Dvizhenie dekabristov. Vol. 1. Pp. 304–42; Pugachev. Dekabrist M.F. Orlov. Pp. 82–114; Landa. Dukh revoliucionnykh preobrazovanii. Pp. 152–217.

33 Oksman (Ed.). Dekabristy. P. 114.

Pushkin was an unexpected opponent of Orlov and came up with an alternative project of a republic. Orlov's wife, Ekaterina Nikolaevna, wrote to her brother A.N. Raevskii from Kishinev on November 23, 1823: "We see Pushkin often, he comes to argue with my husband about various topics. His latest hobby—the *perpetual peace of Abbé de Saint-Pierre*. He believes that governments will perfect themselves slowly and will introduce general peace and then no blood will be shed other than the blood of people of strong character and passions, and adventurous spirit, whom we now call the great men and who then would only be thought as breakers of public peace."[34]

Historians have long noticed the connection between this letter and Pushkin's notes on "eternal peace."[35] Pushkin presented ideas from Rousseau , who in turn had retold a multivolume work by Saint-Pierre with his own commentaries. Pushkin's notes consisted of two parts. The first included three main points relevant to the problem. He stated a need to recognize the ridiculous cruelty of war, then the incompatibility of constitutional order and permanent armies, and finally the necessity to send people of great passions and military talents to the guillotine: "La société se soucie fort peu d'admirer les grandes combinaisons d'un général victorieux" (Society cares very little to admire the grand combinations of a victorious general). The "victorious general" referenced here is certainly Orlov, who received the capitulation of Paris in 1814.

In the second part, Pushkin went back to Rousseau and quoted his commentary on the idea of perpetual peace. Finally, he commented on this commentary. Pushkin understood "horrible means" by Rousseau as revolutions and wrote that these had become reality and that there was now a chance to establish a new order in Europe, based on the ideas of Saint-Pierre. Here, the poet gave an opinion of his opponent, easily recognizable as Orlov: "le témoinage d'un petit garcon comme Rousseau qui n'a jamais gagné seulement un pauvre bataille ne peut avoir aucun poids" (the testimony of a greenhorn like Rousseau who has never won even a small battle can have no weight). A "petit garcon" who had not won even a small military engagement was certainly a reference not only to Rousseau but also to Pushkin as viewed by Orlov.

Their argument was about the results of a revolution. Orlov thought that a revolution should result in the victory of a new leader, a savior of his country who would dictate his laws to the nation, but for Pushkin this scenario meant

34 Alekseev. Pushkin i problema "vechnogo mira." Pp. 176–77.

35 Tomashevskii. Pushkin i vechnyi mir; Alekseev. Pushkin i problema "vechnogo mira"; Rudnickaia. Mirotvorcheskaia paradigma russkoi obshchestvennoi mysli.

not the end of the revolution but only the replacement of one despotic regime by another. The poet contrasted this cycle to the establishment of a principally new order that would exclude mass bloodshed. If Orlov counted on his military division to achieve his goals, what did Pushkin count on?

Pushkin's heated discussions with Orlov proves that Pushkin saw his historical role as nearly equal to that of Orlov and intended to be on equal terms with him. An unfinished and unsent poetic epistle to Vladimir Fedoseevich Raevskii, "It's Not That That I'm Proud of, My Bard," written in autumn 1823, shows that the poet strongly felt his high mission at this time (the same period in which the earlier quoted letter from Ekaterina Orlova to Raevskii was written). Several key lines from stanza 8 in the second chapter of *Eugene Onegin*, also written in autumn 1823, point to a similar high mission. Notably, these lines were absent from the first printed edition of 1826:[36]

> That there existed chosen vessels,
> Holy friends of the human race
> Immortals clasped in fate's embrace,
> Who with radiant light would wrestle,
> One day, to illuminate and bless
> A future world with their caress.[37]

Boris Tomashevskii linked these lines with Pushkin's poem to Raevskii.[38] Yuri Lotman further developed this idea and saw in these lines "a hint to a secret society, or, at least, to a group of conspirators."[39] It seems that the style of these lines makes it possible to determine which group of conspirators was meant. It was certainly not the southern society of the Decembrists, and not the Kishinev group of General Orlov. Pushkin used a different style when he wrote about these—take, for example, the line "we will partake of a cup of blood" from his poem to Vasilii L'vovich Davydov. The passage from *Eugene Onegin*, in contrast, is dominated by the language of peace: "friends," "immortals," "bliss." The implication here is of people ready for a peaceful, moral coup. Its aim is evidently connected to the ideas of perpetual peace that interested Pushkin. As for the means, these certainly referred to the Masonic tradition.

Two years before writing these poems, Pushkin was a member of the "Ovid" Masonic Lodge. The information about the lodge is scarce and has been explored

---

36 Lotman. Roman A. S. Pushkina "Evgenii Onegin." P. 184.

37 Pushkin. Polnoe sobranie sochinenii. Vol. 5. Pp. 39–40.

38 Tomashevskii. Pushkin. Vol. 2. Pp. 161–62.

39 Lotman. Roman A. S. Pushkina "Evgenii Onegin." P. 184.

by scholars.[40] I would stress only one aspect, the significance of which has been overlooked. The lodge united the Decembrists and the members of the Filiki Eteria (the Society of Friends), the movement for the liberation of Greece from Ottoman rule. The meetings of the lodge took place at the house of one of its members, Mikhalaki Kacika. The lodge was founded by General Pavel Sergeevich Pushchin, and its meetings were opened by P.I. Pestel'.[41] There is no doubt that the "Ovid" lodge was overtly political in its character. It will be enough to quote a letter of January 1826 sent by A.S. Pushkin to V.A. Zhukovskii: "I was a Mason in the Kishinev lodge, the one that was the reason all lodges in Russia were destroyed."[42] The membership of Pestel', Raevskii, and Pushchin is telling. The most interesting question, however, is this: why did the Decembrists, who had joined Masonic lodges at earlier stages and used them as schools in organizing their secret society, go back to Masons at the time when the northern and southern societies were established, both aimed at revolution? Unfortunately, sources do net let us offer even a guess. It is certainly possible that members of various societies who met at the "Ovid" lodge had different agendas. In this case, we are interested in Pushkin's view of the compatibility of Masonic work and revolutionary activities. Lotman analyzed a poem that Pushkin addressed "To General Pushchin," writing that Pushkin wrote,

> a paradoxical combination of the Masonic "hammer" and a political call for liberty, evidently comical in the eyes of the Decembrists who were used to Masonic texts, [it] ended with a stanza, which was an ironic comment on the attempt to put the Decembrists in Masonic cloths. Masonic terminology, clearly recognizable by the audience (the image of the "dark city," "enlightened" by the light of "Brother Masons") created a comic contrast with the imagery of the first stanza. Masonic vocabulary was combined with ironic voice. And clear stylistic contrast between revolutionary and civil pathos and irony, typical for the Kishinev poems by Pushkin, shows how he viewed the "Ovid" lodge, its essence, and its trappings.[43]

The stylistic irony noticed by Lotman does not answer the question about the ideological compatibility of Masons and the revolution, and it does not explain why Pushkin selected Pushchin, and not Raevskii or Pestel', as the main character of this poem. It seems that the comparison between Pushchin and Spanish revolutionary Don Antonio Quiroga in the first stanza, set alongside the comparison

40 Kul'man. K istorii masonstva v Rossii. P. 343–73; Semevskii. Politicheskie i obshchestvennye idei dekabristov. Pp. 313–21; Lotman. Besedy o russkoj kul'ture. Pp. 369–76.

41 Serkov. Russkoe masonstvo. P. 1017.

42 Pushkin. Pis'ma. P. 3.

43 Lotman. Besedy o russkoi kul'ture. P. 374.

between Orlov and Napoleon, had a particular meaning. Quiroga, commander-in-chief of the revolutionary army in Spain, did not follow Napoleon's way to power. The Spanish revolution did not lead to a military dictatorship but to the restoration of the constitution and the election of Cortes. While in France Napoleon overthrew a constitutional body—the Directory—and became a tyrant, in Spain Quiroga and Rafael del Riego destroyed the absolutist power of Ferdinand VII and helped establish constitutional rule, after which Quiroga withdrew from public life. Events in Spain, according to Pushkin, opened the way to eternal peace in Europe. The comparison between Pushchin and Quiroga shows, first, that Pushkin saw him as an antipode to General Orlov, and, second, that Masonic ideas of peaceful enlightenment of the people appealed to Pushkin as a possible path toward the peaceful transformation of Europe and Russia in the postrevolutionary period.

Thus, Pushkin set the "Napoleonic" plans of Orlov in opposition to the utopian ideas of Saint-Pierre as interpreted by Rousseau, on the one hand, and to the similarly utopian ideas of Masonic enlightenment, on the other. Pushkin's project of a Masonic republic can also be seen in opposition to the Holy Alliance, which, in the words of Abbé Pradt was an "alliance of monarchs against the peoples." If monarchs united against the peoples, then the latter should also unite to oppose them; Masons could serve as an example of an international brotherhood, its political dimension engendered by European revolutions of the 1820s.

Thus, we see a heterogeneous image of republican projects construed by the members of the Russian opposition in the 1810s and 1820s. Pestel''s Russian Truth presented a classical republican vision. Murav'ev offered a liberal project that united republic and monarchy on a constitutional basis. The model offered by the Order of Russian Knights, in my opinion, is an imperial republic, which implied personal dictatorship and aggressive foreign policy. Finally, Pushkin's republic, in which humankind enjoyed perpetual peace, can be seen as an alternative to all projects by the Decembrists, which did not exclude violence and bloodshed as part of the process of implementation.

List of references

Alekseev, Mikhail. Pushkin i problema "vechnogo mira." In: Alekseev, Mikhail. Pushkin. Sravnitel'no-istoricheskie issledovaniia. Leningrad, 1984. Pp. 174–281

Arkhiv brat'ev Turgenevykh. Vol. 3. Dnevniki Nikolaia Ivanovicha Turgeneva za 1811–1816 gody. Vol. II. St. Petersburg, 1913

Chernov, Sergei. U istokov osvoboditel'nogo dvizheniia. Saratov, 1960

Constant, Benjamin. Cours de politique constitutionnelle ou collection des ouvrages publiés sur le gouvernement representatif. Vol. 2. Paris, 1861

Druzhinin, Nikolai. Revoliucionnoe dvizhenie v Rossii v XIX v. Moscow, 1985

Gel'vecii, Klod. Sochineniia: V 2-kh tomakh. Vol. 1. Moscow, 1974

Kul'man, Nikolai. K istorii masonstva v Rossii. Kishinevskaya lozha. In: Zhurnal ministerstva narodnogo prosveshcheniia. (1907) # 10. Pp. 343–73

Landa, Semen. Dukh revoliucionnykh preobrazovanii. Moscow, 1975

Livii, Tit. Istoriia Rima ot osnovaniya goroda. Vol. 1. Moscow, 1989

Lotman, Iurii. Besedy o russkoi kul'ture. St. Petersburg, 1994

Lotman, Iurii. Izbrannye stat'i: V 3-kh tomakh. Vol. 2. Tallinn, 1992

Lotman, Iurii. Roman A.S. Pushkina "Evgenij Onegin." Kommentarii. Leningrad, 1983

Nechkina, Milica. Dvizhenie dekabristov. Vol. 1. Moscow, 1955

Oksman, Iurii (Ed.). Dekabristy. Otryvki iz istochnikov. Moscow-Leningrad, 1926

Orlov, Mikhail. Kapituliaciia Parizha. Politicheskie sochineniia. Pis'ma. Moscow, 1963

Pugachev, V.V. Dekabrist M.F. Orlov i moskovskii s'ezd Soiuza blagodenstviia. In: Uchenye zapiski Saratovskogo universiteta. Vol. 66 (1958). Pp. 82–114

Pushkin, Aleksandr. Pis'ma / Pod red. i s prim. B.L. Modzalevskogo. Vol. 2. Moscow-Leningrad, 1928

Pushkin, Aleksandr. Polnoe sobranie sochinenii v 10-ti tomakh. Vol. 5. Moscow, 1962

Rudnickaia, Evgenii. Mirotvorcheskaia paradigma russkoi obshchestvennoi mysli v kontekste evropeiskogo Prosveshcheniia. In: Evropeiskoe Prosveshchenie i razvitie civilizacii v Rossii. Mezhdunarodnyi nauchnyi kollokvium 2–6 sentiabria 2001 g. Saratov, 2001. Pp. 198–206

Semevskii, Vasilii. Politicheskie i obshchestvennye idei dekabristov. St. Petersburg, 1908

Serkov, Andrei. Russkoe masonstvo 1703–2000. Enciklopedicheskii slovar'. Moscow, 2001

Trubetskoi, Sergei. Materialy o zhizni i revoliucionnoi deiatel'nosti. Vol. 1. Irkutsk, 1983

Tomashevskii, Boris. Pushkin. Vol. 2. Moscow, 1990

Tomashevskii, Boris. Pushkin i vechnyi mir. In: Zvezda. (1930) # 7. Pp. 227–30

Vosstanie dekabristov. Materialy. Vols. 1–23. Leningrad-Moscow, 1925–2016

2 monographs on P + republicanism
4 Kiianskaia, O'Meara (Pestel)

18 pp

Lorenz Erren

Russia a Republic? Some Remarks on the National Consciousness of the Decembrists

1. The Puzzle

The Decembrist movement puzzles all European intellectuals when they first read about it. What did its members have against Tsar Alexander I? How did the liberal nobility come up with the idea of killing a liberal monarch? How did such a ruthless attitude emerge toward a ruler who had done no serious harm to them? Why did they not resort to milder measures? Was there no hope left to witness the constitutional reforms that had been announced by the tsar himself?

Moreover, did they not fight against their own interests? What made these nobles argue for the abolition of noble privilege? Why were they so eager to put an end to the "golden age of nobility," still so coveted by most teachers of Russian literature? Could these estate owners sincerely feel sympathy for their serfs? Did these "counts and princes" really want to "turn into shoemakers"?[1] Why did they name their secret association the "Union of Salvation," when Mother Russia had already, so long before, been saved from Napoleon? What sort of calamity was hanging over the Russian Empire? Did the Russians not possess—in contrast to the Germans, the Polish, and the Hungarians—their own state, in fact the most powerful in Europe? What were they really missing? Moreover, if it is so difficult to explain their motives convincingly, why do later generations still generally approve of and sympathize with them? What is the foundation of the ever-popular Decembrist myth? 15 Qs culminating in

In his 1963 monograph on the Decembrists, Hans Lemberg drew attention to the fact that one of the Decembrists' dominant motives may have been the problem of national identity.[2] In this chapter, I will try to further develop that idea through a focus on the chain of events that resulted in the officers' mutiny

1 More or less the same questions are posed by: Parsamov. Dekabristy. Pp. 212–24. The last question was traditionally ascribed to Count Fedor Vasil'evich Rostopchin (Russkii biograficheskii slovar'. Vol. 17. P. 295).

2 Lemberg. Die Nationale Gedankenwelt. See also: Rogger. National Consciousness.

on Senate Square on December 14, 1825.[3] I would like to emphasize that this chapter's conclusions are not the result of long-term research but rather a kind of improvisation, and they should be read as an invitation to debate.

2. Contrasting Rome with the Barbarian West

The Decembrists emulated Brutus's example. They were sincere in their aim to assassinate the tsar; they did not just say so in order to boast their revolutionary aspirations. According to legend, Lucius Junius Brutus founded the Roman Republic by deposing the last Etruscan king and banishing him from the city. One of his direct descendants, Marcus Junius Brutus, killed Julius Caesar 450 years later because the latter wanted to wear the king's crown. Since the Roman Senate and People did not stand any kings, the first emperor, Octavian Augustus, legitimated his rule on the claim that he had supposedly restored the republic, and he owed his political power solely to his personal authority and his informal status of the *primus inter pares*, or *Princeps*, the "first citizen among peers." Consequently, the Roman Empire remained a republic to the end of its days, with the Roman Senate and People as nominal bearers of sovereignty.

As Anthony Kaldellis has recently shown, the same was true for medieval Constantinople.[4] In neither Rome was the state ever treated as the private property of the ruler or his family. The Decembrists' admiration for Rome was—contrary to some widespread theories—not only a result of influence from the Western Enlightenment. It also stemmed from older sources, partly fostered by the Russian elite's nostalgia for the Byzantine Empire and the Boyar Duma. After the coronation of Ivan III, and even more so after the election of Michail Romanov in 1613, Moscow had adopted Byzantine state doctrine to describe its own place within the world.[5] Russians, however, were less inclined than Europeans to contrast Eastern Rome with its Western predecessor. Instead, Moscow tsars, boyars, and intellectuals saw themselves as inheritors of both parts of a single empire, which they perceived as a whole. As with all Orthodox Christians, Russians were familiar with the realities of ancient Rome; their knowledge stemmed from the gospel, the martyrs' legends, the fathers' scriptures, and last not least, holy icons, which

---

3 Within the movement, there was a wide range of ideological convictions and opinions as to which methods should be applied. See: Parsamov. Dekabristy; Kiianskaia, Dekabristy.

4 Kaldellis. The Byzantine Republic. Pp. ix–xvi, 89–117.

5 Ekkehard Kraft went so far as to call the seventeenth century "Moscow's Greek age." Kraft. Moskaus Griechisches Jahrhundert.

frequently presented prominent saints (including Archangel Michael or George the Victorious) as Roman soldiers. Identification of Russia with Rome became a commonplace for the simple reason that Rome/Constantinople remained the epitome of statehood. As a result, Romanov tsars never regarded the state as their private property. Peter I acted within this tradition when he styled himself as "first servant of the state" rather than as the state's embodiment.[6]

Since the end of the seventeenth century, influence from the Polish-Ukrainian baroque reinforced Moscow elite's inclination to adopt Roman history as a valid precedent, if not as a national symbol of patriotic virtue—this applies to Sofiya Alekseyevna and Silvestr Medvedev as well as to Peter I and Feofan Prokopovich. Until the end of the eighteenth century, Russian noble patriots like Nikita Ivanovich Panin, Aleksandr Sumarokov, and Michail Shcherbatov made "Roman virtue" a symbol of national resistance against Western dynastomania in general and the pretensions of the German houses of Brunswick-Wolfenbuttel and Schleswig-Holstein-Gottorf in particular. In the 1750s, Araja's opera *Clemency of Tito* displayed the mildness of the truly Russian Empress Elizabeth Petrovna , a ruler whose core virtue so favorably differed from the despotism of her immediate predecessor, Anna I, who had been controlled by overambitious, vengeful German favorites. In 1759, the first issue of Sumarokov's journal *Busy Bee* (*Trudoliubivaia pchela*) bluntly stated that "there is no history that is closer to our age than that of ancient Rome"[7]—and it was no accident that the author of these words, Grigorii Kozickii, adhered to the intellectual circle of Panin, Sumarokov, and Denis Fonvizin, sometimes called "aristocratic fronde." By the 1760s the Rome motif had become, according to Stephen Baehr, "what Ernst Cassirer has called a 'mythic metaphor,' a substitution where what seems to our subsequent reflection as a sheer transcription is mythically conceived as a genuine and direct identification."[8]

Under Catherine II , the Roman discourse gradually radicalized. In the 1760s, writers such as Mikhail Kheraskov praised the legendary king Numa, who had made Rome flourish, to voice their desire for a peaceful foreign policy that would create conditions for domestic prosperity. By the late 1780s, Shcherbatov had already begun to venerate the name of Brutus, the king-killer.[9] At the same time, playwright Iakov Kniazhnin (1740–91) finished his tragedy *Vadim from*

---

6 This choice was in visible contrast to Louis XIV. See also: WHITTAKER. Russian monarchy. P. 39.

7 KOZICKII. O pol'ze mifologii. Pp. 17–18; quoted in BAEHR. From History to National Myth. P. 1.

8 BAEHR. From History to National Myth. P. 10; SCHIERLE. Syn otechestva. Pp. 357–58.

9 SHCHERBATOV. O povrezhdenii nravov v Rossii. P. 8.

Novgorod, whose plot can serve as an illustration of how Roman and Russian past now formed a unique mythological space. Vadim is a mythological hero who can easily be identified as a Russian Brutus. According to the play, Vadim was an outstanding citizen of what had been the Republic of Novgorod—until the citizenry dropped into civil war and invited Rurik to rule them as an autocrat. Although Rurik resembles an ideal monarch much like Julius Caesar and Octavian Augustus , Vadim cannot come to terms with the loss of freedom—and chooses to kill himself.[10]

For the Decembrists, that equation made sense: Russia was Rome—not the "third one," not the "Eastern one"—simply Rome without any numerical and geographical restrictions. It was an identity imposed not by a religious apocalyptic wait for doomsday but by the secular need to distinguish their own Roman-Russian republican patriotic idea of the state from German-French patrimonial-dynastic monarchism.

Western or Western-oriented Russian scholars may be perplexed by this perspective,[11] one that was no longer dominated by the opposition of barbarian Russia and civilized Europe, inert (Eastern) Byyantine Empire and dynamic (Western) Roman Empire, and the like. Instead, Russia embodied Roman statehood—and therefore it was strongly opposed to aggressive Western royal dynasties that could not base their selfish claim to rule the world on a better argument than their descent from barbarian chiefs who had captured, destroyed, and looted the Western Roman Empire 1,400 years before.[12]

However, the East took a different path. On two occasions, not so long ago, during the Time of Troubles and in the years of the Great Northern War, the Russian people had proved able to repel invaders who called themselves serv-

---

10 Kniazhnin finished *Vadim* few months before the outbreak of the French Revolution. Ekaterina Dashkova, for deciding to publish the tragedy in print, earned the displeasure of Catherine II, who ordered the copies burned (Dashkova. Zapiski kniagini. Pp. 203–11). Shakespeare's *Julius Caesar* was removed from bookstores for the same reason (Whittaker. Russian monarchy. P. 172).

11 The reevaluation of stereotypes has a long tradition within Russian thought. Nikolai Danilevskii named "inclination to violence" (*nasil'stvennost'*) a typical trait of the Western (Germano-Romanic) mentality in 1895 (Danievskii. Rossiia i Evropa. Pp. 223–49).

12 On the popularity of Henri de Boulainvilliers's theory, which based French nobles' privilege on the Germanic conquest of western parts of the Roman Empire, see: Asch. Europäischer Adel. P. 14. For a rejection of that idea, see: Siéyès. Qu'est-ce que le Tiers état? Pp. 17–18.

ants of the "King of the Goths and the Vandals."[13] But Moscow and Rome had much more in common than a common enemy. In both cases, autocracy and sovereignty of people, imperial and republican foundations, were seen as not mutually exclusive but as two sides of one coin.[14] According to Western notions, absolute power of the king was obtained only via succession, whereas the sovereignty of a chosen king was subject to limits. Western observers and historians have long been puzzled by the fact that Michail Romanov was elected to unlimited autocratic power. This difference between Western and Eastern notions existed at least until the French Revolution (if not until now). Peter I, Ivan V, and even Anna Ioannovna became sovereigns, "chosen by all the people."[15] Acceptance of the title of Roman emperor implied the ongoing existence of the (Roman) republic, and its very institutions, namely the Senate and the Synod, vested Peter the Great with this honor while speaking in the name of the whole nation. Cicero, the most prominent defender of the Roman constitution, was silently remembered by the title *Pater Patriae*, given to Peter I the same day.[16] The full restoration of the republic of Octavian Augustus was accomplished with the 1722 Law of Succession, which gave the monarch the right to choose his successor. In defense of that law, Feofan Prokopovich referred to the precedent of the first Roman emperors, who had transferred their power to their adopted children.[17] Throughout the eighteenth century, Russian political culture stayed faithful to a set of values that was more "Roman" than "European": a strong emphasis on the "common good", a resentment of foreign dynasties and dynastic warmongering,[18] the elite's insistance on the active role of military corporations (i.e., "the people") in state affairs, and rhetorical invocations of "the Russian na-

13 As a descendant of the House of Wasa, the Polish king Sigismund III bore that title to underline his claim to the throne of Sweden.

14 As for Byzantine Empire, see: KALDELLIS. The Byzantine Republic. Pp. 89–117.

15 On elections in Russian political culture, see: WHITTAKER. Chosen by "All the Russian People"; IDEM. Russian Monarchy.

16 The manifesto itself, it must be said, made reference not to Marcus Tullius Cicero but to Emperor Maximilian I (1459–19). See: Akt podnesenii Gosudarju Tsariu Petru I titula Imperatora Vserossiiskago i naimenovaniia: Velikago i Otca Otechestva. 22 Oktjabrja 1721 goda. In: PSZ. Vol. 6, Pp. 444–46.

17 Among forty-seven precedent cases enumerated by Prokopovich, numbers five to twenty-seven were drawn from Roman history. PROKOPOVICH. Pravda Voli Monarshei. Pp. 45–48.

18 Peter III's obsession with Holstein affairs was the ultimate reason for his downfall. As late as the 1770s, Mikhail Shcherbatov articulated his fundamental criticism of dynastic marriage (SHCHERBATOV. O povrezhdenii nravov v Rossii. Pp. 101–11).

tion" and, occasionally, of the Roman past. Most or all of these features showed up in the 1718 trial of Aleksei Petrovich,[19] the 1741 and 1762 palace coups, and, finally, the Decembrist movement.[20]

The Decembrists' passionate self-identification with ancient Rome and Brutus was a reaction to what they perceived as a desire on the part of Emperors Paul I and Alexander I to eradicate republican elements from Russian statehood. It was not accidental that Pavel Pestel' handpicked as his main authority, from among all contemporary theorists, Antoine Destutt de Tracy, whose most important book was essentially a critique of Montesquieu's monarchism. Destutt de Tracy disagreed with Montesquieu's division into republican, monarchic, and despotic forms of government. Instead, Destutt de Tracy presented what he deemed to be the defining principle of people's sovereignty: he distinguished between "national" and "particular" (or "private") forms of rule. "National" forms acknowledged that the ruler and his government received power from the people and could use it only in the name of the people and only for the welfare of the people.[21] "Particular" forms, however, implied a claim to rule that stemmed from other sources such as divine right, noble origin, or military conquest.[22] As should be obvious, Destutt de Tracy's categories quite closely reproduced the above-quoted dichotomy of Roman republican and Germanic patrimonial ideas of statehood.[23] Patriots like Pestel' were glad to see that the basis of the ideal republican form of governing could be found not in feudal Western Europe but in their own Byzantine-Russian past.

Against this background it becomes more comprehensible why the Russian plotters were ready to assassinate the emperor: in contrast to their French counterparts, they never believed that divine right stemmed from blood lineage alone.

---

19 It seems to me that it was precisely Peter I's antidynastic attitude—rather than any nimbus of "genius" resembling Homer, Newton, or Voltaire —that induced later Decembrists (such as Turgenev) to include him among the monarchomachs and followers of Brutus. Cf., PARSAMOV. Dekabristy. Pp. 313–14.

20 For a historiographical tradition that stressed this feature, see: WHITTAKER. Chosen by "All the Russian People"; ERREN. Feofan Prokopovich's Pravda voli.

21 A resemblance to the constitution of the United States is not accidental. Destutt de Tracy was in close contact with Thomas Jefferson. See: DVOICHENKO-MARKOV. Jefferson and the Russian Decembrists.

22 DESTUTT DE TRACY. Commentaire sur l'Esprit des lois de Montesquieu.

23 In the Byzantine Empire, "Power was never theorized as absolute. Its republican framework did not so much *limit* the exercise of power, as many historians claim today, as it actually *defined its purpose*" (KALDELLIS. The Byzantine Republic. P. 117; italics in the original).

God may bestow his grace on some ruler during the latter's life, but he is free to take it away from him later. From their point of view, the assassination of the tsar was at worst an ordinary crime, not a sacrilege. That is why the Decembrists, in contrast to French Jacobins, did not have to recede from Christianity before considering a tsar's assassination.

3. Landowning Servicemen versus Nobility by Birth

Since Russia was identified with Rome, aristocrats were fond of the idea of likening themselves to Roman citizens—or more precisely, to patrician clans, whose eldest patriarchs were represented in the Senate. Prince Mikhail M. Shcherbatov's pamphlet *On the Corruption of Morals in Russia* began by praising the virtue of Roman citizens Cassius and Brutus, who were not ready to sacrifice their modest life in liberty for a luxurious life in slavery. Using the example of Prince Iakov Fedorovich Dolgorukov, Shcherbatov proved that Russian ancestors had possessed the same Roman virtues as recently as three generations previously. To historians like him, the equation of (pre)Petrine Boyars with ancient Roman Senate aristocrats made irrefutable sense. Their core virtue was moral courage; they were readiness to tell the "truth" immediately, even in the face of a daunting emperor. In contrast to selfish and flattering favorites like Aleksandr Menshikov, true patriots like Dolgorukov always fulfilled their duty for the common good. Thus, Dolgorukov's famous refusal to carry out Peter I's decree to confiscate grain (on the grounds that it would cause harm to the people) was, according to Shcherbatov and his contemporaries, worthy of being eternized in marble (see fig. 1).[24]

---

24 For this anecdote, see: Shcherbatov. O povrezhdenii nravov. Pp. 20, 30; Dolgorukov. Skazaniia o rode kniazei Dolgorukovych. Pp. 64–67. According to the story, Prince Dolgorukov suggested to the tsar that he confiscate supplies from Menshikov rather than collecting grain from the suffering people.

Figure 1. Prince Iakov Fedorovich Dolgorukov burns a decree of Peter I by Mikhail Kozlovskii (1796). State Tretyakov Gallery, Moscow.

Source: Wikipedia Commons (Shakko).

One portrait from the nineteenth century even depicted this descendant of Rurik (Dolgorukov) as an ancient Roman hero—the role in which his scions wanted to see him.[25]

25 Dolgorukov. Skazaniia o rode kniazei Dolgorukovych. P. 46. Hermitage St. Petersburg, Inventory Nr. ERZh-735.

Figure 2. The tomb monument of Nikita Panin by Ivan Martos (1780s). Panin is depicted wearing a Roman toga. The Church of Annuciation/Alexander Nevsky Lavra, St. Petersburg.

Source: Wikipedia Commons (Shakko)

Veneration of Rome and rehabilitation of pre-Petrine Russia, particularly of the Boyar aristocracy, went hand in hand. According to Hans Rogger, some critics even called the founding of St. Petersburg a repetition of Emperor Constantine's "mistake." According to this line of thinking, Constantine, by shifting the seat of his administration to Byzantium, had "removed the Romans from ancestral sites which inspired their patriotic zeal" and finally caused "the decline of Roman virtue and greatness."[26]

26 Rogger. National Consciousness. P. 18; unfortunately, Rogger's only evidence is a quotation from Catherine the Great, who maintained the opposite view. On Sumarokov's sympathy for pre-Petrine Boyars, see: Ibid. Pp. 50–52.

In roughly 1790, playwright Petr Alekseevich Plavilshchikov had demanded that the Russian stage glorify national heroes such as "merchant Minin and Prince Pozharsky" instead of Dido and Aeneas.[27] A monument was erected to these two heroes—Minin and Pozharsky—in 1818 on Red Square. In its caption, Kuzma Minin was labeled a "citizen," a detail that was harshly criticized by Pushkin for not corresponding to the historical truth, for there had been no "Russian citizens" in 1613.[28] But from an ideological point of view this title was correct. Minin deserved to be honored by the title of citizen because of his behavior. In the critical moment, rather than fulfilling the decree of a provisional authority, as submissive subjects would have done, he followed the model of ancient Romans by acting on his own initiative to save his fatherland from the king of the Goths and Vandals.[29]

Russian nobility had one more reason to depict themselves as the Romans: their proverbial inability to conform to standard European criteria of "nobility" or of "noble" distinction and behavior. They lacked the status symbols of their Western peers. Their castles were wooden, their count and baron titles were freshly given, their coats of arms were invented, and their education was not complete. Authentic attributes of ancient origin and high status made no impression on foreigners. Even Russian princes who could trace their origin to Rurik—who thus had longer ancestral lines than most European monarchs—faced difficulty in communicating their real status to their Western cousins, who stubbornly estimated the rank of an aristocrat by the toponyms in his title.

The most painful subject for Russians was widespread doubt among Europeans in the cultural equivalence of knightly honor and Russian nobility. Throughout the eighteenth century, the saying that "Russians have no *point d'honneur*" was a commonplace across Europe.[30] Around 1730 a situation arose when a French priest of low origin, who occasionally happened to visit Russia, lectured Russian aristocrats in their own house that honor was an unknown virtue in their country.[31] This bitter reproach took root in the Russian national consciousness. One hundred years after the death of Peter the Great, Prince Petr Vladimirovich Dolgorukov denied the very existence of an old Russian aristocracy by the commonplace Western argument that people "doomed to a life-long service obligation,

27 Giust. Die Rezeption der italienischen opera. Pp. 180–82.

28 Pushkin. Primechanie o pamiatnike kniaziu Pozharskomu i grazhdaninu Mininu.

29 "Grazhdanin" had a propagandistic status in Pushkin's time. See: Schierle. Syn otečestva. P. 361; Zorin. Kormia dvuglavogo orla. Pp. 159–86.

30 Mervaud. Le knout et l'honneur des Russes; see also Auerbach. Der Begriff "Adel" im Russland des 16. Jahrhunderts; Berelowitch, Plaidoyer pour la noblesse moscovite.

31 Jubé. La Religion, les moeurs et les usages des Moscovites. P. 136.

subjected to public corporal punishment, cannot be called aristocracy."[32] Indeed, he stated, Russian elites were no more than "high-ranking slaves." This westernized Russian emigré differed in his opinion from the Decembrists in one crucial respect: although both fervently condemned corporal punishment (a punishment that would have seemed outrageous to Roman citizens and French aristocrats alike)—for many of the Decembrists, corporal punishment's existence was the driving factor for assassination plots)—they differed on their views of military service. The Decembrists considered military service to be a patriotic duty, while Petr Dolgorukov saw it as a life-long yoke.

Roman discourse gave Russians a possible link to the Roman tradition that avoided the influence of Western nobility standards. Western nobility based their privileges on the doubtful merits of the destruction of the Roman Empire. Their rights and privileges, as upheld against their kings, originated in a claim for a share of the captured loot. The Russian service noblemen, however, regarded their responsibility as protecting the realm from foreign invaders, such as Tatar nomads and Teutonic knights.

Russian noblemen had not taken part in the destruction of any part of the Roman Empire and therefore did not have an opportunity to develop the Frankish feudal system on captured lands. They therefore had neither obtained the privilege of a class of feudal seigneurs nor developed chivalric mentality, values, and passions. On the other hand, Russian service noblemen were superior to their Western cousins in certain respects: they had the ability to take part in ruling the state, an ability garnered according to their place in the service hierarchy. Unlike in Western Europe, central corporations in Russia maintained their political importance. Besides their military and bureaucratic functions, these associations collectively represented the state as a whole and identified with its main purposes: to defend Orthodox belief and national identity. The Russian service nobility, whose noble class corporations were essentially the same as the bureaucratic and military institutions of the centralized service state, saw itself not as a soulless tool in the monarch's hands but as a collective subject that disposed of a political will of its own.[33]

According to Montesquieu's well-known formula, monarchies were based on honor, and republics on virtue. From this formula, Russian nobles may have drawn the following conclusion: if they notoriously lacked honor, they yet had plenty of virtue; and if the Holstein Monarchy had no use for the Russian nobles'

32 Dolgorukov. Vremia imperatora Petra II i imperatricy Anny Ioannovny. P. 13.

33 Zernack / Kerski (Eds.). Polen und Russland. P. 134.

virtue, it was time to replace the monarchy with a republic. Decembrist Matvei Aleksandrovich Dmitriev-Mamonov spoke from a place of injured pride when he claimed that a "citizen of Rome is nobler than a crowned head."[34]

Acknowledging this chain of conclusions is difficult for Western historiography for two reasons: this line of thinking does not match the stereotype of Russian despotism, and likewise, it does not match the thinking of Western elites, who regarded all vassals (including knights) as passive servants of the prince whom they have sworn to serve. According to Western conceptions, nobles could legally defend their rights only in class assemblies and courts. When they joined a monarch's military service, they lost their political voice. The very idea that military detachments would interfere in politics seemed fearful and awful for the West. There were almost no military uprisings until the French Revolution, even in the course of previous revolutions.[35]

This question clearly reveals the contrast between the moral code of Western and Russian officers. The Decembrists viewed themselves as patriotic Roman citizens, but from the Western point of view they were treacherous Praetorian guards who stabbed their master in the back. European aristocrats wanted to be noble knights faithful to their master, while Decembrists viewed them as greedy mercenaries who had cynically abandoned their fatherland.[36] Herein lies the main difference between the French Jacobins and Russian Decembrists despite their seemingly uniform goals: For the French, revolution meant a radical breakup with a past that everybody had previously considered to be great. Russian service nobility, on the contrary, could see its own pattern of existence historically justified by the latest French events. Had not France, the most powerful country in Western Europe, by abolishing hereditary monarchy and feudal privileges of its faineant aristocracy, adjusted itself to Russian standards? By 1793, the "great nation" had proclaimed itself a republic with explicit reference to the Roman precedent. There remained great differences, however. Although Decembrists proved to be no less disposed than the Jacobins to kill their monarch, they never felt occasioned to desecrate the churches of the Kremlin ("this capitol of Modern times"[37]) or the

34 Such was the creed of Matvei Aleksandrovich Dmitriev-Mamonov, who insisted that the current emperors "were not Romanovs at all, but stemmed from the Holsteiners" (Lotman. Matvei Aleksandrovich Dmitriev-Mamonov. Pp. 303, 310).

35 Until the nineteenth century, official history regarded political soldiers like Wallenstein or Cromwell as disgraced villains.

36 Lemberg. Die nationale Gedankenwelt.

37 Dmitriev-Mamonov, quoted in Lotman. Matvei Aleksandrovich Dmitriev-Mamonov. P. 306.

necropolis of the great princes and tsars. To them, Russia's misfortune was not rooted in the Middle Ages, but in its recent past, according to Germaine de Stael's dictum: "Freedom is old, despotism is new."[38]

It must be emphasized that this new despotism had its roots, according to the Decembrists, not in the East (Mongol or Byzantine) but in the Romano-Germanic West—in feudal and absolutist Europe, no matter how "enlightened" it might appear. In their minds, the tyranny of Tsars Paul I and Alexander I was closely connected to the "Germans' domination" at the court, about which they had soughed since Biron's times.[39] Modern historiography usually views such complaints as xenophobic or merely the result of career envy. Such feelings undoubtedly remained a firm feature of Petersburg court life throughout two centuries, causing tensions between officers of different origins time and again. But that was hardly true for the Russian patriots among the Decembrists (many of whom originated from Germany). Most Decembrists acted not out of petty envy but out of their sentiment toward the obvious aspirations of the Schleswig-Holstein-Gottorf monarchs to exorcise the Roman republican spirit from Russia and to replace it with Western European patrimonial monarchical statehood.

The republican project of the Decembrists proceeded from the necessity to thwart this tendency and thus to further the existence of Russia as a political nation. The spread and relevance of this attitude can be illustrated by the memoirs of Ivan Dmitrievich Iakuskin, an officer of the Semenovskii regiment of the guards. His memoir opens with the statement that "the War of 1812 awakened the Russian people for life and became an important period in their political existence."[40] But whom did Iakushkin have in mind when he spoke about "the Russian people"? As becomes clear in his subsequent remarks, this concept refers to both the nobility and the common people, including the great mass of unfree serfs. He undoubtedly was influenced by the French Revolution and the anniversary of the popular levy of 1612. This time, however, Russia not only defended itself, it strove to liberate all European nations from despotism, including the French. From Iakushkin's point of view, Alexander I saved France from his own allies who wanted to tear it piecemeal like "greedy wolves." He guaranteed the French constitution that provided considerable rights to the French people and the possibility of "[continuing] the line of 1789."[41] "This time the republican

38 Parsamov. Dekabristy. Pp. 203, 432.

39 Criticism of Anna I remained an important matter for Kondratii Ryleev; see his "Dumy" cycle of poems: Ryleev. Polnoe sobranie sochinenii. Pp. 120–92.

40 Iakushkin. Zapiski. P. 1.

41 Ibid. P. 3.

La Harpe could only be glad for the actions of his tsarish disciple," Iakuskhin remarked, and one might assume that he shared this glad attitude. In 1814, the world of the future Decembrist was in perfect order: Germany was and persisted to be the stronghold of feudalism, while Russia was the engine of republican progress. The real vanguard inside Russia was the officer corps, at least, in the Semenovskii regiment, where two political demands were greatly favored: first, the abolition of physical punishment, and second, the liberation of serfs. But why were the Decembrists desperate to abolish serfdom, their source of livelihood? Iakuskhin spoke from a position common to many Decembrists, that of an army officer who had marched with his soldiers from Russia to France and then back to Russia. Military camps in Europe may have been the place where the idea emerged that ordinary soldiers of serf origin must be included in the nation and given civil and political rights. There could be military reasons for that: future warfare required soldiers who were highly motivated. The existing order, wherein the emperor possessed unlimited power over the nobility and the nobles held unlimited power over the serfs, was completely rotten. This point of view, in combination with a fervent rejection of patrimonial statehood, fit well into the Decembrists' conception of history, according to which serfdom was a rather young institution, introduced only by Boris Godunov.

Ivan Iakushkin was both an officer and a landowner, and the patriotism of the former won out over the selfishness of the latter—and according to his memoirs, the same happened to his fellow officers. Against this background, the officers' claim for total abolition of corporal punishment implied more than a simple inclination to humanize army discipline; it was a political symbol of antifeudal protest.

In 1814 many Russians still hoped that the liberal emperor would head a liberal movement. Iakushkin's memoirs, however, read as a chronicle of gradual disillusionment. In 1815, Alexander I forbade collective newspaper readings for the officers of Semenovskii regiment because "these officer meetings did not please him."[42] The same year, the tsar reduced in rank some artillery officers who had, according to Colonel Taube, treated Taube without due respect. It seems that Iakushkin perceived this episode as an expression of mutual hostility between officers of German and Russian origins. In the very next passage, he quoted a widespread rumor, according to which the emperor assured the duke of Wellington that each Russian was "either a cheat, or a fool" and that

42 Ibid. P. 6.

all war merits belonged to foreign officers.[43] Since postwar regimental service essentially consisted of exercises and drills, Iakushkin decided to resign.[44] Nevertheless, due to the influence of existing secret societies, the Semenovskii regiment maintained its political profile and outlook. Officers continued discussions about politics and mostly subscribed to the call for total abolition of corporal punishment.[45] When Grand Duke Mikhail Pavlovich appointed Colonel Fedor Shvarc as new commander of the regiment, on the recommendation of Aleksei Andreevich Arakcheev, (who had convinced him of the necessity to restrengthen discipline), the officers likely perceived the appointment as an act of political repression. According to the account of Philipp Menger, the new commander established draconian measures. He resorted to corporal punishment for even the smallest infractions, even for soldiers who had fought against Napoleon and had therefore been decorated with the St. George Cross. Shvarc even was reported to spit in the face of soldiers.

Therefore I doubt the prevailing opinion that the 1820 Semenovskii uprising was a simple military affair with no hidden political causes.[46] The political meaning of this event can be easily deciphered if one considers that this regiment at this moment had become a symbol of Russia itself—more precisely, of the patriotic progressive nobility's aspirations to make Russia a political nation. Later widespread opinion that Alexander I "hated Russia" was a reference to his scorn for the officer corps. And he scorned them for their desire to participate in the political process, a desire that was in keeping with the Russian tradition, in contrast with a Western tradition that would have required unconditional faithfulness to the sovereign. Exposing Russian officers to corporal punishment meant humiliating and enslaving the whole Russian nation, especially as the men charged with carrying out the punishment bore German surnames.

In 1820, the world of the Russian Decembrists was deeply disturbed, but national roles were distributed in the same way that they had been six years before: a yearning for freedom and humanity inherent in Russia confronted age-old European despotism in the slightly updated variation of the Metternich age. Such a dichotomy can be illustrated with one of Iakushkin's episodes, which had taken place in 1816:

43 Ibid.

44 Ibid. Pp. 6–7.

45 Ibid. Pp. 34–35.

46 Menger. Die Heilige Allianz. P. 347; Bogdanovich. Bezporiadki v Semenovskom polku 1820 g.

> there were discussions between commanders about how to punish the soldiers: a little but often, or rarely but severely, and I remember quite clearly that the commander of the second battalion baron Damas, who later in France during Charles X's reign became the minister of foreign affairs, expressed the opinion that soldiers should be punished rarely, but never given less than two hundred stick strikes, and it should be noted that this cruel punishment was used not only in the case of misbehavior, but sometimes for a small misdeed in service or for a slip in marching.[47]

4. Characteristics of Alexander's Epoch

In the epoch of Alexander I the ways of Russian and European development crossed. Old intentions to make Russia a hereditary monarchy finally succeeded under Nicholas I—and just at the same time, Western Europe turned away from the principle of dynastic legitimacy and moved toward constitutionalism and the idea of "people's sovereignty."[48] The most delicate situation lasted from 1804 to 1814. The usurper Napoleon , who had advanced himself from the rank of "Roman Consul" to that of "Emperor of the French," later claimed to have spent an hour trying to convince Alexander I of the advantages of hereditary monarchy, advantages that were supposedly denied by Alexander, a dynastically legitimate emperor.[49] Whether the German princes followed this discussion is not known, but they had already begun to believe that Napoleon would protect them from their own subjects more reliably than would Alexander. They were, of course, mistaken, as were their subjects, who had expected the liberal tsar to support German nationalism. In an article of the 1815 Treaty of Paris, the document that formed the Holy Alliance, the Russian emperor, the Prussian king, and the Austrian emperor claimed themselves to be designated by Providence as the rulers of their lands and peoples, which were declared to be branches of one family: the rulers and their subjects belonged to a single Christian nation, the only sovereign of which was God.[50] The lead-up to and initial plan for this treaty are the subject of many discussions in historiography, but contemporaries across Europe certainly viewed the quoted proposals as a rejection of the principle of national states and national sovereignty. In Russia, that fact may have caused great indignation: Russia's sovereign, with

---

47 Iakushkin. Zapiski. P. 35. Although Iakushkin writes "Dallas" here, this is an obvious error for Ange Hyacinthe Maxence, Baron de Damas (1785–1862).

48 On "constitution" and "fundamental laws" in political discourses in this time, see the article by Sergei Polskoy in this volume, Pp. 135–166.

49 Las Cases. Mémorial de St. Hélène. Vol. 1. P. 250.

50 Dross. Quellen zur Ära Metternich. P. 45.

the help of two German monarchs, confirmed himself to be a representative of a pan-European monarch family and made an alliance with them that was aimed against the political emancipation of the subjects of all three powers. Pushkin's poem[51] "Noël. A Fairy Tale" alluded to these circumstances: "So hear, my Russian people / What all the world knows well / A Prussian and an Austrian uniform / I tailored for myself."

Future Decembrists considered themselves to be part of a pan-European national movement that made still no clear distinction between republicanism and patriotism: political emancipation of "the people" and national sovereignty were perceived as two sides of the same coin. They were still unaffected by romantic folkish nationalism and its claim of ethnically homogeneous states and societies. The line of conflict was drawn not between various ethnic groups but between hereditary monarchs and the nations oppressed by them. The Russians, the Polish, the Czechs, the Hungarians, and the Germans could feel the same way. From this point of view, unimpeded territorial growth of the Russian Empire, annexation of Poland, and fragmentation of Germany into thirty-five independent principalities were calamities for all of these nations. The Concert of Europe, as restored by Talleyrand, Metternich, and Nesselrode, was a shame because it impeded the emergence of political nations and extended the existence of Western-style "despotism" (i.e., unlimited hereditary monarchy). This is why soldiers of St. Petersburg guard regiments hated their German commanders so much but felt sympathy toward German nationalism.

There was no Semenovskii regiment in Germany—but there was Jena University. Both corporations were strongholds of national movements, and both became the target of the Russian monarch's anger. Russian counselor of state Alexander Sturdza, who according to recent research may have been the actual inventor of the Holy Alliance, warned European monarchs about the danger coming from German universities, which had disseminated unrest since Luther's time.[52] German students and other nationalists reacted to this statement with indignation. Some months later, Karl Sand, a student of Jena University, killed the tsar's counselor August von Kotzebue, who was seen as an evil slanderer who had denigrated the German student movement in his reports to the tsar. This assassination was aimed at the emperor himself and was therefore

51 The original poem reads: "Noël. Skazka / Uznai, narod rossiiskii, / chto znaet celyi mir / I prusskii i avstriiskii ia sshil sebe mundir."

52 Martin. Die Suche nach dem juste milieu. Pp. 81–125.

warmly welcomed by the future Decembrists. Pushkin wrote his poem "The dagger" in commemoration of Sand:[53]

> Oh my righteous youngling, the fatal chosen one,
> Oh Sand! Your life was snuffed out on the block;
> But by your holy virtue
> You kept your voice within your slayed remains

In these words, some may hear a certain envy of the murderer, whose name would be undoubtedly "written on the ruins of autocracy."[54]

5. The Defeat of Alexander

The epoch of Alexander I was the last in which Russian autocracy included a republican, "Roman" component. From Senate Square, its path turned. In the aftermath of the Decembrists' mutiny, Nicholas I expelled the republican demon from the soul of the Russian monarchy, and from that time on he ruled as a German monarch on Russian land. He possessed the empire that, according to Petr Chaadayev, represented a gap on the map of the world civilization, stretching from the Bering Strait to the Oder.[55]

Rome was defeated, and on its ruins aristocrats had to find a new role, be it a privileged slavery in the service of an odious oppressor or martyrdom in the catacombs of the emerging revolutionary movement. The Decembrists lost their battle for power, but this defeat led them to a complete cultural victory; their defeat became the foundation of the myth with which the Russian nation continues to eagerly identify, even today.

What can we say about Alexander I himself, the hero of his age? His is the case of a wise and smart monarch with kind intentions who still fails in his "scenarios of power," in his propaganda. Even if he did realize the problem of Russian political identity, he proved unable to solve it. He had no myth, no idea, and no constitution with which the patriotic elite could identify. This finding is also reflected in his nickname "Sphinx," and the often-remarked difficulty in describing his epoch in a convincing narrative.

---

53 The original poem, titled "Kinzhal," reads: "O iunyi pravednik, izbrannik rokovoi, / O Zand, tvoj vek ugas na plakhe; / No dobrodeteli sviatoi /Ostalsia glas v kaznennom prakhe."

54 Consider Yuri Lotman's comments on the last line of Pushkin's poem "To Chaadaev": "I na oblomkakh samovlastiia / napishut nashi imena!" (Lotman. Alexander Puschkin. Pp. 76–78).

55 Chaadaev. Filosoficheskie pis'ma. P. 11.

List of references

Asch, Ronald G. Europäischer Adel in der Frühen Neuzeit. Köln, 2008

Auerbach, Inge. Der Begriff "Adel" im Russland des 16. Jahrhunderts. In: Cahiers du Monde Russe. Vol. 34 (1993). Pp. 73–88

Baehr, Stephen L. From History to National Myth. Translatio imperii in Eighteenth-Century Russia. In: Russian Review. Vol. 37 (1978). Pp. 1–13

Berelowitch, André. Plaidoyer pour la noblesse moscovite. À propos des affaires d'honneur au XVIIe siècle. In: Cahiers du Monde Russe. Vol. 34 (1993). Pp. 119–38

Bogdanovich, Modest. Bezporiadki v Semenovskom polku 1820 g. In: Vestnik Evropy. (1870) # 11. Pp. 55–84

Bugrov, Konstantin. Gosudarstvennye instituty i grazhdanskie dobrodeteli v politicheskoi mysli N.I. Panina (60–80-e gg. XVIII v.). In: Cahiers du Monde Russe. Vol. 53 (2012). Pp. 507–22

Bugrov, Konstantin. Monarkhiia i reformy. Politicheskie vzgliady N.I. Panina. Ekaterinburg, 2015

Chaadaev, Petr. Filosoficheskie pis'ma. Kazan', 1906

Danilevskii, Nikolai. Rossiia i Evropa. Vzgliad na kult'turnye i politicheskie otnosheniia Slavianskogo mira k Germano-Romanskomu. St. Petersburg, 1895

Dashkova, Ekaterina. Zapiski kniagini. Vospominaniia. Memuary. Minsk, 2003

Destutt de Tracy, Antoine. Commentaire sur l'Esprit des lois de Montesquieu. Paris, 1822

Dolgorukov, Petr V. Skazaniia o rode kniazei Dolgorukovych. St. Petersburg, 1840

Dolgorukov, Petr V. Vremia imperatora Petra II i imperatricy Anny Ioannovny. Moscow, 1997

Dross, Elisabeth. Quellen zur Ära Metternich. Darmstadt, 1999

Dvoichenko-Markov, Eufrosina. Jefferson and the Russian Decembrists. In: American Slavic and East European Review. Vol. 9 (1950). Pp. 162–68

Erren, Lorenz. Feofan Prokopovich's Pravda voli monarshei as Fundamental Law of the Russian Empire. In: Kritika. Vol. 17 (2016). Pp. 333–60

Giust, Anna. Die Rezeption der italienischen opera seria von Anna I. bis zu Katharina II. In: Lorenz Erren (Ed.). Musik am russischen Hof, Herausgegeben von. Berlin, 2017. Pp. 164–81

Iakushkin, Ivan. Zapiski. Leipzig, 1874

Jubé, Jacques. La Religion, les moeurs et les usages des Moscovites. Texte présenté et annoté par Michel Mervaud. Oxford, 1992

Kaldellis, Antonios E. The Byzantine Republic: People and Power in New Rome. Cambridge, Mass., 2015

Kiianskaia, Oksana. Dekabristy. 2. izd. Moscow, 2017

Kozickii, Grigorii. O pol'ze mifologii. In: Trudoliubivaia pchela. (1759) # 1. Pp. 5–33

Kraft, Ekkehard. Moskaus Griechisches Jahrhundert. Russisch-griechische Beziehungen und metabyzantinischer Einfluss 1619–1694. Stuttgart, 1995

Las Cases, E. Mémorial de St. Hélène. Vol. 1. 1842

Lemberg, Hans. Die nationale Gedankenwelt der Dekabristen. Köln, 1963

Lotman, [Iurii] Jurij. Alexander Puschkin—Leben als Kunstwerk. Leipzig, 1989

Lotman, Iurii. Matvei Aleksandrovich Dmitriev-Mamonov. Poet, publicist i obshchestvennyi deiatel'. In: Lotman, Iurii. Izbrannye stat'i v trekh tomakh. Tallinn, 1992. Pp. 282–349

Martin, Alexander. Die Suche nach dem juste milieu. Der Gedanke der Heiligen Allianz bei den Geschwistern Sturdza in Russland und Deutschland im napoleonischen Zeitalter. In: Forschungen zur osteuropäischen Geschichte. Vol. 54 (1998). Pp. 81–125

Menger, Philipp. Die Heilige Allianz. Religion und Politik bei Alexander I. (1801–1825). Wiesbaden, 2014

Mervaud, Michel. Le knout et l'honneur des Russes (à propos de deux articles de l'Encyclopédie). In: Recherches sur Diderot et sur l'Encyclopédie, Nr. 14 (1993), Pp.111–24

Parsamov, Vadim. Dekabristy i russkoe obshchestvo 1814–1825 gg. Moscow, 2016

Pushkin, Aleksandr. Primechanie o pamiatnike kniaziu Pozharskomu i grazhdaninu Mininu. In: Pushkin, Aleksandr. Sobranie sochinenii v 10ti tomakh. Tom 6. Moscow, 1962. Pp. 241–42

Prokopovich, Feofan. Pravda Voli Monarshei… Moscow, 1722

Rogger, Hans. National Consciousness in Eighteenth-Century Russia. Cambridge, Mass., 1969

Russkii biograficheskii slovar'. Sankt-Peterburg, 1896–1913

Ryleev, Kondratii. Polnoe sobranie sochinenii / Red., vstupitel'naia stat'ia i kommentarii A.G. Ceitlina. Moscow, 1934

Schierle, Ingrid. "Syn otečestva." Der "wahre Patriot." In: Peter Thiergen / Martina Munk (Eds.). Russische Begriffsgeschichte der Neuzeit. Beiträge zu einem Forschungsdesiderat. Köln, 2006. Pp. 347–67

Shcherbatov, Michail. O povrezhdenii nravov v Rossii. Leipzig, 1876

Siéyès, Emmanuel-Joseph. Qu'est-ce que le Tiers état? 3e édition. 1789

Whittaker, Cynthia H. Chosen by "All the Russian People": The Idea of an Elected Monarch in Eighteenth-Century Russia. In: Acta Slavica Iaponica. Vol. 18 (2001). Pp. 1–18

Whittaker, Cynthia H. Russian Monarchy: Eighteenth-Century Rulers and Writers in Political Dialogue. DeKalb, Ill., 2003

Zernack, Klaus / Kerski, Basil e.a. (Eds.). Polen und Russland—zwei Wege in der Europäischen Geschichte. Ein Gespräch mit Basil Kerski, Robert Traba und Klaus Zernack. In: Historie. Jahrbuch des Zentrums für historische Forschung Berlin der polnischen Akademie der Wissenschaften. Vol. 4 (2010/2011). Pp. 132–43

Zorin, Andrei. "Kormia dvuglavogo orla." Literatura i gosudarstvennaia ideologiia v Rossii v poslednei treti XVIII–pervoi treti XIX veka. Moscow, 2001

V. provocative article & flawed by unwarranted & misleading generalisations re Ds, Semenovsky Regt, heritage of Rome in AI's Russia, etc.

3 Redistribution of power in Imperial Space and Politics

This section would have benefitted from a map (or two).

Alsu Biktasheva

Russian Governors during the Reign of Alexander I: Mechanisms of Appointment and Dismissal in the Context of Administrative Reform

Russian governors were appointed and dismissed by the emperor, and this act held a special significance. In practice, high-ranking state officials served as intermediaries at the appointments of governors. In the eighteenth century, the right to present candidates for the position of governor belonged to the Senate, but in 1802, when governors were made accountable to the Ministry of Internal Affairs, appointments also came to be managed by this department. From that time, the minister of internal affairs presented selected candidates for gubernatorial vacancies to the emperor. We will analyze the ministry's mechanism of appointments in full detail through a careful reading of surviving documents: records of the Ministry of Internal Affairs,[1] official correspondence, governors' files, and private documents. A complete study of documents collected under the rubric "On the Appointment and Dismissal of Governors" at the Rossiiskii Gosudarstvennyi Istoricheskii Arkhiv (RGIA)[2] made it possible to find form listings of candidates for gubernatorial positions. The form included information about a candidate's administrative career, recommendations from a number of persons, and petitions from influential state officials and relatives. All this information helped establish formal parameters of gubernatorial appointments, allowing us to inspect the criteria used.

Russian law provided only vague guidelines for the selection of candidates; a legal mechanism for this process was not fully developed. For example, the imperial decree of May 11, 1801, "about the appointment of governors and the selection of candidates for it in some governorates" stated that the Senate was to "choose the worthiest and most capable candidates for the positions of governors

1 Rossiiskii Gosudarstvennyi Istoricheskii Arkhiv (hereafter, RGIA). F. 1284. Departament ispolnitel'noi policii and F.1286 Departament obshchikh del Ministerstva vnutrennikh del. (Records of the Department of Executive Police and of the Department of General Cases of the Ministry of Internal Affairs) (1826).

2 RGIA. F 1286. Op. 1. Ll. 13, 117, 256 f.

and deputy governors."[3] In December of the same year, the emperor ordered the Senate again to present ten candidates.[4] The text of this decree gave a more detailed description of the "worthiest" candidates—these candidates would be those whose moral qualities and worldviews made them aspire for social justice. In the reality of the early nineteenth century, however, it would have been very difficult to establish a competitive procedure of gubernatorial appointments according to the above-mentioned parameters, thus the decree was, in fact, a less-authoritative declaration. At the same time, it reflected the view of the young emperor on the existing mechanism of appointments made by the Senate.

1. Ministerial Appointments

Russia needed specialized high schools in order to increase the pool of available candidates for state offices. Partially compensating for the lack of these schools in the early nineteenth century was a pool of high-ranking army officers, who remained the main source of staff for civil administration. Usually, these officers were retired, older colonels who had transferred to civil service. Military service was the only school of administration available in the empire, thus the office of governor was often seen by Russians as a reward for feats of arms. It was thought that a commander of a regiment, a division, or a corps could become an educational district head, a senator, or a minister.[5] The situation began to change with the establishment and development of the educational system—first with the founding of specialized high schools, and then with the founding of universities and the system of higher education. For example, the Imperial School of Jurisprudence in St. Petersburg was founded in 1835, and specialized "preparatory" courses at the Ministry of Internal Affairs were created in this same period. State administration only became professional in the second half of the nineteenth century when, in the eyes of bureaucrats, university education and experience in administrative work became preferable to ancestry and rank.

During the reign of Alexander I, the major development that concerned Russian governors was their subjection to the Ministry of Internal Affairs,[6] as also took place in France and, slightly later, in Belgium and Italy. With the 1802 emergence of the ministerial system, all records of appointments, transferals, recognitions, and dismissals of governors were brought to the Ministry of Internal Affairs.

3 PSZ I. Vol. 26. № 20005, 9.09.1801.
4 PSZ I. Vol. 26. № 20071, 8.12.1801.
5 Berendts. O proshlom i nastoiashchem russkoi administracii. P. 109.
6 PSZ II. Vol. 21. № 20406, 8.09.1802.

Now the procedure of appointing heads of local administrations was as follows: special ministry departments produced individual "presentations" for each candidate, the minister selected candidates, the minister made a report to the emperor, and their conversation resulted in a decree of appointment that would later be presented to the Senate to be confirmed. Later, in accordance with long-standing tradition, a decree of "the Sovereign of All Russia from the Governing Senate" was issued, addressed to the minister of internal affairs, and this act appointed a governor.[7] This procedure preserved the fiction of the Senate's participation in gubernatorial appointments. In fact, the appointment of governors was controlled by the minister of internal affairs. A decree of May 3, 1829, "About the procedure of appointments in the Ministry of Internal Affairs" obliged the minister to present lists of candidates to the emperor through the Committee of Ministers. The procedure of dismissal was to follow similar steps.[8] In practice, however, this rule was rarely followed. Gubernatorial appointments remained solely under the Ministry of Internal Affairs, although, legally, it was only upon the 1837 publication of the "Instruction to governors" that governors were listed among the offices of this department.[9]

There were more than enough aspiring candidates for coveted gubernatorial positions. Some petitioned for these positions and waited years for a vacancy. The chancellery of the Ministry of Internal Affairs received letters of recommendation from various state officials, as well as personal petitions from influential relatives of candidates. Internal affairs officials prepared documents about each candidate "for the attention of the minister" and then produced lists of candidates for gubernatorial vacancies to be presented to the emperor. Similar "extracts" existed in the eighteenth century when a *Geroldmeister* (King of Arms) entered the Senate with a "presentation."[10] The form of the document changed over time, but the practice of making lists remained.

The records of the chancellery of the Ministry of Police holds a file entitled "About the candidates intended for civil governors," dated August 26, 1810.[11] It contains three sheets of paper, which have information about fifteen candidates who aspired to fill gubernatorial vacancies. Each sheet was divided into four columns: the first three contained a number, surname, office and rank, length of state service, and names of persons who had petitioned for candidates to

---

7 RGIA. F. 1286. Op. 1. Ll. 13 f., 117, 256.

8 PSZ II.Vol. 4. № 2857, 5.11.1714.

9 PSZ II. Vol. 12. № 10303, 13.09.1754.

10 Gotie. Istoriia oblastnogo upravleniia. P. 141.

11 RGIA. F. 1284. Op. 1. Kn. 3. Ll. 18, 78–81.

be included on the list. For example, Active State Councillor Egor Borisovich Fuks, who was at the top of the list, waited four years for a vacancy in one of the Baltic governorates, and Active State Councillor Egor Andreevich Torsberg was a protégé of Empress Maria Fedorovna for two years. Others seemed to have been added to the list belatedly, like Major General Dmitrii Egorovich Leslie, who was included upon the petition of Ivan Ivanovich Dmitriev, the minister of justice, and who had been a candidate for only four months at the time the list was compiled. The former minister of justice Petr Vasil'evich Lopukhin petitioned for two candidates (the deputy governor of the Caucasus and the chair of the Kostroma civic chamber), while the minister of finance Dmitrii Gur'ev petitioned for six deputy governors who served as few as ten and as many as thirty-five or forty years in their previous office. In other cases, the length of administrative service was not mentioned.

The last column, which described the decision made, was filled in for only three cases. Major General Prince Grigorii Segeevich Golicyn, whose petition was "presented by Private Councilor Novosil'cev," was appointed to Penza "with transferal to civil rank," which he, however, "did not recognize as he wished to preserve his military rank" (Golicyn's governorate lasted for five years, until he was replaced in 1816 by Mikhail Speransky). State Councilor Brionn, the head of the Crimea committee of "land division," was appointed governor of Voronezh, but something prevented him from taking the office, and March 1811 Matvei Petrovich Shtern was appointed governor of Voronezh.[12] Active State Councillor Pavel Sergeevich Pushchin was to be appointed to Orenburg.

Patronage, as is clear, worked in the ministry through recommendation. It was considered, systematized, weighted, and turned into a career factor. A patron's social weight and influence could help a candidate obtain office, while all responsibility for the decision remained with the minister of internal affairs. Recommendations and petitions constituted a lever that started a machine of appointment-making. The quoted document shows that other ministers, for the most part, contributed to the list of candidates, and the office of deputy governor was considered a "school" for civil governors. By the mid-nineteenth century, the list included one more column—a reference to the candidate's education.[13] Thus, education, together with recommendations, experience of administrative work, and length of service opened the way to the office of governor. It is difficult to see personal "influence" behind appointments because backstage intrigues are hard

12 Morunov / Samokhvalov (Eds.). Gubernii Rossiiskoi imperii. P. 90.

13 Shumilov. Mestnoe upravlenie. P. 207.

to reconstruct, but surviving records of the Ministry of Internal Affairs shed some light on these manueverings. We will look into particular cases.

Major General Boris Aleksandrovich Mansurov was a protégé of the minister of internal affairs Viktor Kochubei. On December 18, 1803, Mansurov was made active state councillor in civil service and appointed governor to Kazan.[14] The background of this appointment is as follows. The retired and widowed general lived in Penza with his family and looked for a chance to continue in service. There was talk that he was related to the senator and future minister of justice Ivan Dmitriev. Mansurov sent Kochubei a petition asking the minister to help him be appointed civil governor of Penza in case of vacancy. He was recommended by a general of the infantry, Prince Pavel Dmitrievich Cicianov. The motivation behind his search for an appointment was clear: the necessity to provide for three young children.[15] The petition was written in August 1803. The governor of Penza, Filipp Filippovich Vigel', had suffered an illness on July 28, and the administration of the governorate was entrusted to his deputy.[16] Mansurov was likely inspired to seize a chance at promotion and present his candidature for the supposed Penza vacancy after hearing rumours of Vigel's anticipated death. However, Vigel' recovered, and Mansurov was appointed to Kazan. This position was considered to be more prestigious, and the Mansurov family had connections to the city of Kazan. The governor's father, Brigadier Aleksandr Iakovlevich Mansurov, had served as ober-commandant of Kazan for a long period of time.[17] Mansurov, as a newly appointed governor, received a decree of appointment and a sum of three to five thousand roubles "for transportation and settlement," its exact amount depending on distance covered.

On March 14, 1804, Mansurov arrived at Kazan. His period in office stood out from other gubernatorial appointments and dismissals of the Alexandrine era because of its length and stability. Mansurov was the governor for eleven years, survived a number of senatorial inspections, and died "in office." Nikolai Dubrovin, who studied corruption in early nineteenth-century administration, listed him among the rare governors with untarnished reputation, respected by contemporaries and grateful descendants alike. Apart from Mansurov, this list includes the governors of Perm, Vyatka (Kirov), and Nizhny Novgorod—Gottlieb Hermes (Bogdan Andreevich Germes), Fedor Ivanovich von Bradke, and Andrei

---

14 RGIA. F. 1286. Op. 1. D. 256. Ll. 174, 176.

15 Ibid. L. 175.

16 Ibid. Ll. 92 f.

17 Rossiiskii Gosudarstvennyi Arkhiv Drevnikh Aktov (hereafter, RGADA). F. 286. Op. 2. Kn. 89. L. 591.

Maksimovich Runovskii, respectively.[18] Notably, all these civil governors were protégés of Viktor Kochubei.

The appointment of Count Ilia Andreevich Tolstoi (Leo Tolstoy's grandfather) made a big stir. Earlier, he had spent twenty years, beginning in 1793, as a retired brigadier, living in his manor in the Tula governorate, and serving as president of the court of conscience, elected by local noblemen.[19] From January 1813, influential relatives of Tolstoi repeatedly petitioned thc chancellery of the Ministry of Police to restore him to active service. The minister of army Prince Andrei Ivanovich Gorchakov asked the minister of police Sergei Kuzmich' Viazmitinov to appoint Tolstoi (Gorchakov's relative) as governor, characterizing him as "an honest and good man."[20] On February 21, 1814, a case was opened "concerning the dismissal from service of Active State Councillor Ivan Ivanovich Bakhtin, governor of Sloboda Ukraine, and the appointment of Brigadier Ilia Tolstoi to this vacancy."[21] Another influential relative who asked for Tolstoi to be appointed to this position was Count Nikolai Ivanovich Saltykov, the head of the Council of the State and of the Committee of Ministers.[22] It would have been unthinkable to reject his petition, considering his rank and social standing. And yet, there is an inscription at the margins of the document: "I cannot." On May 17, 1815, the governorate of Sloboda Ukraine was given to Active State Councillor Vasilii Gavrilovich Muratov. He remained head of the governorate for the next twelve years.

Archival documents describe cases when people not included on any list were promoted to governorship, or even appointed against their will. The emperor could grant governorship as a reward to his closest servants—an authoritative and conscientious administrator, say, or a trustworthy general—bypassing highly recommended candidates and other power brokers. Provincial life, however, was self-correcting. A governor appointed by the highest authority was supposed to demonstrate not only good professional qualities as an administrator, but also knowledge of the life of the governorate "entrusted" to him, and some did not succeed. Administration of the inner governorates differed greatly from the outer ones, and not only in the amount of power given and in the specific administrative tasks performed. In regions with noble land ownership, corporate power of nobility and gentry made the governor listen to the opinion of local aristocratic leaders. If he did not, the governor remained a hostage to fortune.

---

18 Dubrovin. Russkaia zhizn'. P. 497.

19 RGIA. F. 1284. Op. 1. Kn. 47. D. 11. Ll. 199 f.

20 RGIA. F. 1284. Op. 1. Kn. 47. D. 11. L. 198.

21 RGIA. F. 1284. Op. 1. Kn. 65. D. 1.

22 RGIA. F. 1284. Op. 1. Kn. 65. D. 1. L. 10.

2. Methods of Firing

If gubernatorial appointments were decided by power struggle in the capital, their dismissal depended on local circumstances. The procedure of dismissal could be initiated by complaints and denunciations made by gubernatorial bureaucrats and local nobles and sent to the Senate or the emperor. Governors, formally ranked as generals, did not have any defined terms of service; as a rule, the emperor dismissed governors upon request ("presentation") of the minister of internal affairs. As a consequence of this imperial act, one could be promoted, transferred to another governorate, dismissed from office with prohibition to continue in active service, or put on trial. Voluntary retirement was also possible on the grounds of ill health, family circumstances, or old age. The procedure of dismissal was as follows: upon ministerial presentation, the emperor made his decision public in his decree, which was confirmed by the Senate. After that, a decree of the Senate was issued to the minister of internal affairs to dismiss a governor "for corruption and disorder," "for abuse of power," or "for weakness in executing his office." The texts of these decrees declared the will of the emperor, without any personal comments, details, or explanations.

The legal mechanism for gubernatorial dismissals was not fully developed, with legal codes merely referring to procedural norms of criminal and administrative law. It was the "Instruction to governors" of June 3, 1837,[23] that systematized the practice of dismissals based on previous norms. The document explained when governors were to be held responsible and how they were to be punished. Punishments ranged from reproof to official reprimand, trial, and dismissal upon the "Highest order." At the same time, the "Instruction" clearly referred to the mediation of institutions and officials responsible for the dismissal of governors. These included the Senate, the Committee of Ministers, governor-generals, senators, inspectors, and personal envoys of the emperor. From 1816, the initiative of making official reprimands or levying any other sanctions against governors belonged "only to the persons of ministers and with their signatures."[24] Earlier, this right had belonged to the Senate; now it was given to the Committee of Ministers—that is, to bureaucratic hierarchy.

Disciplinary measures were taken against governors not as a result of legal action but by authority of higher-ranking officials. For "abuse of office," governors could also face criminal or civil court. Criminal cases implied retribution for an abuse of power, while civil cases implied the duty to pay compensation for losses

23 PSZ II. Vol. 12. № 10303, 13.09.1754. Cols. 324 f.

24 PSZ I. Vol. 33. № 26493, 13.10.1816.

that occurred because of errors made by the governor when in service.[25] Trials for abuse of power happened upon presentations made by the First Department of the Senate. Guarantees of the legality of administration were necessary. This guarantee lay in the system of power and in the development of institutions. For governorships, the "limits of power" were preserved by administrative control. At the gubernatorial level, it existed in the form of reports, inspections by the Senate, and constant explicit and implicit surveillance. This oversight made the possibility of abusing one's power as governor less likely.

At the beginning of his reign, Alexander I dreamed of establishing the rule of law in Russia. He presided over the redefinition of the functions of the Senate, as executive power was slowly taken from it and concentrated in the ministries. The Senate turned into the highest court of appeal. In the opinion of Sergei Korf, it was this circumstance that led to the emergence of an administrative judiciary in Russia, "unbeknown to the legislator himself," which revealed itself during the reign of Alexander I.[26] In nineteenth-century legal practice, an administrative judiciary implied court appeals to administrative acts. With an orderly system of administrative judiciary, a private person acquired a right to initiate an administrative case. However, this practice was not fully developed in imperial Russia. One can discuss only some elements of the administrative judiciary under the First Department of the Senate. Notably, in 1810 a commission was set within the Council of State to receive and consider petitions to the "Highest name,"[27] and from 1812 one more channel to petition the Emperor was opened—HIM Own Chancellery. In a situation wherein reformed central institutes (the ministries, the Senate) were often set in opposition to the archaic system of governorates, the inspections of the Senate became the main way to control the local administration. The mechanism of administrative control was initiated by the local population through a particular genre of communication—complaints and denunciations.

We do not know the total number of senatorial inspections that took place, but judging by the surviving documents, between 1800 and 1915 the Senate held approximately 120–125 inspections.[28] Three-fourths of these (90) took place in the first half of the nineteenth century, and in the second half these happened less often. According to my calculations, 52 inspections took place during the first quarter of the century, while only 38 took place during the reign of Nicholas I,

---

25 Elistratov. Osnovnye nachala. Pp. 324 f.

26 Korf. Administraivnaia iusticiia. P. 271.

27 PSZ I. Vol. 31. № 24064, 1.01.1810. Cols. 88–113.

28 See: [Nol'de / Chechulin (Eds.)]. Istoriia Pravitel'stvuiushchego senata. Vol. 2. Pp. 96–600; Vol. 4. Pp. 513–15.

in the second quarter.[29] Senatorial inspections thus played an important role in the Alexandrine system of administration. The state spent a good deal of money on the inspections. On average, one inspection cost the government between five and ten thousand roubles[30] and lasted for up to four months. These inspections were called "supra-ministerial," which emphasized the fact that they were separate from the Ministry of Internal Affairs, but their punitive nature struck a blow to the prestige of the office of governor. If one compares the surviving statistics of senatorial inspections of the first quarter of the nineteenth century with a list of Russian governors and their terms in office,[31] a clear pattern emerges: most dismissals of Russian governors coincided with periods of senatorial inspections.

The senatorial judicial procedure for governors' cases lasted for five to six years and stimulated the increase of new legal documents connected to the investigation. These files usually accumulated negative information about the actions of the governors. Even with these materials, it is not easy to understand real causes for the dismissals of governors. Let us look into particular cases. A focus on a single governorate renders nuances of political decisions more pronounced. The localization of the study makes it possible to correlate policy with reality, demonstrates ways in which governors' authority was interrupted, and reveals conflicts that transcend the framework of institutionalized relations.

3. Senate Revisions in the Careers of Kazan Governors

A case study here is the governorate of Kazan, the governorate that was most visited during the course of Alexandrine senatorial inspections.[32] Legal documents of the time named it as an "inner" governorate, and it was seen as one of "Greater Russia." In terms of geography, it united the European and the Asian parts of Russia, and economically, it was a typical agricultural region with an urban industrialized center. Local nobles were medium and small landowners. The style of administration typical for the inner governorates (with noble land ownership)

---

29 Ibid. Vol. 2. Pp. 503–8.

30 Ibid. Vol. 3. P. 636.

31 Morunov / Samokhvalov (Eds.). Gubernii Rossiiskoi imperii.

32 The governorates of the Volga region saw twenty-four senatorial inspections: the governorate of Kazan in 1801, 1803, 1808, 1810, 1815, 1819; the governorate of Vyatka in 1801, twice in 1807, and in 1813; the governorate of Simbirsk in 1826; the governorate of Perm in 1808, 1809, 1817; the governorate of Penza in 1808, 1815, 1826, 1828; and the governorate of Saratov in 1802, 1808, twice in 1826, and in 1837. See: [Nol'de / Chechulin (Eds.)]. Istoriia Pravitel'stvuiushchego senata. Vol. 4. Pp. 513–15.

was clearly different from those of border governorates in Siberia, the Caucasus, and the Baltic region. Here the governor often clashed with the head of the local nobility, and governors had to pay attention to noble opinion, thus the presence of noble self-administration is a characteristic of the region.

It has already been mentioned that under Alexander I, the governorate of Kazan was repeatedly subjected to senatorial inspections (in 1801, 1803, 1808, 1810, 1815, and 1819), and each of these inspections ended a career. Materials of the six inspections of Kazan, put together, reveal persistent and widespread conflict between local nobility and the representatives of the central government. Out of nine governors of Kazan who served under Alexander I, six were dismissed by court decision: five of these by the public decision of the First Department of the Senate (Pavel Pushchin, Aleksandr Il'ich Mukhanov, Nikolai Ivanovich Kacarev, Fedor Petrovich Gur'ev, Il'ia Tolstoi) and one (Petr Andreevich Nilov) was forced to retire by decision of the Committee of Ministers. The senatorial inspection of 1819–20, sent in response to a denunciation made by the leader of the Kazan nobility, paralyzed the local administration. Each dismissal of a governor from St. Petersburg resulted from conflict with a local noble "faction." Kazan nobility clearly wanted to have a puppet governor and to control his administration.

The first conflict played out between the local leader of nobility Court Councillor Grigorii Nikiforovich Kiselev and deputy governor Filipp Gur'ev, who was acting governor at the time. In 1815, fourteen representatives of the nobility were elected in the governorate of Kazan, but only seven of them were confirmed. Acting within his rights, the governor did not confirm certain elected candidates as jurors of *uezd* courts. Kiselev complained about this refusal to the Senate and other departments.[33] Gur'ev was severely reprimanded and was shortly dismissed from office after being accused by local landlord Mosolov of taking bribes.[34] This pattern of events often happened when governors wanted to fill local vacancies with central administrators. Local nobility saw governors' actions as an attack on their corporate interest. If a governor failed to build a working relationship with the leader of the local nobility, all means were used to remove the governor from office.

This is exactly what happened to the next governor of Kazan, Count Il'ia Andreevich Tolstoi. Tolstoi soon found himself at the center of a conflict with local nobility. Many were annoyed by his lifestyle, and the reason for his appointment seemed obvious. Prince Dmitrii Vasil'evich Tenishev inspired and organized the

33 Nacional'nyi Arkhiv Respubliki Tatarstan (hereafter, NART). 168. Op. 1. D. 32. Ll. 1–59.
34 NART. 168. Op. 2. D. 46. Ll. 1–49.

opposition to the governor. Tenishev's father was a well-known governor of Kazan. The younger Tenishev had served in the Preobrazhenskii Lifeguard Regiment before beginning his civil career as deputy governor of Kazan. Later he was appointed governor of Astrakhan, but he was dismissed and put on trial "for dereliction of duty at the time of epidemics." Two years later the Senate found him not guilty,[35] but he remained bitter at his unfair dismissal. Tenishev's experience in administration, secret resentment, and jealousy of Tolstoi all make it safe to conclude that he wanted the governorship of Kazan for himself.

Beginning in 1817, Kiselev wrote a number of complaints to the Senate and to the minister of justice about the debates on particular candidates at local elections of noble representatives. However, unlike in Gur'ev's case, these complaints did not have the desired effect. The governor and Kiselev conflicted openly at the next election of noble representatives, in March 1818. Kiselev's addressed his next denunciation "about the abuse of local authority over road duty" to Count Aleksei Arakcheev, the head of HIM Own Chancellery. In 1819, upon the report of Arakcheev, the Committee of Ministers recommended sending two senators to Kazan—Private Councillor Sergei Sergeevich Kushnikov and Count Petr L'vovich Santi. The denunciation of the abuse of road duty was well thought out. No order or justice existed in the distribution of road duty between Russian peasants and noble landlords. And no one looked into the legality of orders. In all of Russia, road duty was one of the harshest assignments, and it opened ways to "abuse."

The inspection of the governorate started on October 12, 1819. On February 5, 1820, Governor Tolstoi was dismissed. The serious accusations proved too much for him, and he died soon thereafter. In the same month, a "Temporary commission of investigation" was created, with Prince Tenishev and six of his cronies at its head. Their desire was granted: the hated governor was dismissed, and the local administrator was replaced. A new civil governor, Petr Andreevich Nilov, arrived at Kazan; he was to deal with "disorder." From the very beginning, Nilov braced for conflict. His actions were aimed at the leaders of the "noble faction" (Prince Tenishev and Kiselev). The "Temporary commission of investigation" was dissolved on April 15, 1822. Nilov managed to organize an early election of the leader of nobility by accusing Kiselev of taking bribes, sending other people's serfs as recruits, and embezzling money donated by the nobility. These measures, however, did not endear the governor to the nobility, and conflict intensified. St. Petersburg was flooded with complaints about the actions and behavior of the governor. To deal with the issue, Senator Vladimir Iur'evich Soimonov was sent

35 Arkhiv Gosudarstvennogo Soveta. Pp. 124–28.

to Kazan. He was given the rights of a governor-general. Nilov was forced to leave Kazan and, after a prolonged investigation, was dismissed from the office of the civil governor of Kazan by the decision of the Committee of Ministers.

Looking at these reasons for conflict between nobles and governorates, as well as the ways in which disputes were initiated and resolved, we see that the nobility's interference and participation in the administration of governorates was not bound by institutional framework but did have a good deal to do with dismissals and transferals of governors. A rival was destroyed by the means available within the existing system of administration: by denunciations, appeals of decisions made by governors, and accusations of bribery that resulted in senatorial inspections.

By the end of the reign of Alexander I, the government's policy was reoriented toward the strengthening of the hierarchy of executive power, the reasons for which are to be found in the local circumstances of governorates. Control over provinces remained a prerogative of the Senate, while executive power was with the Committee of Ministers. Numerous senatorial inspections caused violations of laws were sent as punishments, but these inspections did not change the situation. At the same time, the government was overwhelmed with complaints and reports of local abuses. As a solution, the institution of governors-general was revived, but these figures undermined the authority of ministers and the administrative functions of the Senate.

Senatorial inspections failed as a permanent mechanism of establishing order while bypassing local administration. "Society," which Alexander I saw as a pillar of law and order, proved to be an independent social force, and its interests did not always coincide with those of the local administration or the central government. Clashes of personality in the governorate of Kazan are clear examples of this trend. An attempt to build civil society failed. Efficient bureaucracy and detailed and sophisticated laws were clearly needed. Further, "citizens" were often loyal to their group or their region first and would put group interests above those of the state—while the state's interests were interpreted in different ways, depending on whether one was a governor, a leader of the nobility, or an inspector sent by the Senate.

Flaws of the mechanism of public and senatorial control became evident. In governorates, the prestige of the representatives of the central government was low, and the office of governor lost its former attractiveness. The government saw a solution in the strengthening of the executive branch, in further centralization and bureaucratization of administration.

List of references

ARKHIV GOSUDARSTVENNOGO SOVETA. Vol. 3: Tsarstvovanie Aleksandra I (1801–1810). St. Petersburg, 1878

BERENDTS, EDUARD. O proshlom i nastoiashchem russkoi administracii (zapiska, sostavlennaya v dekabre 1903 goda). Moscow, 2002

DUBROVIN, NIKOLAI. Russkaia zhizn' v nach. XIX veka. In: Russkaia Starina. Vol. 98 (1899). Pp. 481–508

ELISTRATOV, ARKADII. Osnovnye nachala administrativnogo prava. Moscow, 1914

GOTIE, IURII. Istoriia oblastnogo upravleniia v Rossii ot Petra I do Ekateriny II. Vol. 1. Moscow, 1913

KORF, SERGEI. Administrativnaia iusticiia v Rossii. Vol. 1. St. Petersburg, 1910

MORUNOV, IURII / SAMOKHVALOV, NIKOLAI (Eds.). Gubernii Rossiiskoi imperii: Istoriia i rukovoditeli, 1708–1917. Moscow, 2003

[NOL'DE, ALEKSANDR / CHECHULIN, NIKOLAI (Eds.)]. Istoriia Pravitel'stvuiushchego senata za dvesti let, 1711–1911 gg. Vols. 1–5. St. Petersburg, 1911

SHUMILOV, MIKHAIL. Mestnoe upravlenie i central'naia vlast' v Rossii v 50-kh–nach. 80-kh gg. XIX veka. Moscow, 1991

Oddly, no mention of предводителя дворянства or of the noble assembly (дворянское депутатское собрание) or of their respective roles+ at губернский/уездный levels (+in elected office)
How typical was the Kazan case? (Very!)

Elizaveta Sysoeva

Alexander I's Governor-General Experiment in the Volga Region: A.N. Bakhmetev's Experience

The early decades of the nineteenth century were a period of "proactive" improvement and "balance of the imperial situation,"[1] both in the content of administrative projects and in their implementation in practices of territorial administration in the Russian Empire. However, Alexander I's attempt at reforming local administration in 1816–25 remains understudied. The emperor, known for his cautiousness and indecision, endorsed the ideas of Aleksandr Dmitrievich Balashov[2] and Viktor Pavlovich Kochubei,[3] who called for introduction of viceroyalties (*namestnichestvo*) as administrative units in the empire. It is still unknown whether Nikolai Nikolaevich Novosil'cev or A.D. Balashov was the true author of the project,[4], but without the political will of the monarch, implementation would have been impossible. The empire was to be structured in accordance with a document titled "The List of Governorates and Their Distribution across Viceregal Regions" (*Spisok gubernii s raspredeleniem po namestnicheskim okrugam*). Amended in 1823–24, it was included in the Book of Civil Statutes (*Kniga shtatov po grazhdanskoi chasti*)[5] and preserved in the archives of the secret "Committee on December 6, 1826." At the end of the nineteenth century, this list of governor-generalships—as found in the committee papers—was published in the *Sbornik Rossiiskogo Imperatorskogo Obshchestva*, with further amendments simply ignored.[6] This version of the text is most referenced by scholars.

As for the question of the relation between the terms "viceroyalty" (*namestnichestvo*) and "governor-generalship" (*general-gubernatorstvo*) in the time of Alexander I, no clear answer exists. The introduction of viceregal rule throughout the empire was stipulated in the Project for Establishing Viceroyalties (*Proekt*

1 Gerasimov / Mogilner / Glebov. Novaia imperskaia istoriia Severnoi Evrazii.

2 Zhurnaly Komiteta ministrov. Pp. 505–7.

3 Sb. RIO. 1894. Pp. 2–17.

4 Raskin / Lukovskaia / Cherkesov. Institut general-gubernatorstva i namestnichestva. P. 72.

5 PSZ I. Vol. 44. Kniga shtatov. № 29865.

6 Sb. RIO. 1894. Pp. 212 f.; Kochubei. Zapiska o polozhenii imperii.

utverzhdeniia namestnichestv) of 1816[7] and the draft State Charter of the Russian Empire (*Ustavnaia gramota Rossiiskoi Imperii*) of 1820,[8] while the List of Governorates was intended as an appendix to these two documents. Two regions excepted from the list were the Kingdom of Poland, which already had viceroyalty status (1815), and the Grand Duchy of Finland, administered by a governor-general since 1809. However, only the head of the executive adminstration in Bessarabia was promoted to viceregal status, in which he joined Vasilii Sergeevich Lanskoi, then viceroy of the Kingdom of Poland. After 1819, the empire's internal governorates saw the introduction of governor-generalships rather than viceregal rule. This applied to the governorates of Ryazan', Tula, Oryol, Voronezh, and Tambov; Arkhangelsk, Vologda, and Olonets; Vitebsk, Mogilyov, Smolensk, and Kaluga; Nizhny Novgorod, Kazan, Simbirsk, Saratov, and Penza; Pskov, Liefland, Estland, and Courland; and finally, Novorossia.

The institution of viceroyalty as a model for administering imperial borderlands with their specific (sometimes constitutional) internal structure has received much attention from historiographers. In contrast, current research of the "viceregal project" and the 1816–25 reform of local administration in the internal regions of the Russian Empire is largely limited to A.D. Balashov's governor-generalship over five governorates in central Russia—those of Voronezh, Oryol, Ryazan, Tambov, and Tula.[9] This fact, sadly, is due to the lack of survival of source documentation. In addition, A.D. Balashov attended in person the sessions of the December 6 Committee, where the fate of the viceregal project was discussed.[10] Ample information on his "experiment" was preserved in the committee registers, while archival data on other viceregal regions was simply lost. Balashov's "experiment" is often linked to the State Charter and the implementation of its provisions.[11] Nevertheless, the history of other governor-generalships, their creation and functioning, is today more frequently the subject of scholarship.[12] Narratives focus

7 Sokolov / Raskin / Korneva. Institut general-gubernatorstva i namestnichestva. Pp. 36–57.

8 Gosudarstvennaia ustavnaia gramota Rossiiskoi imperii. P. 11.

9 Anuchin. Istoricheskii obzor razvitiia administrativno-politseiskikh uchrezhdenii v Rossii. Pp. 12–30; Kalachov. Razbor sochineniia g. Andreevskogo. Pp. 45–71; Vernadskii. Gosudarstvennaia Ustavnaia Gramota Rossiiskoi Imperii; Predtechenskii. Ocherki; Akul'shin. General-gubernator A.D. Balashov. Pp. 170–80; Skrydlov. Na sluzhbe Rossii.

10 Sb. RIO. Vol. 74. Pp. 116–30.

11 Vernadskii. Gosudarstvennaia Ustavnaia Gramota Rossiiskoi Imperii.

12 Arutiunian. General-gubernatorstva pri Aleksandre.

on M.M. Speransky's appointment as governor-general of Siberia,[13] or Aleksei Fedotovich Klokachev's appointment as governor-general of Arkhangelsk and chief executive of the Olonets and Vologda governorates,[14] or the renaming of the military governor of Kherson as the governor-general of Novorossia.[15] Another manifestation of the "viceregal program" in the Volga-Urals region can be found in the office of the interim governor-general Vladimir Iur'evich Soimonov.[16]

An important provision in both the Project for Establishing Viceroyalties of 1816 and State Charter of the Russian Empire was the idea of setting up a viceregal council with deliberative powers in every viceroyalty, with heads of regional offices of ministries of state as council members.[17] The two documents disagreed on the council's structure. According to the draft State Charter, the council had to include a governing council and a general assembly with wider functions, and every region was to have a private sejm (*duma*). The presence or absence of such a council in any given region can be used as a criterion to assess the degree and objective of reforms of the empire's administrative structure. We can also use this criterion to assess whether these reforms matched the original designs or reflected ad hoc practices of implementation.

According to notes in the December 6 Committee register, the governorate- and *uezd*-level councils that were established by A.D. Balashov[18] were done so at his behest alone and did not match the original designs. In this respect, should we see Balashov's strategy as the first step toward implementing the constitutional programor as merely a modernization of administrative policy? Since Balashov's region was followed by other governates-general in the internal areas of the Russian Empire, studying "the Balashov experience" can help us reconstruct the agenda of local administration reform and of the introduction of constitutionalism and "federalization" of the political space of the empire.

---

13 Vagin. Istoricheskie svedeniia o deiatelnosti grafa M.M. Speranskogo; Dameshek / Dameshek / Zinov'ev. Sibir' v sostave Rossiiskoi Imperii.

14 Efimova. Olonetskaia guberniia pod upravleniem general-gubernatora A.F. Klokacheva. Pp. 143–56; Idem. Prichiny vvedeniia i otmeny general-gubernatorstv pri Aleksandre I. Pp. 145–62.

15 PSZ I. Vol. 38. № 29031. P. 191; Kravchuk. Institut general-gubernatorstva v Tavricheskoi gubernii.

16 Biktasheva. Ot unifikatsii k spetsifikam. Pp. 147–63.

17 Vernadskii. Gosudarstvennaia Ustavnaia Gramota Rossiiskoi Imperii. Pp. 34–47; Sokolov / Raskin / Korneva. Institut general-gubernatorstva i namestnichestva. P. 52.

18 Sb. RIO. 1891. Pp. 146–47.

This chapter represents an attempt to compare A.D. Balashov's administrative experiment in five governorates of central Russia with Aleksei Nikolaevich Bakhmetev's work in the Volga region, which similarly consisted of five governorates but was established in 1825. As the deliberative bodies established by Balashov were different from those envisaged by either the 1816 viceroyalty plan or the draft State Charter, the first section of the chapter investigates the reasons for these transformations and the gradual demise of the council. In the second section, I attempt to explain why the region's center was fixed at Nizhny Novgorod and examine the details of establishing the Office of the Governor-General of the Downstream (*Nizovye*) Governorates.

1. Viceregal Council

I view the 1816 Project for Establishing Viceroyalties, the List of Governorates and Their Distribution across Viceregal Regions as preserved in the papers of the December 6 Committee, the State Charter, and Balashov's practical experiment as elements of a single policy aimed at developing a new administrative model or improving the efficiency of local administration. Introducing the viceregal council became the key issue in the whole viceroyalty project, since this council would allow vicegerents (de facto governors-general) to maintain local supervision over every aspect of the administration.

That the original designs were corrected in 1820–22 can be seen from the contents of a draft Instruction for Governors-General (*Proekt nakaza general-gubernatoram*) discovered among the Koz'ma Grigor'evich Repinskii archives in the manuscript department of the National Library of Russia. Repinskii, a close associate of M.M. Speransky, wrote the following on the title page of the manuscript: "This work, dating back to 1821 or 1822, was discovered among the private papers of His Majesty Emperor Alexander I upon his demise, with amendments in his own hand, and handed over to the December 6, 1826, Committee, established by royal decree, with V.P. Kochubei as its chairman and Count Petr Aleksandrovich Tolstoi, Nikolai Vasil'evich Vasil'chikov, Prince Aleksandr Nikolaevich Golicyn, M.M. Speransky, Hans Karl von Diebitsch, Dmitrii Nikolaevich Bludov, and Dmitrii Vasil'evich Dashkov as its members. It is evident that this paper is nothing more than a reworking of the Establishment of Viceroyalties [*Uchrezhdenie Namestnichestv*], which had been critiqued by M.M. Speransky early in 1821."[19] Indeed, the document is an almost verbatim copy of the 1816 Project for

19 Otdel Rukopisei Rossiiskoi nacional'noi Biblioteki (hereafter, OR RNB). F. 637. Repinskii K.G. D. 767. "Proekt nakaza general-gubernatoram, 1821–1822." L. 1.

Establishing Viceroyalties, but it has no provision for setting up viceregal councils, and what had been referred to as "viceroy" (*namestnik*) was replaced by "governor-general" throughout. Among the December 6 Committee archives, this document appears together with the 1816 Project, the List of Governorates and Their Distribution across Viceregal Regions, two memoranda by the minister of finance Dmitrii Aleksandrovich Gur'ev dated 1817, and anonymous responses to those.

As early as 1817, at the request of the monarch, Gur'ev listed the weaknesses of the viceregal project as he saw them. His point was that if the governor-general was to be entrusted with every aspect of administration, aspects that were at the time distributed among various local ministry offices, he would never be able to do it efficiently.[20] Sooner or later he would focus on improving a single sphere of administration—the one he understood best—and in dealing with the rest, he would have to rely on the judgment of his associates, transforming himself into a mere "instrument of others' designs."[21] Gur'ev held that administration could only be efficient if all elements of local power were responsible to the central offices. Ministers would then be able to "see and act along every line of administration," and no external power would divert or hold sway over those lines.[22] Speransky also found several faults in the project. He thought that the more a viceroy was involved in administration, the less time he would have for supervision, since he "would have to supervise himself":[23] "an integral feature of any supervision is not to enter into affairs of day-to-day administration. However, supervision can be accompanied with administration in several aspects, but these have to be few, important, and set down with highest precision."[24]

Thus, critics of the 1816 Project for Establishing Viceroyalties were exclusively ministers, who would have lost the power of giving direct orders to "persons and places." Supporters of enhancing the ministerial power held that viceregal councils should act as consultative and mediatory bodies but not expert ones. The fact that the draft instruction lacked any provision on the viceregal councils explains the complex solution: the original plan of territorial redivision was preserved, but the governors-general would have supervisory rather than administrative

---

20 Sokolov / Raskin / Korneva. Institut general-gubernatorstva i namestnichestva. P. 70.

21 Ibid. P. 72.

22 Ibid. P. 68.

23 OR RNB. F. 637. Repinskii K.G. D. 752. "Primechanie k proektu ob uchrezhdenii namestnichestv M.M. Speranskogo.1821." L. 4.

24 Ibid. L. 7.

(*upravitel'naia*) power.[25] According to Balashov, it was the latter that they had been supposed to enjoy originally.

Vladimir Arutiunian describes the body under Balashov's command as a huge chancellery office and ten ad hoc officers, rather than a full-scale council. The office included the head section, which dealt with the affairs of governorate-level councils; governorate directories (*pravleniie*); and chambers. The chancellery's second section was the supervisory police; and the third, the expedition of special-purpose institutions—hospitals, charity institutions, penitentiaries, statistical offices, and so forth. The fourth section was responsible for reviewing pleas; the fifth for workflow control; and the sixth comprised the ad hoc officers. Under Balashov, all section heads sat together on a "council similar to those of directors under a minister of state," but this, Arutiuniuan says, was not a deliberate body in the direct sense: it was composed of officers of the chancellery rather than of administrators. A large body of work fell on the shoulders of the ad hoc officers.[26] All these facts lead to the conclusion that the councils set up by Balashov differed in their composition and functions from the original plans and were started as his private initiative.

Some historians[27] see the draft Instruction for the Governors-General as the earliest project (or at least one of the first) related to the governorates-general. It is, however, evident that the issue of viceregal councils has been broached as early as in the Gur'ev memoranda, which means that setting up these bodies was under discussion in 1817. The text of the royal edict issued to Balashov on January 19, 1820, mentioned the "present instruction" prepared for governors-general.[28] Nevertheless, no such instruction was received, and governors-general had to rely mostly on the emperor's oral admonitions. It is quite possible that "present instruction" might have referred to the draft Instruction preserved among the December 6 Committee's papers. Thus, after 1820 the government more frequently recognized the need for local administrative reform by strengthening the vertical avenues of power headed by the ministries. Also important was the need to account for regional features and to explore opportunities for implementing the viceregal program in particular region.

---

25 Rossiiskii Gosudarstvennyi Istoricheskii Arkhiv (hereafter, RGIA). F. 1409. Op. 1. D. 4074. "Vypiska iz otcheta general-ad"iutanta Balasheva o deistviiakh ego s 1820 po 1826 v dolzhnosti General-Gubernatora." Ll. 94–95.

26 Arutiunian. General-gubernatorstva pri Aleksandre. P. 222; Sb. RIO. 1891. Pp. 119–20.

27 Arutiunian. General-gubernatorstva pri Aleksandre. Pp. 92–101; Pisar'kova. Gosudarstvennoie upravlenie Rossii. P. 291–92.

28 PSZ I. Vol. 37. № 28106. P. 21.

2. The Viceregal Experiment Continues: The Bakhmetev Experience in the Volga Region

To expand our view on regional varieties in the viceregal program, we will now examine the appointments of other governors-general in Russia's internal governorates[29]—those that followed in the wake of Balashov's experiment. In both its number of governorates and its "internal" locations, the Balashov experiment was comparable to that of A.N. Bakhmetev, who was put in charge of the five governorates along the Volga (Nizhny Novgorod, Kazan, Simbirsk, Saratov, and Penza) by the decree (*ukaz*) of August 30, 1825.[30] This region was listed eleventh in the Structure of the Governorates under Governors-General (*Raspisanie gubernii po upravleniiam general-gubernatorov*) and ninth on the original List of Governorates and Their Distribution across Viceregal Regions.[31] Bakhmetev was the last governor-general to be appointed by Alexander I, and his region of governorship existed until December 6, 1828.[32] Notably, this regional experience has never before been compared to that of Balashov or studied alongside either the 1816 Project for Establishing Viceroyalties or the State Charter.

Bakhmetev's relations with local elites in Nizhny Novgorod were described in detail by Igor Makarov in his book *Governors and Police Commissioners* (*Gubernatory i politsmeistery*)[33], which largely follows F.F. Vigel's narrative. Bakhmetev' appointment to Nizhny Novgorod was also the subject of several articles by R.N. Kipiatkov,[34] but his governor-generalship has never been examined in the general context of the empire.

By the time he was appointed to the Volga region, Bakhmetev had already made himself a figure of note. As a military governor in the Podolie and the "viceroy plenipotentiary" of Bessarabia, he drafted the Statute of Establishment of Bessarabia

29 Efimova. Prichiny vvedeniia i otmeny general-gubernatorstv pri Aleksandre I. Pp. 145–62.

30 RGIA. F. 1286. Op. 3. D. 297. "Ukaz o bytii Bakhmetevu general-gubernatorom, 1825." L. 1.

31 PSZ I. Vol. 44. № 29865. P. 194; Sokolov / Raskin / Korneva. Institut general-gubernatorstva i namestnichestva. Pp. 58–59.

32 Gosudarstvennyi Arkhiv Rossiiskoi Federacii (hereafter, GARF). F. 109. Op. 59. D. 107. "O chinovnikakh kantseliarii general-gubernatora Bakhmeteva, 1829." L. 1.

33 Makarov. Gubernatory i policmeistery. Pp. 171–87.

34 Kipiatkov. General-gubernator Nizhnego Novgoroda A.N. Bakhmetev. Pp. 217–19; Kipiatkov / Nikolaev. General-gubernatory ne tol'ko polezny, no i neobkhodimo nuzhny. Pp. 190–93.

(*Ustav obrazovania Bessarabskoi Oblasti*),[35] which laid the foundation for administration in the region for the coming decade. His experience in dealing with local elites stemmed from his term as the military governor of the Podolian Governorate (beginning in 1814), whose elites were Polish.[36] According to Vigel's memoirs, Bakhmetev's appointment to Bessarabia was due to Alexander's predisposition to "separate Russia's conquests from the mainland and to his [Alexander's] desire to turn a fraction of his country into a small ideal state with representative rule."[37] Thus, by the time of Bakhmetev's appointment to the Volga region, he had obtained administrative experience, including holding a seat at the collegiate deliberative body—the regional council, composed of the military governor-general of Podolia (himself), the civil governor, his deputy (the vice-governor), chief judges of the criminal and civil courts, four members of the local nobility assembly, and its marshal.[38]

On September 18, 1825, Bakhmetev received an official letter from Count Aleksei Andreevich Arakcheev with a copy of the Royal Decree to the Governing Senate of August 30. The document announced Bakhmetev's appointment as governor-general of Nizhny Novgorod, Kazan, Simbirsk, Saratov, and Penza.[39] The sudden death of Alexander I and Arakcheev's long illness delayed the new governor-general's arrival to his viceregal region. Early in November he wrote to head of general staff H.K. Diebitsch asking to procure royal assent for him to travel to St. Petersburg and to receive royal instructions and orders concerning the governorates freshly under his care. He also asked for instructions for his newly established region, staff lists of officials under his command, and authorized information on his destination. Waiting for response at "a residence of his own" in Podolian Governorate, Bakhmetev asked to make Nizhny Novgorod the center of his viceroyalty.[40] On December 10, his note was handed over to the minister of internal affairs. On December 31, 1825, a memorandum by Bakhmetev "declaring Nizhny Novgorod the place of his permanent residence" was entered on the register of the Committee of Ministers, and on February 6, 1826, it was promulgated by Nicholas I.[41]

---

35 PSZ I. 41. № 27357. P. 222. For more information regarding Bakhmetev's time in Bessarabia, see the article by Victor Taki in this volume, Pp. 317–337.

36 Kushko / Taki. Bessarabia v sostave Rossiiskoi imperii. Pp. 118–24.

37 Vigel'. Zapiski. P. 266.

38 PSZ I. Vol. 41. № 27357. P. 222.

39 Central'nyi arkhiv Nizhegorodskoi Oblasti (in the following: CANO). F. 3. Op. 1. D. 1. "Ukaz na imia Bakhmeteva. 1825." L. 3.

40 RGIA. F. 1286. Op. 3. D. 297. "Otnoshenie Bakhmeteva na imia Dibicha, 1825." Ll. 7–8.

41 RGIA. F. 1263. Op. 1. D. 450. "Zhurnaly Komiteta Ministrov, ianvar' 1826. 1826." L. 105.

Indeed, the List of Governorates under the Command of Governors-General with Mention of Town of Residence for Every Governor-General of April 14, 1824, did not specify which town in the Volga region would be the center of the viceroyalty.[42] This gave Bakhmetev an opportunity to make his own choice; however, it does not explain why he chose Nizhny Novgorod rather than Kazan, as had been intended in the 1818–19 List of Governorates. The reason, quite likely, lay in Bakhmetev's own social connections.[43] His most detailed biography appears in the *Russian Biographical Dictionary* and the reference text *State Councillors of the Russian Empire, 1801–1906*. According to these sources, Bakhmetev was born in Penza Province of Kazan Governorate. By the time that the viceregal program was launched, his ancestral lands had become part of Penza Governorate and thus part of the viceroyalty under his command. It was in Nizhny Novgorod in 1812–13 (as reported by P.A. Viazemskii) that Bakhmetev recovered after being wounded in the Battle of Moscow (Borodino).[44] Finally, of equal importance may have been the fact that one of his sisters was married to the marshal of nobility of Nizhny Novgorod Governorate, gentleman of the royal chamber, Prince Egor (Georgii) Aleksandrovich Gruzinskii.[45] In his memoirs, Vigel' described Gruzinskii as "a man of royal descent, with hot blood of the south, ardent passion and harsh temper." "As a prince of power," wrote Vigel', "he ruled over his rich and large settlement of Lyskovo, on the bank of the Volga, across the river from the small town of Makariev." The town was famous for its annual fair, and many traders and visitors preferred during the event to lodge at the house that Gruzinskii rented out for the purpose. It was a very profitable business, wrote Vigel', but after the fair was moved from Makariev to Nizhny Novgorod, the power of the marshal was shattered.[46] The transfer of the fair to the capital city of the governorate required that the regional authorities take serious measures to adapt Nizhny Novgorod's infrastructure to the annual influx of a huge number of sellers, buyers, and cargo.[47]

Whether high-profile officials in St. Petersburg knew of Bakhmetev's family ties to the marshal of Nizhny Novgorod's nobility is unknown, since Bakhmetev's sister had died years before his appointment. During his term as

---

42 PSZ I. Vol. 44. № 29865. P. 194.

43 Russkii biograficheskii slovar'. Pp. 600–601; Shilov / Kuz'min. Chleny Gosudarstvennogo soveta Rossiiskoi imperii. P. 57.

44 Viazemskii. Polnoe sobranie sochinenii. Pp. 413–17.

45 Shilov / Kuz'min. Chleny Gosudarstvennogo soveta Rossiiskoi imperii. P. 57.

46 Vigel'. Zapiski. P. 239.

47 Seleznev. Pervye lica Nizhegorodskoi gubernii. P. 34–35.

governor-general, he twice received royal orders to investigate the actions of the marshal, who was reported to have exerted undue influence over poorer gentry, abused army recruitment rules, rigged elections, and generally "misemployed his powers."[48] Reports on the progress of the investigation, sent to the head of general staff Diebitsch and head of the Third Section of the Imperial Chancellery Alexander von Benckendorff, revealed a very slack attitude and made no mention of serious measures.[49] The marshal of Nizhny Novgorod nobility was finally brought to Moscow for trial in 1832, after Bakhmetev was no longer governor-general. The Central Archives of the Nizhny Novgorod region have preserved a document titled "Memorandum on the Case of the Ex-Marshal of Nobility Gruzinskii… ,"[50] which was sent to the archives from the joint collection of the Moscow Departments of the Governing Senate. The document reports that "Adjutant General Benckendorff […] has privately received the following news on Prince Gruzinskii, also confirmed by widespread rumors: Governor-General Bakhmetev is a very close relative of Gruzinskii's, whose wife was the former's sister. For a long time, Prince Gruzinskii has been indulging in all kinds of misdemeanors."[51] It follows that Diebitsch and Benckendorff had not originally known of the family ties between the marshal and the governor-general, which were only brought to light in the reports of the gendarmes. Thus, it is not unlikely that Bakhmetev's request for residence in Nizhny Novgorod was purely his own initiative.

Before setting out for his destination, the governor-general had to visit St. Petersburg to receive instructions and to obtain official approval for his chancellery's staff list. A surviving document titled "A Special Register of the Committee of Ministers of January 19, 1826. On the Staff of Chancellery Offices of Governors-General"[52] reports that Bakhmetev had been invited to attend a session of the committee to discuss his chancellery staff list "in comparison with [those of] his counterparts." Having heard from Bakhmetev, the Committee of Ministers granted his chancellery office "a staff list comparable to [that of] Governor-General

48 GARF. F. 109. Op. 3. D. 100. "Otnoshenie nashal'niku Glavnogo Shtaba. 1828." L. 2.

49 Ibid.

50 CANO. F. 1408. Op. 1. D. 507. "Zapiska iz dela o byvshem gubernskom predvoditele dvorianstva Gruzinskom, obviniaemom v pristanoderzhatel'stve beglykh, zapisi v reviziiu ikh pod chuzhimi imenami i drugikh prestupleniiakh. 1828–1831." L. 100.

51 Ibid. L. 104.

52 RGIA. F. 1263. Op. 1. D. 362. "Zhurnaly Komiteta Ministrov, iiul' 1824. 1824." Ll. 369–83.

Balashov, in the total sum of 56,000 roubles."[53] Prior to that decision, the staff lists for chancelleries of governors-general and military governors-general had been drafted by a special committee, established on December 15, 1823, and consisting of heads of departments of the State Treasury Office and the head of chancellery of the military governor-general of St. Petersburg. The number of employees and the stationery expenditure were to increase in direct proportion to the numbers of governorates under command.

The same principle had also been followed by the earliest committee to draw up chancellery staff lists, a committee set up in 1820 and consisting of governors-general themselves. With the expansion of covered territories, the number of files grew, as did the numbers of officials.[54] The members of the 1823 special committee believed that the staff list of a governor-general's chancellery (with the exception of those located in the nation's two capitals) could include the head of chancellery, his secretary, three aides, a register keeper, an executive officer (doubling as a treasurer), a translator, and six scribes. While the territories of "old Russia" and five internal governorates under Balashov's command did not have an interpreter on staff, Podolian Governorate had as many as two.[55] The staff list of a governor-general's chancellery could vary in accordance with the local conditions in the governorates that composed the viceroyalty, and it was also partially dependent on personal requests made by the governors-general.

The staff list granted to Bakhmetev provided that his chancellery would have a director, five secretaries, fifteen aides (of whom three dealt with matters of policing, five with domestic economy, and five with judicial affairs), a journal keeper, a treasurer, fifteen senior scribes and as many assistants, and finally, five ad hoc officers.[56] After the staff list was endorsed and the vacancies filled, on June 15, 1826, Bakhmetev divided the chancellery into five expeditions: 1.

53 Ibid. L. 345.

54 CANO. F. 3. Op. 1. D. 75. "Vypiska iz zhurnalov Komiteta Ministrov 24 iiulia 1824, 24 sentiabria 1825, 19 ianvaria i 16 fevralia 1826 g. 1826." L. 7.

55 Ibid.

56 RGIA. F. 1263. Op. 1. D. 450. "Osobyi zhurnal Komiteta Ministrov genvaria 19 dnia 1826 o shtatakh kantseliarii general-gubernatorov.1826." L. 345; D. 362. "Osobyi zhurnal Komiteta ministrov 24 iiulia 1824 goda i 24 oktiabria 1825 goda po predstavleniiu Upravliaiushchego ministerstvom vnutrennikh del ot 29 maia 1824 goda za № 551 po Ispolnpitel'nomu departamentu o vnov' sostavlennykh Shtatakh Kantseliarii general-gubernatorov i voennykh gubernatorov. 1824." L. 355.

domestic economy; 2. executive; 3. civil affairs; 4. criminal; 5. investigative.[57] In September 1826 he demanded that should any order fail to be executed on time, the secretaries should report the incident through the chancellery's director.[58] The economic expedition dealt with documentation on fiscal issues, services provided by towns and territorial authorities, charity institutions, hospitals, almshouses, prisons, problems related to sowing and harvesting crops, population size, and other issues. The second expedition of the chancellery controlled compliance with the decrees and orders of the Governing Senate, letters of the ministers of state, requests from governmental institutions on implementing compliance orders, registers of tax arrears, and incidents and problems unsolved. The same expedition also kept journals and drafted reports upon receipt of decrees of the Governing Senate. The third expedition dealt with complaints and requests in cases at civil law, while the functions of the fourth and fifth were similar: they received petitions and complaints in criminal cases and during the investigative stage, and they had the power to revise these cases and examine reports on peasants disobeying their owners. All in all, under Bakhmetev's governor-generalship, the chancellery was supposed to employ fifty-eight officials,[59] but in fact it had only twenty-two staff members,[60] and when the viceroyalty was dismantled at the end of 1828 as many as twenty-three.

3. Conclusions

The top-down viceregal project was a complex and multilevel process of reform, whose main direction was guided by the content of expert evaluations, in-depth analysis of and control over the local situation, and the staging of site-specific experiments to investigate potential risks.

Although Balashov and Bakhmetev had the same number of governorates under their command, and governed simililarly situated provinces in the empire, they governed their respective viceroyalties in a very different manners. Balashov, whose term as governor-general began under direct guidance of Alexander I, was open to constitutional activity and experiments, and he governed his region in a markedly proactive way. Bakhmetev's work in the five governorates along the Volga involved no attempts to set up a deliberative body—even though the governor-general had a treasure trove of experience in reforming local adminis-

57 CANO. F. 3. Op. 1. D. 75. Ll. 20–21.

58 Ibid. L. 24.

59 CANO. F. 3. Op. 1. D. 75. L. 3.

60 Ibid. Ll. 26–27.

tration in the western regions of the empire. There was no standard instruction set up for the governors-general. Bakhmetev was the only governor-general selected for participation in the viceregal project by Alexander I but later endorsed and instructed by the new emperor, Nicholas. The governor-generalship model, as it was introduced in the new reign under new circumstances, after the failed uprising of the Decembrists, lost the liberal and constitutional element that had originally been introduced into the program by its creators and Alexander I. At the same time, Bakhmetev's work as governor-general, given the absence of a viceregal council in his region, correlated well with the provisions of the draft Instruction to the Governors-General of 1821–22 and can be seen as an alternative attempt at reforming local administration, one aimed at reaching a compromise between governors-general and ministries in their political and administrative relations in provincial Russia.

List of references

AKUL'SHIN, PETR. General-gubernator A.D. Balashov. In: Otechestvennaia istoriia (2004) # 2. Pp. 170–80

ANUCHIN, EVGENII. Istoricheskii obzor razvitiia administrativno-politseiskikh uchrezhdenii v Rossii s Uchrezhdeniia o guberniiakh 1775 g. do poslednego vremeni: sostavlen po rasporiazheniiu ministra vnutrennikh del chinovnikom osobykh poruchenii pri ministre E. Anuchinym. St. Petersburg, 1892

ARUTIUNIAN, VLADIMIR. General-gubernatorstva pri Aleksandre I. Moscow, 2008. Doctoral dissertation, unpublished manuscript

BIKTASHEVA, ALSU. Ot unifikatsii k spetsifikam: regional'noe upravlenie v Rossiiskoi imperii (vtoraia chetvert' XIX veka). In: Novoe proshloe / The New Past 1 (2017) P. 147–63

DAMESHEK I.L. / DAMESHEK L.M. / ZINOV'EV V.P. e.a. Sibir' v sostave Rossiiskoi imperii. Moscow, 2007

EFIMOVA, VIKTORIA. Olonetskaia guberniia pod upravleniem general-gubernatora A.F. Klokacheva. In: Rossiiskaia Istoriia. (2009) # 3. Pp. 143–56

EFIMOVA, VIKTORIA. Prichiny vvedeniia i otmeny general-gubernatorstv pri Aleksandre I. In: ZHUKOVSKAIA, TATIANA (Ed.). Vlast', obshchestvo, armiia: ot Pavla I k Aleksandru I. St. Petersburg, 2013. Pp. 145–62

GERASIMOV, ILYA / MOGILNER, MARINA / GLEBOV, SERGEI. Novaia imperskaia istoriia Severnoi Evrazii. Vol. 2: Balansirovanie imperskoi situatsii: XVIII–XX vv. Kazan, 2017

Gosudarstvennaia ustavnaia gramota Rossiiskoi imperii = La Charte Constitutionne de l'Empire de Russie / Publ. d'apres l'original des archives de St. Petersbourg. Pref. de M. Theodor Schiemann. Berlin, 1903

Kalachov, Nikolai. Razbor sochineniia g. Andreevskogo "O namestnikakh, voevodakh i gubernatorakh", sostavlennyi po porucheniiu imperatorskoi akademii nauk Nikolaem Kalachovym s prilozheniem dopolnitel'nogo issledovaniia avtora i obozreniia proektov i bumag komiteta 6 dekabria 1826 g., otnosiashshikhsia k gubernskim uchrezhdeniiam. St. Petersburg, 1867

Kipiatkov, Ruslan. General-gubernator Nizhnego Novgoroda A.N. Bakhmetev. Paper presented at Problemy istorii i tvorcheskoe nasledie professora N.P. Sokolova. Materialy mezhvuzovskoi konferentsii 10–11 oktiabria 1997 g. Nizhnii Novgorod, 1998. Pp. 217–19

Kipiatkov, Ruslan / Nikolaev, Dmitrii. General-gubernatory ne tol'ko polezny, no i neobkhodimo nuzhny: zapiska generala ot infanterii A.N. Bakhmeteva. 1826 g. In: Istoricheskii arkhiv. (2008) # 2. Pp. 190–93

Kravchuk, Alexander. Institut general-gubernatorstva v Tavricheskoi gubernii. Simferopol', 2016. Doctoral dissertation, unpublished manuscript

Kochubei, Viktor. Zapiska o polozhenii imperii i o merah k prekrashheniiu besporiadkov i vvedenii luchshego ustroistva v raznye otrasli pravitel'stva sostavliaiushchie. In: Sbornik Rossiiskogo imperatorskogo istoricheskogo obshchestva. Vol. 90 (1894). Pp. 2–17

Kushko, Andrei / Taki, Victor. Bessarabiia v sostave Rossiiskoi imperii (1812–1917). Moscow, 2012

Makarov, Igor. Gubernatory i policmeistery. Seriia: Nizhegorodskie byli. Nizhnii Novgorod, 2005

Pisar'kova, Liubov'. Gosudarstvennoe upravlenie Rossii v pervoi chetverti XIX v.: Zamysly, proekty, voploshchenie. St. Petersburg, 2012

Predtechenskii, Anatolii. Ocherki obschestvenno-politicheskoi istorii Rossii v pervoi chetverti XIX v. Moskva-Leningrad, 1957

Raskin, David / Lukovskaia, Dzhenevra / Cherkesov, Viktor. Institut general-gubernatorstva i namestnichestva v Rossiiskoi imperii. St. Petersburg, 2001

Russkii biograficheskii slovar'. Vol. 2. St. Petersburg, 1992.

Sbornik imperatorskogo russkogo istoricheskogo obshchestva. Vols. 74 and 90. St. Petersburg, 1891–94

Seleznev, Fedor. Pervye lica Nizhegorodskoi gubernii. Nizhnii Novgorod, 2005

Shilov Denis / Kuz'min, Iurii. Chleny Gosudarstvennogo soveta Rossiiskoi imperii. 1801–1906: Biobibliograficheskii spravochnik. St. Petersburg, 2007

SKRYDLOV, ANDREI. Na sluzhbe Rossii: Aleksandr Dmitrievich Balashev. 1770–1837. St. Petersburg, 2016

SOKOLOV, ALEKSANDR / RASKIN, DAVID / KORNEVA, NADEZHDA. Institut general-gubernatorstva i namestnichestva v Rossiiskoi imperii. St. Petersburg, 2003

VAGIN, V.I. Istoricheskie svedeniia o deiatel'nosti grafa M.M. Speranskogo v Sibiri s 1819 po 1822 god. Vol. 1. St. Petersburg, 1872

VERNADSKII, GEORGII. Gosudarstvennaia Ustavnaia Gramota Rossiiskoi Imperii 1820 g. Istoriko-iuridicheskii ocherk. Praga, 1925

VIAZEMSKII, PETR. Polnoe sobranie sochinenii. Vol. 2. St. Petersburg, 1879

VIGEL', FILIPP. Zapiski. Moscow, 2000

ZHURNALY KOMITETA MINISTROV TSARSTVOVANIIA IMPERATORA ALEKSANDRA I. Vol. 2: 1810–1812. St. Petersburg, 1891

Victor Taki

Construction of Center and Periphery in the Reign of Alexander I. The Case of Bessarabia, 1812–1828

According to the Treaty of Bucharest, which concluded the war between the Russian Empire and the Ottoman Empire of 1806–12, the Ottoman Empire ceded to Russia the lands between the rivers Dniester, Prut, and Danube and the Black Sea. The early history of Russian policies in this territory, which soon came to be known as Bessarabia, offers an interesting entry to the more general problem of administrative and political reform in the Russian Empire during the reign of Alexander I.[1] This chapter demonstrates that Alexander I's policy in the new province was conditioned by his attempts to accommodate the political aspirations of the elites of the Western Borderlands and, at the same time, elaborate an overall administrative-political framework for the entire empire. The tsar's experiment with Bessarabian autonomy took place in the context of a discussion about the ministerial/functional and the viceregal/territorial types of government, which contributed to the emergence of distinct administrative formats in the center and the borderland regions.

---

1 The most significant studies of Bessarabian autonomy are: Kushko / Taki. Bessarabiia v sostave Rossiiskoi imperii. Pp. 105–45; Grosul. Genezis Bessarabskoi avtonomii. Pp. 20–31; Idem. Avtonomia Bessarabii v sostave Rossii. Pp. 110–234; Barcaru. Considerații privind instituțiile administrației locale din Basarabia. Pp. 69–86; Melinte / Cernenchi. Unele aspect din istoria. Pp. 215–24; Morozan. Formirovanie i deiatel'nosti administrativnykh organov upravlenia v Bessarabskoi oblasti; Jewsbury. The Russian Annexation of Bessarabia; Ancupov / Zhukov. Reformy v upravlenii Bessarabii. Pp. 145–59; Boldur. Autonomia Basarabiei sub stăpânirea rusească; Kasso. Rossiia na Dunae i obrazovanie Bessarabskoi oblasti. Pp. 190–230; Nakko. Ocherk grazhdanskogo ustroistva Bessarabskoi oblasti. Pp. 109–221. Most of these authors, however, approach the subject of the Bessarabian autonomy from the local or foreign political perspective and do not attempt to relate it to projects of political-administrative reform that were considered and implemented in the rest of the Russian Empire.

1. The Bessarabian Experiment of Alexander I

The first measures on the administrative organization of Bessarabia were taken by the last commander of Russia's "Moldavian" army, Admiral Pavel Chichagov, and his diplomatic chancellery secretary Ioannis Kapodistrias (In Russia also known as Ioann Kapodistira).[2] Their goal was to preserve Russian influence over the Balkan peoples, whose situation in the Ottoman Empire remained uncertain in the wake of the Russo-Turkish War. Since the Treaty of Bucharest, which was hastily concluded on the eve of Napoleon's invasion of Russia, stipulated the return of Serbia, Wallachia, and most of Moldavia to the Ottoman Empire, Bessarabia had to serve as a refuge for those who had compromised themselves in the eyes of Ottoman authorities by their cooperation with the Russians during the war. However, it was meant to be more than a compensation to the former Russian allies and clients. Like the Illyrian provinces of the French Empire on the opposite extreme of the Balkans, Bessarabia had to help project imperial influence in the region. In order to fulfill this function, the newly annexed province had to be a showcase of benevolent Russian rule.

In his letter to Alexander I, Chichagov characterized Bessarabia as "a beautiful country" that offered all sorts of advantages, yet "should be given some respite." Alongside the suspension of taxes for a period of three years and relief from the military draft, Chichagov and Kapodistrias insisted on preserving the local institutions: "One should not do or arrange for anything that would not be in accordance with local needs and local means."[3] Accordingly, the "Rules for the Temporary Government of Bessarabia," which were elaborated by Kapodistrias in summer 1812, did not pursue the goal of bringing "the local institutions in accordance with the Russian ones"; instead they based the provincial government on the local laws and made Moldavian (Romanian) the language of administrative affairs and the courts.[4] In parallel, the first civil governor of Bessarabia, Skarlat Sturdza, was instructed to "draw the attention of the neighboring peoples to this province." According to the instructions, "the last Russian-Ottoman war preoccupied the thoughts of Moldavians, Wallachians, Greeks, Bulgarians, and Serbs," yet the conclusion of peace and the withdrawal of the Russian army to confront Napoleon in the north "could bring the spirit of these peoples down and allow our

---

2 On Kapodistrias, see: Grimsted. The Foreign Ministers of Alexander I; Arsh. Kapodistria i grecheskoie nacional'no-osvoboditel'noe dvizhenie.

3 Bogdanovich (Ed.) Pis'ma admirala Chichagova k imperatoru Aleksandru I. August 6, 1812. Pp. 28 f.

4 Materialy po noveishei istorii Bessarabii. Pp. 109 f.

enemies to take over them." It was therefore necessary to "preserve the attachment of these peoples to Russia and protect them from the influence of our enemies."[5]

Bessarabia came to the attention of Alexander I again almost four years later. After the conclusion of the Congress of Vienna and his return from Europe, the emperor turned to internal affairs that had long demanded his attention. According to Kapodistrias, who in the meantime became the Russian minister of foreign affairs, Alexander I devoted considerable time to the situation in Bessarabia, where administrative chaos and abuses by officials had placed the ambitious vision of Chichagov and Kapodistrias on the verge of total failure. Kapodistrias explained this situation by "the vices characteristic of this country that had so far received only Moldavian—that is, Turkish—upbringing."[6] To correct the situation, the emperor appointed military governor of Podolia Aleksei Bakhmetev[7] as his viceroy in Bessarabia, with the goal of "establishing a civil government in the province that would accord with its mores, customs, and laws." The viceroy was authorized to address the emperor directly on all questions pertaining to administration of the region.[8]

An accompanying memorandum contained instructions on the formation of the government of the province. The viceroy was supposed to form it out of able inhabitants whose knowledge of local traditions could contribute to the final definition of provincial autonomy. "Can one really hope," asked the author of the document, "that the happiness of a people be based on constraint and that a people change its character and adjust it to a completely foreign form of government?"[9] The most important task of the viceroy was the elaboration of a new Bessarabian Statute to replace the "Rules for the Government of Bessarabia" of 1813. The project of the statute was to define the rights and duties of all classes of the population, stipulate the mode of election for the provincial government and

---

5 Ibid. P. 111.

6 Kryzhanovskaia / Rusev (Eds.). Istoriia Moldavii. Kapodistrias to Bakhmetev, 4.06.1816. P. 206.

7 On Aleksei Bakhmetev and his time as governor-general on the Volga, see the chapter by Elizaveta Sysoeva in this volume, Pp. 301–315.

8 PSZ I. Vol. 23. № 26289, 26.05.1816. "Vysochaishee povelenie, obiavlennoie Komitetu Ministrov grafom Arakcheevym. O naznachenii v Bessarabskoi oblasti polnomochnogo namestnika."

9 Rossiiskii Gosudartvennyi Istoricheskii Arkhiv (hereafter, RGIA). 1286. Op. 2. D. 70. "Delo ob obrazovanii Bessarabskoi oblasti i o naznachenii polnomochnym namestnikom Bessarabii Podol'skogo voennogo gubernatora general-leitenanta Bakhmeteva. 1816 g." L. 25.

district administration, provide for the dispensation of justice in the Moldavian (Romanian) language and on the basis of local laws, and contain provisions for the internal police and border guard service.[10]

The appointment of the military governor of Podolia as the Bessarabian viceroy was highly significant. Annexed to the Russian Empire as a result of the second partition of Poland, Podolia was a region dominated by Polish nobility.[11] During the first two decades following the annexation, relations between the Russian Empire and the Polish elite remained undefined, particularly taking into consideration Russia's confrontation with revolutionary and Napoleonic France. Alexander I responded to the creation of the Grand Duchy of Warsaw in 1807 by signaling to the Poles his intention to grant them wide autonomy.[12] Despite the participation of the Poles in Napoleon's campaign against Russia, the tsar proceeded to create a constitutional Kingdom of Poland, which was bound to the Russian Empire only by means of personal union.[13] He also considered the possibility of incorporating into this new kingdom the territories that Russia had annexed in the course of the second and third partition of the Polish Lithuanian Commonwealth, a possibility that caused great discontent among the Russian nobility.[14] In 1816, the policy of cooperation with Polish elites in the Western Borderlands was thus in full swing, and the decision to confer the Bessarabian viceroyalty to the governor of Podolia meant that the emperor considered Bessarabia to be part of Russia's Western Borderlands.

The instructions given to Bakhmetev confirm this hypothesis, noting that the policy with respect to Bessarabia "is fully in accordance with the one that His Imperial Majesty chose to adopt with respect to other territories acquired during

10 Ibid. Ll. 30–33.

11 The case of Podolia is discussed by Constantin Troianowski in this volume; see Pp. 339–360.

12 On Napoleon's policies in Poland, see: Blackburn. Napoleon and Szlachta. On St. Petersburg's policies in the "Polish" gubernias, see: Dolbilov / Miller (Eds.). Zapadnye okrainy Rossiiskoi imperii. Pp. 75–78. For a comparative study of the Russian, Austrian, and Prussian policies in the territories of the former Polish Lithuanian Commonwealth, see: Wadycz. The Lands of Partitioned Poland. On Alexander I's plans to offer the Poles autonomy on the eve of Napoleon's invasion of Russia, see: Czartoryski. Memuary kniazia Adama Chartoryzhskogo. Pp. 151–55.

13 On the creation of the Kingdom of Poland and its existence in the Russian Empire, see: Dolbilov / Miller (Eds.). Zapadnye okrainy Rossiiskoi imperii. Pp. 83–94; Thackeray. Antecedents of Revolution.

14 Dolbilov / Miller (Eds.). Zapadnye okrainy Rossiiskoi imperii. Pp. 90 f.

His reign."[15] This was a clear reference to the Grand Duchy of Finland and the Kingdom of Poland, which implied that Bessarabian nobles were supposed to play the same role in the provincial government as the Polish and Finish elites did in their respective regions. The appointment of the Podolian governor as the Bessarabian viceroy indicated the emperor's willingness to respect the privileges of the Bessarabian nobility, as did his order to elaborate the statute on the basis of local laws, customs, and traditions. It is thus possible to say that Bessarabian autonomy was in a certain sense conditioned by Alexander I's policies with respect to the Polish elites, policies that themselves represented a response to Napoleon's Polish policies. There was not only a generic similarity but also a direct connection: Bakhmetev brought with him to Bessarabia his Polish chancellery, whose head, Nikolai Andreevich Krinickii, then authored the Bessarabian Statute of 1818.[16]

Upon his arrival to Chisinau, Bakhmetev focused on the elaboration of the statute. The fruit of these efforts was the "Project of the Main Foundations for the Formation of the Bessarabian Province," which eventually became the Bessarabian Statute of 1818.[17] The statute presupposed the creation of a Supreme Council, consisting of the viceroy, the civil governor of the province, the vice-governor, the presidents of the criminal and civil courts, and four deputies from Bessarabian nobility elected every three years. The council represented both the highest administrative body and the court of last appeal. Decisions that did not circumvent existing laws were executed immediately, although they could be appealed in the State Council or through the Ministry of Justice. Most members of the criminal and civil courts of the province were also to be elected by the nobility, as were members of district administrative boards (*ispravinchestva*) and district courts.[18]

The project of the statute thus built on the rules of 1813 and represented another step in the affirmation of Bessarabian autonomy on the basis of local peculiarities. Following preliminary approval in St. Petersburg in 1817, the statute was put into force in late April 1818, by Alexander I himself, following his meeting with representatives of the Bessarabian nobility. The statute was thus akin to a contract between the emperor and the local elite. The latter secured wide participation in the local administration on the basis of indigenous legal tradition and administrative practices. In return, the emperor expected Bessarabian nobility to

15 RGIA. F. 1286. Op. 2. D. 70. "Delo ob obrazovanii Bessarabskoi oblasti i o naznachenii polnomochnym namestnikom Bessarabii Podol'skogo voiennogo gubernatora general-leitenanta Bakhmeteva. 1816 g." Ll. 25 f.

16 Vigel'. Zamechaniia na nyneshnee sostoianie Bessarbii. P. 4.

17 Egunov (Ed.). Zapiski Bessarabskogo statisticheskogo komiteta. P. 147.

18 Ibid. Pp. 150, 152.

view "the national character" of the province and "the special form of its government" as something other than a narrow estate privilege. In his official letter to Bakhmetev, Alexander I stressed that "this enormous gift and all related benefits should not be limited to only one group of inhabitants. All should partake of it in just measure."[19]

Remarkably, the statute was approved soon after the first session of the Polish Sejm at which Alexander I declared his intention to extend "legal and liberal institutions" (*zakonno-svobodnye uchrezhdeniia*) to all his domains. The Bessarabian Statute was thus the first realization of this plan and can therefore be considered as a manifestation of the emperor's constitutionalism. The statute was not formally a constitutional charter, but this fact was in keeping with local custom: despite strong Polish influences in Moldavia, relations between Moldavian princes (hospodars) and boyars were not governed by formal legal documents comparable to the Polish Pacta Conventa of 1572. Alexander I's own conflict with the Polish Sejm in the first half of the 1820s demonstrated that the emperor did not consider the constitutional charter that he had granted to the Kingdom of Poland to be equally binding on him and the szlachta. The emperor tended to consider all legislative acts that stipulated forms of government in the borderland regions and defined relations with regional elites to be products of his personal benevolence—regardless of the formal legal status of these acts. This peculiarity of Alexander I's constitutionalism was well expressed by Mikhail Speransky, who wrote that, in contrast to the constitution of other states "that emerge by fits and starts in different epochs and are often the products of violent perturbations, the Russian constitution will owe its existence to the benevolent inspiration of the central authority."[20]

2. Projects of Administrative-Political Reform of the Russian Empire in 1815–1830

Alexander I's Bessarabian experiment was part of a broader process of institutional transformation in the Russian Empire in the early nineteenth century.[21] The emperor paid attention to Bessarabia soon after his return from Europe, at a time when he also signaled his intention to deal with the empire's problems of internal organization. The appointment of the Bessarabian viceroy came at a time when

19 PSZ I. Vol. 35. № 27357, 29.04.1818. "Reskript Aleksandra I A.N. Bakhmetevu." P. 222.
20 Speranskii. Plan vseobshchego gosudarstvennogo obrazovaniia. P. 342.
21 See Predtechenskii. Ocherki obshchestvenno-politicheskoi istorii Rossii; Mironenko. Samoderzhavie i reformy.

the emperor was considering the possibility of dividing the empire into viceroyalties. This idea appears to be the exact opposite of the reforms of the first part of his reign. Whereas the creation of ministries and of the State Council in 1802–11 can be considered a step toward greater centralization and bureaucratization, the division into viceroyalties can be seen as a return to the "empire of the nobles" (*dvorianskaia imperia*) of Catherine the Great, as it created the preconditions for the strengthening of the regional elites.

This dichotomy needs to be nuanced inasmuch as the appointment of governorsgeneral throughout the empire after 1815 was supported by the same people who earlier had played an important role in the creation of central ministries. In a memorandum submitted to Alexander I in 1814, the former (and future) Russian minister of internal affairs Viktor Kochubei found governors-general to be indispensable for assuring unified authority in the gubernia administration, which was plagued by conflicts between gubernia boards and fiscal chambers.[22] Besides raising administrative efficiency, the governors-general, in Kochubei's opinion, could have an important civilizing influence on provincial nobility by bringing the lifestyle of the capital into their provinces.[23] The first Russian minister of internal affairs thus evidently believed that central ministers and governors-general would complement rather than contradict each other.

The same applied to Aleksandr Balashov, who served as minister of police in 1810–19 and who may have been the author of the "Project of the Institution of Viceroyalties" of 1816, which presupposed the division of Russia into ten or twelve viceroyalties.[24] The project drastically redefined the administrative space of the Russian Empire inasmuch as it elevated viceroys to the rank of ministers, empowering them to make changes in the local administration in order to eliminate abuses and even to suspend in some cases the decisions of the Senate and of the

---

22 Kochubei. Zapiska Grafa V.P. Kochubeia o polozhenii v imperii. P. 16 f.

23 Kochubei. Zapiska Grafa Kochiubeia ob ucherezhdenii ministerstv. P. 210.

24 Lukovskaia and Raskin suggest that Aleksandr Balashov and the imperial commissioner in the Kingdom of Poland Nikolai Novosil'cev as the two possible authors of the project of viceroyalties. See Lukovskaia / Raskin. Institut general-gubernatorstva. P. 72. According to John LeDonne, Novosil'cev was unlikely to be the author of the 1816 Project on the viceroyalties, which is very different in content from the Constitutional Charter for the Russian Empire of 1820 that was produced under his direction. LeDonne suggests that the project was produced by someone close to the Ministry of Police. See LeDonne. Administrative Regionalization. Pp. 5–34. On Balashov, see Shilov. Gosudarstvennyie deiateli Rossiiskoi Imperii. Pp. 61 f.; the project of viceroyalties and Balashov are discussed at length in the chapter by Elizaveta Sysoeva in this volume, Pp. 301–315.

central ministries.[25] The creation of viceregal chancelleries and councils of viceroyalties, which replicated the structures of central ministries on a regional level, would certainly have contributed to the consolidation of existing regional elites and to their formation in those parts of the empire where they were still absent. The personal character of viceregal authority was potentially more conducive to the preservation of local traditions.

In 1819, Balashov was appointed the governor-general of Ryazan and four other central Russian gubernias, an appointment that is often seen as a pilot project for the creation of governor-generalships throughout the empire. While the transformation of a minister into a governor-general might be seen as a downgrade, Balashov's tasks in these five provinces in 1819–28 in some respects were not unlike his activities as the minister of police. The Ministry of Police was in fact a superministry that, alongside providing political police, was also placed in charge of general welfare throughout the empire. From the Ministry of Internal Affairs, which it temporarily took over in 1811–19, the Ministry of Police inherited a holistic approach to internal administration, which had characterised the eighteenth-century well-ordered police state.[26] The sheer range of domains that were placed within the purview of the early ministers of internal affairs and police was such as to exclude any active governing on their part and to necessarily limit their functions to those of supervision. In his reports to Alexander I from Ryazan, Balashov characteristically distinguished between the functions of administration (*upravlenie*) and supervision (*nadzor*) and saw the latter as his main task as governor-general.[27] Like Kochubei, Balashov did not treat ministries and governors-general as mutually exclusive precisely because he viewed both institutions as supervisory ones.

The same idea was expressed with greater clarity by Mikhail Speransky, who served as the governor-general of Siberia in 1819–21 after playing a key role in the reorganization of central ministries in 1810–11.[28] Asked to comment on the

25 Proekt uchrezhdenia namestnichestv. Arts. 32 f., 38. In: Materialy sobrannye. Pp. 17, 19, 33 f.

26 On the well-ordered police state, see Raeff. The Well-Ordered Police State. Pp. 1221–43. After the Ministry of Police was abolished in 1819, its functions were assumed by the Ministry of Internal Affairs, which remained a "superministry" for the rest of the nineteenth century.

27 Obozrenie grazhdanskogo upravlenia po guberniam i nekotorye soobrazhenia po semu predmetu Riazanskogo General-Gubernatora General Ad'iutanta Balashova. In: Materialy sobrannye. Pp. 121 f.

28 Speransky's political career is well studied and therefore needs no special discussion here. Raeff's *Michael Speransky* is still the most important contribution. More recent

"Project of Viceroyalties," Speransky sought to place governors-general within the typology of central and local institutions of supervision.[29] In his "Introduction to the Regional Administration," Speransky compared viceroyalties to the institution of periodic Senate revisions of the individual governorates (introduced by Peter the Great), but he argued that the permanent character of viceroyalties would make them more effective. In his definition, a viceroyalty was a "ministry acting on the spot, and belonging to the general structure of all the ministries, the Senate."[30] This definition suggests the indebtedness of the famous Russian reformer to the eighteenth-century practices of senatorial government in which the function of the Senate and other central and provincial administrative bodies consisted in responding to external stimuli (petitions of the subjects, orders of the ruler).[31] Speransky was thus not as attuned with the later notion of the ministries as promoters of policy within a specific domain by means of a developed hierarchy of specialized officials.

The reintroduction of governors-general throughout the empire in the second part of Alexander I's reign was thus not in direct contradiction with the earlier creation of central ministries, as long as both the ministers and governors-general were deemed to be supervisors rather than active policy-makers. At the same time, governors-general or viceroys did not guarantee the preservation of regional peculiarities and could in fact contribute to standardization of administrative practices. This combination of decentralization and standardization characterized the gubernia reform of Catherine the Great of 1775, which for the first time introduced the institute of the viceroys. The reform shifted much of the administrative

---

treatments include Tomsinov. Speranskii; Wisenhunt. In Search of Legality; Morozov. Gosudarstvenno-pravovye vzgliady; Idem. Politicheskie vzgliady i konstitucionnye proekty; Chibiriaev. Velikii russkii reformator.

29 Speranskii, "Vvedenie k namestnicheskomu (oblastnomu) ucherezhdeniiu." In: Materialy sobrannye. P. 74. Speransky's appreciation of the "territorial" organization of administration after 1812 resulting from his involvement in local affairs becomes even more notable in light of the fact that by supporting the division of the empire into viceroyalties, he sided with Balashov, the likely author of the 1816 Project of Viceroyalties, who as minister of police in 1811–12 brought about Speransky's downfall in March 1812.

30 Speranskii. "Vvedenie k namestnicheskomu (oblastnomu) ucherezhdeniiu." In: Materialy sobrannye. Pp. 74, 77. A similar idea of ministerial supervision as a complement to the procuracy and Senate supervision can be found in Troshchinskii. Zapiska o ministerstvakh. P. 43.

31 On the Senatorial government, see: Yaney. The Systematization of Russian Government. Pp. 77 f.; Christian. The "Senatorial Party" and the Theory of Collegial Government. Pp. 298–322.

work from the center to the provinces and, at the same time, led to the abolition of local institutions in some of the borderland regions.

The same logic characterized the most ambitious and comprehensive reform project of Alexander I's later years—the Constitutional Charter of the Russian Empire, which was elaborated in Nikolai Novosil'cev's chancellery in 1818–20. Just as with the Project of Viceroyalties of 1816, the charter presupposed the division of the empire into viceroyalties, including several gubernias, each "according to the population, distance, and size and taking into consideration the mores, customs, and particular local laws that bring people together."[32] At the same time, the charter manifested the constitutional aspirations of Alexander I and called for the creation of representative assemblies on the regional level. The legislative assemblies of the viceroyalties (sejms) had to take part in the elaboration of local laws, whose final approval, however, depended entirely on the emperor.[33]

The constitutional charter represented an attempt to expand to the rest of the empire the political-administrative arrangements that were being tested in the Western Borderlands. However, its implementation would have eliminated the peculiar status of the Kingdom of Poland, the Grand Duchy of Finland, and Bessarabia within the empire by elevating other regions to their level. Although legal and cultural peculiarities had to serve as the basis for the formation of viceroyalties, the project presupposed the abolition of the Polish Constitutional Charter of 1815 on the ground that it was unreasonable to have two constitutions in one empire.[34] The Kingdom of Poland itself would have to become a viceroyalty. This projected trivialization of the (quasi-)constitutional arrangements that had earlier been adopted in the Grand Duchy of Finland, Poland, and Bessarabia represented Alexander I's response to the resentment of Russian nobility caused by the adoption of the Polish Constitutional Charter in 1815 and the opening of the Polish Sejm in 1818.[35]

Despite the secrecy with which Alexander enveloped the elaboration of the charter, rumors about it circulated in the military and the officialdom, and there was some intimation that the division of the entire empire into governor-generalships (completed by 1823) was preparation for the adoption of a constitution. Thus Ivan Dibich (Hans Karl Freidrich Anton von Diebitsch, appointed

---

32 Schiemann (Ed.). Gosudarstvennaia ustavnaia gramota Rossiiskoi imperii. P. 11.

33 Ibid. P. 25.

34 A draft of the corresponding decree was published in: Vernadsky. Gosudarstvennaia ustavnaia gramota Rossiiskoi imperii. Pp. 42 f.

35 For the reaction of the Russian nobility to Alexander I's speech before the Polish Sejm, see Mironenko. Samoderzhavie i reformy. Pp. 159–61.

head of staff in 1823 and retaining this post under his personal friend Nicholas I) told the famous memoirist Aleksandr Mikhailovskii-Danilevskii in 1829 that "by means of governor-generalships Alexander I sought to introduce constitutional government starting with the inclusion of a number of deputies from each governor-generalship in the [State] Council."[36] The complications that Alexander I faced with the Polish Sejm in September 1820, a new round of revolutions in southern Europe, and the mutiny of the Semenovskii regiment made him postpone the introduction of the charter. Nevertheless, the emperor remained interested in this project until the end of his days, as is clear from a conversation that he shared with Karamzin in 1825.

The personality of Nicholas I and the circumstances of his succession to the Russian throne in December 1825 put an end to the constitutional aspects of the reform projects of the final ten years of Alexander I's reign. These factors, however, cannot fully explain the abandonment of the viceregal government that was de facto implemented in the first half of the 1820s, when the empire was effectively divided into twelve districts each under the command of a governor-general.[37] From the beginning, the Project of the Viceroyalties encountered strong opposition from proponents of a functionally organized administration that was inimical to local and regional autonomy and favored central bureaucratic control. This clash between "territorial" and "functional" notions of administrative organization led to the institution of a midway solution that would define the structure of the Russian Empire until 1917.

The most important critic of viceregal government in the late 1810s and early 1820s was the minister of finance Dmitii Gur'ev. An advocate of the separation of administrative and judicial authority, he opposed the idea of their unification in the hands of a viceroy. He was also against the idea of endowing the viceroys with both administrative and supervisory functions. According to Gur'ev, the appointment of viceroys with such wide prerogatives would destroy the existing ministerial system of government. In Gur'ev's vision, the ministry was similar to a panopticon operating in a completely homogeneous administrative space, perfectly transparent for minister's orders and uncompromised by any other *loci* of power (i.e., viceroys): "Each ministry must have its own sphere clearly defined, so that the *radii* could freely penetrate from the center to the very limits of the sphere and the minister could use each *radius* to translate his orders to the most

36 Quoted in: Mironenko. Stranicy tainoi istorii samoderzhaviia. P. 40.

37 The list of these districts and of the gubernias that composed them is published in: Sbornik Imperatorskogo Russkogo Istoricheskogo Obshchestva (hereafter, Sb. RIO). Vol. 90 (1894). Pp. 212 f.

distant limits of the state without the interference of any other power."[38] In order to secure the operation of this principle, each ministry should have "dependant middle and lower governmental bodies in gubernias and districts, through which the ministry could act on the whole expanse of the empire."[39]

In Gur'ev's representation, a ministry emerges as some ideal, centrally located controller totally commanding the administrative space and undisturbed by regional and local concentrations of power and administrative regimes (such as what viceroyalties would create). "If local circumstances require any deviations from the general order, they should reflect the care and circumspection of the central government rather than the insistence of the local administration."[40] According to Gur'ev, the latter would lead each territory to fight for its own interests and each viceroyalty to present its own demands. Pointing to the successful experience of administrative unification in England and France, as well as to the problems experienced by heterogenous Spain and the Habsburg Monarchy, the minister of finance wondered whether it was worthwhile to "sow the seeds of divergent interests and introduce the elements of a federal system" in a country that had always been unitary.[41]

Gur'ev's memorandum is remarkable not only for his criticism of the viceregal government but also for his understanding of the ministries, an understanding that was quite different from that of Speransky and Balashov. Whereas the latter two viewed the ministries and governors-general as mutually complementing institutions of central and regional supervision, for Gur'ev, each ministry was an institution of administration (*upravlenie*) that formulated and actively promoted policy within its specific domain by means of its own agents in the provinces. This vision of the ministries may have reflected Gur'ev's experience at the Ministry of Finance, which—in contrast to the Ministries of Internal Affairs and Police—was never in charge of the general wellfare but instead focused on the "narrow" and clearly definable area of finances. Whereas the minister of internal affairs dealt with the gubernia administration in general, the minister of finance sought to secure control over one specific segment of the gubernia administration—namely, the fiscal chambers.[42] Other central ministries—Justice, Education, or

38 Gur'ev. Mnenie Ministra Finansov o proekte ucherezhdeniia o Namestnikakh, soobshchennoe emu po Vysochaishemu poveleniiu. In: Materialy sobrannye. P. 48. Emphasis added.

39 Gur'ev. Ob ustroistve verkhovnykh pravitel'stv Rossii. P. 64.

40 Ibid. P. 49.

41 Ibid. P. 50.

42 The latter became subordinated to the Ministry of Finance in 1837. Yaney. The Systematization of Russian Government. P. 219.

State Domains—would follow the example of the Ministry of Finance in trying to establish control over a corresponding segment of the gubernia administration or create its own set of local agents in each of the provinces.[43] For its part, the Ministry of Internal Affairs would consolidate its control over gubernia governors, who were required to submit to it yearly reports from 1828 onward.[44]

Although Gur'ev's vision of the ministries as policy-making rather than supervisory bodies ultimately prevailed, the victory of the functional principle of administrative organization over the territorial one was not complete. The Russian Empire never became a unitary state in which the orders of the ministers unproblematically reached "the most distant limits." Instead, the late 1820s witnessed the adoption of a formula that combined the functional and territorial principles and that defined imperial Russia's institutional development for the rest of its history. The key role in the formulation of this compromise belonged to the Committee of December 26, 1826, which Nicholas I established in order to review the projects of reform that were left by his late brother. The committee included some of the foremost statesmen of Alexander I's reign: Kochubei, Speransky, and the former procurator of the Holy Synod Aleksandr Golicin, as well as the military men Illarion Vasil'chikov, Petr Tolstoi, and H.K. Diebitsch. Dmitrii Dashkov and Dmitrii Bludov , who would later become the ministers of justice and internal affairs, respectively, served as the committee's secretaries.

On May 4, 1827, upon listening to materials concerning the governors-general as well as the personal report of Balashov, the committee recommended abolishing governor-generalships in central Russia. In its opinion, the division of the empire into twelve governor-generalships would produce twelve separate domains. Doubting the effectiveness of a governor-general's supervision, let alone his rule over four or five million people, the committee pointed to the fact that the "Project of Viceroyalties" left his authority and relations to the higher state and lower gubernia institutions undefined. The key to the improvement of local administration was the "right choice of officials rather than the limitlessness of their power. [...] The desired order in the local government will only be established when precise and uniform rules are defined for all administrative and judicial bodies and when all these bodies are dependent on a supreme central authority." At the same time, the committee recommended retaining governors-general in the capitals, Siberia, the Orenburg region, the Caucasus, Novorossiia, and the Baltic provinces, where

43 On the development of the institution of regional delegates of various central ministries over the first quarter of the nineteenth century, see: LeDonne. Administrative Regionalization. Pp. 5–34.

44 Orlovskii. The Limits of Reform. P. 31.

"location and other circumstances oblige the governors to take care of various matters unrelated to administration, such as diplomatic relations and trade."[45]

Whereas the sympathizers of the 1816 "Project of Viceroyalties" sought to combine viceroyalties with ministries by defining both institutions as forms of supervision over gubernia administration, the "compromise" solution suggested by the committee consisted in assigning the two forms to different kinds of territories. While the administration in the center of the empire was to be established in accordance with the "ministerial" model, the borderland territories were to be governed by governors-general. This solution seems all too natural in retrospect. Yet, in order to arrive at it, several things had to be made obvious: 1) that the gubernia government was not a "self-sufficient" territorial unit encompassing all aspects of administration (as it had been under the 1775 Gubernia Statute) but rather included several "branch" sections directly subordinated to central ministries; 2) that a ministry was not a form of central supervision over the functioning of autonomous "territorial units" (as it was defined by Speransky in 1821) but rather a body monopolizing all effective policy-making in a given sphere and turning some parts of gubernia administration into its lower agencies; and 3) that a viceroyalty was not a form of permanent local *supervision* over the functioning of the self-sufficient gubernia administration (as in the 1816 Project of Viceroyalties or in Speransky's project) but rather a "territorial" form of *government* that could potentially be in contradiction to the ministries.

3. The Curtailment of Bessarabian Autonomy during the 1820s

Alexander I did not have the chance to see the fruits of his Bessarabian experiment. This assessment was made by a different person—Mikhail Semenovich Vorontsov, who was appointed the governor-general of Novorossiia and viceroy of Bessarabia in May 1823. The son of Semyon Vorontsov, the Russian ambassador in London and a famous Russian anglophile, Mikhail Vorontsov was initially sympathetic toward the Polish nobility. At the time of the Napoleonic Wars, he expressed a desire to serve in Podolia or Volhynia, and eventually, like Bakhmetev, he married a Polish aristocrat. After a series of clashes between the Bessarabian nobility and both Bakhmetev and Ivan Inzov (Bakhmetev's immediate successor, who served in 1820–23), Mikhail Vorontsov's appointment brought the Bessarabian nobility into a state of euphoria and led it to expect "complete freedom."[46]

45 See minutes of the proceedings from May 4, 1827 in: Sb. RIO. Vol. 74 (1891). Pp. 144–47; and February 19, 1828. In: Materialy sobrannye. P. 59.

46 Vigel. Zapiski. P. 99.

And yet, Vorontsov would drastically curtail Bessarabian autonomy at the end of the 1820s.[47]

In order to understand this somewhat paradoxical outcome, one has to take into consideration the difference between the first and the third Bessarabian viceroys. Whereas Bakhmetev governed a province in which the Polish nobility—on the basis of historical privilege and a peculiar legal tradition—retained their dominance, Vorontsov combined the Bessarabian viceroyalty with the government of a region that for half a century constituted a space of colonization policies. Whereas the identification of Bessarabia with the Western Borderlands led to an emphasis on "historical privileges" and local customs, its reclassification as part of Novorossiia during the 1820s put forward the discourse of the "civilizing mission."[48] Vorontsov's predecessors in Odessa the Duke of Richelieu and Alexandre-Louis de Langeron (in Russia also known as Aleksandr Lanzheron) were rather typical "enlightened administrators" who operated within this framework of the civilizing mission. Neither of them was directly involved in the administration of Bessarabia. However, Richelieu played an important role in the resettlement of the Nogais from the Budzhak steppe (the southernmost part of Bessarabia) in 1807, opening this space for Bulgarian, German, and Russian colonists.[49] As for Langeron, his memoirs of the Russo-Turkish Wars of 1787–91 and 1806–12 characterized Moldavia and Wallachia as "barbarian," "despotic," and susceptible to improvement only through rational and enlightened rule.[50] Further, Vorontsov's Polish wife, Elizaveta Vorontsova, was Grigorii Potemkin's niece. In the words of Filipp Vigel', the appointment of Vorontsov as the governor-general of Novorossiia and viceroy of Bessarabia therefore was a matter of "coming into possession of his rightful inheritance."[51] This logic helps to explain why Vorontsov continued Potemkin's approach and ultimately came to view Bessarabia as a space of colonization rather than of nobility-based self-rule.

---

47 Rhinelander. Prince Michael Vorontsov. Pp. 67–93.

48 This is a nice illustration of the difference between governors-general of Western Borderlands and those of the steppe regions. Whereas the primary task of the former consisted in securing the loyalty of the local elites, the latter focused on colonization. In a similar way, Kimitaka Matsuzato speaks about "ethnobonapartist" versus "economic" governors-general in the second half of the nineteenth century. See Macuzato. General-gubernatorstva Rossiiskoi imperii. P. 427–58.

49 On the resettlement of the Nogais from Bessarabia, see: Sunderland. Taming the Wild Field. P. 112.

50 See Langeron. Journal des campagnes faites aux services de la Russie. Pp. 160–392.

51 Vigel. Zapiski. P. 91.

Vorontsov did not curtail Bessarabian autonomy single-handedly. He quickly found support in the person of the deputy minister of internal affairs Dmitrii Bludov. The latter became convinced that "crying abuses" in the Bessarabian administration reported by Vorontsov's subordinates reflected not so much the pitfalls of particular individuals as "the beautiful customs, and noble ways of this dear country" and that it was a big mistake to turn these customs into the "fundamental laws."[52] As a ministerial official, Bludov particularly did not like the Bessarabian Supreme Council, which "concentrated all kinds of authorities and branches of administration and could thus be used to paralyze the course of government." Bludov was also skeptical of the project of codification of Bessarabian laws that was initiated by Kapodistrias.[53] Fortunately, the provisional character of Alexander I's approval of the Bessarabian Statute in 1818 left the possibility to implement reforms that would "bring the province closer to the institutions that exist in the interior of the empire, in order to gradually eliminate the differences between provinces and achieve uniformity of laws and administration, which would ultimately bring about the unity of mores and interests desirable everywhere and especially in Russia given her unprecedented expanse."[54]

Supported by Bludov, Vorontsov appointed a committee for the elaboration of a new statute. This project was received and approved by the Committee of Ministers in November 1824, and in 1826 a draft of the new statute was submitted to the consideration of the State Council. During his extended stay in St. Petersburg in 1826–28, Vorontsov spared no time or effort in convincing the emperor and council members of the advantages of the new document.[55] The Bessarabian Supreme Council was replaced by the Council of the Province with only one elected member (the Bessarabian marshal of nobility). All the rest were members ex officio or appointed by the Senate on the recommendation (*po predstavleniiu*) of the governor-general. In comparison to the 1818 statute, the new settlement reduced by more than half the number of elected officials in the provincial administration. The elected positions were distributed in such a way as to eliminate any pockets within the local administration that would be beyond the effective control of the viceroy. With the exception of the provincial and district marshals of the nobility, all elected positions were concentrated in the provincial and district courts. By

52 Bartenev (Ed.). Arkhiv kn. Vorontsova. Bludov to Vorontsov, December 29, 1823. P. 295. Bludov essentially repeated the idea from Vorontsov's own letter to him dated December 4, 1823. In: Ibid. P. 291.

53 Ibid. Bludov to Vorontsov, December 29, 1823. Pp. 296 f.

54 Ibid. Bludov to Vorontsov, October 8, 1823. P. 289.

55 Rhinelander. Prince Michael Vorontsov. P. 70.

contrast, all administrative positions were to be filled by appointment. A special section of the new statute stipulated the relations between different parts of the provincial administration as well as its overall subordination to the Russian Senate, the ministries, and the viceroy in administrative, fiscal, and judicial affairs.[56] Further, within five years, Russian replaced Romanian as the language of official correspondence (*deloproizvodstvo*).

The drastic curtailment of Bessarabian autonomy at the end of the 1820s has frequently been interpreted as the result of centralization and bureaucratization of the imperial government in the second quarter of the nineteenth century. Undoubtedly, Bludov's words about the necessity of bringing institutions and laws of different parts of the Russian Empire closer together illustrate the logic of administrative standardization. However, the decisive role in the curtailment of Bessarabian autonomy belonged to the viceroy rather than to the deputy minister of internal affairs. Nicholas I's reign was certainly marked by bureaucratization and the reduction of the role of the provincial nobility in local administration. And yet, the principal measures in this respect followed rather than preceded the decision to reduce Bessarabian autonomy. At best, this nascent tendency could have facilitated Vorontsov's project, which reflected his own desire to establish firm control over local administration.

At the same time, Vorontsov did not turn Bessarabia into a Russian gubernia. During the period under consideration and in the decades that followed, it continued to be a borderland province. However, the period of 1812–28 is important inasmuch as it defined what kind of borderland Bessarabia was going to be. Whereas Kapodistrias envisioned Bessarabia as a showcase of the Russian Empire in the Balkans, and Alexander I viewed it as part of Russia's Western Borderlands and an element of an attempt to reorganize imperial governance on the new "territorial" principle, for Mikhail Vorontsov Bessarabia was part of Novorossiia. As a successor of the grand project of Catherine the Great and Potemkin, Vorontsov viewed Bessarabia as part of the space of colonization.

In a more general sense, the history of Bessarabian autonomy and its curtailment makes it necessary to reconsider the conceptual duality of autonomy and centralization, which is often used in the description of imperial absorption of a new province. One should not perceive the history of Russian empire-building through the prism of eternal centralism that inevitably prevails over local peculiarities and circumstances. The process of assimilation does not always follow the

56 PSZ II. Vol. 3. № 1864, 11.03.1828. "Vysochaishe utverzhdennoe mnenie Gosurastvennogo Soveta."

linear logic of replacement of the local institutions and administrative practices by those that exist at the center. The imperial center itself is not a preexisting core that gradually absorbs the borderlands. Instead, both the center and the peripheries emerge simultaneously alongside each through the application of distinct administrative formulas to different areas of the empire.

Until the end of the 1820s, there was no irreversible difference between the administration of the borderland regions and what would eventually become known as "internal governorates." Catherine's reform of 1775, which delegated much of the authority to the viceroys and the provincial nobility, left few differences between the Mogilev and the Ryazan gubernias from a purely administrative point of view. Although Alexander I combined the establishment of central ministries with grants of wide autonomy to the newly annexed territories, the second part of his reign was marked by attempts to extend viceregal government and "legal and liberal institutions" to the entire Russian Empire, an action that would have necessarily trivialized the privileges of the Polish, Finish, and Bessarabian elites. Only the failure of this attempt and a comprehensive revision of Alexander I's administrative legacy by the Committee of December 26, 1826, established by Nicholas I, produced a familiar combination of the ministerial government in the historical core of the Russian Empire and the viceroyalty/governor-generalship in the borderland regions, a combination that would persist until 1917.

List of references

ANCUPOV, IVAN / ZHUKOV, VASILII. Reformy v upravlenii Bessarabii s 1812 po 1828 gg. In: Uchenye zapiski Kishinevskogo universiteta. Vol. 26 (1957). Pp. 145–59

ARSH, GRIGORII. I.A. Kapodistria i grecheskoe nacional'no-osvoboditel'noe dvizhenie 1809–1822. Moscow, 1976

BARCARU, SILVIA. Consideraţii privind instituţiile administraţiei locale din Basarabia reflectate în actele legislative ruseşti din anii 1812–1837. In: Revista de istorie a Moldovei. Vol. 4 (2009). Pp. 69–86

BARTENEV, PETR. (Ed.). Arkhiv kn. Vorontsova. Vol. 38. Moscow, 1892

BLACKBURN, CHRISTOPHER. Napoleon and Szlachta. Boulder, Colo., 1998

BOGDANOVICH, MIKHAIL. (Ed.). Pis'ma admirala Chichagova k imperatoru Aleksandru I. Sbornik Imperatorskogo Russkogo Istoricheskogo Obshchestva. Vol. 6 (1871). Pp. 1–66

BOLDUR, ALEKSANDRU. Autonomia Basarabiei sub stăpânirea rusească in 1812–1828. Chişinău, 1929

Chibiriaev, Stanislav. Velikii russkii reformator: Zhizn', deiatel'nost' i politicheskie vzgliady M.M. Speranskogo. Moscow, 1993

Christian, David. The "Senatorial Party" and the Theory of Collegial Government, 1801–1803. In: Russian Review. Vol. 38 (1979) #3. Pp. 298–322

Czartoryski, Adam. Memuary kniazia Adama Chartoryzhskogo i ego perepiska s Aleksandrom I. Vol. 2. Moscow, 1913

Dolbilov, Mikhail / Miller, Aleksei (Eds.). Zapadnye okrainy Rossiiskoi imperii. Moscow, 2006

Egunov A.N. (Ed.). Zapiski Bessarabskogo statisticheskogo komiteta. Vol. 3. Kishinev, 1868

Grimsted, Patricia Kennedy. The Foreign Ministers of Alexander I. Berkeley, Calif., 1969

Grosul, Ia.S. Avtonomia Bessarabii v sostave Rossii (1812–1828). In: Iakim Grosul (Ed.). Trudy po istorii Moldavii. Kishinev, 1982. Pp. 110–234

Grosul, Vladislav. Genezis Bessarabskoi avtonomii v sostave Rossii: K 200-letiu prisoiedinenia Bessarabii k Rossii. In: Slavianovedenie. Vol. 3 (2012). Pp. 20–31

Gur'ev, Dmitrii. Ob ustroistve verkhovnykh pravitel'stv Rossii, December 1, 1815. In: Sbornik Russkogo Istoricheskogo Obshchestva. Vol. 90 (1894). P. 39–106

Jewsbury, George F. The Russian Annexation of Bessarabia, 1774–1828: A Study of Imperial Expansion. Boulder, Colo., 1976

Kasso, Lev. Rossiia na Dunae i obrazovanie Bessarabskoi oblasti. St. Petersburg, 1913

Kochubei, Viktor. Zapiska Grafa Kochiubeia ob ucherezhdenii ministerstv 28-go marta, 1806 g. In: Sbornik Russkogo Istoricheskogo Obshchestva. Vol. 90 (1894). Pp. 199–211

Kochubei, Viktor. Zapiska Grafa V.P. Kochubeia o polozhenii v imperii i o merakh k predotvrashcheniiu bezporiadkov i vvedeniu luchshego ustroistva v raznye otrasli pravitel'stvo-sostavliaiushchie, dekabria 1814-go g. In: Sbornik Russkogo Istoricheskogo Obshchestva. Vol. 90 (1894). Pp. 5–26

Kryzhanovskaia, K.P. / Rusev, Evgenii (Eds.). Istoriia Moldavii. Vol. 2. Kishinev, 1957

Kushko, Andrei / Taki, Victor. Bessarabiia v sostave Rossiiskoi imperii, 1812–1917. Moscow, 2012

Langeron, Alexandre. Journal des campagnes faites aux services de la Russie. In: A.I. Odobescu (Ed.). Documente privitoare la istoria Românilor. Vol. 3. București, 1889. Pp. 160–392

LeDonne, John P. Administrative Regionalization in the Russian Empire, 1802–1826. In: Cahiers du Monde Russe. Vol. 43 (2002). Pp. 5–34

Lukovskaia, Dzhenevha / Raskin, David. Institut general-gubernatorstva i namestnichestva v Rossiiskoi imperii. St. Petersburg, 2001

Materialy po noveishei istorii Bessarabii. In: Aleksandr Egunov (Ed.). Zapiski Bessarabskogo oblastnogo statisticheskogo Komiteta. Vol. 3. Kishinev, 1868. Pp. 105–54

Materialy sobrannye dlia Vysochaishe uchrezhdennoi Komissii o preobrazovanii gubernskikh i uezdnykh uchrezhdenii. St. Petersburg, 1870

Macuzato, Kimitaka. General-gubernatorstva Rossiiskoi imperii: Ot etnicheskogo k prostranstvennomu podkhodu. In: Il'ia Gersimov (Ed.). Novaia imperskaia istoriia postsovetskogo prostranstva. Kazan, 2004. Pp. 427–58

Melinte, Veronica / Cernenchi, Eugen. Unele aspect din istoria creării instituţiilor autoadministrării locale în Chişinău (1812–1818). In: Revista de istorie a Moldovei. Vol. 4 (2009). Pp. 215–24

Mironenko S.V. Samoderzhavie i reformy. Politicheskaia bor'ba v Rossii v nachale XIX veka. Moscow, 1989

Mironenko, Sergei. Stranicy tainoi istorii samoderzhaviia: Politicheskaia istoriia Rossii pervoi poloviny XIX stoletiia. Moscow, 1990

Morozan, Vladimir. Formirovanie i deiatel'nosti administrativnykh organov upravleniia v Bessarabskoi oblasti v nachale XIX v. In: Klio. Zhurnal dlia uchenykh. Vol. 1 (2005). Pp. 125–34; Vol. 2 (2005). Pp. 152–61

Morozov, Viktor. Gosudarstvenno-pravovye vzgliady M.M. Speranskogo: Istoriko-teoreticheskoe issledovanie. St. Petersburg, 1999

Morozov, Viktor. Politicheskie vzgliady i konstitucionnye proekty M.M. Speranskogo. St. Petersburg, 2000

Nakko, Aleksei. Ocherk grazhdanskogo ustroistva Bessarabskoi oblasti s 1812 po 1828 gg. In: Zapiski Odesskogo obshchestva istorii i drevnosti. Vol. 22 (1900). Pp. 109–221

Orlovsky, Daniel T. The Limits of Reform: The Ministry of Internal Affairs in Imperial Russia, 1802–1881. Cambridge, Mass., 1981

Predtechenskii, Anatolii. Ocherki obshchestvenno-politicheskoi istorii Rossii v pervoi chetverti XIX-go veka. Moscow, 1957

Raeff, Mark. Michael Speransky, Statesman of Imperial Russia, 1772–1839. Westport, Conn., 1990

Raeff, Mark. The Well-Ordered Police State and the Development of Modernity in Seventeenth- and Eighteenth-Century Europe: An Attempt at a Comparative Approach. In: American Historical Review. Vol. 80 (1975) #5. Pp. 1221–43

Rhinelander, Anthony. Prince Michael Vorontsov: Vice-Roy to the Tsar. Montreal, 1990

SCHIEMANN, THEODOR (Ed.). Gosudarstvennaia ustavnaia gramota Rossiiskoi imperii 1820 goda. Berlin, 1903

SHILOV, DENIS. Gosudarstvennye deiateli Rossiiskoi Imperii, 1802–1917. St. Petersburg, 2002

SPERANSKII, MIKHAIL. Plan vseobshchego gosudarstvennogo obrazovania. In: Speranskii, M.M. Rukovodstvo k poznaniiu zakonov. St. Petersburg, 2002

SUNDERLAND, WILLARD. Taming the Wild Field: Colonization and Empire on Russian Steppe. Ithaca, N.Y., 2004

THACKERAY, FRANK W. Antecedents of Revolution: Alexander I and the Polish Kingdom, 1815–1825. Boulder, Colo., 1980

TOMSINOV, VLADIMIR. Speranskii. Moscow, 2006

TROSHCHINSKII, DMITRII. Zapiska o Ministerstvakh. In: Rossiiskogo istoricheskogo obshchestva. Vol. 3, (1867). Pp. 23–162

VERNADSKY, GEORGE. Gosudarstvennaia ustavnaia gramota Rossiiskoi imperii 1820 goda. Prague, 1925

VIGEL', FILIPP. Zamechania na nyneshnee sostoianie Bessarbii. In: F.F. VIGEL'. Zapiski. Vol. 6. St. Petersburg, 1892. Pp. 1–34

VIGEL', FILIPP. Zapiski. Vol. 6. St. Petersburg, 1892

WADYCZ, PETR. The Lands of Partitioned Poland, 1795–1918. Seattle, 1993

WISENHUNT, WILLIAM B. In Search of Legality: Mikhail M. Speranskii and the Codification of Russian Law. Boulder, Colo., 2001

YANEY, GEORGE L. The Systematization of Russian Government, 1711–1905. Chicago, 1973

Copy-editor? Numerous typos + translit errors.

Moldovan sources
Well researched but the line of argument is not always totally convincing (or clear).

Most refs are to RGIA
20 pp

Constantin Troianowski

"The Volhynian Revolution": An Episode from the History of Relations between the Polish Nobility and the Imperial Government in the Age of Alexander I

In 1883 *Kievskaia starina*[1] published a 122-page-long piece under the title "The Volhynian Revolution of the First Quarter of the Nineteenth Century." It was presented as a series of three seemingly authentic letters written in 1818 by a certain Opytov, supposedly a Russian official of counsellor rank (*statskii sovetnik*). The letters were addressed to a certain Countess Starozhilova. While traveling from St. Petersburg to Vienna to Rome, Opytov passed through the Russian province of Volhynia, where at the request of the countess he made inquiries about recent events that had caused the removal of Volhynian governor Mikhail Ivanovich Komburlei (allegedly a relative of Starozhilova). In Volhynia Opytov met an unnamed Russian official who recounted the story of a Polish conspiracy that brought down Komburlei. This narrative is the central element of the letters, which recount in detail the development of the alleged plot organized by Volhynian Polish-speaking landlords under the leadership of the gubernia's marshal of nobility Bartołomey Giżycki and Senator Józef August Iliński, his brother-in-law. The plotters aimed to remove Russian gubernial and district administrators and replace them with local Polish officials. Slander and unjust complaints to St. Petersburg about abuse of power by local authorities were their weapon of choice. As a result of this grand intrigue, Governor Komburlei lost his office and went to trial "without any guilt."[2] The letters' apparent purpose was to lodge a defense of Komburlei, whom the author presented as an innocent victim of vile Poles who eventually succeded in their "revolution."

Kievskaia starina's editors prefaced the publication with very short comments on the provenance of the manuscript (found in the archives of Vasilii Stepanovich Popov, an associate of Prince Grigorii Alekseevich Potemkin) and its content.

---

1 *Kievskaia starina* (Kiev's Past) was a historical, ethnographic, and literary magazine. It was published in Kiev between 1882 and 1907.

2 Volynskaia revoliuciia pervoi chetverti XIX stoletiia. Pp. 121–44, 319–65, 774–828.

They admitted their failure to identify the real name of the letters' author, who had hidden himself and his addressee behind pseudonyms. The editors also suggested that the letters were apparently designed for circulation within a limited circle of familiars. The publication's title ("Volhynian Revolution") was borrowed from the letters' content.[3]

Historians disagree on whether to accept these texts as authentic letters. Nikolai Petrovich Chulkov, author of the entry on Bartołomey Giżycki in the *Russian Biographical Dictionary* called the letters "a contemporary pamphlet."[4] Daniel Beauvois wrote that "the testimonial of this traveler is interesting in that it more openly exposes stereotypes held by Russian conservatives than official reports."[5] G.V. Makarova treated Opytov's letters as an "unofficial document" written by a certain official who probably used a pseudonym.[6] Beauvois and Makarova referred to different copies of the letters' manuscript and were apparently unacquainted with their publication in *Kievskaia starina*. O.V. Markevich, who authored an article on Komburlei, also does not openly doubt the authenticity of this source.[7]

However, the overall presentation and some details raise doubts about this document as authentic letters. K.B. Egorova interpreted the letters as a literary work that reflected real events in a grotesque form.[8] I would agree that Opytov's correspondence belongs to the realm of literary production. Yet the exceptional richness of detail and very good knowledge of events demonstrated by the unknown author or authors of the letters make me think that they were based on authentic sources, probably daily records, letters, or an oral narrative of Komburlei himself or someone close to him. The good literary style of the letters betrays a professional writer or a journalist as their author/authors.[9] The quality of the writing was important since the pamphlet was likely intended to circulate in the upper echelons of government in order to sway opinions in favor of Komburlei and influence the outcome of his trial in the Senate and the final verdict of the State Council. The pamphlet of letters was, notably, unfinished. The third letter concludes with an announcement of a story to come and an enumeration of its

3 Ibid. Pp. 121–22.

4 Russkii biograficheskii slovar'. Pp. 175–76.

5 Bovua [Beauvois]. Gordiev uzel Rossiiskoi imperii. P. 213.

6 Makarova. Rossiia i sozdanie konstitucionnogo Korolevstva Pol'skogo. Pp. 100–101, fn. 89.

7 Markevich. Fenomen M.I. Komburleia. P. 60.

8 Egorova. Pis'ma o volynskoi revoliucii.

9 One might hypothesize that these persons were linked to N.M. Karamzin's milieu.

main points.[10] The letters were likely actually composed between 1818, the year they were dated, and 1821, when Komburlei died (while still under trial), thus bringing this early nineteenth-century public relations campaign to an end.

Besides its quite accurate recounting of the facts, the most interesting feature of the pamphlet is that it presents a sample of the anti-Polish discourse that would dominate the Russian public sphere nearly a decade later, after the uprising of 1830–31 in Poland and the empire's western provinces, when the official view on Poles drastically changed. Also possible is that the letters were produced as a posthumous defense of Komburlei, on commission from his relatives. Komburlei's two daughters—Elizaveta and Ekaterina—married Dmitrii Petrovich Buturlin, later a senator and chairman of the infamous censorship committee (1848–49), and Count Mikhail Dmitrievich Tolstoi, respectively.

The events of 1814–16 in Volhynia are not well known to historians and have mostly been ascertained from publications in *Kievskaia starina* in 1883. The present chapter examines the events through official documents of the Committee of Ministers, which are stored in the Russian State Historical Archive (RGIA). It contributes to an ongoing historiographical discussion of Polish nobles' attitude toward and willingness to cooperate with their new rulers in the aftermath of Poland-Lithuania's partitions.[11]

1. Wartime Hardships in Vohlynia as a Prelude to the Conflict between the Nobility and the Local Imperial Administration

Mikhail Ivanovich Komburlei (1761–1821) was a son of a Greek émigré who made a career under Prince Grigory Potemkin in Novorossiia. Before being appointed governor of Volhynia in 1806, Komburlei served as marshal of nobility in Ekaterinoslav gubernia and, for a short 1.5 years, as governor of Kursk.[12] Having proven himself as an energetic and effective administrator, Komburlei was made a senator in April 1811 and governor-general in Volhynia in January 1813.[13] In the first years of his rule, Komburlei established amicable relations with the local aristocrats, who presented him with a golden snuffbox with gems as a sign of their gratitude for his good rule of the gubernia.[14]

10 Volynskaia revoliuciia pervoi chetverti XIX stoletiia. P. 828.

11 Lane. Szlachta outside the Commonwealth. Pp. 526–28, 541–42.

12 Murzanov. Slovar' russkich senatorov. P. 215.

13 Arutiunian. General-Gubernatorstva pri Aleksandre I. P. 81.

14 Markevich. Fenomen M.I. Komburleia. P. 65.

With the start of the Napoleonic Wars, the borderland Volhynia became an arena of large-scale logistical operations for the Russian army. The year 1812 was a pinnacle of wartime strain for the province. The troops of the Second army of Prince Petr Ivanovich Bagration, the Third ("Observation") army of Aleksandr Petrovich Tormosov, the Danubian army of Petr Vasil'evich Chichagov, and the thirty-thousand-strong Malorossiian militia were stationed in or passed through Volhynia. In the same year a quarter of the gubernia was occupied by the troops of the Grande Armée's Austrian corps under the command of Prince Karl Philipp von Schwarzenberg. In October 1814 one hundred thousand troops of the Russian army passed through the province on their way home from France. The main burden of supplying these men fell to the local peasants and their landlords. Troops that quartered in villages needed substantial amount of food supplies and firewood for the personnel and oats, hay, and fodder for the horses. Local landowners were obliged to supply horses and oxen with carts as well as drivers recruited from serfs (who very often did not return home) to meet the army's transport needs. To prize supplies or services from the landowners, the local police often organized various forms of forced requisition. Additional soldiers were stationed in landowners' estates and the number doubled each day until the demands of the military were satisfied.

The army's quartering had the detrimental effect of causing an outbreak of the plague among the peasant population. The relative economic prosperity of Volhynia was seriously undermined. Many landlords came to the brink of bankruptcy, having received from the Russian army quartermasters only paper receipts instead of money for grain and other supplies. Moreover, to the gentry's chagrin, overzealous Komburlei did not accept any excuses and began sequestering land estates of those nobles who went into tax arrears, despite the fact that the sum of receipts held far exceeded the total of their tax arrears. The situation heightened tensions that were already raised between Komburlei and local nobility. Years before, in 1809, several hundred Volhynians had secretly crossed the border to join the troops of the Grand Duchy of Warsaw in the fight against the Habsburg Monarchy.[15] Komburlei, then governor, sequestered defectors' estates and sent to the Russian interior provinces those nobles whose loyalty was suspect.[16]

---

15 On the scale of defections, see: Bovua [Beauvois]. Gordiev uzel Rossiiskoi imperii. Pp. 196–200.

16 The pamphlet accuses patriotic Polish activists in the Grand Duchy of Warsaw (created in 1807 by Napoleon) of instigating Volhynian nobles to launch an intrigue against Komburlei. Allegedly they saw him as the main hindrance to their plans of restoring the ancient Polish kingdom (see:Volysnkaia revoliuciia. P. 130). This passage was

While fighting Napoleon in Europe in 1813–14 Alexander I received disturbing signals about the grave economic situation and ruined landlords in the western provinces of Russia. Polish aristocrats intended to send a delegation to Alexander I in order to beg for help and remind of his previous promises to restore Poland. However, the tsar agreed to receive delegates only after his return to St. Petersburg.[17]

In 1814 nobles of each imperial province were allowed to send delegates to St. Petersburg to congratulate the tsar on his victory over Napoleon.[18] In June of that year, the Volhynian nobility elected the leading local dignitaries with connections in St. Petersburg as their delegates—imperial senator Count Józef August Iliński[19] and marshal of nobility Bartołomey Giżycki,[20] among others.[21] In August the emperor held a separate audience with delegates from the Polish provinces.[22] The Volhynian delegates used this opportunity to address a letter of grievances to Alexander I.

Earlier, in January of that year, Senator Iliński sent to Alexander I a letter describing the deplorable state of Volhynia. Most importantly, Iliński complained about abuses and rampant corruption of the local police. His main point was that the nobility of the province suffered not so much from the burden of taxes and wartime expenses but from the manner in which taxes were collected. In his words, extortions from local police nearly doubled the amount of taxes and services required by the state. Nobles were so terrified by the threats of vengeance that did not dare petition higher authorities about abuses of imperial administration at the district level. In the name of all nobility of the province, Iliński asked the tsar to redress grievances and send to Volhynia an inspector selected from senators who came from the former Polish-Lithuanian lands. He suggested a list of suitable candidates including Prince Adam Czartoryski and Counts Michał Kleofas Ogiński, Leon Worcell, and Walerian Antoni Stroynowski.[23] The latter two senators along with Iliński were natives of Volhynia and possessed large landed estates there.

---

apparently designed to elevate Komburlei's significance for the empire, presenting him at the forefront of the struggle with clandestine separatists.

17 Mémoires de Michel Oginski. Vol. 4. P. 151–55.

18 Shil'der. Imperator Aleksandr. P. 253.

19 Also known in Russia as Avgust Ivanovich Il'inskii or Ilinskii (1766–1844).

20 Known in Russia as Varfolomei Kaetanovich Gizhitskii (1775–1826).

21 Sverbiguz. Starosvits'ke panstvo. P. 132.

22 Mémoires de Michel Oginski. Vol. 4. Pp. 159–61.

23 Rossiiskii Gosudarstvennyi Istoricheskii Arkhiv hereafter, RGIA). F. 1409. Op. 1. D. 979. "Pismo senatora grafa Ilinskogo na vysochaisheie imia." Ll. 1–2 ob.; RGIA. F. 1151. Op. 1. 1819. D. 18. "Zapiska iz vsepoddaneishego doklada po delam o zloupotrebleniiakh, otkrytykh senatorom Siversom pri revizii Volynskoi gubernii." Ll. 3 ob–4.

Iliński appeared to be one of the most suitable members of the Polish-speaking elite—Russian subjects by now—to present the province's grievances to the throne. His career in Russia proved that he was a man willing to work with the Russian imperial authorities. In 1796 Volhynian nobles had elected him to be the first provincial marshal of nobility. In the same year, together with other nobles' delegates from the Polish provinces, he had an audience with Catherine II in St. Petersburg and received the court rank of chamberlain (*kamerger*).[24] According to a memoirist, Alexander I (while still a grand duke) met his future long-time mistress Princess Czetwertyńska (Maria Naryshkina) at Iliński's apartment when the latter was on a trip to St. Petersburg as Volhynian marshal.[25] Iliński managed to enter the inner circle of the crown prince Paul I in Gatchina and was elevated to the rank of senator after Catherine II's death.[26] Apparently he was one of Paul I's most important counselors on Polish affairs. After the accession of Alexander I, a similar role had passed to Adam Czartoryski. Nevertheless Iliński, as a senator, must have kept some influence on decisions relating to the Polish provinces.

Polish nobles' petitions of the imperial government had a mixed history of success. The act of presenting the province's grievances and needs to the throne could result in serious problems for the petitioners themselves. In 1797 nobles of the newly acquired Polish lands were invited to send delegates to Moscow to attend the coronation ceremony of Paul I. After electing six delegates at a special assembly in February of that year, nobles of the Braclaw gubernia (in present-day Ukraine) drafted a petition that contained nine demands and was signed by the provincial marshal Tadeusz Kozłowski.[27] Upon their arrival in Moscow, the delegates learned that some of the Braclaw nobility's demands were already being met by the new monarch (for example, restoration of the Polish-Lithuanian legal system). Consequently they decided to redraft the petition, omitting unnecessary items. The new petition, with only four items, was submitted to Paul I in March 1797. Because collective petitions were forbidden by the new emperor, it was signed just by one delegate—Onufry Szczeniowski, a former judge of the Braclaw voievodeship.[28] The petition raised grievances relating to issues caused by the administration of former general-governor Timofey Tutolmin. Paul I per-

---

24 Polski Słownik Biograficzny. Vol. 8. P. 152.

25 Pamętniki Szymona Konopackiego. Vol. 1. P. 125.

26 Polski Słownik Biograficzny. Vol. 8. P. 152.

27 RGIA. F. 1345. Op. 98. D. 854. "Ob'iasnenie podsudka zemskogo byvshego voevodstva Bratslavskogo Onufria Shcheniovskogo." Ll. 27–28 ob.; Ibid. "Naypokornieysza Prozba podana od Zgromadzenia Szlachieckiego Guberniy Braclawskiey." Ll. 32–33 ob.

28 Ibid. Ll. 6–6 ob.

sonally disliked Tutolmin and had immediately removed him from office after assuming supreme power.[29] An investigation of the grievances was commissioned by the Senate, which delegated this task to local imperial authorities. Relying on their reports, the Senate found Onufry Szczeniowski guilty for making unjust denunciations of the imperial administration, denunciations that he later failed to substantiate with evidence. In March 1804 Alexander I approved the Senate's report and ordered Szczeniowski to be tried.[30]

The trial of the nobility's delegate, who had acted on behalf of all provincial nobles, outraged the local community. Bypassing legal ban on admitting persons under trial to ballot, local nobles reelected Szczeniowski to the office of district marshal. The district court availed themselves of the general pardon proclaimed at Alexander I's accession to fully acquit Szczeniowski. The main gubernial court, which was also stuffed by local nobles, backed this verdict.[31] Disagreeing with the court's resolution, Governor-General Magnus Gustav von Essen (in Russia known as Ivan Nikolaevich Essen)[32] thought it necessary to fine Szczeniowski and other delegates two hundred roubles each and remove Szczeniowski from office.[33] The case continued to drag on in 1808, as the Fifth department of the Senate awaited a report on the findings for one of the grievances.[34] Whether Onufry Szczeniowski finally received any penalty for his mission is unclear. He remained in the office of Winnica district marshal until 1809.[35]

Tutolmin was fully acquitted after spending one and a half years in prison in Peter and Paul Fortress.[36] Apparently, in the wake of Szczeniowski's affair, the imperial government became cautious in regard to grievances and protests coming from Polish nobles who were personally unknown in St. Petersburg. This skeptical view was noticed by a memoirist.[37]

Quite an opposite outcome met petitions submitted to Alexander I by a delegation of Vilna nobility in summer 1810. The author of the initial address was,

---

29 Senatskii arkhiv. P. 19.

30 RGIA. F. 1345. Op. 98. D. 854. "Vsepoddaneishii doklad Senata." Ll. 187–214.

31 RGIA. F. 1345. Op. 98. D. 854. "Prigovor Pervogo depertamenta Podol'skogo glavnogo suda ot 20 iiulia 1806." Ll. 226–69.

32 Known in Germany as Magnus Gustav von Essen.

33 RGIA. F. 1345. Op. 98. D. 854. "Raport general-gubernatora Essena 1-go Senatu ot 30 sentiabria 1806." L. 270–97.

34 Ibid. "Opredelenie 5-go departmenta Senata ot 9 sentiabria 1808." Ll. 445–502.

35 Mesiatsoslov. P. 441.

36 Shilov. Gosudarstvennye deiateli. P. 811; Senatskii arkhiv. P. 348.

37 Heleniusz. Wspomnienia lat minionych. Vol. 1. P. 125.

most likely, Prince Michał Kleofas Ogiński,[38] a Polish-Lithuanian aristocrat whom Alexander I made a senator and privy councilor (*tainyi sovetnik*).[39] After receiving the monarch's encouragement, the other representative of the Vilna nobility—gubernial marshal Kazimierz Sulistrowski—submitted another petition with a more detailed list of the gubernia's needs (containing eight items on the nobility's self-government, courts' administration, and economic issues). Most of these demands were fulfilled by Alexander's *reskript* of October 6, 1810.[40]

2. Senator Sievers's Inspection of Volhynia and the Unfolding Conflict

Alexander I was well aware of the dire economic circumstances of the western provinces stemming from wartime exigencies. In 1813 Prince Czartoryski informed his crowned friend that "the five governments of Lithuania are [...] suffering under an administration more unjust and arbitrary than any of those that have preceded it."[41] As the signal from Volhynia—in the form of Iliński's petition—was more specific in detail, the emperor could take immediate action to remedy wrongs. The petition passed to the Committee of Ministers, which in September 1814 delegated the investigation of the nobility's grievances to the Volhynian gubernial authorities—that is, to governor Komburlei himself. However such a bureaucratic move did not satisfy the petitioner and his fellow nobles. In January 1815 Senator Iliński addressed the committee's chairman, Prince Nikolai Saltykov, with a complaint about Komburlei. According to Iliński, the governor had demanded that all those landowners who had any grievances should present them personally at Zhitomir, the gubernia's capital town. Otherwise they had to sign a remission of claims for the district police at home.[42] The governor's intention was clear: Komburlei hoped that landowners would remit their claims out of a reluctance to journey to the capital city, which was located at the far eastern corner of the gubernia.

38 Godek. O stanie i potrzebach guberni litewskich. P. 50.

39 Murzanov. Slovar' russkich senatorov. P. 319.

40 Godek. O stanie i potrzebach guberni litewskich. Pp. 57–69, 75–83.

41 Makarova. Rossiia i sozdanie konstitutsionnogo Korolevstva Pol'skogo. P. 70. Quoted from: Memoirs of Prince Adam Czartoryski. P. 239.

42 RGIA. F. 1263. Op. 1. D. 84. "Zhurnal komiteta ministrov ot 4 dekabria 1815 g. Zapiska iz byvshikh v komitete ministrov del o zloupotrebleniiakh po tamozhennoi chasti v Radzivillovskom okruge i o obrevizovanii Volynskoi gubernii." Ll. 91 ob.–92.

Another important signal that drew St. Petersburg officials' attention to Volhynia came from the military quarters. Field marshal Michael Barclay de Tolly[43] forwarded to the tsar reports from General Alexandre Andrault de Langeron[44] on the large-scale smuggling of goods into Volhynia and corruption at the infamous Radzivillov customs house.[45]

On January 9, 1815, the Committee of Ministers decided to send a senator to Volhynia for an inspection. The initial choice was A.U. Bolotnikov, but because of his illness, Friedrich Wilhelm von Sievers[46]—former governor of Courland and senator of the Fourth department—was appointed.[47] Inspections of the provinces by one or occasionally two senators was an established practice in the Russian Empire. It was perceived by the ruling elite as an instrument to repair wrongs of the local administration.[48] In 1815, besides Volhynia, four other provinces (Kazan, Kostroma, Penza, and Tula) were subject to inspection.[49]

The initial stage of inspection did not foretell anything bad to the Volhynian gubernial administration. In April 1815 Sievers reported to St. Petersburg that upon inspecting most of the governmental agencies in Zhitomir, he found file-keeping and general business dealings to be well in order. Governor Komburlei, Sievers found, was "just, energetic, diligent, and loyal to the emperor and the fatherland." To substantiate his statement, the inspector indicated that out of 1,247 landowners who were questioned by the police, 921 acknowledged that they had no claims on the state treasury. Many esteemed aristocrats told Sievers that they received protection at the hands of the governor. Sievers concluded that the main point of nobles' grievances was indignation at the local police for extorting bribes from the landowners.[50]

At the end of April, Sievers left the gubernia's capital to travel to Radzivillov—a town with a customs house on the Austrian border—to investigate whether re-

43 Known in Russia as Mikhail Bogdanovich Barklai de Tolli.

44 Known in Russia as Aleksandr Fedorovich Lanzheron.

45 RGIA. F. 1263. Op. 1. D. 84. "Zhurnal komiteta ministrov ot 4 dekabria 1815 g." L. 92.

46 Known in Russia as Fedor Fedorovich Sivers (1748–1823).

47 RGIA. F. 1263. Op. 1. D. 84. "Zhurnal komiteta ministrov ot 4 dekabria 1815 g." Ll. 92–92 ob.

48 On senatorial inspections of gubernias, see: Biktasheva. Kazanskoe gubernatorstvo. Pp. 57–71.

49 Istoriia Pravitelstvuiushchego Senata. P. 504.

50 RGIA. F. 1263. Op. 1. D. 86. "Zapiska ministra iustitsii D.P. Troshchinskogo v komitet ministrov ot 11 maia 1815 g." Ll. 28–30 ob.; RGIA. F. 1409. Op. 1. D. 1067. "Donesenie F.F. Siversa Akeksandru I ot 24 maia 1815 g." L. 9.

ports of smuggling were true. On his inspection tour, the senator visited nine district towns. In each location Sievers encountered the local marshal and a crowd of petitioners who complained about oppression by the police and the gubernia's crown authorities.[51] Bartłomiej Giżycki, the gubernia's marshal of nobility, claimed that before Sievers arrived in Volhynia, police authorities such as land captains (*zemskie ispravniki*) and sheriffs (*gorodnichie*) had pushed many landowners to write letters to the governor that they had no claims on the treasury.[52] Now in the presence of the senior governmental inspector, nobles felt able to express their grievances.

As the complaints of the local nobles piled up, the inspector's opinion of Komburlei changed. On August 11, 1815, Sievers wrote to Saltykov that he had completely altered his opinion of Komburlei.[53] Sievers reported to the tsar that the nobles had "great dissatisfaction" with the governor. They believed that Komburlei groundlessly doubted their loyalty to Russia. This attitude of the governor, according to the nobles, was the cause of "undeserved censure" from the government and oppression by the local administration.[54]

In mid-July after Sievers returned to Zhitomir, Gizycki gave him a general petition on behalf of all Volhynian nobility. It summarized the previous complaints and contained eighty-four points. The majority of concerns mentioned in the petition were devoted to the missing compensation for wartime expenses and losses, the tax burden, the landowners' economic well-being, the arbitrariness of imperial officials, and a desire for wider participation of nobility in administration of the gubernia. Most importantly, the petitioners demanded that M.I. Komburlei, Vice-Governor Aleksandr Dmitrievich Khrushchov, and other crown officials be discharged of their offices.[55]

---

51 RGIA. F. 1263. Op. 1. D. 84. "Zhurnal komiteta ministrov ot 4 dekabria 1815 g." Ll. 58, 107 ob.

52 RGIA. F. 1263. Op. 1. D. 87. "Prilozhenie k zhurnalu komiteta ministrov ot 30 oktiabria 1815 g." Ll. 103 ob.–104.

53 RGIA. F. 1263. Op. 1. D. 84. "Zhurnal komiteta ministrov ot 4 dekabria 1815 g." L. 110 ob.; RGIA. F. 1398. Op. 1. D. 1143. "Vsepoddanneishii doklad Senata po delu o zloupotrebleniiach volynskogo gubernatora Komburleia i vitse-gubernatora Khrushchova." L. 172.

54 RGIA. F. 1409. Op. 1. D. 1067. "Donesenie F.F. Siversa Akeksandru I ot 24 maia 1815 g." Ll. 6–7.

55 RGIA. F. 1151. Op. 1. 1819. D. 18. "Zapiska iz vsepoddaneishego doklada po delam o zloupotrebleniiakh, otkrytykh senatorom Siversom pri revizii Volynskoi gubernii." Ll. 4 ob.–14 ob.

Earlier Giżycki had asked Komburlei to allow nobles to assemble in district towns and submit their complaints. The governor had not rejected this proposal outright but responded that every noble could address him personally with any grievances. Yet when Giżycki repeated his appeal and stated that Volhynian nobles wanted to assemble in district towns to discuss their *soslovie* (noble corporation) needs, Komburlei rejected it and turned to the Committee of Ministers for endorsement.[56] Reporting to St. Petersburg that he was not sure of district marshals' and their deputies' commitment to Russia,[57] the governor had craftly played on the history of some Polish nobles' disloyalty to Russia in 1809–12. On June 12, 1815, the government supported Komburlei's decision and instructed him to monitor marshals' activities.[58]

Komburlei once again had pretext to report about Giżycki's suspicious activities when the governor learned that, in February, the marshal had asked nobles to collect money for local needs, unbeknownst to imperial authorities. The Committee of Ministers not only forbade the nobles to raise money but commissioned Sievers to remove Giżycky from the office unless he explained the purpose of the fund-raising[59]. Komburlei thus succeded in stirring up the Russian ruling elite against Giżycki. Later the Senate passed a resolution to the effect that the Volhynian marshal should have been relieved of his office and put on trial for "insolence" against the governor.[60]

Komburlei continued to demonize the leader of the Volhynian nobility as the prime agent of subversive activities. At th end of July he informed the government that Giżycki had organized the marshals' assembly in Zhitomir, persuaded them to sign unjust complaints, and instigated them against the gubernia's administration. Touching the delicate chords of the top officials' fears, Komburlei warned that things may go out of control in his gubernia.[61]

The event that Komburlei referred to in his report was the nobles' assembly that was organised by Giżycki shortly before he was summoned by order of the

56 RGIA. F. 1284. Op. 4 b. Kn. 10. D. 191. "Kopiia s predstavleniia Komburleia glavnokomanduiushchemu v Sankt-Petersburge S.V. Viazmitinovu." Ll. 231–37.

57 RGIA. F. 1263. Op. 1. D. 84. "Zhurnal komiteta ministrov ot 4 dekabria 1815 g." Ll. 100–102 ob.

58 Ibid. Ll. 102–102 ob.

59 Ibid. Ll. 103–5.

60 Ibid. L. 107.

61 Ibid. Ll. 109–109 ob.

emperor to join the army of Barclay de Tolli.[62] On July 17, 1815, marshals on behalf of all Volhynian nobles submitted to Sievers a general petition of their grievances containing eighty-four points.[63]

After Giżycki's departure, the relieved governor asked St. Petersburg to confirm Count Jan Choloniewski as marshal.[64] Choloniewski was the candidate most palatable to Komburlei because he was not known for his involvement in Volhynia's public life and instead spent much time traveling abroad. The governor, in endorsing Choloniewski, passed over two district marshals—Henryk Iliński (son of Senator Iliński) and Joseph Malynski—who had been chosen by the nobility at the 1814 elections to be the first and second candidates after Giżycki to the office of marshal. Agreeing with the main motive expressed by Komburlei—the avoidance of further disrespect from the nobility and erosion of the governor-general's power—the government confirmed Choloniewski on July 13.[65]

After this move, the local nobility demonstrated open indignation of Komburlei. General Major Giżycki was highly respected by the Volhynian Polish-speaking elite. In August 1814 he had been elected as gubernia's marshal at the regular nobles' assembly.[66] Shortly before this, he had been elected along with Senator Iliński and several other nobles of Volhynia to a delegation to St. Petersburg. At his audience, Alexander I had summoned Giżycki back to military service.[67] However, in December 1814 in response to the petition of Volhynian nobles, the government had allowed him to resume the office of the nobility's marshal.[68]

---

62 RGIA. F. 1284. Op. 4 a. Kn. 91. D. 234. "Raport Komburleia ministru vnutrennikh del O.P. Kozodavlevu ot 1 iiulia 1815 g." Ll. 186–186 ob.

63 RGIA. F. 1151. Op. 1. 1819. D. 18. "Zapiska iz vsepoddaneishego doklada po delam o zloupotrebleniiakh, otkrytykh senatorom Siversom pri revizii Volynskoi gubernii." Ll. 4 ob–5.

64 RGIA. F. 1263. Op. 1. D. 84. L. 105 ob.

65 Ibid. L. 106 ob.

66 RGIA. F. 1284. Op. 4 a. Kn. 89. D. 208. "Spisok o chinovnikakh, izbrannykh dvorianstvom Volynskoi gubernii i utverzhdennykh v raznye dolzhnosti." L. 212.

67 RGIA. F. 1284. Op. 4 a. Kn. 91. D. 234. "Predstavlenie ispravliaiushchego dolzhnost' volynskogo marshala Zaleskogo senatoru Komburleiu." Ll. 173–75. Gizycki initially entered Russian military service after the dissolution of the Polish troops. In 1798 he was promoted to the rank of major general. He commanded a cavalier brigade at the Battle of Austerlitz. In 1808 Gizycki was given an honorable discharge with a right to wear his general's uniform. See: Russkii biograficheskii slovar'. Vol. 5. Pp. 175 f.

68 RGIA. F. 1284. Op. 4 a. Kn. 91. D. 234. Ll. 178–79.

3. Tensions between Two Senators: Governor Komburlei and Inspector Sievers

The presence of the senator-inspector in the gubernia encouraged the nobles to defend the autonomy of their corporation from intrusions by local administration. Komburlei's May 1815 ban on the communications practice employed by the marshals caused an uproar. Marshals normally sent circular letters on issues of public interest either directly to the landowners or through lower police officers with the envelopes sealed. From now on, district marshals were obliged to dispatch all circulars only through the local police, so that the administration could be informed of their content. Considering this prescription as an intrusion into the nobility's local affairs and a sign of distrust, seven district marshals protested and attempted to resign to Sievers. Yet the government supported Komburlei's decision and did not accept the marshals' resignation.[69]

Feeling threatened not only by the local Polish elite but by the diligent inspector, Komburlei cunningly managed to stir the Committee of Ministers against Sievers himself. In a series of reports to the Senate, Komburlei tried to drive home the message that Sievers' inspection caused a disturbance of the public order, which could lead to general unrest. Citing the refusal of several Polish nobles to provide provisions and horses to the military, the governor wanted to prove that "the grievances campaign" that had unfolded under Sievers's patronage undermined imperial power in the province.[70]

Sievers, admittedly, routinely resorted to heavy-hand measures. When inspecting the town of Berdichev, he ordered a company of soldiers to round up Jews involved in the sale of smuggled goods. Another motive for this action was to spot and register those Jews who had been previously omitted from tax rolls.[71] Vice-Governor Khrushchov reported that the inspector ordered an announcement posted in Jewish schools to the effect that those who did not comply with the requirements of authorities would be shot.[72]

69 RGIA. F. 1263. Op. 1. D. 81. "Zhurnal komiteta ministrov ot 7 sentiabria 1815 g." Ll. 184–87; RGIA. F. 1409. Op. 1. D. 1067. "Kratkoe izlozhenie raportov senatora Siversa Aleksandru I ot 26 iiunia 1815 g." L. 14 ob.

70 RGIA. F. 1263. Op. 1. D. 91. "Zhurnal komiteta ministrov ot 11 ianvaria 1816 g." Ll. 162–62 ob.

71 RGIA. F. 1409. Op. 1. D. 1067. "Pis'mo Siversa Aleksandru I ot 26 iiunia 1815 g. na frantsuzkom iazyke." Ll. 13–13 ob.

72 RGIA. F. 1398. Op. 1. D. 1143. "Vsepoddanneishii doklad Senata po delu o zloupotrebleniiach volynskogo gubernatora Komburleia i vitse-gubernatora Khrushchova." Ll. 188 ob.–189 ob.

Though nominally accountable to the Committee of Ministers, Sievers maintained an independent position. After receiving his April 21 report about the investigation in progress, the committee received nothing from him for more than two months.[73] Sievers felt responsible only to the tsar. In contrast Komburlei frequently reported to the ministers, presenting Sievers's activities in a critical light.

One incident caused the ministers open indignation because of the supposed arbitrariness of the senator-inspector. Sievers restored Count Iakov Nikolaevich Bulgari to the office of the Radzivillov customs district chief without notifying the minister of finance. Then he allowed Bulgari to take a leave and dispatched him to Alexander I in Vienna.[74]

As storm clouds gathered over his head, Komburlei asked permission to travel to St. Petersburg, presumably to defend himself, but he was required to stay in his gubernia until the completion of the Sievers inspection.[75]

In order to resolve the growing tensions in Volhynia, the Committee of Ministers recommended in late July that Sievers wrap up his inspection and return to St. Petersburg.[76] Perhaps by coincidence, at this same moment Sievers wrote to Saltykov that his inspection was almost finished. He admitted that his previous opinion about Komburlei had completely altered. Describing "abuses" in the gubernia, Sievers dispatched to St. Petersburg the original complaint of the nobility with the demand to remove the governor and other crown officials. Sievers reported that Komburlei tried to hinder his investigation of the smugglers in Berdichev. He suggested that Komburlei should be immediately summoned to St. Petersburg and that Khrushchov should be discharged even before the investigation was completed.[77]

Confident in the tsar's support, Sievers defied the committee and stayed in Volhynia to continue his inquiry in Berdichev. He had a purpose that the committee could not ignore. The senator informed the ministers that he had received secret papers from the emperor on the smuggling affair and was awaiting a resolution on his reports.[78] The ministers could do nothing but grudgingly acknowledge the

---

73 RGIA. F. 1409. Op. 1. D. 1699. "Zapiska o revizii senatorom F.F. Siversom Volynskoi gubernii." Ll. 1–2.

74 RGIA. F. 1263. Op. 1. D. 84. "Zhurnal komiteta ministrov ot 4 dekabria 1815 g." L. 108 ob.

75 Ibid. Ll. 108–108 ob.

76 Ibid. L. 110.

77 RGIA. F. 1263. Op. 1. D. 81. "Zhurnal komiteta ministrov ot 4 dekabria 1815 g." Ll. 319 ob.–320 ob.

78 Ibid. Ll. 317–18.

priority of Sievers's secret task. All the committee could do was express concern that inspectors' judgments about the officials' guilt were often unfounded and warn the inspector not to interfere in the current administration of the gubernia.[79]

Meanwhile Komburlei bombarded the committee with reports of Sievers's arbitrary and biased approach. He wrote that several local officials had been discharged on the basis of complaints that were not supported by any documentation. The governor insisted that the nobility's complaints about him contained nothing but slander and defamation.[80] He tried to convey to St. Petersburg the idea that Giżycki and "a party of schemers" who cobbled together hundreds of complaints had taken advantage of Sievers's benevolence and created a dangerous atmosphere of disobedience.

Losing patience, the committee passed a resolution on August 21, 1815, that appeared to be in favor of Komburlei. Sievers was reminded to wrap up his inspection of Volhynia and to hurry to the capital in order to present his findings. At the same time Komburlei would finally be allowed to take a leave and travel to St. Petersburg as soon as the government appointed an official to act as the civil governor. Tacitly acquiting Komburlei, the committee acknowledged that in view of Sievers's findings, Vice-Governor Khrushchov could not fill this position.[81] On September 18, the committee appointed Count Armand Charles Emmanuel de Saint-Priest, the governor of the neighboring gubernia of Podolia, to act as the temporary head of Volhynia for the time that Komburlei was in St. Petersburg.[82] The committee, thus, seemingly took into account the wishes of the nobility, who viewed the governor of Podolia as a prudent and just administrator. This decision was not unanimous. Three members of the committee—Nikolai Semenovich Mordvinov, Aleksei Kirillovich Razumovsky, and Aleksandr Semenovich Shishkov thought that Komburlei should stay in Zhitomir for two reasons: first, to keep control over the administration of the province in the current difficult circumstances and, second, to avoid rumors that his leave was the result of Sievers's inspection.[83]

4. Komburlei's Removal and Indictment

Busy with the affairs of Europe, Alexander I did not interfere in Volhynian issues until November 1815. He regularly received reports from Sievers and met with

79 Ibid. Ll. 320 ob.–323.

80 Ibid. Ll. 191–93, 482–84; RGIA. F. 1263. Op. 1. D. 84. Ll. 215–19.

81 RGIA. F. 1263. Op. 1. D. 84. Ll. 111–12.

82 Ibid. L. 116 ob.

83 RGIA. F. 1263. Op. 1. D. 81. Ll. 311–12 ob.

the people who were dispatched by the inspector—Henryk Iliński, Bartłomiej Giżycki, Iakov Bulgari, and most probably others—who apparently supplied the tsar with first-hand accounts of Volhynian affairs.

Only after signing in Warsaw the constitutional charter of the Kingdom of Poland did Alexander I publicly react to the ongoing wrangling between Sievers and the Committee of Ministers. On November 28, 1815, the emperor signed a decree to the Senate that was aimed at resolving the situation. Backing Sievers, the tsar rebuked the ministers for attempting to recall the inspector before he finished his investigation.[84] More importantly the tsar relieved Komburlei and Khrushchov of their offices and ordered them to be put under investigation.[85]

On January 21, 1816, the emperor instructed the Senate to examine the case of "abuses in Volhynia gubernia."[86] By now Alexander I viewed Komburlei as a corrupt official and treated his critique of Sievers's inspection as an attempt to cover up his crimes. The tsar expressed his trust of the inspector and forbade complaints from Komburlei.

In the final stage of his mission, Sievers resolved his investigation of smuggling over the Austrian border, a case that had long bothered the Russian government. The inspector managed to uncover an illegal fund run by Jewish merchants in Berdichev, which was set up to pay off local police and customs authorities for allowing the forbidden imports. Sievers charged Komburlei and Khrushchov for not only knowing and taking no action but for patronizing this criminal operation. According to the inspector's findings, a range of middle- and top-level gubernial officials regularly received pay-offs and profited from selling the smuggled goods. The investigation led Sievers to compile a list of charges against Komburlei that implicitly indicated his corruption and graft. Aside from mismanagement, negligence of police "abuses," and complicity in the Berdichev smugglers' fund, the inspector accused him of receiving gifts from kahals for covering Jews who were not registered during the tax revision. In Berdichev and Radzivillov, the inspector uncovered 2,500 Jews (about half the total population of these towns)

gloss?

84 Not fully trusting his top officials, Alexander delegated to Aleksei Andreevich Arakcheev on December 24, 1815, a task to make presentations to and supervise the activities of the committee. On the date, see: Shilov. Gosudarstvennye deiateli. P. 54.

85 RGIA. F. 1263. Op. 1. D. 84. Ll. 41 ob.–44; Sbornik istoricheskikh materialov. Vol. 4. № 219.

86 RGIA. F. 1151. Op. 1. 1819. D. 18. "Zapiska iz vsepoddaneishego doklada po delam o zloupotrebleniiakh, otkrytykh senatorom Siversom pri revizii Volynskoi gubernii." Ll. 2–3.

not included in the tax rolls. Further investigations in five districts found that over seventy thousand male Jews and peasants were omitted from the tax rolls.[87]

Another grave accusation carried politically sensitive overtones. According to Sievers, the former governor was duplicitous in his reports to St. Petersburg on the state of affairs in Volhynia. To cover up his own misdeeds and those of his subordinates, Komburlei depicted Volhynian nobles as perfidious and rebellious subjects.[88] Yet after Alexander I granted amnesty to Poles implicated in anti-Russian activities (1814), this charge was not followed up. Most probably Komburlei overstated the case in order to exploit early nationalist feelings among some Russian ministers.

Komburlei's case was heard first in the Fifth department of the Senate and then in the State Council. Because of dissenting opinions in these institutions, the trial over the former governor dragged on until his death in October 1821 and was formerly closed only in 1827.[89]

5. Success of the "Volhynian Revolution" and the New Imperial Policy in the Western Provinces

Events in Volhynia and Sievers's inspection took place against historically significant developments linked to the restoration of Poland by Alexander I. Sievers himself noted that in the course of inspection he altered his opinion about Komburlei. Was this change brought about by the news from Vienna and Warsaw, where the Russian emperor had defended his pro-Polish stance? Did the tsar's open sympathies to the Polish cause lead the senator to trust local Poles in Volhynia more than Russian officials? The sources examined for this chapter do not provide direct evidence to support this conclusion. Nevertheless, Sievers could not ignore the pro-Polish stance of Alexander I's policies after the "Bases de la Constitution" were approved and the establishment of the Kingdom of Poland was officially proclaimed in May–June of 1815. The investigation in Berdichev, and its implication of Komburlei, likely also served to ruin the governor's reputation in Sievers's eyes.

These events inaugurated the tsar's new approach to the governance of the western provinces—the appointment of local Polish-speaking aristocrats to the

87 RGIA. F. 1398. Op. 1. D. 1143. "Vsepoddanneishii doklad Senata po delu o zloupotrebleniiach volynskogo gubernatora Komburleia i vitse-gubernatora Khrushchova." Ll. 173–200, 238–414.

88 RGIA. F. 1151. Op. 1. 1819. D. 18. Ll. 14 ob.–15.

89 Ibid. Ll. 100–117 ob., 119–21 ob.

highest positions in the gubernial administration, a practice that followed the standard already set for Poland. Its constitutional charter stipulated that public offices in the kingdom were to be filled only with Poles (art. 28).[90] This principle was a continuation of the line formulated in the constitution of the Grand Duchy of Warsaw (art. 83). Alexander I had already approved of this idea.[91]

Prior to the events with Komburlei, the appointment of a Pole to the governor's office in the former Polish-Lithuanian provinces of Russia was a rare exception. However, starting from 1816, the exception became the rule. The new pattern was set forth in January 1816 when the marshal of the Grodno province Prince Franciszek Ksawery Drucki-Lubecki, an official highly trusted by the imperial authorities, was appointed civil governor.[92]

The new policy quickly spread to other Polish gubernias of the empire. In April 1816 Bartłomiej Giżycki was appointed as Volhynian civil governor.[93] The Russian emperor was known to be deliberating on the idea of joining the Polish provinces of the empire with the Kingdom of Poland. Yet Alexander I understood well that this action, though ardendly desired by Polish-speaking nobility, would be seriously opposed by their Russian counterparts. In these circumstances the tsar tried through practical and symbolic actions to demonstrate that he was willing to fulfill the wishes of his Polish subjects. New appointments of local Poles to high administrative positions were warmly welcomed by the local noble community, which perceived these appointments as the first step toward the western provinces' integration into the Kingdom of Poland.[94]

Having found an accommodation with the Poles, Alexander I was also ready to alleviate potential concerns of the Russian ruling elite. In the same year, the tsar commissioned the Project for Establishing Viceroyalties[95] (the idea of reestablishing governor-generalships had circulated since at least 1812).[96] The project envisaged the introduction of viceroys or governors- general to supervise areas

---

90 Konstitutsionnaia Khartiia Carstva Pol'skogo. P. 529.

91 A clause to this effect was included in the project of setting up the Grand Duchy of Lithuania with autonomy within the empire, a plan that was presented to the tsar by Michał Kleofas Ogiński in October 1811. See: Mémoires de Michel Oginski. Vol. 3. Pp. 77–80.

92 Smolka. Polityka Lubeckiego. Pp. 61, 437.

93 Polski Słownik Biograficzny. V. 8. P. 21.

94 Smolka. Polityka Lubeckiego. Pp. 63, 66.

95 Arutiunian. General-Gubernatorstva pri Aleksandre I. P. 84; LeDonne. Administrative Regionalization. P. 14.

96 Arutiunian. General-Gubernatorstva pri Aleksandre I. P. 78.

covering several gubernias and overseeing civil governors. In the case of the western provinces, newly appointed Polish-speaking governors would have been safely controlled by a viceroy.

The tsar addressed the concerns of the Volhynian nobles and appeared to be sympathetic to their needs and requests. He restored their right to elect members of the district police and made some other changes to administrative regulations. Special "liquidation" commissions were to set up in each province with the task of taking stock of requisitions made by the troops and estimating compensation of landowners for wartime expenses. To redress the grievances of the Volhynian nobles and to elaborate measures to improve the economic status of the gubernia, the tsar set up a special senatorial committee headed by Sievers.[97]

6. Conclusion

The episode with the "Volhynian Revolution" can also be viewed as a case of power interplay between the local imperial administration and the local noble corporation in the lands of the former Polish-Lithuanian Commonwealth—*Rzecz Pospolita*. In the first decade of his reign, Alexander I strengthened the office of the gubernial marshal of nobility, hoping to engage the support of its holders for his reform program.[98] According to Alsu Biktasheva, the situation in some provinces of Russia could have been described as a stand-off between civil governor and marshal of nobility. A governor as an agent of the central authorities ex officio pursued the state interests, which did not always correspond to the concerns of the provincial nobility voiced by its marshal.[99] In Volhynia this balance was tilted in favor of the imperial representative when Komburlei became governor-general in January 1813. By that time he was already perceived by most Volhynians as a corrupt and arbitrary official. In this situation they appealed directly to the supreme arbiter—the Russian emperor.

Leaders of the Vohlynian nobility—a body that had produced three senators of the empire—were attuned to the changes in the Russian political situation and to the tsar's sentiments. They chose a felicitous moment for an appeal to the throne, when Alexander I began fulfilling his long-time pro-Polish intentions. At the same time the nobles' remonstrance might have served as an additional stimulus for Alexander I to do favors for his Polish subjects.

97 Sbornik istoricheskikh materialov. Pp. 219–21.

98 Biktasheva. Kazanskoe gubernatorstvo. P. 134.

99 Ibid. Pp. 169, 255.

The conflict between the two senators—the inspector and the governor-general—was closely monitored by central authorities and was only resolved with the intervention of the tsar himself, who decisively sided with the inspector. The resultant removal of gubernial officials was hardly a rare occurrence following a senatorial inspection.

The conflict between the provincial imperial administration and the nobility's marshal in Volhynia was similarly not a unique occurrence in the Russian Empire at that time. Biktasheva notes growing opposition among provincial nobles to local imperial administrations after the Napoleonic Wars. In the governorate of Kazan, such attitudes brought about open conflict between the governor and the marshal.[100] Investigating the same time period, Jörg Ganzenmüller demonstrated that conflicts between these two figures in the Polish provinces should not be seen as stemming necessarily from an inherent opposition to Russian power among the local nobility. Rather, the roots of such conflicts could be found in personal antagonisms.[101]

Bartołomey Giżycki and Józef August Iliński could hardly be ranked among ardent fighters for Polish independence. Instead they were willing to work with imperial authorities. Their initiative was not an intrigue: the petition reflected indignation at officials' corruption in a province that was left in dire economic straits after the Napoleonic Wars. Certainly, the pro-Polish mood of Alexander I also encouraged this initiative. Yet the conflict between the imperial administration and the nobility's leaders in borderland Volhynia, with the subsequent replacement of the Russian officials by Polish dignitaries, was used by Russia's early nationalists to interpret this matter as a political and subversive intrigue. The aim of the Opytov-Staroszilova fictitious letters was to present Poles in the darkest light in order to whitewash Komburlei. The "Volhynian Revolution" piece was later welcomed by the journalists of *Kievskaya starina* as a fitting illustration of duplicity and cunning in Poles. The text served the political needs at a time of growing Russian nationalism and anti-Polish attitudes among the public.

List of references

Arutiunian, Vladimir. General-gubernatorstva pri Akeksandre I. Moscow, 2008. Doctoral dissertation, unpublished manuscript

Biktasheva, Alsu. Kazanskoe gubernatorstvo pervoi poloviny XIX veka. Bremia vlasti. Moscow, 2014

100 Ibid. P. 135.

101 Ganzenmüller. Russische Staatsgewalt. Pp. 355, 358.

BOVUA [BEAUVOIS], DANIEL. Gordiev uzel Rossiiskoi imperii: Vlast', shliachta i narod na Pravoberezhnoi Ukraine (1793–1914) / Avtorizovannyi perevod s frantsuzskogo Marii Krisan'. Moscow, 2011

EGOROVA, KSENIIA. Pis'ma o volynskoi revoliucii: konspirologicheskie motivy kak kliuch k ponimaniiu teksta / Tezisy dokladov na seminare "Konspirologicheskie siuzhety v russkoi kul'ture: problemy issledovaniia." St. Petersburg, 16–17 noiabria 2015 g. http://www.pushkinskijdom.ru/LinkClick.aspx?fileticket=7a2CoShxDjU%3D&tabid=36 [18.10.2018]

GANZENMÜLLER, JÖRG. Russische Staatsgewalt und polnischer Adel. Elitenintegration und Staatsausbau im Westen des Zarenreiches (1772–1850). Köln, 2013

GODEK, SŁAWOMIR. O stanie i potrzebach guberni litewskich w roku 1810 w świetle protokolów czynności delegacji szlacheckiej w Petersburgu. In : Zeszyty Prawnicze. Vol. 14 (2014) # 3. Pp. 37–85

HELENIUSZ, EU. Wspomnienia lat minionych. Vols. 1–2. Kraków, 1876

ISTORIIA PRAVITELSTVUIUSHCHEGO SENATA za dvesti let 1711–1911. Vol. 4. St. Petersburg, 1911

KONSTITUTSIONNAIA KHARTIIA CARSTVA POL'SKOGO. In: Pol'sha i Rossiia v pervoi treti XIX veka. Iz istorii avtonomnogo korolevstva Pol'skogo 1815–1830. Moscow, 2010

LANE, HUGO. Szlachta outside the Commonwealth. The Case of Polish Nobles in Galicia. In: Zeitschrift für Ostmitelleuropa-Forschung. Vol. 52 (2003) # 4. Pp. 526–42

LEDONNE, JOHN. Administrative Regionalization in the Russian Empire 1802–1826. In: Cahiers du monde russe. Vol. 43 (2002) # 1. Pp. 5–34

MAKAROVA, G.V. Rossiia i sozdanie konstitutsionnogo Korolevstva Pol'skogo. In: Pol'sha i Rossiia v pervoi treti XIX veka. Iz istorii avtonomnogo korolevstva Pol'skogo 1815–1830. Moscow, 2010

MARKEVICH, O.V. Fenomen M.I. Komburleia abo khronika pravlinnia volyn'skogo gubernatora. In: Problemy istorii Ukrainy XIX – pochatku XX st. Politichni studii. Vol. XIX. Pp. 59–72

MÉMOIRES DE MICHEL OGINSKI. Sur la Pologne et Ler Polonais. Depuis 1788 jusqu'a la fin de 1815. Vols. 3 and 4. Paris, 1827–83

MEMOIRS OF PRINCE ADAM CZARTORYSKI and His Correspondence with Alexander I. Vol. 2. London, 1888

MESIATSOSLOV S ROSPIS'IU CHINOVNYKH OSOB, ili Obshchii shtat Rossiiskoi Imperii, na leto ot Rozhdrstva Khristova 1809. Vol. 2. St. Petersburg, 1809

MURZANOV, NIKOLAI. Slovar' russkikh senatorov. 1711–1917 gg. Materialy dlia biografii / Izd. podgot. D.N. Shilov. St. Peterburg, 2011

PAMĘTNIKI SZYMONA KONOPACKIEGO. Vols. 1–2. Warszawa, 1899

POLSKI SŁOWNIK BIOGRAFICZNY. Vols. 8 and 10. Wrocław-Warszawa- Kraków, 1959–64

RUSSKII BIOGRAFICHESKII SLOVAR'. Vol. 5. St. Petersburg, 1916

SBORNIK ISTORICHESKIKH MATERIALOV, izvlechennykh iz arkhiva sobstvennoi ego imperatorskogo velichestva kanceliarii. Vol. 4. St. Petersburg, 1891

SENATSKII ARKHIV. Vol. 1. Imennye ukazy imperatora Pavla I. St. Petersburg, 1888

SHIL'DER, N.K. Imperaror Aleksandr Pervyi. Ego zhizn' i carstvovanie. Vol. 3. St. Petersburg, 1897

SHILOV, DENIS. Gosudarstvennye deiateli Rossiiskoi imperii. Glavy vysshikh i central'nykh uchrezhdenii, 1802–1917. Biobibliograficheskii spravochnik. St. Petersburg, 2002

SMOLKA, STANISŁAW. Polityka Lubeckiego przed powstaniem listopadowem. Vol. 1. Kraków, 1907

SVERBIGUZ, VOLODYMYR. Starosvits'ke panstvo. Warszawa, 1999

VOLYNSKAIA REVOLIUCIIA pervoi chetverti XIX stoletiia. In Kievskaia starina. (1883) # 1. Pp. 121–44; # 2. Pp. 319–65; # 4. Pp. 774–828

Abbreviations

ASPbII RAN	Arkhiv Sanktpeterburgskogo Instituta Istorii RAN (Archive of the St. Petersburg Institute of History of the Russian Academy of Sciences), St. Petersburg
CANO	Centralnyi arkhiv Nizhegorodskoi oblasti (Central Archive of the Nizhny Novgorod Region), Nizhny Novgorod
GARF	Gosudarsvennyi Arkhiv Rossiiskoi Federacii (State Archive of the Russian Federation), Moscow
LATh-HStA Weimar	Landesarchiv Thüringen—Hauptstaatsarchiv Weimar
NART	Nacional'nyi arkhiv Respubliki Tatarstan, Kazan
OR RNB	Otdel rukopisei Rossiiskoi Natsional'noi Biblioteki (Manuscripts Department of the National Library of Russia) St. Petersburg
ORRK NBL KFU	Otdel Rukopisei i Redkikh Knig Nauchnoi Biblioteki Kazanskogo Federal'nogo Universiteta (Manuscripts and Rare Books Department, Research Library of the Kazan Federal University), Kazan
PSZ	Polnoe sobranie zakonov Rossiiskoi imperii
RGADA	Rossiiskii Gosudarstvennyi Arkhiv Drevnikh Aktov (Russian State Archive of Ancient Acts), Moscow
RGIA	Rossiiskii Gosudarstvennyi Istoricheskii Arkhiv (Russian State Historical Archive)
RGVIA	Rossiiskii gosudarstvennyi voenno-istoricheskii arkhiv (Russian State Military History Archive), Moscow
Sb. RIO	Sbornik Imperatorskogo Russkogo Istoricheskogo Obshchestva
SAA	Stadsarchief, Amsterdam
VPR 1	Vneshniaia politika Rossii XIX i nachala XX v. Dokumenty rossiiskogo Ministerstva inostrannykh del. Seriya 1 (Vol II). Moscow, 1961
VPR 2	Vneshniaia politika Rossii XIX i nachala XX v. Dokumenty rossiiskogo Ministerstva inostrannykh del. Seriia 2 (Vol. I (IX)). Moscow, 1974
VVA	Voûte Vereniging, Amsterdam

Index

Authors

Alsu BIKTASHEVA—Doctor of Sciences in History, Professor, Department of Philosophy, The State University–The Higher School of Economics, Moscow, Russia

Benjamin CONRAD—Dr.Phil, Teaching Coordinator, Department of History, Humboldt-University, Berlin, Germany

Lorenz ERREN—Dr.Phil., Research Associate, Department for Eastern European History, Johannes-Gutenberg-University at Mainz, Germany

Alexander KAPLUNOVSKY—Dr.Phil., Research Associate, Department for Eastern European History, Johannes-Gutenberg-University at Mainz, Germany

Jan KUSBER—Dr.Habil., Professor, Chair of Department for Eastern European History, Johannes-Gutenberg-University at Mainz, Germany

Aleksandr ORLOV—Doctor of Sciences in History, Professor, Department of Modern and Contemporary History, Institute of History and Politics, Moscow Pedagogical State University (MPGU), Moscow, Russia

Vadim PARSAMOV—Doctor of Sciences in History, Chief Research Fellow, Poletayev Institute for Theoretical and Historical Studies in the Humanities; Professor, Faculty of Humanities, The State University–The Higher School of Economics, Moscow, Russia

Sergei POLSKOY—Candidate of Sciences in History, Associate Professor, Faculty of Humanities, The State University–The Higher School of Economics, Moscow, Russia

Maike SACH—Dr.Phil., Research Associate, Johannes a Lasco Bibliothek Große Kirche Emden, Emden, Germany

Franziska SCHEDEWIE—Dr.Habil., Associate Professor, Chair for Eastern European History, Friedrich-Schiller-University, Jena, Germany

Elizaveta SYSOEVA—M.A. in History, Ph.D. Candidate, Faculty of Humanities, The State University–The Higher School of Economics, Moscow, Russia

Victor TAKI—Ph.D. in History, Sessional Instructor, Concordia University of Edmonton, Alberta, Canada

Constantin TROIANOWSKI—PhD in History, Associate Lecturer, Institute for Medical Education, Almazov National Medical Research Centre, St. Petersburg, Russia.

Elena VISHLENKOVA—Doctor of Sciences in History, Leading Research Fellow, Poletaev Institute for Historical-Theoretical Studies in the Humanities; Professor, Faculty of Humanities, The State University–The Higher School of Economics, Moscow, Russia

TRANSFORMATIONEN – DIFFERENZIERUNGEN – PERSPEKTIVEN
MAINZER STUDIEN ZUR NEUZEIT

TRANSFORMATIONS – DIFFERENTIATIONS – PERSPECTIVES
MAINZ STUDIES ON THE MODERN AGE

Herausgegeben von / Edited by Michael Kißener, Jan Kusber, Andreas Rödder und / and Matthias Schnettger

Band 1 Stephanie Mayer-Tarhan: Zwischen Diktatur und Europa. Joaquín Ruiz-Giménez und der spanische Katholizismus, 1936-1977. 2017.

Band 2 Matthias Gemählich: Frankreich und der Nürnberger Prozess gegen die Hauptkriegsverbrecher 1945/46. 2018.

Band 3 Fabian Spreier: Kontinuität oder Diskontinuität? Das westfälische Anwaltsnotariat 1945-1961. 2019.

Band 4 Tanja Herrmann: Der zweite deutsch-französische Städtepartnerschaftsboom (1985-1994). Akteure, Motive, Widerstände und Praxis. 2019.

Band 5 Alexander Kaplunovsky, Jan Kusber, and Benjamin Conrad (eds.): The Enigmatic Tsar and His Empire. Russia under Alexander I. 1801–1825. 2019.

www.peterlang.com